'Stanford – a practising Catholic and the former editor of the *Catholic Herald* – conveys brilliantly to a secular atheist like me the nature of the internal battle that Luther underwent . . . what makes this work so valuable is the writer's belief that religion is important and that the relationship of the believer to God requires explanation. I wonder whether an atheist like me would have been half so effective a communicator of Luther's true importance.'

David Aaronovitch, *The Times*

'An honest but sympathetic portrait of a profoundly complicated and at times contradictory individual, seen in the heated context of his times . . . Stanford has managed a rare thing: an easy, pleasurable read through difficult concepts and hard choices. Yet he also conveys Luther's most admirable qualities, not least the absence of self-satisfaction and the presence of what the author calls "sheer, selfless courage". In his quest to declaim his truth, Martin Luther's constant resting place was discomfort: a lesson in conscience for his times, and for ours.'

Jenny McCartney, *The Mail on Sunday*

'Readable, tolerant, intelligent . . . Stanford humanises the "little monk" once seen as a man full of flaws, but whose courage in standing almost alone against clerical abuse and corruption changed the course of history.'

Nigel Jones, *The Observer*

'Stanford – himself a Catholic – has developed a reputation as a first-class biographer . . . [he] skilfully traces the course of the Reformation [   ] to great lengths to make Luther's theology acc[   ]eology, he argues rather convin[   ] . . If you think this is a religious [   ]e wrong.'

The Irish Independent

To Fiona Fraser,
The tireless champion every writer needs

Unless indicated otherwise, Scripture quotations are taken from the The
New Jerusalem Bible published and copyright © 1974 by Darton, Longman
and Todd Ltd and Doubleday, a division of Random House Inc.

Every reasonable effort has been made to trace the copyright holders, but if there
are any errors or ommissions, Hodder & Stoughton will be pleased to insert
the appropriate acknowledgements in any subsequent printings or editions.

First published in Great Britain in 2017 by Hodder & Stoughton
An Hachette UK company

This paperback edition first published in 2017

A CIP catalogue record for this title is available from the British Library

ISBN 978 1 473 62167 1
eBook 978 1 473 62168 8

Typeset by Hewer Text UK Ltd, Edinburgh
Printed and bound in the UK by Clays Ltd, St Ives plc

Hodder & Stoughton policy is to use papers that are natural, renewable
and recyclable products and made from wood grown in sustainable
forests. The logging and manufacturing processes are expected to
conform to the environmental regulations of the country of origin.

Hodder & Stoughton Ltd
Carmelite House
50 Victoria Embankment
London EC4Y 0DZ

www.hodder.co.uk

MARTIN LUTHER

Catholic Dissident

Peter Stanford

HODDER

Also by Peter Stanford

Judas: The Troubling History of the Renegade Apostle

How To Read a Graveyard:
Journeys in the Company of the Dead

The Death of a Child (editor)

The Extra Mile: A 21st Century Pilgrimage

C Day-Lewis: A Life

Why I Am Still A Catholic:
Essays in Faith and Perseverance (editor)

Heaven: A Travellers' Guide to the Undiscovered Country

Bronwen Astor: Her Life and Times

The She-Pope: A Quest for the Truth
Behind The Mystery of Pope Joan

The Devil: A Biography

The Outcasts' Outcast: A Life of Lord Longford

Cardinal Hume and the Changing Face of English Catholicism

Catholics and Sex (with Kate Saunders)

Believing Bishops (with Simon Lee)

Contents

Part Three:
'Pope' Martin

A Brief Note on Sources

To mark the 400th anniversary of Martin Luther's birth, work began in Weimar on compiling a complete collection of all his writings, collectively known as the Weimarer Ausgabe. *When it was finally completed in 2009, it ran to a total of 80,000 pages, spread over 121 volumes and published by Hermann Böhlaus Nachfolger. There is also an online edition, and a CD-ROM, now in various languages.*

The volumes fall into four groups: fifteen given over to his translation of the Bible (Die Deutsche Bibel); *eighteen to his correspondence* (Briefwechsel); *six to his Table Talks* (Tischreden); *and seventy-two to his other works* (Werke). *All notes in this biography referring to material in these volumes are listed as* WA, *except for the Table Talks, listed as TT with their number.*

In seeking the best and clearest rendering in English of Luther's words, I have found of particular use Off The Record with Martin Luther: An Original Translation of the *Table Talks, translated and edited by Charles Daudert (Michigan, 2000), as well as the edition of Luther's Works by the official publishing house of the Lutheran Church in the USA (Concordia, 1967).*

All Bible quotations that I use are taken from my now dog-eared but beloved 'popular edition' of The New Jerusalem Bible *(London, 1974), the first translation of the whole Bible into modern English to appear. It has just celebrated its fiftieth birthday. Luther would have raised a glass. Indeed* The New Jerusalem Bible *is another of his legacies.*

Finally, a stylistic note: there has been much debate as to whether Luther was a monk or a friar. Monk is often preferred as it is more readily understandable to a secular audience, but since he was a member of an Augustinian order known in England as the Austin Friars, it must surely be friar. And so it is, save when I am quoting others who call him a monk. Which leads to whether he lived in a monastery, a friary or a cloister. The final one may be technically the most accurate, but to modern ears it makes him sound as if he was cohabiting with nuns, so I have fudged it and used all three, as and where each contributes to the clearest picture.

Martin Luther: A Timeline

Parallel events in italics

1483   Born in Eisleben on 10 November

1492   Columbus discovers the Americas

1493   Peasant unrest breaks out in southwest Germany

1497   Sent to school in Magdeburg

1498   Switches to a school in Eisenach

1500   Silver guilders introduced into Germany

1501   Enrols at the University of Erfurt

1502   Graduates as a Bachelor of Arts on 29 September

*1502   Elector Friedrich of Saxony establishes a university at
Wittenberg*

1503   Julius II elected as Pope

1505   Receives his Masters at Erfurt on 7 January
Starts studying law
Vows to become a monk when trapped in thunderstorm
on 2 July
Enters Augustinian cloister in Erfurt on 17 July

1506   Johann Tetzel starts selling indulgences in Germany

1507   Celebrates his first mass following ordination as a priest
on 2 May

1508   Temporary posting at the University of Wittenberg

1508   *Maximilian I elected Holy Roman Emperor*

1510   Travels to Rome on business for his order

1512   Moves to Wittenberg permanently as Professor of Biblical Studies

1513   Begins the first of his series of lectures

1513   *Leo X (Giovanni de Medici) elected as Pope*

1514   *Prince Albrecht of Brandenburg buys Archbishopric of Mainz*

1516   *Erasmus publishes his Greek New Testament*

1517   Sends letter of protest about the sale of indulgences, along with Ninety-Five Theses, to his archbishop

1518   Summoned to defend his writings at Diet of Augsburg

1518   *Philipp Melanchthon arrives at University of Wittenberg*

1519   Participates in Leipzig debates with Johann Eck in July

1519   *Emperor Maximilian dies and his grandson, Charles V, is elected in his place*

1519   *Ulrich Zwingli starts preaching at Zurich's main Catholic church*

1520   Declared a heretic by Pope Leo X and threatened with excommunication

1520   *Anabaptist movement starts in Zurich*

1521   Formally excommunicated by the Pope in January
        Refuses to recant before the Diet of Worms in April and outlawed by Edict of Worms
        Is held in Wartburg Castle from May

1522   Returns to Wittenberg in March
Publishes his German translation of the New Testament
in October

1522   *Hadrian VI elected as Pope*

1523   *Clement VII (Giulio de Medici) elected as Pope*

1523   *Diet of Nürnberg delays action against Lutheran rebels*

1524   Peasants' War breaks out across Germany

1525   Peasants' War crushed by German princes with Luther's
backing in May
Marries Katharina von Bora in June

1525   *Elector Friedrich dies and is succeeded by his brother
Johann*

1526   Publishes the German mass

1527   *Imperial army of Charles V sacks Rome and imprisons
Pope*

1529   Confronts more radical reformers at Marburg

1529   *Ottoman Turks lay siege to Vienna*

1529   *Diet of Speyer labels all reformers as 'Protest-ants'*

1530   Is absent when the *Augsburg Confession* is rejected by
the Imperial Diet

1530   *Emperor Charles crowned in Bologna by Clement VII*

1530   *Protestant German princes form Schmalkaldic League*

1531   *Henry VIII declared supreme head of the Church in
England*

1531   *Zwingli killed in battle at Kappel*

1534   Completes his translation of the Bible into German

1534   *Paul III elected as Pope*

1540   Privately sanctions bigamous second marriage of Philipp of Hesse

1542   Appoints his first 'Lutheran' bishop

1544   *Paul III calls for a general council of the Church at Trent*

1546   Dies at Eisleben on 18 February

1547   *Protestants defeated in Germany by Catholic forces in Schmalkaldic War*

1547   *Wittenberg surrenders to Imperial Army on 19 May*

Introduction

'I pray thee, stay with us; go not to Wittenberg.'
Gertrude in *Hamlet* Act 1, Scene II

Wittenberg: summer 2016

An almighty August thundercloud is stuck fast over Wittenberg, venting its considerable anger. Sheltering from the downpour in a doorway, I am counting the gaps between each clatter from the bruised sky, hoping they will get longer and signal the storm will soon pass. But they don't. It's going to be a long wait.

In front of me is a main square presided over by a bronze statue of Martin Luther, the first Protestant (a word his Catholic opponents chose for him) and unambiguously Wittenberg's most famous old boy. Café workers are scurrying to put away chairs and clear the outdoor tables where moments before I have been eating. Each clap of thunder prompts a chorus of terrified dogs to howl.

Once that fades away, a silence falls before the next boom. The stillness feels curious because, since my arrival in this small provincial town on the River Elbe in central Germany, there has been the steady buzz of building works, dawn to dusk. Wittenberg is busy smartening itself up, ready to greet an expected influx of visitors come to mark the 500th anniversary of 31 October 1517, the day when, legend has it, Luther fired the starting gun on the Reformation by nailing Ninety-Five Theses to the door of the Castle Church.

A thunderstorm is part of his story, too. Or, at least, it was when Luther told it. On 3 July 1505, he was a twenty-one-year-old university student, set fair on a career as a lawyer. He was walking back through open countryside from a visit home when he was caught in a deluge of biblical proportions. There was that day no equivalent of my doorway available for him to cower in, and so, vulnerable to the elements, he grew ever more convinced that a bolt of lightning was about to strike, killing him and depositing his soul at the gates of heaven. Terrified, he made a promise to Saint Anne, the Virgin Mary's mother. If he survived, he would enter a monastery.

And survive he did; to him a miracle, though today we have a better statistical grasp of how remote his imagined fate would be. True to his pledge, Luther entered an Augustinian cloister. What he saw, heard and experienced as a friar was, twelve years later, to prompt those Ninety-Five Theses.

My jeans are now so wet they might as well be soggy cardboard. To distract myself, I wonder what, if anything, it would take in the midst of today's apocalyptic thunderstorm to bring a similar oath to Luther's to my own lips. After all, I am sufficiently Catholic still to resort, when things around me are going awry, to my own prayers of supplication via the saints of my childhood, offering eternal gratitude if they intervene with God to rescue me. Of late, I have even returned to the habit learned from my Liverpool Catholic mother of saying novenas (patterns of prayers, repeated over cycles of nine days) as I am going to sleep and my head won't stop spinning with worry about my own children.

But I am still a country mile away from being able to think myself into Luther's promise, which may have something to do with the gap of half a millennium. If indeed he did utter it, and wasn't just making up the story, then that vow belongs to another age. In late medieval Europe, Catholicism was dominant, part of every aspect of life, and pretty much universally embraced and observed. Vocation to the religious life was therefore common-place, and was often a standard career choice for clever young men of slender means, such as Luther, brought up at a time when it didn't occur to most to make any distinction between the secular and the religious.

By contrast, that particular distinguishing line is drawn with heavy underscore today in the West. Religion is often discredited and exiled from the public square, widely blamed for the world's ills and regularly accused of having caused wars all through history, including the conflicts between Catholics and Protestants in the hundred years after Luther's death, which brought a greater devastation to swathes of Germany than the Second World War. And, anyway, young men and women simply have so many other options in terms of life choices and social mobility nowadays. Recruitment to seminaries and religious orders is, as a consequence, in free fall.

These more sceptical times have also taken their toll on Luther's reputation. Try Googling him. It is more a modern reflex than an infallible test, but at least gives a pointer as to where society's current enthusiasms lie. Luther comes up, of course, as the one who started the Reformation in Wittenberg because he objected to the Pope selling places in heaven through slips of parchment called 'indulgences'. But before you get to the bottom of the first page of available links, he is overwhelmed by references to Martin Luther King, whose contemporary relevance (in terms of race relations and fundamental equality) is so much more readily recognised than that of the man after whom he was named.[1]

And what of 'justification by faith', Luther's great theological insight that became one of the dividing lines in the Reformation disputes? It is a long, long way down the list on Google, buried beneath references to DCI John Luther, the troubled and obsessive TV detective played by Idris Elba. 'Justification by faith' has become one of those impenetrable technical phrases, the religious equivalent of quantitative easing. Yet Luther was talking about the most important issue in his own terms and those of his age: how to achieve salvation. Eternal life remains the most enduring of religious promises. And salvation remains an issue still, though couched in very different terms of life after death. Many may now reject any formal religious attachment – scorn talk of God, even – but poll after poll reveals that a majority still hankers after heaven or hopes that there should be something beyond the grave.

So there is an obvious link for a modern audience to Luther, but he doesn't count as an easy man for our age to embrace. The best known of his obsessions – his terrible constipation and his fear of the devil – invite repulsion and derision rather than engagement. When I mentioned on a literary festival platform recently that I was researching a biography of Luther, my fellow speaker, the historian and broadcaster Professor Peter Hennessy, challenged me to find a single joke that Luther had ever told. It earned him a round of applause.

So all that building work that had been going on in Wittenberg until the storm broke, and which will doubtless shortly resume its drone when the clouds clear, could well be unnecessary. Here, a year before the big anniversary, Luther is only attracting a trickle of visitors, though it may be that the stay-aways have taken the sensible precaution of consulting the weather forecast.

As the raindrops keep falling, I distract myself by conducting an unscientific survey of those I have encountered so far over breakfast at Wittenberg's Luther Hotel, themed throughout with waist-high statues of the man himself in every conceivable alcove and every conceivable colour. They look so like giant candles that I have even checked the top of them for a protruding wick.

The majority of the other guests are domestic arrivals from Germany, where Lutherans (including the Chancellor, Angela Merkel, daughter of a Lutheran pastor), make up most of the 30 per cent who define themselves as Evangelical Christians

(Evangelical was Luther's preferred label for himself). Germans retain a special affection for Luther as one of their own. At the end of 2014, the toy company Playmobil launched a £2 plastic figure of him, complete with outsized quill pen, engaged in translating the Bible into German, one of his greatest achievements, and said to have had a greater influence on the development of the modern German language than any other book. The Playmobil Luther quickly became the fastest-selling toy its makers had ever put on the market in Germany. Thirty-four thousand were sold in seventy-two hours. One is sheltering from the rain in my soaked trouser pocket.

At the hotel, I have also spotted a significant bloc of Scandinavians, who have made the journey down from the Baltic to Wittenberg. The established churches of Denmark, Norway, Iceland and Greenland are Lutheran, and it retains the status of 'national church' in Sweden and Finland. And while half of the world's approximately seventy million Lutherans are Europeans, the eight million-strong community in North America, established in the mid-seventeenth century and augmented by a rush in the nineteenth after schisms in the Church in Germany, is engagingly represented in the hotel breakfast room by two couples who have told me over *Wurst* and *Brötchen* that they hail from the 'Scandinavian Upper Mid-West'. In states such as Minnesota, Wisconsin, Michigan and the Dakotas, Lutheranism is still thick on the ground. And, to complete the picture, when I was handing in my room key this very morning, I met a Taiwanese Lutheran, product of the various centres of Lutheran missionary activity in Asia and Africa that have developed since the nineteenth century.

So some visitors will definitely be coming next year, but however great their numbers, they are unlikely to reflect the debt that Europe in particular owes Luther: for breaking the stranglehold of the late medieval Catholic Church over all aspects of life, religious or otherwise; for his championing of ideas of individual responsibility, freedom of conscience and worship; and for show-ing how powerful, well-entrenched elites can be confronted and vanquished, if only you have the courage.

Of late, Luther's life and achievements have, though, more widely become something of a minority pursuit, restricted to those who call themselves Lutherans (another tag that Luther disliked, since again it had been first coined by an opponent), and in literature to an army of academics who take advantage of the exceptionally large and well-organised archive of mate-rial by and about Luther to research aspects of this complex man. It is sometimes said that more books and papers have been written about Luther than anyone else except Jesus, but they have failed in recent times to distil his life in such a fash-ion that his fascination reaches the general audience that it surely deserves.

*

My shoes are starting to fill up with water, and no amount of musing and mulling can prevent me noticing the squelching when I wiggle my toes. I need to find somewhere rather more watertight than this too-shallow doorway. After one more burst of thunder again sets nearby windows rattling loudly in their frames, I make a short but sopping-wet dash for sanctuary across the square and in through the open door of the twin-towered Stadtkirche, or 'Town Church', of Wittenberg.

This is where Luther is reported to have preached more than two thousand sermons, the basis for its stated claim to be the Mother Church of the Reformation, just as the infinitely and expensively grander Saint Peter's in Rome likes to describe itself as the Mother Church of Catholicism. A sandwich board propped up in the porch catches my eye. It announces daily services in English. Providentially, the small print says the next one starts in ten minutes. Luther would have taken that as God's invisible hand guiding me, but it is a touch on my arm from a friendly usher that points me towards where it is happening in the Corpus Christi Chapel, tucked away in one corner of this medieval building.

En route, it is impossible not to pause to take in the vast and vivid (even in the menacingly gloomy light) altarpiece by Lucas Cranach the Elder, another local Wittenberg boy-made-good, a close collaborator of Luther's and the sometime guardian of Mrs Luther before her wedding. If only for its scale and shape (akin to a vast projector screen), it stops you in your tracks.

Lucas Cranach's vast altarpiece in Wittenberg's Town Church places Luther with the apostles at the Last Supper and features the three sacraments Luther retained from Catholicism's list of seven.

It is formed of a triptych, with a fourth panel – or predella – running underneath the other three. In the largest of the main scenes, Luther is seated at the Last Supper, along with Jesus and His twelve apostles. Judas Iscariot is unmissable, three seats to Luther's left, with red hair and an elaborate money-bag, and in the backdrop, seen through an open window, just as unmistakable, is the Wittenberg skyline, dominated by Luther's home, the Black Cloister. Luther, though, is in disguise, hiding behind a thick beard. The image is based on a portrait that Cranach painted during his friend's ten-month exile, from May 1521 to March 1522, in Wartburg Castle, after the Diet of Worms had acceded to the wishes of the Pope and the Holy Roman Emperor and declared Luther a heretic who must be sought out and handed over to Rome for punishment.

A bearded Luther, the disguise he wore while hiding in Wartburg Castle, joins in the first ever Eucharist, in Lucas Cranach's Last Supper panel in his 1547 altarpiece in Wittenberg's Town Church.

Cranach wasn't claiming that Luther had actually been at the Last Supper, but he may have been suggesting that he should have been, such was his importance. Luther, though, would have scoffed at the very idea. When someone once placed him right up there alongside the apostles, he protested that he was just a 'stinking afterthought', a typically earthy remark from one capable of still shocking vulgarity, but also of passages of sublime beauty, often found side by side in tracts carrying headlines that could have been penned by a modern keyboard warrior, spoiling for a fight.

There is, though, another subtext to this panel. The Last Supper was the first eucharist, when Jesus shared the bread and wine, and described them to His apostles as His body and blood. Cranach was reminding congregations, staring forward from the pews on a Sunday at the altar of Luther's favourite church, that eucharist was one of just three of Catholicism's seven sacraments that Luther retained in his radical reforms of Romish practice. The discarded quartet, he held, had no authority in the gospels, and did nothing to help believers know God better.

This shaking up of the familiar pattern of worship in Catholics' everyday lives was where Luther made his most immediate impact. Some opponents regarded it as the moment he crossed the Rubicon. His contemporary, the Dutch Humanist, Desiderius Erasmus, called this action of Luther's – rather than the posting of the Ninety-Five Theses – the moment his breach with Rome became irreparable.

Maintaining his sacramental theme, to the left of the Last Supper, Cranach has painted a baptismal scene, another of the three sacraments retained by Luther. It features his closest collaborator and later hagiographer, Philipp Melanchthon, pouring water over a reluctant infant. There is artistic licence here, since Melanchthon was never an ordained minister. And a bit of point-scoring. Once Luther had forced open the door to reform in Catholicism, others quickly crowded through and vied to outdo him, including those more extreme Protestants, notably the Anabaptists (direct forerunners of today's Amish and Mennonites, and more general inspiration for 'born-again' Christians) who advocated adult baptism, when the individual could make a mature statement of commitment to God. Here, then, Cranach is affirming once more, as Luther had to do repeatedly in his later years, that retaining Catholicism's preference for infant baptism was the correct course.

And on the right the artist puts a confessional scene. By his own account Luther spent many a long and tortured hour while a young friar with his confessor, mentor and religious superior, Johann von Staupitz. He was struggling with his own despondency, despair and depression, something that he gathered under the umbrella description of *Anfechtung*. It is a word that defies simple translation into English but carries with it a real sense of physical assault.[2] Luther was convinced at the time that God was angry with him, and hence had turned His back on him. It was Luther's determination to defeat this angst that, in part at least, pushed him back on the Bible and the authority of Scripture, which in turn led him to demand an overhaul of Catholicism so that it might better serve individuals struggling as he did with faith.

It is, however, the predella panel that provides one of the best-known images of Luther. He is standing in his favourite spot, the Stadtkirche pulpit, preaching the gospel as he instructed every Lutheran pastor to do as their main task. His outstretched right hand reaches towards an outsized depiction of the suffering Jesus Christ on the cross. It was through that sacrifice of His Son on Calvary, Luther came to believe, that God revealed His mercy to humankind. It was what gave him some hope of salvation, and a partial cure for his *Anfechtung*.

It went to the essence, too, of what he meant by 'justification by faith'. The 'good works' done by any individual during a lifetime, including buying indulgences, played no role in God's judgement. It was all a question, Luther insisted, of having faith and trusting in God's mercy and grace, as revealed by the sacrifice on the cross of His Son.

Introduction

It is one to ponder, and to explore more thoroughly, but the friendly usher is once more at my elbow. The service is about to begin. And so I exchange the altar for the Corpus Christi Chapel.

*

Catholicism isn't a fan of informality when it comes to any sort of liturgy, so I am immediately wrong-footed as I step in through the door of the chapel and am welcomed by a benign elderly American in a dog collar, short-sleeved black shirt and pale trousers of a type more suited to an Alpine hike. He clasps my hand and introduces himself as the Rev. Cliff from Wichita, one of a team of retired pastors who come to Wittenberg each summer for two-week spells to run these services to give visitors a sense that Lutheranism isn't just a piece of history, but a living, breathing faith, as much part of the twenty-first century as it was of the sixteenth.

When we are all greeted and seated, the Rev. Cliff's Brazilian-born wife, Lois, gets things rolling from the front row by leading us, a cappella, in Luther's best-known hymn, 'A Mighty Fortress Is My God'. I've read the lyrics before and listened to recordings, but never before heard them in the flesh.

With singing in church, I tend to operate on the basis that hymns are rather like those seven basic plots that cover all stories. Once you know seven tunes, you can find your way through anything in the hymnal. And, the occasional duff note to one side, what the Rev. Cliff calls 'the hymn of the Reformation' fits the pattern. It may be my first time, but by verse four it feels as if I have been singing it all my life.

One lyric in particular leaps out as a variation on another of those phrases most often associated with Luther. At the Diet of Worms (a good way of getting over the schoolboy sniggers at how strange this sounds in English is to pronounce the W in the German way as a V), Luther would not be cowed by the might of the papacy and the presence of the Holy Roman Emperor, Charles V. He refused to recant his writings critical of the Catholic Church of his day, ending with a fine rhetorical flourish: 'Here I stand. I can do no other.' Or as his hymn (written subsequently) has it: 'we tremble not, unmoved we stand/They cannot overpow'r us.'

By the time the Rev. Cliff embarks on the formal prayers, the standing and kneeling, the rituals of moving around the chapel's ancient altar, I'm feeling pleasantly at home, save for the wet patch I am leaving on the very clean floor. It is all remarkably like what I am used to in my usual Sunday Catholic mass back home.

The overlap that exists today between the two branches of the Christian family is brought home at the bidding prayers, when the Rev. Cliff highlights Father Jacques Hamel, the eighty-six-year-old Catholic priest who had been murdered the previous week by two followers of Islamic State on the altar of his church of Saint-Etienne-du-Rouvray near Rouen.

Such mutual concern is a relatively new development. The century of 'religious wars' that followed Luther's death in February 1546 was also a battle over territorial claims and 'big power' rivalries in Europe: in modern terms, the political, social and economic as well as the religious. But it was undeniably fuelled by Catholic rhetoric so vituperative as to be an incitement to violence. One twisted account of Luther's life, by his contemporary and sworn enemy, the Catholic controversialist, Johannes Cochaleus, painted the reformer as a seven-headed serpent, manipulative in his theology, spurred on by lust and personal ambition, and worse than the notorious prisoner Barabbas, who features in the gospel accounts of Jesus' trial and crucifixion.[3] Cochaleus invented quotations and whole episodes to paint Luther in the worst possible light.

Once Germany and those who used it as a battleground had been exhausted by a hundred years of war following Luther's death, and the fighting came to an end, the borders between Catholic and Lutheran territories were every bit as excluding as the theological divisions that had been erected. For more than three hundred years these Christian cousins didn't even acknowledge each other's existence if they met in the street, so thoroughly were they estranged. It took until the middle of the twentieth century for two Catholic scholars, Joseph Lortz and his student Erwin Iserloh, to refute Cochaleus's poisoned pen and the portrait of Luther it had produced, which still prevailed as gospel in Roman circles. But it was the reforming Second Vatican Council, held in Rome between 1962 and 1965 and attended by the world's Catholic bishops in modernising mood, that finally began a meaningful dialogue between the two faiths, aimed at addressing their turbulent past.

The Council produced a decree on ecumenism (*Unitatis Redintegratio*) and initiated the first, official Catholic–Lutheran talks. These took place over four phases from 1967, growing in confidence and trust over the decades and resulting in 1999 in the 'Joint Declaration on the Doctrine of Justification', issued by both parties, and stating that 'a common understanding' had been reached. A mere 453 years after Luther's death, the core theological dispute had been laid to rest.

It was a ridiculously long amount of time to take, it goes without saying; the sort of delay that is another factor in explaining modern intolerance of religion. Yet such a laying-to-rest of the ghosts of the Reformation, however long-winded and drawn-out, should not be lightly dismissed as too little, too late, or irrelevant. It sends out a different message to our own age, more troubled by religious intolerance and antagonism than any in living memory, a hopeful sign that wrongs done, wounds inflicted and divisions apparently set in stone can, eventually, be overcome.

And that healing process between the Reformation rivals is now in full swing. If the Rev. Cliff Winter has welcomed me with open arms to his service in Luther's church in Wittenberg, even after I have confessed myself a Catholic and dripped all over the floor, then 2017 will see an abundance of opportunities for the two churches to go an ecumenical step further. In preparation for the anniversary, Germany's Catholic bishops have already been hailing Luther as 'a religious pathfinder, gospel witness and teacher of the faith', quite a change of tone since Pope Leo X in 1518 had referred to him as 'a son of iniquity'.[4]

To mark the anniversary of Luther's attack in the Ninety-Five Theses on papal authority and Catholic practice, the Lutheran World Federation, representing the vast majority of Lutherans around the globe, and the Rome-based Pontifical Council for Christian Unity, on behalf of 1.3 billion Catholics, are jointly planning what they describe as a 'joint *fest* for Jesus Christ' to show the world that 'despite the Reformation period, [we] have more in common today than what divides [us]'.[5]

It represents quite a turnaround. The two churches describe their various shared plans (including a common pilgrimage to the Holy Land and a two-day celebration in Malmö, Sweden) as something for 'the age of globalisation'. The jargon, though, should not distract from the unparalleled nature of what was contained in an announcement that has largely gone unheralded.

The text of a prayer service has been made available to local Lutherans and Catholics anywhere who want to use liturgy to find out more about each other and put behind them past battles. 'Thanks be to you [God],' reads one of the set prayers, 'for the good transformations and reforms that were set in motion by the Reformation or by struggling with its challenges.'

That neatly touches both bases: the teaching on which Luther built his distinctive Church, and the Counter-Reformation, agreed by the Council of Trent, meeting between 1545 and 1563, whereby Catholicism responded to the questions Luther had posed, and the exodus from its pews that he had caused, by reforming itself (though not along the lines he proposed) and thereby ensuring that it is still around today.

Another prayer urges that both Catholics and Lutherans be given space 'to experience the pain over failures and trespasses, guilt and sin in the persons and events that are being remembered'. It is nothing short of a joint *mea culpa*, as my Christian Brother teachers long ago taught me to describe saying sorry. Or 'through my fault', as Luther would have preferred we put it, rejecting the excluding use of Church Latin in favour of German, arguing that it was the language that his congregations spoke.

It was Benedict XVI, the former Cardinal Joseph Ratzinger and the first German Pope in a millennium, who translated all these fine words about reconciliation between Catholics and Lutherans into something more tangible than conferences of theologians and printed materials for dedicated ecumenists. In November 2008, in the same Saint Peter's that Luther had seen being built on a visit to Rome as a young man, a sight that convinced him the papacy was the Antichrist, Benedict addressed himself directly to the question of 'justification by faith alone', as Luther was later to amend his formula. 'Being just simply means being with Christ and in Christ,' the Pope said. 'And this suffices. Further observations are no longer necessary. For this reason, Luther's phrase "faith alone" is true.'[6]

What pain the world might have been spared if one of his predecessors had uttered those words during Luther's lifetime, but here, finally, was the head of the Catholic Church treating Luther as an equal, not an irritant, and acknowledging that he was essentially right. Two years later, on his first visit to his homeland as Pope, Benedict went to the former Augustinian monastery at Erfurt, where the young Luther had lived and studied. 'We should give thanks to God for all the elements of unity which he has preserved for us and bestows on us anew,' he told his mixed (Catholic and Lutheran) audience.

The language was so positive that it gave rise to speculation that Luther's excommunication from the Church of his birth and upbringing, announced in the papal bull *Exsurge Domine* by Leo X in 1520, was about to be lifted. But this process of healing wasn't about rewriting the past, but rather moving forward with Lutherans in a spirit of mutual respect.

And forward it is going. In November 2015, Benedict's successor, the Argentinian Pope Francis, visited the Lutheran church in Rome – something that has now become commonplace for Catholic bishops, and another sign of how far things have been changing. In one of the meet-the-people, question-and-answer sessions that have become his hallmark, Francis was challenged by a Lutheran woman. She was married to a Catholic, she told the pontiff, but was not allowed to receive communion in her husband's church, whereas he could in hers.

Her observation touched on another central issue of the Reformation: some Protestants held that the bread and wine Jesus used in the first eucharist were merely a symbol of His body and blood. Luther, for his part, said they were more. He maintained a belief in the 'real presence' – that the bread and wine are really bread and wine that, through the mystery of God's grace, really become His body and blood. His position, though, was still some way short of Catholicism's rather more theologically involved doctrine of transubstantiation, a gap that means, ever after, Lutherans cannot take communion in a Catholic Church.

No doubt conscious of the deep theological waters in which he was swimming, Francis replied to the woman that he did not 'dare to give permission' for her to join her husband at the communion rails, alluding to the upset it would cause traditionalist Catholics, but still went on to puzzle over why the 'explanations' and 'interpretations' that separate Catholic and Lutheran approaches to the eucharist should necessarily make inter-communion impossible. 'Life,' he said, well capturing the attitude of many today in the pews, and more still beyond, 'is bigger than explanations and interpretations ... I ask myself: but don't we have the same baptism? If we have the same baptism, shouldn't we be walking together?'[7]

*

Before that can happen, there is undoubtedly more progress that needs to be made. Even after half a millennium, schism cannot just be magicked away by time, goodwill, fine words, or even the leadership of a Pope more open than any other in the modern era. But the degree of rapprochement between Catholicism and Lutheranism today is such that, when I emerged from the Stadtkirche in Wittenberg into suddenly blue skies, I found myself considering one of those historical what-ifs. What would Luther make of the modern Catholic Church? Might he want to remain a member of it rather than leave and set up on his own?

There is still a local Catholic church in Wittenberg, an undistinguished twentieth-century building, tucked away out of sight on a back street, well off the main tourist trail, where workmen have now re-emerged after the deluge and are back at work weeding between the cobbles at the side of the road with great precision, and then burning away any remaining roots with a blow torch.

I am trying to conjure up a picture of Luther as a pin-up in the dissident ranks of the so-called 'liberal' or 'à-la-carte' Catholics who now vocally challenge their own bishops for change. There are plenty of them in Germany, where some Catholics even attend services led by women priests. The Vatican says they are illicitly ordained, but they still attract quite a following.[8] Most surveys suggest that anywhere between 50 and 80 per cent of church-going Catholics in the developed world now want to see their Church reformed in some way.[9] Implicit in this is a questioning of papal authority, which leaves the liberals not so very far apart from Luther's stance.

Before I get carried away, though, I remind myself that Luther is not a time-traveller, and, moreover, that the Catholic Church, as currently constituted, would quite simply not be in the form it is today without the impetus to reform itself that was so rudely provided by the Reformation Luther led. He cannot both head the charge 500 years ago, and then return to reap the benefits of the process he set in motion.

And Luther was definitely no liberal. Though he helped instigate the liberalisation of Europe, by moving from the collective approach to religion and worship of Catholicism towards a greater emphasis on the individual, with each one following his or her conscience before God, Luther would have been horrified by what has subsequently developed from that breakthrough in the wider interaction between the state and the citizen. He was by nature conservative, a man rooted in his own late medieval age.

Yet I am reluctant to let go of the daydream of a still-Catholic Luther. What is striking is the degree to which those more recent reforms that have reshaped Catholicism, especially at the Second Vatican Council, have in many ways followed Luther's prescription. In my lifetime, for example, the vernacular has replaced Latin as the language of the mass, just as he advocated. When I go to receive the eucharist at Catholic mass on Sunday, I can now do so in 'both kinds' – the bread *and* the wine – which again Luther instituted as a way of demolishing the clerical–laity divide that continued to see the wine reserved for priests in Catholicism until the late 1960s.

Moreover, I even receive bread and wine at my local Catholic parish church in north Norfolk from a married priest. Luther discarded the rule that clergy had to be celibate. The Church of Rome still hasn't quite fallen into line with that yet. Married clergy remain the exception rather than the rule as far as the Vatican is concerned. My Norfolk priest is part of a concession granted in the 1990s to that small number of Anglican vicars with wives who were prompted by changes within their own Church to convert to Catholicism, but who still felt a calling to ministry.

Pope Francis has, though, hinted that he would like to extend this and drop altogether the rule that ordinarily Catholic priests must be celibate. As Luther pointed out, it is a man-made regulation and has no basis in Jesus' teaching in the gospels. But, so far, it has only been a case of hints.

Francis, however, has been busy making other reforms that Luther would have applauded. He has shown himself keen, when tackling such matters as the treatment of divorced and remarried Catholics, to devolve decision-making away from Rome to bishops in their dioceses. Luther was a powerful advocate of German Catholics choosing for themselves, when and where appropriate, rather than having decisions imposed from far away by the Pope.

Francis is also subjecting the Vatican curia to a painful overhaul in order to tackle just the sort of corruption, arrogance and centralism that Luther objected to so strongly, a stance that won him the support of many Germans who felt simultaneously exploited financially and ignored spiritually by Rome. And, of course, the sale of indulgences, the initial spur for the Ninety-Five Theses, stopped many moons ago – though Catholics are still asked, but not required, to make a donation if they apply for a mass to be said for a deceased friend or relative.

What a reborn Luther would surely find most conducive in the modern Catholic Church is the extent to which it now echoes not just his practical reforms but also his own words. For example, one of the most resonant and inspiring phrases of the Second Vatican Council has an unmissable ring of Luther. In his 1520 *Appeal to the Christian Nobility of the German Nation*, Luther argued for 'the priesthood of all baptised believers'. It was his strongest weapon in his fight against clergy and monks imagining that they had a faster track to salvation than those in the pews.

He was savaged for such a suggestion by his Catholic critics at the time. It was, they said, a recipe for chaos and anarchy. And yet, in November 1964, in *Lumen Gentium* ('The Light of Nations'), the dogmatic constitution of the Catholic Church set out by the Second Vatican Council, is found the promise that clergy and laity should henceforth be equal partners as 'the people of God', an equality rooted in a 'shared priesthood' of all Catholics, received at baptism but lived out thereafter in different ways. That's pure Luther.

*

My day has come full circle. I am sitting at the same outdoor table at Tante Emma's Bier und Café Haus in the main square that had been mine before the thunderstorm broke. Only the puddles on the ground, fast disappearing under a strong, warm sun, remain to show that it hasn't been a perfect summer's day. And my still-damp clothes and shoes. Hoping they will dry out of their own accord is probably as fanciful as wanting the wounds of 500 years of division between Catholics and Lutherans to evaporate.

There are, inevitably, outstanding issues. Luther's most significant complaint, as laid out in the Ninety-Five Theses, was with the papacy's claim to overarching authority. That remains unchanged in the theory, if not in the current practice of Catholicism. And, among other barriers, the Church of Rome continues to insist on its seven sacraments, whereas Luther limited his list to three.

Yet his Reformation was never a straight rejection of everything Rome stood for. It began in the Ninety-Five Theses as a desire to see change, that most potent of slogans down the centuries. It only escalated into something more when his appeal was contemptuously dismissed by the Vatican. Pope Leo X is said to have brushed off Luther (revealing much of Roman attitudes to Germany) as just another drunken German who would regret his outspokenness once sober. Catholic theologians took their lead from such high-handedness. They based their subsequent repudiations of Luther and the invitation to debate he offered (that was, after all, what the Ninety-Five Theses were – a plea for a discussion, not an alternative manifesto) on a blanket assertion that the Pope's word was final. As a result, the gap grew wider and deeper, and the barbs of both sides more poisonous.

Once Luther had been excommunicated in 1521, any way back was immeasurably harder, especially once he started building a Church within a Church in those areas of Germany that sided with him. Even so, there remained a real and live possibility in his lifetime that the breach could be repaired, not least because so many German princes were pushing for it. Luther's public persona was as one unwilling to compromise, and he played up to it, maintaining his anti-papal rhetoric right up to the year before his death when he penned *Against the Papacy at Rome, Founded by the Devil*, another of his characteristically provocative titles.

Yet behind such eye-catching outpourings, Luther appreciated the argument for compromise, that certain Catholic 'abuses' might have to be tolerated to achieve a bigger goal of limited reform and eventual reunion, a position advanced most powerfully by his close collaborator Philipp Melanchthon. It was Melanchthon who, with Luther's full support, wrote the *Augsburg Confession*, a statement of Lutheran belief that, in 1530, represented the best chance in Luther's lifetime of achieving that. Its language was diplomatic, and the issue of papal authority deliberately relegated to smooth the way forward.

It failed to achieve the desired result, but, unlike his contemporary, fellow Protestant and sometime rival, Ulrich Zwingli, Luther never thereafter formally declared independence for his fledgling organisation from the Catholic Church. Instead he worked in parallel with Catholicism, pondering increasingly as he neared death as to what exactly the Church was: the hierarchical structure run by the Pope and his bishops; or the assembly of those individuals gathered to share the Scriptures, hear a sermon and worship God? By the second definition, Lutheranism was still part of the whole, not a breakaway. There was even a part of him, Luther on occasion admitted, that missed his Catholic days.

*

The nature and extent of any continuing attachment, and its relevance today, is part of the story I now want to tell: of how Luther came to fall out with the Church of his birth, upbringing and formation; why the disagreement grew and such a chasm opened up between the sides; and to what extent it developed its own momentum, or was driven by Luther. None of what happened was inevitable, certainly not predictable, though what did come to pass shaped Europe and the world ever after in ways that the participants could never have imagined. Or that we, today, truly appreciate.

Luther's tale is now too often sidelined as a chapter in the history of Christian fragmentation, at a time when Christianity itself is increasingly overlooked in our secular, scientific and sceptical age. Yet Luther is one of those key individuals who explains why the world is as it is now. His biography is not then just for believers, of whatever denomination, but for all who want to understand how we have arrived at the state we are in.

There have been, granted, many who have told the story of Luther before me, but none so far, to my knowledge, in the particular setting of a 500th anniversary that will see Catholics and Lutherans edging closer than ever before to putting past disagreements behind them. That focus informs the pages that follow and gives the book its title.

The most obvious way of getting under the skin of Luther is to hear his voice as much as possible. There are, after all, few other figures from the first half of the sixteenth century about whom so much original material exists, and none where the archives are so well organised, annotated and easily accessible in English as well as German as those about Luther, thanks to the tireless efforts of scholars. Indeed, there is so much (the American edition of

Luther's collected works currently runs to fifty-five volumes) that there are always new insights to be gleaned by those with suffi-cient curiosity and stamina. As Samuel Taylor Coleridge once remarked in the journal *The Field* of the written footprint Luther has left behind: 'perhaps there is no subject for which so many unused materials are extant.'[10]

And what a voice he had! Luther's turn of phrase was remark-able. It could be sublime, or it could be the crass, crude swagger that we might now more readily associate with a football manager. But it was compelling and all his own. You would not mistake a piece of his writing or oratory for another's.

Accordingly, in what follows, I try, wherever practical, to strip back the accumulations of 500 years and let Luther tell it for himself, whether via his private letters or his public outpourings with his pen or in the pulpit. They were hugely popular in his day, as the newfangled printing presses churned them out and the artists with their woodcuts dressed them up so that they reached into every corner of Europe. Even the cardinals in Rome were rumoured to have a secret stash of his latest tracts and sermons.

And in this biography, Luther will talk like Luther. That means drawing on his *Tischreden* or *Table Talk* from the last quarter of his life. Some scholars downplay them, since they were recorded by professed admirers and uttered with the bene-fit of hindsight by the great man they had come to hear. They do, indeed, have their obvious drawbacks. Memory can be unre-liable, and those at the centre of events often strain every sinew in later life to secure a particular reading of their contribution, or 'legacy'. When appropriate this danger will be highlighted, but balanced with the realisation that in the *Table Talk* we can unmistakably hear the real Luther, at his most confessional, at his most charismatic, and using his most accessible language. They span the gap between our age and his more effortlessly than any of his formal texts.

For all their manifold historical shortcomings when it comes to the facts, the *Table Talks* do nevertheless manage authoritatively to challenge some of the best-known aspects of Luther's story as it is told today. The year 2017 will see a celebration of his nailing of the Ninety-Five Theses to the door of the Castle Church in Wittenberg, but nowhere in *Table Talk* does Luther mention ever doing that. Nor, for that matter, in his letters and other documents.

He certainly produced the text, and sent it to his archbishop, who in turn sent it to Rome. Quite how and why it caused such a stir is so much more complicated than the traditional image of an angry friar putting up a petition on the church door. Some famous men and women have their whole lives boiled down in popular history into a series of gobbet-sized anecdotes. In Luther's case, there was the thunderbolt, the nailing of the Ninety-Five Theses, and then his outspoken and still-repeated words of defiance before the Diet of Worms.

These edited highlights have to be properly scrutinised. I am reluctant to be the killjoy who tones down splashes of colour in Luther's story, but they don't always seem authentic, while the facts about him are just as vivid and revelatory. Understanding Luther's complex personality is one of the three principal goals of this biography. The second is to explain his theology in a way that includes rather than excludes those many without formal theological training, a sound knowledge of the Bible, or sufficient experience of the rituals of a Christian church service to guide them through what, in an age of disbelief, can be off-putting and even irrelevant jargon. This biography will be Luther for the general reader, curious about our past, not Luther for the converted or the specialist.

And the third strand is history. Luther's theology was not startlingly original. Others had said the same things before him. The key fact about Luther, and why we remember him, is that he succeeded while others who had walked the same path in rebelling against Catholicism's claim to ultimate authority had paid with their lives for having the temerity or conviction to speak out. The Bohemian priest Jan Hus, for instance, was burned at the stake on the orders of the Church in 1415 for proposing very similar ideas to Luther.

So how did Luther get away with it? The answer lies in the convoluted politics of his day: in the complacency of Rome and the corruption of the papacy; in new theological currents of Humanism that had created a climate more amenable to reform; in the rise of nationalism as well as economic and social discontent in Germany; in the disintegration of the Holy Roman Empire; in the jockeying for position between the great powers in Europe; and in the existential threat to medieval Christendom posed by the advance of the Ottoman Turks.

Weave these many threads together successfully and the backdrop becomes more defined and therefore enables Luther to step clearly into the centre of the picture. Like any of Shakespeare's best-known plays, with Luther's life the details, the characters and even the dialogue may be familiar, but each new telling has the potential to afford fresh angles and insights for its times.

A final thought delays me in front of Luther's statue in the main square before I trudge back in my waterlogged shoes to the Luther Hotel to change into something dry: does a biographer have to like his or her subject? Those I have written about before have, for the most part, been either alive or recently deceased, and thus sufficiently within reach for me to make a real connection with them and develop a genuine sympathy, even as I understand their flaws. Elsewhere, when I have strayed further back in history, my subjects may or may not have existed at all (the devil, Judas, Pope Joan).

So Luther is my first undeniably flesh-and-blood subject examined at such a distance in time. And he is a difficult figure to like, as the stout, grey-green statue in front of me makes once more abundantly clear. His mouth is not only unsmiling: it turns down at the corners. His eyes and whole countenance are fierce and he brandishes an open Bible in front of him more as a weapon than a shield.

He has the same look in almost every other surviving portrait of him, which may account for his enduring reputation as dour to the point of depressive, punitive, pious and unbending, none of them compliments as far as the modern age (or any other) is concerned.

And yet, I remind myself, for sheer, selfless courage, Luther is impossible to outdo and cannot but be admired. Behind that unappealing exterior lies a hero to rival any other. For a thousand years before he came along, the Catholic Church had been one of the great powers on earth, so powerful it even fixed the calendar the world still uses, taking as its pivot the birth of Jesus Christ. It had grown bloated, corrupt and complacent in its rule, until along came Martin Luther, a relatively lowly born monk from the backwoods of Germany. He had the courage to take it on, to challenge its bishops, distinguished theologians and even popes, not to mention the princes who were their allies. He did so in the full and certain knowledge that it would most likely cost him his life. He was confronting the might of the first truly universal religion, and doing so in person and often alone with an extraordinary passion, intensity and energy that is all the more admirable for his selflessness. And most remarkable of all: not only did he survive, but he triumphed, and we are all better off because of him. What's not to like about that?

PART ONE:

Friar Martin

'Luther was a rather endangered young man [who] found a spiritual solution.'

Erik Erikson, *Young Man Luther* (1958)

CHAPTER ONE

Growing Up: A Lawyer in the Making

'I am the son of peasants. My great grandfather, grandfather and father were all simple farmers.'

Martin Luther, *Table Talk*[1]

For one who in later life enjoyed talking about himself at length and apparently unguardedly, Martin Luther left behind very few clues as to his childhood. The six volumes of his *Tischreden*, or *Table Talk* – all recorded in his Wittenberg home from 1531 onwards by his admirers, making notes as the most famous man in Europe part reconstructed, part embroidered his own biography – provide much more detail about Luther's life than is available for any other early sixteenth-century public figure. Yet, in them, the references to his upbringing are scant.

When they do surface, they can be misleading. Take Luther's claim, which opens this chapter, that he was from peasant stock. His father, Hans, did indeed hail from a poor, rural, farming background in Möhra, in Thuringia, a wooded, hilly region that sits in the centre of modern Germany. Back then it was part of the 'Holy Roman Empire of the German Nation', a loose assembly of territories of differing sizes, each with their own ruler. Those who have delved into Hans Ludher's family history, though, paint him as one step above what was usual for rural 'peasants' who eked out a subsistence existence on the land.[2] 'Yeoman farmer' might capture it better. And there is evidence, too, that Luther's mother, Margarethe Lindemann, was connected by birth to the emerging merchant class in towns and cities where fledgling capitalism was displacing the prevailing late medieval system.[3] She had a nephew who was a priest and a cousin who taught medicine at Leipzig University. She was even, some have suggested, sufficiently educated to instil in her son a precocious love of words and reading in what was an age of widespread illiteracy.[4]

This was not the impression Luther was seeking to convey when, in January 1533, he remarked at table: 'In my youth, my father was a poor miner. My mother carried all the wood needed on her back. That is how I was raised.'[5] He might just as well have added that they were bent double and had no teeth. Not only was he from peasant stock, Luther was asserting, he also had a peasant upbringing, but the truth is rather different.

According to the custom of the day, Hans, as the eldest son, didn't inherit the yeoman Ludher family's agricultural lands in Möhra. Instead, they went to a younger brother, leaving Hans to find work in the copper and silver mines that ran through the hills of Thuringia like rabbit burrows. By dint of hard graft, commercial acumen and good fortune in what were notoriously dangerous working conditions, Hans prospered. He ended up owning the extraction rights to six mineshafts as well as two copper smelters, and employing his own workforce. So well respected did this 'peasant' become that he is recorded as one of four 'lords' on his town council.

So why would Luther claim humbler origins for himself than he had – especially when, as a young friar, he had apparently been intent on travelling in the opposite direction, swapping the coarse-sounding Ludher in favour of the more refined, Latin- and Greek-influenced Luther? Those who rise from modest beginnings are often prone as they grow older to exaggerate their lowly start in life, conveying just how far they have risen up the social scale ('if you think you're having it hard, when I was a child . . .'). Luther has few rivals in this regard. By the time he shared his description of his downtrodden mother and father, his name was known all over Europe, he counted princes among his friends, and he lived in style in a large former monastery, the four-storey Black Cloister in Wittenberg.

There may, though, have been a more specific purpose behind his caricature of his roots. His revolt against the Catholic Church had initially drawn widespread support from the peasant classes, who regarded him as one of their own and their champion. In his words they read not just a spiritual message but one that echoed their economic and social grievances. Yet in 1524, when they rose up against their rulers to right those grievances, expecting Luther's support, he had sided with the German princes. So here he was, nine years on at his table in Wittenberg, trying to heal the breach by insisting to the peasant class that he was still essentially one of them.

And, in fairness to Luther, there may have been more than a grain of truth in that hard-pressed picture of childhood he conveyed. At least in the early days of their marriage, his parents would have been thrifty. Hans was setting out to make his fortune, and Margarethe supported him by running a tight household for their expanding family.[6] Why waste money on fuel when there was plenty to be gathered simply by walking around the forests that covered large swathes of the neighbourhood? It was what many people did.

Johannes – always shortened to Hans – and Margarethe had married in her hometown of Eisenach in 1479, aged 20 and 16 respectively. By the time Martin came along on 10 November 1483,[7] the couple had moved to Eisleben. The only portraits that survive of them date from much later, shortly before their deaths. Both are by Lucas Cranach the Elder, court painter to the Electors of Saxony and a close friend and supporter of Martin Luther. He affords neither sitter any airs and graces.[8]

Hans Ludher has the rough countenance of one who has fought his way to get where he is, from his crooked nose, fiery, impatient eyes and ill-kempt hair to the battered, earthenware hands that sit awkwardly in his lap, at odds with the plush fur trimming on his jacket collar, symbol of the hard-won respectability he has acquired. Margarethe, by contrast, is dressed with stark simplicity, as any woman back then working in the fields might have been, though her clothes are clean and pressed. Her hair and brow are covered by a crudely woven peasant scarf, and her hollow cheeks are browned by the sun. Unlike her husband's, her eyes are still and passive, her whole demeanour one of stoicism in the face of all that this world could throw at her.

Four years separate their marriage from Martin's birth. They may have had other children before he came along, who did not live long, but records are opaque. Infant mortality was common in the late medieval age. The resulting fear that their newborn son might not survive caused the Ludhers to follow the prevailing custom and baptise Martin as soon as possible after his arrival. Church teaching was explicit that any child not christened (and therefore cleansed of the stain of original sin that all humans carry because of the misdeeds of Adam and Eve in the Garden of Eden) would be denied salvation in heaven and consigned to *limbus puerorum* ('Limbo of the Infants'). So within twenty-four hours of his arrival, the Ludhers presented their baby son for baptism at the Church of Saints Peter and Paul in Eisleben. They chose for him the name of the saint whose feast day occurred on 11 November – Martin de Tours, a fourth-century martyr, traditionally depicted cutting his cloak in half to share it with a beggar.

Within a few months, baby Martin and his parents had shifted again, this time the ten miles to the town of Mansfeld, in the heart of the mineral-rich Harz Hills, where there were opportunities aplenty for an ambitious miner such as Hans, keen to provide for his family. Some speculative accounts suggest that he had been sacked from his job in Eisleben (and even that Margarethe worked in a brothel) but they are based on too literal a reading of the personal insults and slights casually flung about by both sides at the height of the Reformation's war of words.[9]

Social mobility

Crucially for their son's future, the Ludhers became – by their own efforts – sufficiently well-heeled to pay for education; in effect, in Hans's case, and like many a father since, ensuring that his offspring enjoyed a better start in life than he had. Young Martin began in the local school in Mansfeld, which would have run the standard curriculum of the time in Latin, music and grammar. The emphasis was on learning by rote, memory and recitation, with mistakes ironed out by corporal punishment. 'Some teachers are as horrible as hangmen,' Luther recalled. 'Even I one morning was whipped fifteen times because I had not learned to decline and conjugate.'[10]

If the regime sounds brutal, it was unremarkable for the time, and Luther did not appear any more traumatised by the experience than his classmates. Indeed, he was ever after a passionate proponent of education. That 'even I' hints at a good and diligent pupil.

The true mark of the Ludhers' affluence – or at least of their willingness to scrimp and save in order to be in a position to pay – was shown at Easter of 1497, when Martin was able to continue his studies beyond the age of thirteen, a privilege available to only a small percentage of boys of his age and only a tiny number of high-born girls. He was sent north as a boarder to a school in the cathedral city of Magdeburg on the River Elbe. He was later to describe the school as linked to the Brethren of the Common Life, a significant lay movement of Dutch origin within the Catholic Church. Its devotees lived together in community, sharing their goods, but without taking religious vows. They adhered to the '*Devotio Moderna*' – or 'Modern Devotion' – which stressed simplicity above all, as well as the importance of penance, meditation and prayer in building a personal relationship with God. Such beliefs were the basis of the curriculum the Brethren offered in schools across northern Europe. These provided greater opportunities for learning to the sons of those from modest backgrounds. The best known among their alumni was Thomas

à Kempis, whose *Imitation of Christ*, a book of devotional medita-
tions on the life and teaching of Jesus, was popular in the late medieval period, and remains a spiritual classic.[11]

There are, potentially, links aplenty between the theological
arguments Luther advanced as an adult and his early training
with the Brethren, but recent research has indicated that the movement had no school of their own in Magdeburg. What Luther
may have been referring to was that some among his teachers in
the city were somehow linked with, or inspired by, the Brethren
and their ideals. Even so, he only spent a year in their care. It
should not be treated as a life-changing experience.

One episode from that year did, however, stick in his memory
ever after. One day, in the street in Magdeburg, he saw Prince
Wilhelm of Anhalt. Wilhelm was a scion of a local Saxon ducal
family, but he had given up his blue-blooded privileges and all his
worldly goods to enter a friary, whose members survived by
begging in the street. It was not an uncommon choice in the medieval era – Saint Francis of Assisi is the best-known example, turning his back at the start of the thirteenth century on a carefree life
as the son of a wealthy merchant draper to live as a mendicant[12] –
but Luther never forgot Prince Wilhelm's admirable example or his
emaciation. 'With my own eyes I saw him . . . carrying the sack like
a donkey. He had so worn himself down by fasting and vigil that
he looked like a death's head, mere skin and bone. No one could
look upon him without feeling ashamed of his own life.'[13]

Aged fourteen, Luther switched schools to Saint George's in
Eisenach, his mother's home town. It may have represented, in the
eyes of the ambitious Hans Ludher, a more prestigious place of
learning for his son. Or the change could have been about money.
In Eisenach, Martin could lodge with Margarethe's relatives and
save on the costs of boarding. Or perhaps this small-town boy
was homesick in the big city of Magdeburg, and the promise of
family close at hand in more modest Eisenach influenced his

parents' choice. What is sure is that his three years at Saint George's, with its traditional Latin-based curriculum, paved the young Luther's way into university. The debt he felt to the place is made clear from the invitation he sent to his teacher there, Wiegand Guldenapf, to attend his first mass as a priest.[14] On the same guest list was Father Johann Braun, a local priest in Eisenach, who organised evenings of discussion and music for the students, and to whom Luther wrote fondly in 1507 as 'his dearest friend in Christ' in what is claimed as the earliest surviving authentic letter in his handwriting.[15]

And it may also have been in Eisenach that Luther began to play the lute, an instrument that later inspired in him a love of Church music. In his *Table Talk*, he remembered how, in his 'home town', he was part of a group of youngsters who went from house to house 'singing for sausages'.[16] This was evidently a local custom in Eisenach, rather than evidence that the pupils were going hungry.

After Saint George's, there was a choice of Leipzig or Erfurt for his university education. In another decision that confirms his high ambitions for his son, Hans plumped for Erfurt, the grander of the two. Established in 1379 in the Thuringian capital, it had been the third university to be set up in Germany and quickly had become the largest. Arriving in May 1501, and signing himself as 'Martinus Ludher ex Mansfeldt', Luther joined the Faculty of the Arts.[17]

His later recollections of his university days swung violently from one extreme to the other. Sometimes, he would conjure up Erfurt as 'a new Bethlehem', with orchards and vineyards, surrounded by fields of flax and saffron (used there in the manufacture of dyes), and a skyline dominated by steeples and spires.[18] On others, he would decry it as 'nothing better than a whorehouse and beerhouse. The students have been the most diligent in obedience to the study of those two subjects. Among them are no professors, no preachers.'[19] Such mood swings, as will become apparent, were an essential part of Luther's make-up.

Erfurt had grown rich as a commercial centre, at the crossroads of trading routes, and its prosperity was on full display in the city's cathedral. It housed an organ said to rival that of Saint Peter's in Rome, as well as numerous expensively purchased relics of saints that, though of questionable provenance, attracted pilgrims. This 'religious trade' meant that, within Erfurt's fortified walls, twelve major religious orders were present, including Dominicans, Franciscans and Augustinians, as well as eighty religious institutions, and an estimated one thousand priests, monks, friars and nuns, out of a total population of close to twenty thousand.

Luther's reference to brothels and *Bierkeller* prompts inevitable questions as to how he spent his time there. Though he later spoke of 'lustful thoughts [that] come upon us without any special invitation, like fleas and lice',[20] he never gave any specific indication that in his youth and later as a friar he himself had found the Catholic Church's demand that he abstain from sexual relationships difficult to follow. He was not, it seems, a lusty young student keen to enjoy his newfound independence. Though he was married by the time he made the remark, he once said, 'nor am I tempted to be unchaste, because I have enough of that, and need no more.'[21] It suggests his libido was healthy but controlled.

Of the dangers of drinking to excess, however, his later warnings were to sound apocalyptic. 'The love of beer will yet lead to the downfall of the universities', he railed, adding with his usual rhetorical flourish that he 'often cursed the first beer brewer' for turning grain into 'dung water ... which we later piss on the wall'.[22] There might just be the guilt of a misspent youth lurking behind the vehemence of such remarks, and a drop of hypocrisy, for the older Luther certainly liked a drink. 'I booze a little myself,' he confessed (though he blamed it on his many responsibilities).[23] Yet the evidence of his Erfurt contemporary, Johann Crotus, recalling in 1520 his now famous fellow student, appears to dispel such notions: 'you were once', he wrote, 'the musician and learned philosopher of our company.'[24]

By music, Crotus was surely referring to Church music. Luther was no wandering troubadour with a lute. 'Music is certainly the greatest of the divine gifts,' he once pronounced, 'because it is the greatest enemy of the devil, with which many great torments of the soul can be driven away.'[25]

The young man who arrived in Erfurt was, then, a thorough-going conformist, well-suited to the regime at universities that, as largely Church-run and Church-controlled institutions, had more in common with a monastery than a modern hall of residence or 'frat' house. Students lived in austere student lodgings, where they rose early to fit in prayers, devotions and mass before attending lectures. The front door was locked by 8p.m.

Driven to learn and to achieve, Luther tackled the *trivium* of grammar, dialectic (logic) and rhetoric. It was largely a continuation of what he had been studying in school. What was remarkable, though, was the intensity that he displayed, so much so that he gained his bachelor's degree in just one year, the shortest possible time allowed by the university's statutes. His awareness of how much it was costing his parents to maintain him at Erfurt was probably the spur, but there is, too, already a sense that Luther was predisposed to fling himself into his work with prodigious, even manic energy.

Father and son

The most powerful influence on the young Luther was undoubtedly his father. Over the centuries it has prompted much speculation, based on the crumbs of information contained in the *Tischreden* (just twenty-seven mentions of Hans in 7,000-plus entries).[26] At its most extreme, this approach has ascribed the whole upheaval of the Reformation to Luther's determination either to find in God a substitute for his brutal, pushy father, or else to do down the hierarchical, patriarchal Catholic Church, headed by a father-figure in the form of the Pope, as a way of avenging himself on Hans.[27] This is too extreme by half, over-simplifying a complex character and a tangled period of European history, but the theory does prompt more measured reflection on, for example, Luther's reluctance to reflect on how he was 'parented'. When he was otherwise so unusually forthcoming, by the standards of his era, in analysing aspects of his life, was his silence part of burying childhood pain?

Of the very few lines about Hans in *Table Talk*, the one most often quoted is: 'my father once whipped me so that I ran away and felt ugly toward him, until he was at pains to win me back.'[28] It neatly encapsulates how tricky both father and son seem to have found each other. Had Hans Ludher really been the never-to-be-satisfied ogre of legend, then the reference to his efforts to 'win back' his son strike a jarring note. Or perhaps not. Developing knowledge of how controlling characters operate points, in general terms, to a cycle in their behaviour, with destructive periods of aggression followed by equally extreme efforts at winning their target back round with blandishments. Was that what Luther is describing in his father? And while whipping your son was commonplace at the end of the fifteenth century, his words about feeling 'ugly' towards Hans because of the beating indicates a deeper tension behind what was otherwise a routine act of discipline.

There was, though, something approaching love for his father on Luther's part. When Hans died in 1530, he wrote to Philipp Melanchthon, his closest confidant, lamenting the loss of 'my dearest father', and referring to 'my affectionate relationship with him'. An emotional response caused by grief? Perhaps. 'I have rarely ever', Luther added, 'despised death so much.'[29] He may have had a tendency to play to the gallery in some of his *Table Talk* remarks, but with Melanchthon there was a greater bond of intimacy. So these sentiments about his father, even when read in the context of Luther's failure to attend Hans's deathbed in Mansfeld,[30] must be taken more soberly.

He was also happy to acknowledge publicly the debt he owed his father for providing the education that enabled him to become the man whose name was known all over Europe. In a 1530 sermon on 'keeping children in school', Luther remarked: 'my dear father lovingly and faithfully kept me at the university of Erfurt, and by his bitter sweat and labour helped me to get where I am.'[31]

There were undoubtedly shared traits between father and son. Friedrich Nietzsche, the nineteenth-century German philosopher, though no fan of institutional religion, spoke approvingly of Luther as a *Bergmannssohn* – 'a miner's son' – on account of his penchant for peppering his high-blown theological debates and writings with the sort of vulgar language more often heard among working men, and suggested it had been learned sitting on Hans's knee.[32] To which inheritance should also be added Luther's regular bouts of anger, apparently typical too of Hans. Nietzsche furthermore attributed Luther's refusal to be intimidated into recanting when faced by the full might of the Catholic Church at the height of the Reformation struggle to an inherited 'peasant stubbornness' that had not been eradicated by his highfalutin education.[33]

Elsewhere, though, when Luther made reference to his father, his feelings are, at best, ambiguous. In an early 1533 *Table Talk*, he was preaching to his dinner guests on a favourite passage from Saint Paul's Letter to the Ephesians in which the apostle[34] urges respect for the Old Testament commandment 'honour your father and mother'.[35] Luther highlighted how Paul saw this dictate through the eyes of the child, and then added a word of warning: 'parents never drive your children to resentment.' Is such resentment what he meant when he spoke of feeling 'ugly' towards his father?

In the same *Table Talk* on Paul, Luther also instructed that children be 'given the rod when they deserve it', but insisted that this be 'mixed with praise so that they are not discouraged and then expect nothing good from you'.[36] Honouring, he implied, was a two-way process. For all his efforts to excel, Luther could have felt that nothing was ever good enough to please his father. 'It is very bad', he went on, 'when a son loves another more than his father. A father must somehow recognise that he must not destroy everything. For simply laying down the law accomplishes nothing, and is unbearable.'[37, 38]

Mother and son

And what of Luther's mother? He was even more reticent in his *Tischreden* about Margarethe than about Hans. This cannot simply be ascribed to the widespread chauvinism of the age, for Luther showed himself perfectly willing in the same forum to acknowledge the strengths of women.[39] He did pay Margarethe one compliment, attributing to her his own good manners,[40] but that pales next to a remark he was reported to have made in the spring of 1537, where he was blaming his parents for his decision to become a friar. 'My parents kept me under a very strict discipline, to the point of making me timid. My mother once whipped me over a nut until the blood flowed. It was such strict discipline that finally forced me into the monastery.'[41]

In many biographies of Luther, this is the single fact included about Margarethe. She beat her son over something as trivial as taking a nut to eat and did so until she made him bleed, her regular resort to discipline so brutalising him that he had no other escape route than to become a friar. Even if we put to one side modern notions about the wickedness of corporal punishment, and allow for a degree of hyperbole in Luther's remark, how credible is such a claim? It is also said of Margarethe that she was profoundly religious, even zealous, and so vocation might naturally have been precisely how she wanted her son to spend his adult life. In which case, his choice of a monastery was less escape than fulfilling his mother's wishes.

There is also a school of thought that questions the translation of the final words of Luther's apparently damning remark about his mother. In German they are *in die Möncherei*, but rather than 'into the monastery', some have rendered them in English as 'into monk-ery' – i.e. that Margarethe's general coldness may have propelled her son into the ascetic world of religious life.[42] The impression is reinforced by a song that Luther reported his mother as having sung to him when he was a child. While he superficially framed it as a happy memory, the lyrics are bleak: 'For me and you, no-one cares; for that we are both guilty.'[43]

There can, however, be no mistaking the chill in Luther's letter to the widowed Margarethe, written in the short period between Hans's death and her own in 1531. Though he addresses her at the outset as 'dearly beloved mother', Luther's attempts thereafter to reassure her of his concern at what proved to be her final illness are mechanical. 'I will seek to do my part and, in keeping with my duty, acknowledge myself as your child and you as my mother, as our God and Creator has made us and bound us by mutual duties, so that I may add myself to the number of your comforters.'[44] It might be a letter written after a long estrangement, or a half-hearted attempt at a deathbed reconciliation. Luther certainly proved elsewhere in his writings that he had the words within him to do better, had he so wished. Yet here he is, potentially saying goodbye to his mother, and including not a single shared recollection, or offering one ounce of thanks to her for bringing him up. Having written at length on 'the boundless goodness and mercy of our Heavenly Father' in deciding her fate in the afterlife, and egotistically congratulating her for joining him in breaking with Rome, he simply signs off with a rudimentary reference to his own wife and children followed by: 'And with this I commend your body and soul to His mercy, Amen.' It is the letter of a pastor to a member of his congregation, not a son to his mother.[45]

Traditionally Margarethe has been cast as the more pious of Luther's parents – partly inspired, no doubt, by that stoical peasant woman's face in Cranach's portrait.[46] The Catholic faith that Luther grew up with was, by his own account, typical of the late medieval age in parts of Europe like Thuringia, far removed from the great cities and centres of learning where theological debates, experiments and even dissent were modernising Christianity. 'From childhood on,' Luther remembered, 'I knew I had to turn pale and be terror-stricken when I heard the name of Christ; for I was taught only to perceive him as a strict and wrathful judge.'[47]

In reaching such a conclusion, he was drinking in all that was around him. The standard image to be found in medieval churches was the 'Doom' painting or fresco, where Christ sits in final judgement of the dead, sending the fortunate few to salvation in a beautiful, golden heavenly garden, and others (usually the vastly greater number) to eternal damnation in hell, where they are broken by hard labour, tortured by fire, and tormented by an array of terrifying demonic creatures, following the devil's orders. It was an image designed to make those in the pews quake, and therefore make them stick close to the Church, doing as it told them, as their only chance of salvation. Hence the regular round of religious processions, ringing of bells, and church attendance that would have shaped Luther's childhood. These activities – 'good works' – were all part of paying your dues on earth in the hope of better to come if you kept on the right side of the Church. So life was measured out by the calendar of saints' feast days – each affording another opportunity to appeal for protection from above and help in atoning for sins before an angry God. For even the most indefatigable church-goer, hope of that serene heaven, often barely glimpsed in the top corner of the 'Doom' painting, was understood to be remote, and efforts at living Christian lives ultimately pitifully inadequate, but nevertheless all that they could do. The best that most aspired to was a spell in purgatory, first mentioned by the Church in the twelfth century (with little scriptural underpinning) as a kind of halfway house. In some depictions, it was a blank waiting room where the souls of the dead waited for the call to heaven, but in many more it was unpleasantly overheated, perpetually licked by the fires of hell beneath it.

The Catholic Church offered an array of support that the living could give to the 'souls' in purgatory. These included various officially approved ways to shorten their wait for the gates of heaven to swing open: by regular attendance at the sacraments; by keeping up a volley of prayers for intercession on their behalf by the saints; by making pilgrimages to see and touch the relics of the same saints; by paying for masses to be said by a priest for their dead relative; or by purchasing 'indulgences', where a sum was placed in the Church's coffers in exchange for remission from purgatory.

In the medieval imagination, salvation wasn't just a distant hope, something to worry about as we might now grow anxious about passing an examination. Every individual's fate, and that of family members who had already died and gone to meet their Maker, loomed large as a daily concern. It went in parallel with a widespread belief in malign spirits. In one *Table Talk*, Luther refers to his mother's belief in witches.[48] One of their neighbours, he reports, was thought locally to be a witch, and attributed with the power to make children ill with her potions. When the priest punished the woman for her alleged sorcery, in Luther's recollection, she placed a spell on him and he died. Such were the snares that faced the living who were struggling to follow God's laws and attain salvation.

The *Malleus Maleficarum*, a manual popularly known as 'The Hammer of the Witches', played a prominent role in the Catholic Church's efforts, through the Inquisition with its torture racks and summary justice, to track down, demonise and expunge all those who stood outside the Church's orbit. It was written by a

German layman and first published in 1486, running through fourteen editions by 1520.[49] 'Witchcraft', it instructed in its opening pages, 'is high treason against God's majesty.' It effortlessly conflated those accused of witchcraft with the devil. 'And if it be asked whether the devil is more apt to injure men and creatures by himself than through a witch, it can be said that there is no comparison between the two cases. For he is infinitely more apt to do harm through the agency of witches.'[50]

It all contributed towards a commonly held view of the world as a threatening place, from which a stern God held Himself remote, waiting to be appeased. Meanwhile, the devil was ever-present and ever-ready to fill the vacuum. As an outlook, it chimed readily with the tenuousness of life itself in late medieval Europe: where flood or famine destroyed livelihoods apparently on a devilish whim; where a flea-born pandemic known as the Black Death had swept across the continent in the fourteenth century, bringing dark blotches on the skin and swellings under the arms that had wiped out between a quarter and a half of the population; and where marauding armies, or robber knights, would appear from nowhere in towns and villages, intent only on plunder and murder. Life, in a very real sense, was hanging by a thread, turning thoughts ever more insistently to salvation.

New currents of thought

If this was the backdrop to Luther's early years, then his progress through schools and on to university slowly made him aware of other ways of seeing the world and God's role in it. Far off in Rome, the centre of the Catholic world, something more empowering of human potential in this life was in the air. From the start of the fifteenth century, successive Renaissance popes, worldly in their deeds, appetites and ambitions, had undertaken large-scale rebuilding works to make their city a celebration of their own and humankind's capacity to shape this world, at the same time as focusing on the next. Alongside the construction boom and the lavish patronage of artists such as Raphael, Bramante, Michelangelo and Leonardo (often funded by the sale of indulgences), there was a lively theological discourse.

Scholasticism had been the prevailing theological orthodoxy in Catholicism since the twelfth century, shaped by the likes of Thomas Aquinas and Peter Lombard, and finding inspiration in ancient Greece, most notably in Aristotle. It relied heavily on logic, discourse and debate as the means of re-examining and re-shaping Christianity into a coherent system that could, for example, 'prove' the existence of God by providing a series of irrefutable answers to fundamental questions. As a seat of learning, Erfurt was broadly supportive but not staunchly traditional in its adherence to Scholasticism. There is evidence to show that students – including Luther[51] – were also accessing the new thinking of Christian Humanist writers such as the Dutch priest and biblical scholar Desiderius Erasmus, often known as Erasmus of Rotterdam. His *Enchiridion militis christiani* – *Handbook of a Christian Knight* – was published in 1501, the same year Luther arrived at the university. Though it shared Scholasticism's respect for Greek learning and rational discourse, it also challenged the high premium placed on reason. Such an approach, Erasmus claimed, 'treated the mysteries of revelation in the tangled fashion of the logician . . . [and] strangled the beauty of revelation'. Reason could only get you so far, he argued. Since humankind was made in the image of God, it should not always be regarded as intrinsically sinful. Instead, he appealed for a greater value to be placed on God's grace, which was not governed by reason or logic, to bring out the best in human nature.

Erasmus was challenging precisely the sort of Christian life that Luther had grown up with. Dutiful adherence to rites and rituals was no substitute, he insisted, for living out the Christian gospel through works of charity. 'Charity does not consist in many visits to churches, in many prostrations before the statues of saints, in the lighting of candles, or in the repetition of a number of designated prayers. Of all these things, God has no need.'[52]

If Erasmus's writings were known and indeed available at Erfurt, the university's own preferred approach to any shortcomings in Scholasticism was a milder form of revisionism, known as Occamism, the school of thought named after the fourteenth-century English Franciscan, William of Occam. His criticism of the Scholastic norm was that it tried too hard to contain and constrain God, who was all-powerful and essentially beyond logic. 'Only faith,' William wrote in Summa Logicae, 'gives us access to theological truths. The ways of God are not open to reason, for God has freely chosen to create a world and establish a way of salvation within it apart from any necessary laws that human logic or rationality can uncover.'[53]

As a theologian, William had enjoyed the patronage of Louis IV, the Holy Roman Emperor (1282–1347), and was based for much of his life at Louis' court in Munich. His enduring influence was most strongly felt, therefore, in Germany, notably in the work of his follower Gabriel Biel (1420–95), who had studied and taught at Erfurt. Unlike the more direct challenge posed to Scholasticism (and by association the whole Catholic theological approach) by Erasmus and his fellow Christian Humanists, the Occamist/Biel approach was more of a gentle nudge to broader thought. And in Erfurt, as a university town, where the influence of religion was felt everywhere, even those students such as Luther reading subjects other than theology would have been hard pressed to ignore the interplay between the different currents flowing through the Catholic Church at the time.

But did any of this discussion about the future direction of the Church have a real and sustained impact on Luther in his student years? The marks of William of Occam are certainly detectable in his later thinking. At its most obvious, William was not one who accepted wholeheartedly papal sovereignty over the Church, a position Luther came to share. But it went further. 'Occam doubted that reason could do more than suggest that God exists,' according to Richard Marius, 'and he was not always sure that reason proved even that. This was a view that Luther himself was to espouse in later life.'[54] God, for Luther, could never be fully known and calibrated as Scholasticism had claimed.

Erasmus's influence on Luther is more significant, but equally is harder to pin down, though there is no mistaking the rivalry between the two. 'Erasmus is an eel,' Luther snapped in 1531, 'he has become an amazing piece of work of the devil.'[55] Their rivalry will play out as part of Luther's story.

For now, his bachelor's degree attained, Luther began 1502 focusing all his energies on his master's, the next stage in his university studies. With each progression up the academic ladder, he was moving into ever more elite groups. This time he was one of just seventeen students. Based on the *quadrivium* ('four ways') of arithmetic, astronomy, geometry and music, the curriculum also required him to take on more of a teacher's role in debates and lectures. His public persona was starting to emerge on the small stage of Erfurt University.

By April 1505 he had completed his master's, again as quickly as possible. Unlike his bachelor's, however, where speed had meant shortcuts in terms of quality, cost him marks and resulted in an undistinguished degree, this time round he managed to come second overall among his peers. His parents were so delighted that they came to his graduation, watching their son process through the city in the torch-lit parade. A proud Hans acknowledged Martin's new stature when he addressed him with the formal personal pronoun *Sie*, rather than the familiar *du*.

He gave him, as a graduation present, a copy of the *Corpus*

Juris, the standard tome on civil law. It was a none-too-subtle sign of what he expected the next step to be. Hans wanted Martin to become a lawyer, then in the Holy Roman Empire, as elsewhere in Europe, a springboard into work with the growing corps of professional public administrators, somewhere those of humble birth might escape the rigid social divisions of the time, first as magistrates and then, for some, as counsellors to kings and princes. Luther went along with his father's plans, though how willingly is a matter of dispute. In the spring of 1543, he returned once again in his *Table Talk* to that passage from Saint Paul's Letter to the Ephesians about honouring your father and mother. This time he concluded that what the apostle wanted to convey was the need for parents to act 'in such a way that they do not make their children timid'. A harsh, stern father, Luther went on, 'makes his children either dispirited or hopeless, and drives them into doing what they would otherwise avoid'.[56]

No one would call the adult Martin Luther timid, though it is a word he uses of his younger self more than once, and here he appears to indicate, with the benefit of hindsight, that, aged twenty-one, on the threshold of adulthood, his choice to study law in the spring of 1505 had been dictated by a father whom he dared not contradict.

With a master's, a student could continue studying for a further two years at the university to prepare themselves more fully for their chosen career. There were three faculties to chose between: medicine, theology and law. Medicine did not enjoy a good reputation at Erfurt. So Luther was left with theology and law. For Hans, there was no debate. Luther did not disagree, though later he suggested nagging doubts were there. 'When I was a young man at the University of Erfurt, I came across a Bible in the library, and read a section from the Book of Samuel. But the bells called me to the next lecture. I was very intent on reading the entire book. But at that time I never had opportunity to do so.'[57]

CHAPTER TWO

Lightning Strikes: Into the Monastery

'Our Lord God always starts a downpour with a blast of thunder . . .'

Martin Luther, *Table Talk*[1]

In the countryside outside the village of Stotternheim near Erfurt, a granite column marks the spot where, on 3 July 1505, twenty-one-year-old Martin Luther is said to have sheltered in the middle of a thunderstorm as he walked back to university in Erfurt after visiting his family in Mansfeld. The simple inscription labels it 'consecrated ground', for it was here that Luther grew so terrified that he was about to be killed by a bolt of lightning that he vowed, out loud, to Saint Anne to become a monk if she allowed him to escape with his life. And because he did survive, and was a man of his word, a fortnight later he fulfilled his pledge to the Virgin Mary's mother, turned his back on his studies in law, and presented himself at the gates of a monastery in Erfurt.

Later, as we have already seen, when it came to explaining such an abrupt change of direction, Luther would blame his own mother, who had driven him 'into monk-ery' by her 'strict discipline'.[2] He was, at least, acknowledging that there was more to his vocation than a promise to Saint Anne made in the heat of the moment, but the story is more complicated still. The choice to abandon law was most obviously a rejection of his father's influence. Hans was, Luther reported, 'very angry' at the turn of events. There was, he recalled, some sort of family dispute over his act of defiance, but he had 'stood by my decision'.[3] For the first time, he had asserted his independence. The adult Luther was born.

Luther gave no hint in any of his subsequent retellings of the thunderstorm narrative that he had been secretly nurturing a vocation before lightning panicked him. Or that – however conventionally pious he had been in his youth – he had previously felt specially picked out by God to serve Him by taking religious vows. Yet here he was joining the clerical and monastic elite. The consequences of that decision were to be so profound that this place outside Stotternheim has become known, in subsequent generations, as the very spot where the Reformation was born. The granite column was put up in 1917, when Germany was in the midst of the First World War and its national spirit was judged in need of a morale boost. The patch of 'consecrated ground' was designed as a potent symbol of the greatness of the whole nation and a highly visible reminder of its pre-eminence, dating back to Luther, in shaping modern Europe.

But can Luther's account of how he arrived in a monastery really be taken at face value? It is just so neat, like one of those perfectly rounded moral tales found in sugary hagiographies of saints, popular in late medieval times, where the hand of God intervenes at just the right moment to redirect the subject away from worldly excess towards spiritual fulfilment. Luther would, of course, have been all too familiar with the genre. Had he created his own myth?

The first reference to the story of his 'road to Erfurt' conversion is attributed to Johann Crotus. In 1517, he described the lightning storm that had floored Luther and the vow it produced.[4] He even went so far as to highlight the parallel between what happened to his fellow student at Erfurt and Saint Paul's hearing the voice of God on the road to Damascus and his conversion, going from being early Christianity's great persecutor to its most articulate advocate.[5]

Crotus seems to have got the details of the lightning story from Luther himself. It may be that he had heard him tell the tale in the student lodgings of Erfurt as a quick and easy way to explain his sudden decision to switch from university to monastery. Yet the clearest source for what has become another integral part of every thumbnail sketch of Luther's life is the man himself.[6] Three decades on – by which time he was anxious to fit his choice of the monastic life into a divine plan to put him somewhere he could not fail to see the corruption of the Church – Luther came up in a *Table Talk* with all the aspects of the now familiar narrative.

It is never a pleasant experience for any walker to be caught in open countryside in the middle of a thunderstorm, but Luther's version of his reaction still sounds curiously extreme. Yet that shouldn't stop it passing the plausibility test. Like many medieval Christians, he saw God's hand everywhere, including in the weather. In 1533, for example, when a storm hit Nürnberg, knocking over trees and ripping off roofs, he spoke in a *Table Talk* of great gusts of winds as spirits that could be angels or demons.[7]

Then there was the all-pervasive fear of death. Luther's response came not from today's health and safety culture, but rather out of the prevailing orthodoxy that death was stalking every individual, picking its moment to strike. Such a thought might well have been uppermost in his mind when the storm struck, so much that he made his promise to Saint Anne – and by implication to God.

So far so good. Luther was undoubtedly someone with a particularly heightened fear of death, even by the standards of his times, as Professor Richard Marius has illustrated in his detailed 1999 study of him.[8] He points especially to the abundance of gloomy medieval treatises and illustrations that would have served to encourage an impressionable Luther to brood on the '*quattuor novissima*' – the 'four last things' – that the Church taught every individual they would face: death, judgement, heaven and hell. It was a phrase taken from the Book of Ecclesiasticus: 'in all your works, remember the last things and you will not sin against the eternal.' Less sensitive souls might have been able to take on board such a message, and yet still live life to the full outside the shadow of death. If not, the medieval age would have ground to a halt. But not, it seems, Martin Luther.

With such a predisposition, his retreat into a monastery was him seeking a haven where he hoped to conquer his fears – of life, of death, of God's judgement and of missing out on salvation. He was not therefore opting to be a monk to get away from his father's plans, but rather as a means of escaping his own terrors. That has a certain logic. One attraction then of dedicating your life to God was well summed up by the popular belief that those who 'died in a monk's cowl' would receive preferential treatment in death, up to and including a fast track to heaven. Life was shaped first and foremost by the dictates of achieving salvation. There was even a popular superstition that, if you were not a monk, you might trick your way into a better sort of afterlife if you could borrow a cowl for your burial.

The monastery, alongside the papacy, was one of the pillars of the medieval Church. Thomas Aquinas wrote eloquently in his *Summa Theologica* of monastic vows as a kind of 'second baptism' – something that allowed the adult sinner the chance, not available to anyone else, to restore himself to a state of innocence in preparation for meeting his Maker.[9]

The view that Luther was terrified into the monastery by his own exaggerated preoccupation with death and judgement gains further traction in a dedicatory letter to his father, which formed the preface to his 1521 treatise, *On Monastic Vows*. In reflecting back on the time in 1505 when the two had been at loggerheads over his change of direction, Luther explained: 'Suddenly surrounded by terror and the agony of death, I felt constrained to make my vow.'[10]

The Road to Erfurt

But are there other ways of reading his change of heart? Luther may have only been six weeks into his studies in law at Erfurt when he gave it all up, yet he seems already to have harboured doubts about his new academic discipline. That, at least, is a reasonable conclusion from all his subsequent remarks – albeit, as ever, uttered with the hyperbole of hindsight. They are especially damning about those who choose law as their calling. 'A lawyer can well be a scoundrel,' he said at the start of 1532, 'but theology requires a pious man. The reason: a lawyer deals with corporeal matters, a theologian, however, is entrusted by God Himself with heaven and all His gifts.'[11]

Such scorn for the whole legal profession might just be a *post hoc* justification of his choice in 1505. Or, alternatively, it could be a way of expressing his hatred of his father's controlling hand. He was damning the calling his father had chosen for him, and therefore by association damning his father. Luther had referred obliquely to a debate in the family after the thunderstorm over what he now planned to do, but had the subject of his changing academic courses been raised *before* he even set out on that walk back to Erfurt?

In this scenario, Luther wasn't enjoying law and went home to Mansfeld to come clean with his parents that he wanted to swap to theology. The discussion hadn't gone well. Hans had given a dusty answer to seeing his cherished plans for his son discarded. An argument followed, with emotional and financial pressure placed on the young Martin to continue to do his father's bidding.

This fits with the general picture Luther presented of his father in that same dedicatory letter to his 1521 treatise on monastic vows. Hans, he wrote, had been anxious to 'chain me up with an honourable and opulent marriage' at the time he chose the monastery.[12] So he had another potential reason to escape and assert his independence.

It wouldn't have been a happy parting, then, as Luther set off back to Erfurt. On the walk, he was troubled, still mulling it all over in his mind, in a state of indecision and agitation, most likely feeling trapped. How convenient, then, was the divine intervention from above? At a stroke, it offered a means of disentangling himself. Better still, the change of course was something that had been imposed upon him by a higher power even than Hans. Though Margarethe was the more devout of the two, Hans Ludher would have been a conventionally religious man of the age, and therefore not one lightly to dismiss or doubt his son reporting that he had received a sign from God to the effect that he should enter a monastery.

In this regard, Luther's invocation of Saint Anne is potentially crucial. Though later he criticised the Catholic reflex to summon up the company of saints in heaven whenever life threw up a challenge, labelling such veneration 'a terrible blindness and money promoter',[13] Luther in his formative years would have regarded certain among the ranks of the saints as akin to family friends. And none more so than Saint Anne.

Though she is nowhere mentioned in the New Testament, the cult of Mary's mother was especially strong in early sixteenth century Germany, with Düren near Cologne housing what were reputedly her relics, brought back by Crusaders from the Holy Land in the thirteenth century, and established with papal blessing as her shrine in 1506. So powerful had devotion to her become in Saxony during Luther's youth that a new town of Annaburg had been built dedicated to her. Statues usually presented her as holding a book, a reminder of the role ascribed to her in Catholic tradition as the one who taught the Virgin Mary to read. Had the pious Margarethe recounted this tale as she sat her son on her lap and instructed him in his letters and words?

Saint Anne would also have been well known in Luther's childhood home for her role as the patron saint of miners.[14] Each day, as Hans went off to work, Margarethe and her son might well have uttered a prayer to her for his safe return from an industry with an appalling safety record.

All of which explains why her name would have sprung readily to Luther's lips when he imagined himself in peril, had the thunderstorm episode really happened. But it works just as well if he had made up the whole episode. If anything was going to cause his father and mother to respect his fabricated account of intervention from above and allow their son to abandon law in favour of theology, the mention of Anne might just have swung it. This was the saint with whom Hans would have been most familiar, to whom he might even have attributed his own survival and success.

Other details from the *Table Talk*, even if treated cautiously, also point to a deep-rooted resistance in Luther to pursuing a career in law. He didn't like the idea that it could make him wealthy – which was presumably one of its main attractions for Hans. Throughout his adult life Luther had an almost total disregard for money. 'The study of law is a base and vile art,' he once remarked, 'and no one would bother with it if it did not fill the purse.'[15]

There are echoes in this remark of his recollections of that teenaged encounter with the pious monk, Prince Wilhelm of Anhalt – 'no one could look upon him without feeling ashamed of his own life'. The young Luther may have nurtured within him a strong yearning for the purer, simpler life. Confronted with the prospect of a future as a lawyer and royal administrator, he despaired and came up with a plan to opt out by going into a monastery.

And – save to Hans – such a switch of tracks would hardly have seemed an earth-shattering step. Erfurt was after all a place where prayer and religious ritual were integral to daily life, certainly for students at the university. Theology rather than law would have appeared at best a gentle readjustment, rather than a radical fresh start. Luther's was not, in essence, as dramatic a conversion narrative as those that had told about various saints. They were often, before they saw the light, individuals who had been luxuriating in all the trappings of this world, or selfishly pursuing their own pleasures without a thought for their morality or the Lord. By contrast, Luther had been a hard-working, hard-pressed, austere and serious student, going to mass and saying prayers daily. Becoming a friar was a natural, unremarkable progression.

Some of his student friends at Erfurt, though, appear to have regarded his decision with a certain reluctance. Luther recalled that a number 'urged me to renounce it', up to and including at a farewell dinner on 16 July. Justus Jonas, another Erfurt graduate and a lifelong associate of Luther's, records this as having taken place in 'Heaven's Gate', a grand library in the Amplonian, one of the student lodging houses attached to the university.[16]

And if his friends were unconvinced, Luther also confessed later to having wavered a little. 'I regretted the oath,' he said of those fourteen days between making his promise to become a friar and acting on it.[17] His words make explicit that he had what we might now call 'cooling-off time' to reflect on his decision, and yet he still went ahead. His entry into the monastery was no knee-jerk reaction to a nasty shock when out walking.

There is a final aspect to the tale that is worth briefly considering. However plausibly Luther's decision may be explained, the speed with which he accomplished the change, as well as the reported surprise in those around him, raise questions about his state of mind. It is well recorded that, throughout his life, he periodically experienced great bursts of energy as well as spectacular collapses. There is, for example, a story, albeit whose authenticity is disputed, that three of his fellow monks in Erfurt recalled the young Friar Martin collapsing to the ground on one occasion in the choir stalls and 'raving' during what sounded like an argument with either God or the devil.[18] At the other end of his life, in March 1537, the *Table Talk* (for once on firmer ground in recording contemporary events rather than looking back on the recent past) tells how Luther was laid low by a 'spiritual illness' which meant that for fourteen days 'he had eaten practically nothing, drunk nothing and also had not slept'. He was, it was reported, awake and quarrelsome, which makes the episode sound more like what would now be routinely referred to as a breakdown.[19] It is one of several similar incidents in the *Table Talk*.

These peaks and troughs may point to what we would now call mental health problems. Psychologist Erik Erikson in the late 1950s certainly surmised something of that nature, though his theory has since been discredited because of the degree of conviction with which he stated his conclusion. Yet, while wary of falling into the modern secular trap that today sees all varieties of religious vocation as a kind of psychological madness, it is surely worth noting that someone with as much respect for religious faith as the nineteenth-century Danish philosopher and theologian Søren Kierkegaard, also confessed himself puzzled when he studied Luther's life by the extreme and erratic switches it contained. Luther, he said, always spoke and acted as if lightning were about to strike him the next moment.[20]

Friar Martin

On 17 July 1505, Luther presented himself at the gate of the Erfurt monastery of the Hermits of Saint Augustine that housed a community of around fifty men.[21] He hadn't been short of alternatives in Erfurt – from the rigorous silence and solitude of the contemplative Carthusians, founded in 1084 by the high-born Saint Bruno of Cologne, to the more cosseted Benedictines, following a rule of peace, prayer and *lectio divina* (meditative reading), or the worldly Dominicans, engaging in 'zealous speaking' as they preached the gospel, or the Franciscans, with their work for the most needy in society.

Luther's choice of the reformed branch of the wider Augustinian family should not be seen as an accident. It was an unusual congregation in that it had been founded by the papacy, something that happened more rarely than might be supposed. In their case, the creation was the work of Pope Alexander IV in 1255, when he invoked the memory of Saint Augustine of Hippo as the basis for the setting up of a new order. Augustine – like Luther – had in 387 changed course to embrace God's calling, in his case after hearing a voice that came to him in a garden directing him to read a passage in Saint Paul. A peerless thinker and writer, Augustine's output (and prejudices) had decisively shaped the Catholic Church's attitudes thereafter. Alexander wanted the saint's strengths in intellectual pursuits and preaching in particular to be the hallmarks of the new order. As a result, they were often therefore to be found in university towns, such as Erfurt. However, the Hermits of Saint Augustine were, he ruled, to be practical not mystical, outward looking on to the world rather than shut away in prayer and contemplation like older-established congregations. That commitment to preaching and communicating the faith was also accompanied by an ethic of forging a close bond with the local laity. In part it was out of necessity. The order held no property of its own and hence relied for funds on donations. But it went further. Alexander had intended that the order would work alongside ordinary people rather than appear apart from them, or above them. The Hermits of Saint Augustine were to listen to and share the joys, miseries and grievances of those around them, a connection that was subsequently to inform Luther's teachings.

The Erfurt Hermits of Saint Augustine were friars not monks. The latter word, derived from the Greek for single or solitary, usually signified those who kept apart from the world. Though not shut off in their cloister, these Augustinians followed a traditional monastic routine based on the 'canonical hours', which divided the day into seven periods of prayer from Lauds at dawn through to Compline (or evening prayer) before going to bed, and added an eighth, when they were required to rise for prayer in the middle of the night.

Augustinians were at the time known in Germany for their printing presses and their libraries, a reputation that must have held a particular appeal for Luther who had, up to that moment, known little else than a sheltered world of books and study. Here, he believed, was a chance to carry forward the academic work at which he had already excelled, but in a different context. How far that unusual link between the Hermits and the papacy influenced him is hard to fathom, yet it is piquant given what was to come.

On admission, Luther was placed in the monastery's guesthouse where, over a number of days, the prior and novice master evaluated him before deeming him suitable to be received into the novitiate. That happened at a modest ceremony and was for an initial period of twelve months. He was asked to swear that he was not married, or infected by any illness. Fear of plague remained high, especially of bringing contagion into the community. He agreed to follow the rule by which the order was governed. If salvation had been foremost in his mind at the moment of entering, Luther would have been especially comforted to hear the prior at his reception ceremony pronounce over him the words, 'not he that hath begun but he that endureth to the end shall be saved'.

He was then given the outward signs of his new life – a tonsured head and a roughly woven blackish-brown robe with a hood that he was to wear for the next twenty years.

His probationary period was akin to a honeymoon. For those first twelve months, he later said, the devil went very quiet,[22] while he immersed himself in the rhythms of the daily life in the monastery and in his studies, some of them at the university. If he had craved more time to read the Bible and devotional works while a law student, now his every mealtime saw the community sit in silence listening as such texts were read aloud for their spiritual nourishment. And the Augustinian tradition also valued music – 'to sing once is to pray twice', the founder had pronounced.[23] Luther's lute had also found a home.

He could, in theory, have been asked to leave at any time during those first twelve months if he had been considered anything but orthodox, but he wasn't. Likewise, had joining a monastery been a rushed decision, for the wrong reasons, he now had plenty of time to repent and change his mind. Again he didn't. Those who were later to suggest that Luther should never have been allowed in a monastery in the first place because his vocation did not include the necessary loyalty demanded of all new clergy to the Pope as the successor of Saint Peter, were speaking with the benefit of hindsight, a blessing not extended to the prior, the monastic community, or indeed Luther himself in July 1506 when he made his final vows of poverty, chastity and obedience as an Augustinian friar.

'To the world,' he would remember fondly of those early years, 'I was totally dead until God decided it was time.'[24] This remark is often quoted to write off this period in his life as essentially a blank, certainly as far as the outside world was concerned, but Luther wasn't giving the full picture. He was too eager to paint his younger self as the stereotypical diligent, bookish young friar on an inward-looking quest for God. 'When I entered the monastery, and left everything behind me, and began to doubt myself, I asked for another Bible. The Brothers gave me one and I read it through carefully, was very impressed by the meaning.'[25] This was the point, he said, at which he embarked on what remained a lifelong habit of reading the Bible, cover-to-cover, twice a year.[26]

In these reminiscences, he tries to place himself far away from the wider theological debates going on in Catholic Europe. Whatever conclusions he reached about Christianity, he implied, he made them on his own, struggling along with just the Bible to sustain him. This is nonsense. The Hermits of Saint Augustine were committed to intellectual pursuits, including theological debates, while the bigger disputes within Catholicism were part of the backdrop to his continuing studies at Erfurt University. As, elsewhere, Luther acknowledged. 'After I had been admitted to the order, they continued my education and gave me sophisticated books. Yet, whenever I had time, I went back to the library and sought solace in the Bible.' Or: 'in the monastery, I discussed it [the Bible] at every opportunity.'[27]

In the community of friars, such debate would have seen him engage with individuals pondering the issue of the future direction of Catholicism. If Luther was 'discussing' with them his thoughts on the Bible 'at every opportunity', they would have responded with their own insights and reading. Luther's tutor, for instance, was fellow friar Johannes Nathin, who taught at Erfurt University and broadly reflected its Occamist perspective that questioned aspects of Scholasticism. A key text at that time, Luther later recalled, was a work on the mass by arch-Occamist Gabriel Biel, recently deceased and regarded with great reverence at Erfurt. Luther labelled it the 'best book' for interpreting divine revelation. [28]

Outside the cloister, too, new thinking was all around. Another of Luther's teachers was Jodcus Trutfetter – 'or Doctor Eisenach as he was sometimes called after his native town,' Luther wrote in 1518, 'a very able professor who deplored the "hair-splitting type" of Scholasticism. He tried to simplify the dialectics of Occam and Biel. He even used a Humanistic style and poetic verse to make his material more popular and effective.'[29] Here are several of the key elements of the wider debate going on in the Church at the time mentioned in a reference to a single individual.

If Luther had spare time to cast his net wider, he need have looked no further to engage his curiosity than to the tombs within the monastery walls. One of his Augustinian predecessors commemorated there had played a part in the 1415 trial of the priest-reformer Jan Hus, whose attacks on the corruption of the Church, on the supreme authority of popes, and even on the selling of indulgences, had led to his execution for heresy – a word which in its original Greek meant opposing the party line. His

'Hussite' followers had continued to worship in their own reformed Church in Bohemia.

Europe on the move

There is slightly more resonance to Luther's claim to have been 'dead to the world' at this time when it comes to other 'non-theological' events that were changing Europe and widening horizons. Already by 1505, and within Luther's lifetime, Christopher Columbus had discovered the Americas, Amerigo Vespucci the Amazon, and Vasco da Gama had become the first European to reach India by sea. The continent was connecting with a 'new world' that would change centuries-old settled patterns of life, social structures and political authority, but the full impact was slow to be felt across Europe. Meanwhile, from the southeast, the Ottoman Turks were advancing, invading Hungary in 1492 and accepting the surrender of the Venetians in 1499. Their Empire was nearing its apex, and the Islamic faith that underpinned it was seen as a threat to the very survival of Christendom. And, elsewhere, the rise of the nation state – in England, France and Spain – was causing still more friction, this time between kings and popes over who should control such matters as the appointment of bishops, hitherto a prerogative the Church had jealously guarded. Such disputes were causing the rulers of the tapestry of German states that made up the Holy Roman Empire to flex their muscles and demand greater autonomy and consequently a reduction in Rome's interference in their lands.

Economically, too, the introduction of silver guilders in parts of Germany in 1500 was the latest stage in the advance of capitalism. The rise of a parvenu class of wealthy merchant-bankers, such as Jakob Fugger in Augsburg, who had made their fortunes in the trade in imported spices, coffee, chocolate and even pineapples from the 'new world', was resented by both high-born and low. The peasants blamed the new merchant-bankers for sweeping away the barter economy and impoverishing them. The upper class took out loans with them, but then resented being in their debt.

Even the thickest monastery wall could not block out all of this turmoil. Reports had been trickling back of the example of Augustinians, in other branches of the tradition, who had forsaken their cloistered lives in Europe to travel to establish missions in the wake of the Portuguese conquerors of Africa. Closer to home, where once monasteries had controlled the spread of the written word, with monks filling the time between the daily round of prayers by producing hand-made manuscripts for a tiny, elite audience, Johannes Gutenberg's pioneering work with mechanical moveable type in 1439 had heralded a printing revolution. The dawn of the age of mass communications was slowly rendering the monk-scribe redundant. Crude printing presses, with texts accompanied by wood-block illustrations and cartoons, facilitated a much more rapid spread of opinions and ideas than hitherto. Many challenged the established order.

There was, overall, a sense of uneasiness that comes when a whole society is changing quickly. One effect was seen in a decline in vocations in the late fifteenth and early sixteenth centuries. Some of the blame was laid at the door of internal critics of the Church such as Erasmus, who had launched a very public and typically witty attack on monks as lazy and lax. They were, argued *The Praise of Folly*, published in 1509 and dedicated to his friend, the English lawyer Thomas More, 'roar[ing] out the psalms in church like braying asses, counting their prayers, but understanding them not at all'.[30] His goal was to reform Catholicism from within by a mixture of learning and laughter, theological insight and sharp ridicule.

Luther was later to concur with Erasmus on the shortcomings of monks and friars – though he chose to couch it in much more dour and angry terms than the Dutch Humanist. 'I took the vow not on account of my stomach but my soul and observed the regulations of our order in the strictest manner,' he wrote, implying that some entered the monastery just to get fed. Yet such rebellious thoughts, he made plain, were not in his head in his early years as an Augustinian. 'I served the Pope with such diligence that I outdid all papists who lived or now live.'[31]

Anfechtung

Hard as he strained to be a diligent, studious, self-effacing friar, Luther found it did not banish his fears for long. If his first brush with a lightning bolt had been on the road to Erfurt in 1501, his second came shortly after his ordination as a priest, when in May 1507 he took his place at the altar in the chapel of the Augustinian monastery to say his first mass in front of guests he had invited. For any priest, it is an occasion to remember. A special joy was his father's presence in the congregation, Hans arriving with a group of his workers plus a handsome donation for the friars. Reconciliation was in the air after a two-year chill.

Yet ever after Luther's clearest recollection of the day was his realisation, in another flash, of his own complete and utter inadequacy before God. It was a feeling that was never thereafter completely to leave him. Human inadequacy before God became one of the central tenets of his belief.

It began as he recited the introductory prayers of the mass, and read the words, 'we offer unto thee, the living, the true, the eternal God . . .' Saying them, he explained, rendered him 'utterly stupefied and terror-stricken'.[32] His collapse wasn't just nerves or a dislike of being in the spotlight. Luther's overwhelming sense at that precise moment, he said, was one of total unworthiness. 'I thought to myself, "with what tongue shall I address such a majesty", seeing that all men ought to tremble in the presence of even an earthly prince? Who am I, that I should lift up mine eyes or raise my hands to the divine majesty? The angels surround Him. At His nod, the earth trembles. And shall I, a miserable little pygmy, say, "I want this, I ask for that"? For I am dust and ashes and full of sin, and I am speaking to the living, eternal and the true God.'[33]

If taking the cowl had been prompted by a desire to make himself feel less alienated from God, he knew in that moment that had singularly failed. A shaken Luther nevertheless managed to steady himself. With encouragement from those around him on the altar, he stumbled on through the rest of the mass, even the consecration, where the priest holds aloft the bread and wine that – according to the Fourth Lateran Council of 1215 – were 'transubstantiated' into the body and blood of Jesus Christ.

The trauma sounds terrifyingly real. 'When I celebrated my first mass at Erfurt,' he later recalled, 'I almost died because of lack of faith. All I thought about was whether I was worthy.'[34] It was something he had clearly already been wrestling with for a long time so, once again, his habit of explaining himself via a single 'bolt-from-the-blue' moment is misleading. Yet on this occasion there are fewer grounds to question the actual details he provides. Every newly ordained priest says a first mass, and most will admit that it is a moment for anxiety, reflection and doubt, when they stand, as the Church teaches, in the place of Jesus Christ at the altar. Studying the words they will speak at the mass as part of preparation for the priesthood in the classroom is, they report, very different indeed from actually being in front of a congregation and pronouncing them, when their full importance and impact can seem startlingly plain.

This second crisis prompted Luther subsequently to give a name to the intense sense of inadequacy he felt when before God. *Anfechtung* is slippery to translate from German into English because it combines elements of temptation, assault and testing all rolled into one. 'Agonising struggles' is favoured by some,[35] but even that doesn't quite capture a concept so crucial to Luther's relationship with God. It lacks the element of physical onslaught that is there in *Anfechtung*. And it is ultimately God who is on the attack, though the actual assault may seem to its victim to come via another route, more often than not in Luther's descriptions from the devil.

For him, *Anfechtung* was every bit as real as if Satan himself had been beating him with fists. He would have rejected fiercely any suggestion that it was 'all in the mind', had such a phrase been in use at the time, or more specifically 'all in his mind'. *Anfechtung*, he wrote in his *Larger Catechism*, a guide for clerics, was a physical affliction suffered by everyone, even the greatest of saints. 'Some feel it in a greater degree and more severely than others. For example, the young suffer especially from the flesh. Afterwards, when they reach middle or old age, they feel it from the world. Others who are occupied with spiritual matters, that is strong Christians, feel it from the devil.'[36]

As the ultimate test that every believer will endure in their life, it was akin to a crucifixion. In 1518, he wrote that the sufferings endured in *Anfechtung* were 'so great and so much like hell that no tongue could adequately express them, no pen could describe them, and one who had not himself experienced them could not believe them'. Luther was here using the third person, but drawing on his own ordeal. 'And so great were they that, if they had been sustained or had lasted for half an hour, even for one tenth of an hour, he would have perished completely and all of his bones would have been reduced to ashes. At such a time, God seems so terribly angry, and with Him the whole creation. At such a time, there is no flight, no comfort, within or without, but all things accuse ... In this moment, it is strange to say, the soul cannot believe that it can ever be redeemed.'

It is a vivid description of desolation, even for readers with no religious faith. That conviction of being lost to God forever, of being beyond salvation, gives some insight into the turmoil Luther suffered in those early years in the monastery. He believed himself to be defenceless and humiliated before God, despite trying all the conventional means the Catholic Church prescribed for approaching God – prayer, ritual, following the rules of his order, even ordination. 'For Luther, death, the devil, the world and hell combine in a terrifying assault upon man,' writes Alister McGrath, Oxford professor of science and religion, 'reducing him to a state of doubt and despair . . . *Anfechtung* is thus a state of hopelessness and helplessness, having strong affinities with the concept of angst.'[37]

Angst is often taken as a sign of mental illness, but for Luther it was more a spiritual failing. And his near collapse at that first mass was not a one-off, especially when in the presence of Jesus Christ's body and blood, in the form of the bread and wine. In his *Table Talk*, he describes taking part, as a priest, in a celebration in Eisleben in June 1515 of the feast of Corpus Christi. 'I was terrified by the sacrament,' he writes, 'carried in the procession.'[38]

Straight after his first mass in May 1507, there was no time to collect himself. He had to face his father at a celebratory meal in the monastery, during which an already overwrought Martin grabbed at the hand of reconciliation that he believed was being offered by Hans. Perhaps he did it a little too desperately, or maybe Hans had been annoyed by the public show his son had made of himself by his faltering conduct at the altar. Soon enough an argument flared up between them. 'Don't you know that it is written that you should honour your father and your mother?' Hans challenged his son, intent on going back over painful old ground. 'And here you have left me and your dear mother to look after ourselves in our old age.'

Luther defended himself by talking of the power of his prayers to support his parents, and began once again to rehearse the details of the thunderstorm and the divine intervention that had caused him to change course in life two years earlier. 'Take care,' his father cautioned, unconvinced, 'that it was simply not a ghost that you saw.'[39]

Some translations of this barb prefer the word 'devil' to 'ghost', and that would most likely have been what Luther took from the remark. It pushed him still closer to the abyss of self-doubt and self-loathing. The devil's ability to disguise himself so as to snare the unwary was a well-understood weapon in the armoury of God's cosmic adversary. Even when you thought you were answering God's call, it could be the devil playing his dastardly tricks. Hans's rebuke hit home with such force precisely because he was enunciating a question that had already been spinning round in his son's head. How could he ever feel confident that he was doing what God wanted? Might it not be the devil who had ushered him into the monastery, and now was making him suffer, shutting him off from God?

After all the guests had left, the doubts remained. Luther's response was to redouble his already punishing efforts in his work, prayer and study in the hope that they might help him banish *Anfechtung*. Or, at least, make it bearable. Among the means he embraced was fasting with ever-greater vigour, pushing his body to the limits.

What lay behind such an approach was a familiar late medieval doctrine, '*facere quod in se est*' – literally 'do what lies within you', more freely 'do your best and God will not withhold His grace'. It had first been heard in the thirteenth century, but had been much favoured by the Occamists and especially by Gabriel Biel,[40] and hence was familiar to all studying at Erfurt University. Acting morally, it taught, would open the individual to the operation of God's grace to forgive sins. And it was forgiveness and grace that Luther hankered after, above all.

With his usual extreme diligence, bordering on the manic, Luther gave 'acting morally' his best shot. He took asceticism to extremes. 'When I became a doctor,' he remarked later in his *Small Catechism*, 'I did not yet know that we cannot make satisfaction for our sins.'[41]

The doctorate to which he refers was awarded in October 1512. Until that point, Luther believed that by 'good works' – a popular but not exact rendering of *facere quod in se est* – he could somehow manage to mitigate God's judgement of him, and achieve salvation, if only he tried hard enough. 'I was very pious in the monastery,' he said, 'but I was sad because I thought God was not merciful to me. I said mass and prayed.'[42]

The harder he tried, though, the more wretched he felt, because of the lack of any answer he could discern. Indeed, he was so pious, so harsh on himself, that he later suggested it may have damaged his health. 'I was a good monk and I kept the rule of my order so strictly that I may say that if ever a monk got to heaven by his monk-ery, it was I . . . If I had kept on any longer, I should have killed myself with vigils, prayers, reading and other work.'[43]

Luther was especially zealous in going to confession, the sacrament that offers the prospect for every repentant sinner of being absolved of their sins through God's mercy. After receiving absolution from the priest who hears their confession, they can begin again with a clean slate. 'When I was a monk,' Luther wrote in his commentary on Saint Paul's Epistle to the Galatians, 'I thought I was utterly cast away, if at any time I felt any evil motion, fleshly lust, wrath or envy against my brother. I went to confession daily, but it profited me not. I was constantly vexed with these thoughts . . . you entered this holy order in vain.'[44]

If Luther had retreated from the world into the monastery in search of spiritual succour, he had never felt more abandoned, inadequate and wretched. He spent long hours, as many as six hours on one occasion, examining his conscience with his confessor, picking over every tiny deed or thought in his daily life that may have offended God. And then, soon afterwards, he would find himself returning as soon as he remembered one more blemish that he hadn't shared on his previous visit. It exhausted the patience of those around him. 'No confessor wanted to listen to me,' he complained. 'That was when I thought, well, no one has this torment of the soul except you, and I became as dead as a corpse.'[45]

Father-figure

His evident suffering and near collapse had started to ring alarm bells. One of those most concerned was Johann von Staupitz. 'If it hadn't been for Dr Staupitz,' Luther wrote later, 'I should have sunk into hell.'[46] This high-born, cultivated, worldly priest, some twenty years Luther's senior, was Vicar-General of the Hermits of Saint Augustine in Germany. He was a man of influence, so respected by Elector Friedrich III of Saxony[47] that he had sought Staupitz's assistance with a vanity project to found a new university in his capital, the unprepossessing town of Wittenberg, northeast of Erfurt. Staupitz had provided Augustinian friars to teach at the university, whose patron was Saint Augustine. In 1502, a year before he was named vicar-general of his order, Staupitz had been appointed by Friedrich as the first dean of Wittenberg's theology faculty.

On his visits to the Erfurt monastery, among his other duties, Staupitz would make time to sit with Luther and listen to his lengthy, tortured confessions.[48] Something about the young man appealed to him. He was diligent, hard-working, serious of purpose and academically gifted, a potential blessing on the order, if only his angst could be soothed. So Staupitz took on the task, thereby becoming a father-figure to the troubled Luther.

A 1524 portrait of Staupitz shows a jowly, balding friar, with small soft eyes and a worldly air. He has a hint of a smile on his lips and an air of general contentment about him. He was, the unnamed artist is seeking to convey, a kindly, tolerant soul. That is certainly how he behaved towards Luther. Analysis of his few surviving sermons and texts reveal Staupitz as a theologian largely untroubled in his faith, and hence broadly typical of mainstream views at the time. He was no radical. He accepted God's ways, even when unfathomable, with an attitude that bordered on resignation, but he laboured to avoid despair by a focus on the gift to humankind of Jesus Christ. Sending His redeeming Son showed the essential love of God for humankind.[49]

Johann von Staupitz in 1522: Luther's superior, confessor and father-substitute – 'if it hadn't been for Dr Staupitz, I should have sunk into hell'.

As a confessor, whether face to face in lengthy conversations or in letters, Staupitz patiently tried to coax Luther towards seeing God as more forgiving of human weakness. At times he took a teacherly tone. He had been in that procession in 1515 in Eisleben, when Luther had been terrified by the sight of the eucharistic bread, in Catholic teaching the body of Christ. 'Afterwards,' Luther recalled, 'I confessed this to Dr Staupitz and he said, "your thoughts are not of Christ". These words were a great comfort to me. That's the way we are. Christ offers Himself to us with the forgiveness of sins, and we flee from His face'.[50]

In other moments, Staupitz would try to assuage Luther's fears by gentle mockery. 'If you expect Christ to forgive you,' he would rebuke him during his lengthy confessions, 'come in with something to forgive – parricide, blasphemy, adultery – instead of all these peccadilloes.'[51]

Luther, though, could not be budged from his conviction that he was sinful to the core, and came increasingly to identify his own particular situation with that of the whole of humankind, with everyone entirely dependent on God's judgement, regardless of their own actions and efforts. This was the predestination that Augustine, the founder of his own order, had taught, with God making an inscrutable choice of who was to be saved at the moment of their death. If He chose to exercise mercy, that was His business. Human achievement or virtue while on earth played no part in salvation.

It was one aspect of Augustine's teaching that was not particularly admired by mainstream theology in Luther's time. Christian Humanism, for example, preferred a more optimistic, empowering tone when it came to eternal fate. Yes, God had absolute power, but He still loved humanity enough to send His Son to this world. And through the operation of free will, multiple devotions and good works, each individual could also show their best side, to which God would respond, a process also captured by Biel's *facere quod in se est*.

'Dear Herr Doctor,' Luther later recalled asking Staupitz, 'our Lord God does so horribly with people all around. How can we serve Him when He smashes people so?' He was raising the question of suffering, which Christianity has always struggled to answer. His mentor replied: 'My dear one, you must learn to see God in another way. If He did not do so, how could He put down the stubborn?'[52]

To facilitate that necessary adjustment, Staupitz tried a variety of means to prompt the unhappy Luther to reconsider.[53] First, he used his patronage to give him a change of scene. In 1508 he appointed Luther to a one-year temporary post at Wittenberg to teach philosophy. Next, he directed him – against the practical spirit of the Hermits of Saint Augustine – towards the writings of some of the medieval mystics, whom he himself admired. Many of these figures, not always popular or well-treated by the Church authorities, had endured their own struggles with a distant, judgemental, unapproachable God, but told how surrendering themselves utterly before Him had enabled them to arrive spiritually at a place where the human and the divine could 'border' on each other, to quote the words of Mechthild of Magdeburg, a revered thirteenth-century Saxon mystic.[54]

Surrender would potentially have meant Luther ceasing to be quite so harsh on himself – with his perpetual fasting and confessions – but he could not accept the idea that sinful man could ever 'border' on the divine. 'Do you not know that God dwells in light inaccessible?' he said in his *Table Talk*, adopting the language of the mystics, but only for the purpose of dismissing their claims. 'We weak and ignorant creatures want to probe and understand the incomprehensible majesty of the unfathomable light of the wonder of God. We approach; we prepare ourselves to approach. What wonder then that His majesty overpowers us and shatters!'[55]

Luther's unmitigated experience remained one of a cruel, unknowable God, and his response oscillated between fury and despair: 'is it not against all natural reason that God, out of mere whim, deserts men, hardens them, damns them, as if He delighted in sins and in such torments of the wretched for eternity, He who is said to be of such mercy and goodness? . . . I was myself more than once driven to the very abyss of despair so that I wished I had never been created. Love God? I hated Him.'[56]

When in Rome

A dispute had developed between the twenty-six Augustinian houses under Staupitz's control about proposed reforms, which required the involvement of the head of the order in Rome. The vicar-general was asked to send two friars to make representations to Italy, and he selected Luther to represent the cloister at Erfurt. The 900-mile pilgrimage, made on foot, to the holiest city in the West, was the longest journey Luther ever undertook, and the furthest he ever strayed from Saxony. Traditionally it has been dated as taking place at the end of 1510 and the start of 1511, but recent scholarship has argued convincingly that it took place twelve months later.[57]

The rounded Luther legend likes to report that the journey to Rome on foot took him forty days – with a gospel echo to the amount of time Jesus spent in the wilderness.[58] When he finally approached the city, Luther reported he threw himself to the ground, and cried out, '*salve, santa Roma*' ('hail, holy Rome').[59] The actual business that Luther had come to carry out was easily sorted, though wheels turned slowly and so he was required to wait around for several weeks for a definitive reply. As Staupitz must surely have intended, he was left free to explore the home-town of the papacy.

Did the vicar-general consciously want to encourage a rebellious spirit in the young friar? Perhaps. Better, he may have reasoned, for Luther to channel his energies into picking a fight with the institution than with God. Like many in the German Church, Staupitz regarded Renaissance Rome as too worldly, too profligate, and stone deaf to the needs of local Churches such as his own. The only purpose Rome appeared to have for German Catholics, some suggested, was to exploit pious souls to line the pockets of the Pope's friends, and to foot the bills for his building projects and his wars. In 1455, the compilers of the *Gravamina*, or list of grievances, of the German people at the unjust demands placed on them by Rome had articulated a desire for reform in their relationship with the papal court. Among their number had been senior prelates and even princes.

This resentment was ignored by Rome but had not gone away, and continued to be felt across the social spectrum by high and low. It was angrily expressed in a document at the Diet of Augsburg in 1518 – one of the regular gatherings of the individual princes from the various component parts in Germany of the Holy Roman Empire with their ruler. 'These sons of Nimrod', it begins, likening the powerful clerics of Rome with the descendant of Noah, who in the Christian tradition grew so mighty and wealthy that he ended up regarding God with contempt, 'grab cloisters, abbeys, prebends, canonates and parish churches, and they leave these churches without pastors, the people without shepherds.'

Rome was busy selling lucrative clerical posts and offices in Germany for profit to wealthy individuals, often Italians, who showed little inclination to take up the pastoral duties that went with the benefices they had purchased, but concentrated instead on raking in the taxes, tithes and rents that their neglected flocks were obliged to pay, however poor the service. 'German money in violation of nature flies over the Alps,' the complaint continues. 'The pastors given to us are shepherds only in name. They care for nothing but fleece and batten on the sins of the people.'[60]

Julius II was on the papal throne at the time of Luther's visit, an extravagant and belligerent figure, who was engaged in rebuilding on a sumptuous scale to reflect as much his own prestige as that of the Church he led. He wanted to make it ever more a magnet for future generations of pilgrims who would ensure the city's prosperity. Michelangelo was at work on the ceiling of the Sistine Chapel and Raphael in the Vatican, but such commissions did not endear Julius to many in the Church. However splendid the face it presented to the world, Rome was beset with all too obvious vices. Erasmus, who lived there from 1506 to 1509, described in his pointed satire, *Julius Exclusus*, how the Pope arrived at the gates of heaven and demanded entry from Saint Peter, boasting: 'I raised the revenue, I invented new offices and sold them . . . I have covered Rome with palaces and I have left five millions in the treasury behind me.'[61]

Unlike the well-travelled Erasmus, however, the deeply provincial Luther did not laugh at the excess and corruption he encountered, much of it funded by his fellow Germans. He was shocked to the core. Among his ambitions for the trip, he later said, had been to find a confessor who might help him shed some of the burden of sinfulness that weighed so heavily on his shoulders. 'The main purpose was that I wanted to do a complete confession of all my sins from my youth on, and had become completely pious, although I had already made such a confession in Erfurt two times.'

If he believed that he might finally discover in Rome the pastoral concern, patience and ultimately the lasting absolution he so craved, he was bitterly disappointed. 'I encountered nothing,' he lamented, 'but completely uneducated men.'[62] Everywhere he looked, the rituals that he followed so assiduously as a way of winning God's favour were treated with contempt. 'I would never have believed it if I had not seen it myself. For so great and shameless is the godlessness and evil there that neither God nor man, neither sin nor shame, are given any notice.'[63] Erasmus might have been able to distinguish between the corruption of individual incumbents and the office of the papacy, but Luther did not make any such distinction.

'I had not been in Rome very long before I had seen much that made me shudder.'[64] Among the most unacceptable behaviour he witnessed was an everyday disrespect for the mass among priests. He recorded overhearing clerics swapping 'crude jokes, laughing and singing out' as they pronounced the words of consecration over the bread and wine. It was all a far cry from his scruples at his first mass. 'Such words hurt very much. What else could I think than, "is this the way they talk so freely at table in Rome? What will it be like when those fellows become pope, cardinals and have celebrated mass here this way?" '[65]

One of the ways in which the papacy generated money for its various pet projects was by charging believers to say masses for their deceased relatives under the pretext that such an offering might accelerate a loved one's progress into heaven. It had turned salvation into an industry, and the masses themselves would be delegated to young priests and undertaken as if on a conveyor belt and without a congregation, one after the other in quick succession. For most of those given the task, it proved tedious, repetitive and meaningless. When Luther was roped in during his stay and took his place on the rota, he inevitably approached it with great seriousness, to the irritation of the other clerics around him. 'Before I had come to the gospel, the priest following me had already laid out his mass and shouted at me, "enough, enough, get through it and get out of there".'[66] Luther was equally appalled by the stories told by priests he met of the sexual licence of clergy, bishops and even popes.[67]

The citizens of Rome did not impress him much either. This country boy was taken aback, for example, by their habit of urinating without embarrassment in the street.[68] From his lodgings in the Augustinian cloister, he went out daily during his four-week stay to explore Rome, seeking out the relics that the Church taught would heap blessings on those who journeyed to stand in their presence and pray. One favourite spot for pilgrims was the Scala Sancta, next to the Basilica of Saint John Lateran, reputedly the steps that a scourged and silent Jesus had ascended on His way to trial by Pontius Pilate, the Roman governor in Jerusalem. Those who climbed the twenty-eight steps on their hands and knees, it had been decreed, would gain an indulgence that would allow the release of a soul from purgatory. As he made the ascent, kissing each step and reciting the *Pater Noster* ('Our Father'), Luther had his dead grandfather in mind, he recalled, but when he reached the top, his doubts had got the better of him. 'Who knows if it is so?' he asked himself.[69]

His impressions were not improved, he remembered, by the ill-health he suffered. Rome was wet and muggy during his stay and caused him to suffer terrible headaches – which he claimed were cured by eating a pomegranate, though this story may have been influenced by the role in Christian symbolism of the pomegranate, open and spilling its seeds, as a sign of Jesus' own suffering.[70]

Carrying such a weight of disillusionment must have made the journey home an ordeal. Luther had set off for Rome in despair because he felt alienated from God, but hoping that the city might ease that sense. Instead he was now also alienated from the institution of the Catholic Church, or at least those who ran it in Rome. The phrase often used to sum it up, and ascribed to Luther, is that he went to Rome with onions and came back with garlic. He travelled with something that smelt bad and returned with something that smelt even worse.[71] Staupitz, however, was not about to be defeated. He had a new plan to tackle Luther's *Anfechtung* – a permanent transfer from Erfurt to Wittenberg.

CHAPTER THREE

Justification by Faith: Finding the Gate to Heaven

'*I was thrown into the battle over the gospel by God without knowing it was happening.*'

Martin Luther, *Table Talk*[1]

Among all the unlikely twists and turns in Martin Luther's story, his appointment in 1512 as 'Doctor in Biblia' at Wittenberg University is right up there. When Johann von Staupitz announced, on Luther's return from what had been a spiritually shattering trip to Rome, that he wanted his protégé to succeed him as a professor of Bible studies at Elector Friedrich's new university, it must have seemed to Luther like another bolt of lightning. Yes, he had been working in Erfurt towards an eventual doctorate, and had previously spent the best part of a year in Wittenberg lecturing on Aristotelian ethics. So teaching at that level was the logical next step, albeit a distant one. Some of his contemporaries would routinely spend twenty years on their doctorates. And his temporary posting at Wittenberg could hardly have been counted a great success – principally because being drafted in to teach Aristotle had only deepened Luther's dislike of the Greek philosopher's reasoned, distant, even abstract handling of God, so very different from his own turbulent day-to-day struggle before the Almighty.

Yet here was Staupitz offering a senior teaching post to someone who was teetering on the verge of a spiritual and mental collapse. It could tip him over the edge, since it is hard to conceive of Luther, in the mess he was in, as well suited to undertake the challenge of instructing tender, inquisitive minds, when his own beliefs were in such a state of flux. And since the focus of his professorship was the Bible itself, his daily toil would offer little distraction from what was already torturing him – namely his conviction that God was angry with him. The Old Testament is, after all, replete with accounts of God's wrath.

There was, though, a degree of calculation in Staupitz's offer. His own moderate reform agenda within the Hermits of Saint Augustine had drawn him into a dispute with Erfurt, as well as several other monasteries under his control. By redeploying Luther he may have been punishing this particular cloister by taking away one of its rising stars.[2] More likely, Staupitz could have simply decided, with every other remedy now exhausted, that it was time for drastic measures if Luther's intelligence, sensitivity to God and moral earnestness were ever to be put to good effect by the friars.[3]

As usual, legend boils this huge step in Luther's life down to a memorable detail. Staupitz is said to have made his offer of a professorship under a pear tree in the monastic court at Wittenberg. There may, though, be some truth in the quaint picture this conjures up. In later years, Luther would point out a particular tree to visitors as another of the physical landmarks on his journey. Consciously or not, he was already shaping his own myth.

Staupitz explained to Luther that his own twin roles teaching at Wittenberg and as vicar-general of the Hermits of Saint Augustine were proving too heavy a burden, so he was giving up the first and wanted Luther to take his place. Predictably, Luther's instant response was that he was unworthy. Next, he came up with a long list of reasons why he shouldn't be handed such accelerated promotion, principal among them being that he didn't yet have his doctorate. That was no problem, Staupitz replied. He could complete it at Wittenberg. But I am too young to receive a doctorate, Luther came back. Again, Staupitz brushed his objection aside.

As they worked their way down the list, Luther switched from practical considerations to issues that give an insight into his deeply troubled mind. He was exhausted, he said. Staupitz still refused to withdraw, so Luther added: 'I know for certain that I am not going to live much longer.' A doctorate would therefore, he claimed, be wasted on him. 'Why should we incur such a great cost?' He was talking more of his spiritual malaise than his medical prognosis. With Luther, body and spirit were never as neatly compartmentalised as elsewhere in mainstream Christianity, so he would often characterise his religious struggles as physical ailments – most vividly in another detail in most one-paragraph accounts of his life, his constant struggle with constipation, which he blamed on the devil possessing his bowels.

Staupitz, though, refused to take no for an answer. With more of the patience and stamina he had already showed in his dealings with his unusual but compelling protégé, he swatted aside even this obstacle. If Luther wanted to fix his gaze on the next world, not this, he replied, then God 'had plenty of work for clever men to do in heaven'.[4] Finally the younger man yielded, no doubt now genuinely exhausted. In his eyes, a key decision had once again been made for him. He felt much more comfortable when he had the sensation of being guided, and therefore could do nothing but go along with the direction in which he was being propelled. It allowed for the possibility of God's hand discreetly at work.

Wittenberg thus became his home – and his stage – for the rest of his life. His doctoral studies were swiftly brought to a conclusion and, on 19 October 1512, he duly became Doctor Luther in the town's Schlosskirche, or Castle Church, at an elaborate ceremony that included swearing an oath to remain obedient to the Roman Church. His sponsor was Andreas von Karlstadt, a priest and theology professor at the university, three years his junior but higher up the academic ladder, and a name subsequently to feature prominently in Luther's story.

Wittenberg in German means white hillock, and true to its name it stands on a gentle rise on the banks of the River Elbe in the midst of the sandy north German plain that stretches to the sea. Luther had swapped the familiar hills and forests of Thuringia for somewhere flatter and more exposed. The town – which numbered 2,500 inhabitants – was much smaller than Erfurt, but had been growing rapidly since the ruling House of Wettin in Saxony had divided its lands in 1485 between two brother princes. Ernst, the elder, had taken the western portion, and the titles of Prince-Elector (Kurfürst) of Saxony and Landgrave of Thuringia. His son Friedrich III, usually known as Friedrich the Wise, had succeeded him the following year. To the east were the domains of his cousin – and rival – Duke Georg, and they included the University of Leipzig, founded in 1409.

With revenues from the silver being mined in the Erzgebirge Mountains (literally 'Ore Mountains' in German) that lay in the southern part of his lands, Friedrich had invested in making Wittenberg a fitting capital for his part of divided Saxony. First had come the ornate Schlosskirche, at the western entrance to the town, with a tower that dominated the landscape for miles, built in late Gothic style and adjoining Friedrich's castle fortress. It had been consecrated in 1499. Three years later, the elector had established his own university, with Staupitz's help. By the time of Luther's arrival, the roll had reached 1,700, marking a dramatic rise in the local population and resulting in a building boom within the town walls of new brick houses.

Wittenberg was in the midst of change. Its traditional role had been as a market for local farmers. Luther rather liked this small-town agrarian backdrop. It appealed to his self-image as the son of peasants. 'To cultivate the fields', he once remarked, 'is a Godly work.'[5] And he quickly grew fond of a place he always referred to as a city,[6] though it hardly moved him to the rhapsodies he had once penned for Erfurt.

Wittenberg's Schlosskirche, or Castle Church, where Luther received his doctorate in theology on 19 October 1512 and swore an oath of obedience to the Roman Church.

> Little land, little land
> You are but a heap of sand.
> If I dig you up, the soil is light
> If I reap you, the yield is slight.[7]

Behind its walls and embankments, Wittenberg's infrastructure remained primitive, but Friedrich's ambitions had caused others to follow suit with construction projects of their own. The Augustinian monastery, known locally as the Black Cloister – because of the colour of the robes its inhabitants wore – was at the eastern end of the town, right up against the walls. It was being substantially enlarged when Luther arrived. In between the two, on one of Wittenberg's three parallel west–east streets, stood the Stadtkirche, or 'Town Church', a large structure, much plainer than the Schlosskirche, and dedicated to the Virgin Mary. Like most medieval towns, the skyline of Wittenberg indicated that it was a place of God, the spires and towers reaching up to the heavens.

A sixteenth-century artist's impression of Wittenberg's skyline: church spires stand out on a site that Luther affectionately labelled 'a heap of sand'.

Elector Friedrich was the dominant figure in the town. A 1496 portrait of him by Albrecht Dürer shows a bearded, serious, scholarly young man, his hand clutching rolled documents and his big eyes shy and enigmatic. He may have founded a university out of dynastic rivalry with Duke Georg, but just as important in his decision was the value he placed on learning. A moderniser in his commitment to education, he also had a medieval side, notably in his approach to religion. A man of great personal piety, he had amassed a huge collection of relics, and is reputed to have collected many of them himself on a six-month pilgrimage to the Holy Land in 1493.

Yet when it came to theology, his was not the closed, backward-looking mind, believed by many in Renaissance Rome to be so typical of German Catholics. Instead he had a great love of the Classics. He referred to his new university as the Leucorea, from the Greek for white mountain, another reference to Wittenberg's elevated position. In his correspondence, Friedrich was in contact with radical and reforming voices in the Church, notably Erasmus and the artist Dürer, both bright lights of the northern branch of the Renaissance, less ostentatious than the Roman variety but similarly concerned with encouraging human potential.

His personal piety, as well as his reputation for thoughtfulness and intellectual backbone, had seen Friedrich's influence spread beyond the boundaries of his particular area of Germany. As a great-nephew of a past Holy Roman Emperor, and a cousin and trusted advisor of the current incumbent, Maximilian I, he was a leader among the German princes.

Staupitz had secured a contribution of 50 guilders from Friedrich to lure Luther to the Leucorea. The money was used to pay for the completion of his doctorate and was given on condition that he remained at the new university for the rest of his career. Both sides were making a commitment, and it was one that would be sorely tested in the years ahead. For the time being, however, there was little hint of that. The elector could not but be aware of the appointment of the clever young friar from Erfurt to the theology faculty at his university but, unlikely though it seems in such a small place, professor and patron always claimed never to have met or conversed face to face. They were in the same room once, it was said, but any communications between them were made via third parties.

That may have been political caution on the part of the shrewd elector, keen to appear neutral in the disputes soon to tear the Catholic Church apart, or a personal religious distaste for Luther's philosophy. Both, though, were to come later. Initially, it was more likely another facet of the shyness of this enigmatic man.

Elector Friedrich the Wise, Luther's patron and protector from the Pope and the Holy Roman Emperor, as depicted by Dürer in 1524. Professor and Prince are said never to have met face-to-face.

Twin tracks

Doctor Luther was allocated a heavy teaching load at the university. He had a series of lectures to deliver each year as well as supervising around half a dozen students at any one time for their masters' in theology.[8] And that wasn't the half of it. At Staupitz's instigation, he had been named as director of theological studies for a whole group of monasteries of the Hermits of Saint Augustine.[9] Whereas in Erfurt he had had times aplenty of silence and solitude in his cell to dwell on his sense of alienation from God, now his days were suddenly very full indeed.

'I could almost occupy two scribes or secretaries,' he wrote to his fellow Augustinian Johann Lang. 'All day long I do nothing but write letters . . . I preach at the monastery, I am lector [reading aloud improving texts to fellow friars] during mealtimes, I am asked daily to preach in the city church [the Stadtkirche], I have to supervise the programme of study, and I am vicar, i.e. prior of eleven cloisters.'[10]

Such a roster of activities brought into sharp relief once more the commercial activities of the Catholic Church, notably in the form of the sale of indulgences. The Pope had taken to himself the power to authorise throughout Christendom the offering of indulgences to the faithful. Most of the proceeds from this trade made their way back to the centre of Catholicism to fund papal ambitions, but where there was a strong national government (in France, Spain or England), such financial matters were the subject of negotiation, and there was often a sharing of spoils. In fragmented Germany collective action by the princes was harder to agree, making it a particular favourite for popes who were short of money. It was, in short, regarded as an easy touch. The Germans had a reputation for gullibility. Between 1486 and 1503, half a million guilders had been raised by a single papal legate on three visits to fund papal action against the Turks.[11]

The Castle Church in Wittenberg was part of the trade. Every 1 November, the feast of All Saints, a time in the liturgical calendar when thoughts were especially directed heavenwards to these role models of outstanding virtue, it would put on a display of relics from Elector Friedrich's personal collection. By 1509 this had grown to an estimated five thousand items,[12] many of them recorded in a catalogue illustrated by the Wittenberg court painter, Lucas Cranach the Elder, and including, *inter alia*, what were claimed as: a thorn from the crown pressed on the head of Christ at the time of His crucifixion; a nail used to fix Him to the cross; a tooth from Saint Jerome, fourth-century compiler of the

Vulgate, or Latin Bible; four hairs from the Virgin Mary; and no fewer than thirteen fragments from the crib of the infant Jesus. Those who came as pilgrims to the Castle Church to venerate could also purchase indulgences.

These had been part of the Church since the days when penance became a private ritual with a priest. Those who had sinned, confessed their sins in good faith to a cleric, and then been given a severe penance to perform, could mitigate it by an indulgence. The devout Elizabeth of Hungary, an early thirteenth-century princess of great piety, for instance, had been ordered by her confessor to suffer physical beatings for her minor misdemeanours and, on one occasion, to share her bed with a leper. Indulgences did not do away with the penance, but reduced it to something more manageable. Typically, this consisted of a commitment to extra prayers, additional fasts or making pilgrimages to shrines to see and touch relics.

As the practice grew in the Middle Ages, specific actions, deemed to be for the benefit of the wider Church, were held to cancel out all of an individual's previous sins – as, for example, in the case of the first Crusaders who, in 1095, set off to liberate the Holy Land for Christianity from its Muslim overlords on a promise from Pope Urban II that their willingness to fight would wipe clean all their past wrongdoings without any further penance.

By the later medieval period, the Church had further developed this concession into a much more elaborate system. Citing the Risen Christ's words to the surviving apostles, 'those whose sins you forgive, they are forgiven',[13] the papacy now claimed to control a 'treasury' of goodness, built up above all by the boundless merit of Jesus' life on earth, as well as by the more limited but still significant efforts of the saints. This capital could then be drawn on by sinners to make amends for their own earthly transgressions, but only by paying for an indulgence. Those who did were in effect cutting a deal with God, with the Church authorities acting as brokers.

In a more recent development of an already shady system, after 1476 indulgences were specifically made available not just for the benefit of the purchaser, but also for release of the purchaser's already deceased loved ones from purgatory.

This racket horrified many in the Church, including Erasmus, who in 1512 visited the English Marian shrine of Walsingham in Norfolk, and labelled it 'Falsingham', after being greeted by legions of salesmen attempting to sell a square of tattered cloth by passing it off as the Virgin Mary's veil, or a bottle of white liquid as her breast milk, and claiming that those possessing such items would earn remission for sins in heaven. Yet, in his early years at Wittenberg, despite his disillusionment on the Scala Sancta in Rome, Luther made no protest when confronted by the way indulgences made a lucrative business out of religion.

He had other things on his mind. However busy his diary, it could never block out his terrors. 'I have my own struggles,' Luther reported to Lang, at the end of the same long letter he had written about all the work he was doing, 'with the flesh, the world, and the devil.'[14] References to the devil litter Luther's writings, as they did the speech and thoughts of most God-fearing folk. For late medieval Christians, their greatest fear was of spending eternity with Satan in his lair, having been inadvertently seduced by him into sinfulness during their lifetime. It is there in one of the hymns that Luther was later to pen.

> In devil's dungeon chained I lay
> The pangs of death swept o'er me.
> My sin devoured me night and day
> In which my mother bore me.
> My anguish ever grew more rife,
> I took no pleasure in my life
> And sin had made me crazy.[15]

Yet, as this autobiographical verse suggests, it was not so much the future prospect of eternity in hell – 'the devil's dungeon' – that preoccupied Luther, but rather Satan's hand in his daily life, causing anguish, extinguishing pleasure, and driving him 'crazy'. That devilish interference covered mental, spiritual and physical ailments. 'In regard to all serious diseases,' he held, 'I believe the devil is author and instigator. First, he is creator of death. Second, Peter said in Acts [10:38], Christ healed not only those who were possessed but also the lame, the blind, and so on. I believe altogether that all dangerous diseases are the stamp of the devil. He uses for his purposes completely natural means.'[16] For Luther, even the most routine malady was proof positive of the devil toying with him.

Although demonstrably devil-obsessed, Luther rarely bothered trying to envisage hell, everywhere else so powerful in the medieval Christian imagination, as epitomised by the 'Doom' paintings in many churches. It may have been that it was just so present in the forefront of Christian imaginations that Luther did not feel the need to add his own descriptions. Yet, on occasion, he appeared almost ready to write it off. 'What hell may be in that last day, I am not altogether sure. I do not believe it is a special place where damned souls now exist like the place painters depict . . . Everyone carries his hell within him, wherever he is, as long as he feels and fears the last necessity of death and God's wrath.'[17] He was making hell sound less a place than an inner torment, or a form of mental disturbance caused by fear of God's wrath.[18]

Comforted by Christ

Luther poured himself into preparing the lectures that were the means by which any professor proved his worth. At Erfurt, when he had lectured as a young friar on Peter Lombard's *Sentences*, a dry treatise on logic that was a pillar of Scholasticism, and later during his 1508 temporary posting at Wittenberg tackling Aristotelian ethics, Luther had been, in his own terms, working with secondary material. Now, as 'Doctor in Biblia', his focus switched to a primary source, the Bible.

For his first series, beginning in August 1513, delivered weekly and lasting for two years, he selected the Book of Psalms. It was an uncontroversial choice and a text that he already knew well – from life in the monastery, shaped as it was by devotional readings of the psalms, spread out over each day. And psalters, illustrated books of the psalms, once the preserve of the wealthy who could afford hand-written, hand-illustrated and hand-bound texts, had become increasingly common in Luther's lifetime with the growth of printing presses, albeit often in crudely produced editions. Indeed, in preparation for his lectures, Luther showed an early taste for working closely with printers to take advantage of the new technology when he commissioned Johannes Grünenberg to make copies for his students of each of the 150 individual psalms contained in the Old Testament text, with spaces left between each for them to add their notes.

The Book of Psalms contains a variety of verses, some more suited to being sung than read aloud. They range from exuberant hymns of thanksgiving to God for His blessings to communal and individual laments at present misfortune. The latter often give voice to fears and doubts about His covenant with His chosen people, the Jews, and refer to the period of their exile in Babylon in the sixth century BCE after Jerusalem had been sacked and its Temple destroyed. The authorship of many of the texts is routinely ascribed to David, the second King of Israel, who reigned in the tenth century BCE, but the constituent parts of the Book of Psalms are the product of many authors and many ages. What is significant about the link with David is that he was, according to the New Testament, an ancestor of Joseph, Mary's husband, and therefore in the Psalms, Christians saw a foretelling of Jesus.

The precise history and context of the Psalms were not of any great concern to Luther, or for that matter any other Christian scholar at the time, with the possible exception of Erasmus.[19] That approach to biblical scholarship was to come in the centuries that followed. Instead, their true value lay in those insights they were believed to give into Jesus Christ's redemptive mission on earth. If proof were needed to endorse such a take, in the gospels of the New Testament were to be found words, on Jesus' lips, that directly repeated resonant phrases from Psalms. This, for Luther and his audience, was a work of prophecy.

The tone he sets in these early lectures is curiously uncertain for one whose historical reputation rests on saying challenging things boldly, sometimes crudely, and without apparent doubt. In his initial efforts as 'Doctor in Biblia', he was, by contrast, nervous of anything too definitive. 'I do not yet fully understand this,' the novice professor confesses to his students on one occasion. Or, 'I did not say that as well the last time as I did today.'[20]

Such gaucheness soon evaporates, but the sense remains that here he is sharing half-formed thoughts. These lectures were, with hindsight, a first tentative public airing of fragments of the key ideas that were later to shake Christendom. Specifically, Luther identifies in Psalms the struggle of faith, the very trauma he was living through as he lectured. 'One should always have the Psalms on hand,' he was to counsel later, 'and constantly and without interruption reflect upon them because we can never adequately appreciate their splendour unless we read them diligently.'[21] In moments of despair, he suggests, no doubt from experience, Psalms offered reassurance.

Beyond searching for ballast in his battle to stay afloat when God appeared to have left him adrift, Luther also drew from the Psalms the necessity of absolute humility before God. This was at odds with the Renaissance spirit to be found overflowing in Rome, which championed the potential of each human being in this life.

But neither did Luther in his lectures endorse traditional, or even moderated Scholasticism. Truth is not arrived at by formulations, disputations and doctrines, he insisted, because it resides uniquely in God. Too much wisdom, he wrote, in what seems like a swipe at Aristotle, is as likely to alienate the believer from God as too much ignorance.

In place of precise formulations and 'proofs', Luther talked to his students in these lectures of the essential mystery of God. It hints at an attraction to the mystical tradition, once prescribed by Staupitz as a cure for Luther's turbulent relationship with God. But here, too, Luther issues words of caution. Too much human striving to draw close to God is as much of a mistake as too much wisdom. He identifies then those approaches to God – standard for the times – that he rejects, but is vaguer on what it is that he is embracing. His own thought was as yet half-formed.

Though never named explicitly in the lectures on Psalms, looming in the shadow of Luther's words is predestination, the belief that God alone will decide each individual's eternal fate, regardless of his or her endeavours, achievements, wisdom, skill in debate and discourse, piety, good works on earth, mystical surrender, or even accumulation of indulgences. If Luther could see any alternative to predestination, it was in a faith that sought to approach God through the figure that the Book of Psalms anticipates and hails, namely Jesus Christ. As God's gift to humankind, He alone could narrow the distance to the Father. Through Him, Luther begins to suggest, could be glimpsed God's mercy and love.

It was a first hint of the emphasis on knowing God through His Son that was to become the cornerstone of Luther's teaching. He would subsequently refer back to Psalm III as 'the pinnacle and head of all Scripture' because: 'it gives an account of the kingdom and priesthood of Christ in the most splendid manner, in that it states it is Christ who rules over everything and comes for everyone, and has everything in His hand. It is an excellent spiritual exposition. The psalm is invaluable, and whenever I am sick, I rely on it.'[22]

And in Psalm 22, which begins with the plaintive cry, 'My God, my God, why have You deserted me?', repeated almost word for word by Jesus on the cross,[23] Luther discerned that Christ too might have suffered His own version of *Anfechtung*. 'For Christ dwells only in sinners ... He descended from heaven, where He dwelt among the righteous, to dwell among sinners. Meditate on this love of His and you will have His sweet consolation.'[24] As Luther did in subsequent verses of his autobiographical hymn 'In devil's dungeon chained I lay':

> Then was the Father troubled sore
> To see me ever languish
> The Everlasting Pity swore
> To save me from my anguish.
> He turned to me His father heart
> And chose Himself a bitter part,
> His Dearest did it cost Him.
> Thus spoke the Son, 'Hold thou to Me,
> From now on thou wilt make it.
> I give My life for thee
> And for thee I will stake it.
> For I am thine and thou art Mine,
> And where I am our lives entwine,
> The Old Fiend cannot shake it.'[25]

'Righteous' is a word that Luther first addressed in detail in his lectures on Psalms. What did it mean to be righteous, he asked, though his fullest, and most challenging treatment was to come later. This was typical of his theological method. He would make an eye-catching remark as part of the debate, giving voice to something that was going on inside his head. Then when it attracted attention, or caused controversy, he would rework and expand on that first airing until he could fully satisfy himself with a definitive statement. 'When I first read and sang in the Psalms *in iustitia tua libera me* [and deliver me in Thy righteousness],' Luther recalled, 'I was horror-stricken and felt deep hostility toward these words, God's righteousness, God's work. For I knew that *iustitia dei* [God's righteousness] meant a harsh judgement. Well, was He supposed to save me by judging me harshly? If so I was lost forever.'[26]

It was a gloomy thought, yet he seemed to accept that, as part of his struggle with faith, knowledge came dropping slowly. 'I did not learn my theology all at once,' he once reflected, 'but I had to always dig deeper and deeper. And it was my bouts of torment that brought me that far, for no one will ever learn anything without such experiences.'[27]

Justification by faith

'I greatly longed to understand Paul's Epistle to the Romans,' Luther wrote in 1545, reflecting shortly before his death on his great breakthrough, 'and nothing stood in the way but that one expression, "the justice of God",[28] because I took it to mean that justice whereby God is just and deals justly with punishing the unjust.' That was how he had seen things thirty years earlier as a young friar and inexperienced professor at Wittenberg. 'My situation was that, although an impeccable monk, I stood before God as a sinner troubled in conscience, and I had no confidence that my merit would assuage Him.'[29] For Luther then, justice had meant only one thing – punishment and probably damnation.

His later remark is a tidy summary of the dilemma he was facing as a scholar and as a sufferer – perhaps too tidy, it could be argued, with Luther producing a rounded account for posterity. But it does provide a first-person account of the insight Luther was to make when reading Saint Paul, from which everything else then flowed.

His two years working on the Book of Psalms had brought him to a point where he could see, in Jesus' death on the cross, that God's wrath was mitigated by His mercy. In the figure of the crucified Christ, therefore, he had hit on what was potentially a way through his own sense of alienation from a condemnatory God. He was beginning to glimpse an answer to his central anxiety – how to be saved.

His next step was to search for a new understanding of God's justice, hitherto in his mind based on the law as laid out in the Ten Commandments, and something which he had found almost impossible to keep without being overwhelmed by a sense of his own sinfulness. How could any concept of God's justice, he asked, sit alongside Jesus Christ's life, death and resurrection?

That was the spur in the autumn of 1515 for Luther to turn his attention as a lecturer to the Apostle Paul and his letters. These were the earliest accounts of Jesus, pre-dating the gospel writers by at least twenty years. And in Paul, the apostle who did most to shape and promote the Christian message, Luther discovered a kindred spirit, someone who was just as concerned as he was with God's justice, and how it could benefit as well as punish humanity.

First, Luther tackled Paul's Letter to the Romans, written in Greek around 57 CE. Like most of Paul's output, it was directed at the fledgling Christian communities of the Middle East and Mediterranean. Addressing the small, persecuted group of his co-believers in Rome, a city he had yet to visit, Paul was reflecting above all on the practical challenges of living out faith. That immediately appealed to Luther, since he remained, at heart, a practical man. His lectures were, at one level, an account of his own battle to live out his faith in practical ways. 'He speaks with such authority,' Luther wrote of Paul. 'Therefore, one should in good conscience pay careful attention to his words. In all my life, I have not read a more serious work.'[30]

Luther offered in that same 1545 recollection a detailed but compelling account of the extraordinary impact that Paul made on his thinking, and on his situation. 'I did not love a just and angry God, but rather hated and murmured against Him. Yet I clung to the dear Paul and had a great yearning to know what he meant. Night and day I pondered until I saw the connection between the justice of God and the statement [in Paul] that "the just shall live by his faith". Then I grasped that the justice of God is that righteousness by which, through grace and sheer mercy, God justifies us through faith. Thereupon I felt myself to be reborn and to have gone through open doors into paradise. The whole of Scripture took on a new meaning, and whereas before the "justice of God" had filled me with hate, now it became to me inexpressibly sweet in greater love. The passage of Paul became to me a gate to heaven . . .'[31] God's justice was no longer a promise of punishment, but the hope of salvation.

It sounds like another thunderbolt and there is, inevitably, a legend around the precise moment this one struck. Based on a free reading of remarks he made in his *Table Talk*, it has been claimed that Luther was sitting on the lavatory in his tower room in the Black Cloister, battling once more with his troublesome bowels. Instead of reading the newspaper while he waited for a movement, he was puzzling over that particular passage in Romans. The Latin phrase he uses to describe the moment – with that vulgar flourish often found in his language – was '*in cloaca*' – 'in the sewer'.[32] That, in the legend, is taken literally as being on the toilet, rather than a more figurative reading as 'in the darkest depths'.

Though the tale conjures up an entertaining, if coarse, image,[33] the reality is that Luther's revelation about 'justification by faith' evolved slowly and gradually, as his studies intensified, just as his hero Paul had taken his time – up to three years and a trip to Arabia, scholars suggest[34] – to digest that moment on the road to Damascus when Christ appeared to him in a flash, and allowed it to grow through prayer and soul-searching into the vision on which he helped build the Christian Church.

The real meaning of 'justification by faith' may not even have dawned on Luther when he was delivering his lecture on this section of Paul's letter. In the original manuscript of the talk, held in the Royal Library in Berlin, he spends just a few sentences on the key phrase before moving on (and there is no mention of a clap of thunder, or a eureka moment in the lavatory). The gate to heaven did not open quite so readily. Whatever the circumstances and precise timing, however, the crucial fact is that he had made the connection between God's justice and 'justification by faith', the phrase that came to define his revolution in Christianity.

So what did it all come down to? In essence, it was the Greek word that Paul used and which was usually translated as justice. Luther argued 'justice', as rendered in the original Greek, embodied not only the enforcement of law (i.e. in standard criminal justice system terms of dispensing punishment to wrongdoers) but also what he deemed the forgiveness of sinners by God (or, to continue the analogy, their rehabilitation). It wasn't that sins no longer mattered. They did. No individual, Luther insisted, has a right to God's forgiveness, but it was available, something to be strived for, fumbling in darkness, relying only on faith, and the belief that by sending His Son, Jesus Christ, God was intent on saving humankind, and therefore that He would keep that promise, albeit in His own mysterious way. Justice – or as Luther put it 'justification' – came by faith in God, nothing more, nothing less.

Central to his understanding was the operation of grace. 'If you have a true faith that Christ is your saviour, then at once you have a gracious God, for faith leads you in and opens up God's heart and will, that you should see pure grace and overflowing love. This it is to behold God in faith . . . He who sees God as angry does not see Him rightly but looks only on a curtain, as if a dark cloud had been drawn across His face.'[35]

If lecturing on Psalms had brought Luther to God's mercy via Christ, his study of Paul's writings had now opened the curtains on His justice and His grace. Although the phrase 'justification by faith' – or 'justification by faith alone', as Luther later put it in his translation into German of the New Testament, adding the extra word to emphasise his key point – was new, the idea that lay behind it was not. Since it came from Paul's text, Luther would naturally say that the credit belonged to the apostle. All he had managed to do was interpret Paul's words correctly.

His insight, however, still required fleshing out, and to accomplish that Luther turned, in October 1516, to lecture on Paul's Letter to the Church in Galatia. This shorter text occupied him until March 1517, when he moved on to the Letter to the Hebrews, thought to have been written around 67 CE in the style of Paul by his followers. 'Galatians', Luther claimed later, 'is my favourite epistle, the one in which I place all my trust.'[36] Perhaps it was Paul's especially fierce tone with a divided Christian community that drew him in. Luther was to imitate it when he felt something passionately. And it certainly provided the ringing endorsement he was looking for about 'justification by faith'.

'What makes a man righteous,' Paul writes in Galatians, 'is not obedience to the Law, but faith in Jesus Christ. We had to become believers in Christ Jesus . . . and now we hold that faith in Christ, rather than fidelity to the Law, is what justifies us, and that no one can be justified by keeping the Law.'[37]

Mere obedience to rules is not sufficient, Paul says. There is no set of steps to take, or boxes to tick, to use a modern phrase, in order to achieve salvation. The apostle goes on to explain: 'If the law can justify us, there is no point in the death of Christ.'[38] And later he adds: 'The Law was to be our guardian until Christ came and we could be justified by faith.'[39]

An original thinker?

Justification by faith, or more broadly the link between right-standing with God and each individual's eternal fate, had been debated endlessly down the centuries by leading Church figures. How would each individual gain salvation? The answers fell into two main camps. For some it was by *doing* – deeds would be guided and enabled by God, and the way in which they were carried out would then shape God's judgement of the individual. For others it was by *being*. Faith in God, regardless of actions, was the sole measurement. Since any achievements in life were down to God's grace, they could play no part in salvation.

The argument between the two stances had played out with particular vigour in the fifth century in the Pelagian dispute. A British-born ascetic and theologian, Pelagius had developed a strong following by his example and his teaching, which included his championing of an innate human ability to attain salvation by such paths as prayer, fasting and 'good works'. This view, though, was disputed by Augustine, inspiration for Luther's own religious order. A sinless life was utterly impossible without faith in God, he insisted, precisely because of the sinfulness of humanity. 'There can be no hope for me except in your [God's] great mercy,' he wrote in his *Confessions*.[40]

There is a distinct echo of Augustine in Luther's lectures on Romans. 'He [God] saves us,' Luther said, 'not by our own merits but by sheer election and His immutable will.'[41] God's choice of who to save is made by criteria that are beyond human understanding. For those eager to influence that choice, Luther had stern words. 'If a man is overwhelmed by the fear that he is not one of the elect, or if he is assailed and troubled about his election, let him give thanks for such fear and let him rejoice about his anxiety.'[42] Just, presumably, as Luther himself could now see that his *Anfechtung* and those tortured early years in the monastery, dominated by his fear of God's anger, had been necessary to bring him to the understanding he had achieved of God's justice and hence of the path to salvation. Without struggle and pain, it was not possible. In 'anxiety' is a realisation of the depth of human sinfulness. And reaching an understanding of God's justice was not an end to that anxiety. For Luther, having faith in God included a readiness for God to deny him salvation and consign him to hell. It is, in that sense, a more brutal form of the surrender favoured by mystics.

In the Pelagian controversy, the Church had sided with Augustine. Pelagius was condemned as a heretic. That verdict was on the curriculum in late medieval theological schools. Yet in Luther's eyes, the Church in his own day had reversed that rejection of Pelagius and was now teaching that God's judgement could indeed be influenced by earthly deeds – as evidenced by its encouragement of 'good works'. In other words, it was repeating Pelagius's error – something that caused Luther to talk of 'fools and pig-theologians'.[43]

By taking one phrase from Saint Paul, Luther had turned the whole medieval system of salvation on its head. 'Good works' might be a means of giving thanks for the offer of salvation, made by God through Jesus' sacrifice on the cross, but they were absolutely not a way of earning it, much less of reserving it in advance. To have any hope of that, faith – in Luther's terms, an almost childlike dependence on God – was everything.

CHAPTER FOUR

The Ninety-Five Theses: Nailing the Corruption of the Church

'I thought I had done him [the Pope] a favour.'
Martin Luther, *Table Talk*[1]

In another time and another place, Martin Luther might have moved forward from his moment (or process) of revelation about 'justification by faith' to develop and debate that theological insight in a series of discourses with fellow friars, clerics and academics, perhaps giving speeches at learned gatherings, or using the new technology of the publishing presses to pour his views into papers or polemical books. The plain fact was that, in theological terms, over the course of his lectures of Psalms and then on Saint Paul's letters, his key breakthrough had been made.

In that same other place and time, Luther might even have convinced sufficient of the decision-makers in Rome to begin a gradual shift in the official approach and ultimately teaching of the Catholic Church. Best of all, as he went about his life in between monastery, university and town church in Wittenberg, Luther might have found a measure of peace in his own troubled relationship with God – perhaps not total, for that was not in his nature, but sufficient to stop him feeling so tortured.

There are no portraits of Luther from 1517, the year he inadvertently wrote his name into the history books, but we can catch a glimpse of how he must have looked from the earliest surviving likeness, dated 1520. It is a woodcut illustration in a book of his writings, and is based on a work by Elector Friedrich's court painter, Lucas Cranach the Elder. A disconcertingly handsome, tonsured Luther is all cheekbones, chiselled jawline and extended cupid-bow lips, almost unrecognisable from later, better-known images, also by Cranach, as he begins to run to fat (so much so that there is still a German phrase that translates as 'as fat as Luther'). The most remarkable feature, though, are his eyes – intense, detached, directed at a far point, high above the messy compromises of this life, fixed on salvation and beyond. And it is the eyes that do not change, mellow or dim in any of Cranach's subsequent portraits of Luther, endowing him ever after with an air of unflinching, otherworldly determination. In the 1523 portrait, the most often used, Cranach records that same ardent gaze, but this time gleaming out from underneath Luther's over-hanging eyebrows and the feathery fringe of a still young-looking man, this last playful detail seemingly at odds with the overall dourness of his countenance and the general thickening in his girth. His tonsure is now gone, but Luther continues to wear his dark Augustinian robe as he clutches his Bible in one hand and clamps the other to his heart, as if a warrior with only his shield, and his fidelity, to protect him.

Both images, however, stand as a reminder that Luther was living at a very specific time and in a very specific set of circumstances which, alongside his inflexible, troubled personality, dictated that there could be no soft landing for his theological conviction about 'justification by faith'. Though nothing could have been further from his thoughts at the start of 1517, he was already in the foothills of his rapid ascent to the heights of European prominence from his quiet backwater of Wittenberg. What drove him on were not just his insights into God's justice that challenged the orthodoxy of the day, but also an array of external factors around politics, dynasties and the exercise of power in the Catholic Church.

The earliest surviving portrait of Martin Luther, a woodcut illustration from 1520 in one of his books, based on a now lost work by Lucas Cranach.

The most familiar image of Luther, again from Cranach, this time in 1523, with his jawline running fat, but a feathery fringe showing him to still be a young man.

Luther began the year with his usual round of lectures, supervision of students, and administrative business in his order. In his New Testament journey, he had – since the previous April – been examining Saint Paul's Letter to the Hebrews, and would continue with the task through to March of 1518. In it he found once again a strong reiteration that it was through Jesus Christ and His sacrifice on the cross that God could be approached.

His reputation as a theologian was growing modestly with the publication of his first book, an uncontroversial commentary in German on seven penitential psalms, drawing on his previous lectures. Getting into print would be a landmark in the life of any professor, then as now. His choice to write in the vernacular is worthy of particular note. Luther's core instinct, as befitted a Hermit of Saint Augustine with its teaching remit, was to broaden participation in the debates of Catholicism. At the time, most tracts were still in the Church language of Latin, and hence excluded all but a chosen few senior clerics, monks and academics. Luther was seeking a broader audience.

Not that he was immune to the pleasures of proficiency in Latin – and increasingly also in Greek. At this stage in his life, with a young man's showy cleverness, he would occasionally adopt the Hellenising fad popular among the Humanists and sign himself 'Eleutherius', a Latin version of the Greek *eleutheros*, meaning 'free'. It was also the name of a second-century Pope, believed to be a freed slave. Modifying his own surname was Luther engaging in the sort of word play that Erasmus or Thomas More sprinkled like sugar in their writings. Here he was claiming, in name at least, to be 'Martin the Freed Man', signifying both his willingness to think freely, and his aspiration to be freed from the crushing weight of guilt and sinfulness that had been his burden for so long. Indeed it may have been his use of Eleutherius that finally sounded the death knell for his birth surname Ludher. Luther was a closer match for his Latin/Greek moniker.

Within the small pond of three-street Wittenberg, Luther's was now a face to notice, whether because of his senior position with the local Augustinians, his sermons from the pulpit of the Stadtkirche, or his lectures. Such minor celebrity wasn't an altogether welcome turn of events, he confided to Johann Lang, his old colleague at Erfurt. 'God's approval declines', he wrote in a letter of 27 January 1517, 'at the same rate that human approval increases.'[2] Fame was never his goal, whatever his critics would subsequently say.

Though his head was far from being turned, there was a newfound self-confidence in Luther, especially in his own abilities as a teacher, which enabled him to play his part in revising the curriculum of Wittenberg's theology department so as to follow a wider trend in Europe. The tide was ebbing on the dry reason of Scholasticism that had dominated his own formation. In its place was a renewed interest in Augustine and Paul. Whether Luther was leading or following within the department is not clear, for he was working with his colleagues Andreas von Karlstadt and Nikolaus von Amsdorf, but in August of 1517 it was Luther who produced *Disputation against Scholastic Theology* for use by his students, in which he set out a new path for training theologians.

It may be that the impetus for change was coming from the students themselves, impatient with prescribed texts, hallowed since the twelfth century. They were eager to bathe in the new theological currents flowing around Europe. Numbers attending lectures on Peter Lombard's *Sentences* – which Luther had once taught at Erfurt – had seen a marked drop, he reported with a measured but unmistakable glee to Lang in a letter of 18 May, while 'our theology and Augustine are progressing well and with God's help rule at our university. Aristotle is falling from his throne and his final doom is only a matter of time.'[3]

No mention, though, of a parallel surge in interest in Christian Humanist texts, such as those by Erasmus. Luther would certainly have been well aware of them, as would his students and colleagues, but if he gave the appearance to Lang of going along with the general trajectory of 'new thinking', in reality he was charting his own course, with his principal guide the Bible. 'Divine Scripture is a very fertile tree,' he once remarked, 'and there is no branch which I have not shaken with my own hands, and knocked down a few apples.'[4]

Pious racket

Luther had witnessed the slow but elaborate and expensive rebirth of Saint Peter's on his visit to Rome. The old fifth-century basilica, the original mother church of Catholicism dating back to when the Roman Empire legalised Christianity, had been built in wood over what was believed to be the grave of the first pope. Now it was being replaced on the Vatican hillside by something more eye-catching. The Renaissance papacy, anxious to celebrate on earth both human achievement and the glory of God, had drawn up plans on the sort of extravagant scale that might now be associated with a Hollywood spectacular. The vast edifice under construction was to be topped with a dome that would outdo in scale and ambition those of its nearest rivals, the Duomo in Florence and Constantinople's Hagia Sophia.

To fund the scheme, when he laid the foundation stone in 1506, Pope Julius II had authorised the sale of a special indulgence for the new Saint Peter's. The building fund was to be promoted by travelling preachers in several parts of Europe, but not initially in Germany, either because of resistance from the princes there, or from a feeling that it had been over-exploited already. That changed in 1516, when Julius's successor, Leo X, wanted to prove his worth by injecting new momentum into the construction, but found himself strapped for cash to pay all the craftsmen and artists required.

The second son of Lorenzo the Magnificent (the Medici patron of the arts and *de facto* ruler of Florence), Leo had been made a cleric at age seven, a cardinal at thirteen, and was pope at thirty-seven. There had been no need to prove his holiness to be elected as Saint Peter's successor. It was his politics and powerful connections that won the day. Though less belligerent and venal than his predecessor, he was just as shameless in his commercial dealings with his flock. By the time of his death in 1521, it has been calculated that there were more than two thousand offices (or jobs) in the papal gift that could be purchased by those prepared to pay the price.[5]

The German indulgence that Leo now authorised was to be a joint venture with Prince Albrecht, younger son of the Elector of Brandenburg, and part of the Hohenzollern dynasty later to rule a united Germany. In 1513, at the age of twenty-three, Albrecht had been named Archbishop of Magdeburg. Among the towns that fell under his ecclesiastical jurisdiction was Wittenberg. But this mighty archdiocese was not sufficient to satisfy the ambitions of the cultured but worldly Albrecht. He was not, in fairness, without interest in religion – like Elector Friedrich, he corresponded with Erasmus and collected relics – yet he was equally attracted by earthly power, and so had set his greedy heart on being Archbishop of Mainz, *Primas Germaniae*, the leading episcopal see in Germany, first held by the revered Saint Boniface in the eighth century as he converted the region to Christianity. Better still, as archbishop of this prosperous city on the Rhine, to the west of Electoral Saxony, Albrecht would also be its elector. His spiritual authority would be accompanied by temporal power.

It was quite a prize, but in order to receive it from the Pope, he had to woo Leo with a substantial donation to the Saint Peter's building fund. The sum required was greater still because Church law did not allow one man to hold two archbishoprics simultaneously. A premium was required for this tiresome detail to be set aside. To pay the bill, Prince Albrecht ended up borrowing heavily from the Fugger merchant-banking house in Augsburg. His debt, it was agreed, would also be paid back out of the funds generated by extending the Saint Peter's indulgence into Germany. Proceeds would be split between the prince-archbishop (and hence his bankers) and the papacy.

Thus it was that in the summer of 1517 the Dominican preacher Johann Tetzel pitched up in Brandenburg to sell his wares. A plump, world-weary Saxon, educated at Leipzig University, he made no great claim to being a first-rank theologian, but if anyone personified the Catholic Church's habit of making a business out of religion, it was him. He had developed quite a reputation as a seller of indulgences, flogging spiritual consolation to the needy. Prince Albrecht employed him so as to maximise the profit in his venture.

A 1619 image of an original poster advertising Johann Tetzel's sale of indulgences. 'Place your penny on the drum,' his sales patter went, 'the Pearly Gates open, and in strolls mum.'

Tetzel had once been a member of the Inquisition, established by the papacy two centuries earlier to root out heresy in the Church by any means, up to and including various forms of torture that would tear the accused limb from limb. Now he was turning his dubious powers of persuasion to selling entry into heaven via indulgences. His sales patter strayed well beyond the guidelines set for him by Albrecht, and beyond the teaching of the Church. Among his catchphrases were said to be, 'Place your penny on the drum/the Pearly Gates open and in strolls mum', and, 'When the coin in the coffer rang, the soul from purgatory sprang'. An indulgence, he is alleged to have claimed, could even redeem a man who had raped the Virgin Mary.[6]

Whether he actually made any of these claims has been questioned by historians who have studied Tetzel, but what is known for sure is that he arrived on Good Friday, 1517, in Jüterbog, just over the border from Saxony in Brandenburg and only twenty-five miles from Wittenberg. News of his commercial activities soon reached Luther. 'All the people ran to him [Tetzel] as though they were possessed. Little by little I began to persuade people otherwise, and to explain to them what grace and forgiveness of sins meant. But ... Tetzel still went shamelessly forward.'[7] Luther dubbed the indulgence-seller 'Junker Tetzel', *Junker* being the term for a nobleman, thus highlighting the gap between the elevated status of the vendor of letters of indulgence, and the poor who parted with a florin to own one.[8]

Tetzel's methods were the antithesis of his own emerging approach to salvation, but Luther was not by any measurement the first to raise concerns about the sale of indulgences. Those who had objected to the crass commercialisation of the forgiveness of sins were manifold, stretching from the Albigensians in southern France in the middle years of the thirteenth century (who rebelled against Rome and were crushed by the newly established Inquisition),[9] to both Staupitz[10] and Erasmus among Luther's contemporaries. In his 1509 satire on priests, *The Praise of Folly*, the Dutch Humanist had sent up the spectacle of greedy clerics trying to measure out time in purgatory 'by the hourglass'.[11]

The focus of most objections lay in the Church's claim that indulgences could be purchased on behalf of a third party and thereby could reduce the wait in purgatory for someone already dead. This extension of the practice had been given papal blessing in 1476 by Sixtus IV, but his critics accused him of encroaching on God's domain. Only God could pass judgement on the salvation of souls, they insisted.

Forgiveness of the past sins committed by the living was, however, usually regarded as a separate issue. Often those sins would be breaking Church-imposed sanctions – man-made rules rather than God's laws, such as the penalty imposed for eating meat on Fridays. And since most of the sinners concerned would, inevitably, go on to offend again, wiping away their transgressions by allowing them to purchase an indulgence prompted less criticism. Some, including Thomas Aquinas, even argued that the benefits of an indulgence obtained in life might even endure when that individual reached purgatory.

Luther, typically, had no time for such fine distinctions. Indulgences, whether for the living or for the dead, the purchaser or a deceased relative, should not be allowed. His objection was not to specific abuses of the system, but to the system itself. Salvation, he believed, was in God's hands. For the Church to claim a role, worse still for them to charge for that role, was anathema to him.

Why suddenly was he so offended? Indulgences had, after all, been sold in the Schlosskirche of Wittenberg since he had arrived there, and no record exists of him raising any objection. When he did take a stand in 1517, Luther claimed that he had 'long hesitated' before speaking out.[12] And that is borne out by his sermons of 1516, when he first started to articulate, in general terms, his concerns. One had been delivered on 31 October 1516, the night before the annual All Saints' Day indulgence in the Castle Church. Luther had questioned the overriding principle that underpinned the system – namely the complete remission of sins that came with the purchase of an indulgence. Surely, he asked, to arrive at such a state required genuine contrition, not just a willingness to pay? Emptying your wallet did not equate to genuine sorrow, and God would not be fooled.

What lay behind his increasing vehemence on the subject, though, was his revelation about 'justification by faith'. Compared to that insight about the nature of salvation, the whole trade in indulgences, especially when exploiting Wittenbergers who had made the day's journey on foot to Jüterbog, was taken by Luther as a personal affront. Salvation, he had come to believe, demanded as a minimum a lifetime's struggle. Tetzel, by contrast, was offering it for a few coins, without even enquiring whether his purchasers regretted the sins they had committed.

Some might have been tempted to turn a blind eye, especially as Elector Friedrich was active in the indulgences market, with the funds raised by sales at the annual All Saints' Day ceremony in the Castle Church used to sponsor Wittenberg's university and keep Luther in a job. Or they might focus their attack on Tetzel's overblown claims. Such a course, had Luther taken it, would doubtless have received the Elector's support, not just because there was a long-standing enmity between the Saxon ruling family and Prince Albrecht's Hohenzollern clan in Brandenburg, but also because Tetzel's efforts threatened to reduce the revenue that Friedrich would receive that November.

Yet Luther was no pragmatist. For him, there could be no distinction between different aspects of what he saw as a single problem. He would speak out, even if it risked alienating his patron. The Elector, Luther reported,[13] had let it be known that the remarks he had made in various sermons in 1516, and again in

February 1517, had not pleased him. Here again was Luther's standard response to pressure or criticism. Faced with the disapproval of their superiors, or mentors, or employer, many would withdraw, apologise, or simply keep silent. Instead Luther deepened and refined his attack, magnifying the offence caused.

There was, to be fair, some trimming of his sails. Rather than involve Elector Friedrich directly in his complaint against Tetzel, he set out his objection in writing to Prince Albrecht as his local archbishop in Madgeburg. Yet his choice of an alternative avenue of protest could hardly have been more misguided. He had no knowledge quite how financially committed Albrecht was to the success of the whole Tetzel road show.

On 31 October 1517, Luther wrote in Latin to his archbishop to warn him about Tetzel's methods, laying out the fundamental error, as he saw it, of offering indulgences. Acknowledging that not everyone shared his view, he proposed staging a debate on the matter. To that end, he attached to the letter ninety-five debating points, or theses, again written in Latin and aimed, in his own words, at initiating a 'disputation on the power and efficacy of indulgences'.

The two texts – letter and theses – each had their distinctive purpose, which dictated their tone. The letter was couched in the moderate tone of a loyal priest reporting a concern to his ecclesiastical superior (though Luther couldn't quite hold back from the occasional sharp remark). In the Ninety-Five Theses, by contrast, he was able to let off steam, on the grounds that debating points, to make any exchange lively, had to be put in a provocative style. This was no sleight of hand to allow himself to express in the Ninety-Five Theses the dissent he really wanted to include in his letter to Albrecht. Luther genuinely did appear to hope that such a face-to-face disputation might be possible, with the archbishop's blessing.

Nailing it

The familiar image, explored countless times over 500 years by artists, is of Martin Luther posting his Ninety-Five Theses on the door of the Castle Church in Wittenberg on 31 October, the eve of the day when the faithful would stream in and purchase indulgences while standing in the presence of a display of relics. If it is an act that sounds eccentric now, it was a routine practice at the time. Those who wished to announce their disquiet about anything happening inside their church, or more generally in Church matters, could do so by fixing a notice on the door. One obvious parallel is with the posting of the 'Twelve Conclusions' on the doors of Westminster Abbey and Saint Paul's Cathedral in London in 1395 by the Lollards, religious reformers who shared

Nailing the Ninety-Five Theses to the door of the Castle Church in Wittenberg: this nineteenth century illustration captures the story of Luther's famous act of defiance, but there is no reference to any such public gesture of rebellion in any of Luther's extensive writings and speeches.

many of the same concerns Luther was soon to air about the power, authority and corruption of the papacy.

In the Lutherhaus, the museum based in Luther's home in Wittenberg, there are plenty of illustrations of him taking his stand at the door of the Schlosskirche. An early seventeenth-century depiction places him there, quill pen in hand, in the midst of writing his theses, as if using the door as his desk. Another, from a century later, shows Luther talking to a passer-by outside the church and urging him to take a closer look at the theses on the door. Once it gets to the nineteenth century, a hammer appears in his hand to nail the paper to the door, though it has been suggested that, at the time, he would have been much more likely to use wax.

How he attached the theses is the least of the many practical concerns raised by the traditional story of Luther's public declaration of rebellion. Even with his uncompromising nature, would he really have posted such a challenge to the sale of indulgences on the door of Elector Friedrich's church, hours before it would be opened in an annual ceremony where money was taken in lieu of the remission of sins? It would have set Luther on a collision course with the patron of the university where he worked.

And, even if he was quite that unconcerned about his own career, how big would the notice have been? Granted each of the Ninety-Five Theses is short, but most run at least to a sentence or two. This was not the equivalent of a petition attached to a noticeboard. The Lollards, for their part, had restricted themselves to twelve in their protest on the actual door, directing readers to a separate fuller list of thirty-seven available inside for those who were sufficiently curious.

There is no suggestion that Luther offered any such option. All ninety-five were, according to the traditional narrative, there on the door. If they were handwritten, then his letters would have had to be very small indeed, unless posting this notice was more akin to hanging wallpaper. The current doors on the Schlosskirche, admittedly replicas of the originals, just about manage to contain the Ninety-Five Theses in printed form, but it is a tight fit top to bottom, and side to side. Recent research may have highlighted a similar document from September 1517, just one month earlier, where Luther had produced a printed broadsheet of theses on another academic topic,[14] but would he really have wanted to risk sharing the potentially incendiary Ninety-Five Theses with a local printer?

It seems a shame to ruin another good yarn about Luther, but the unforgettable picture of him wielding his hammer at the church door, symbolically knocking down the old order and smashing Europe into a Reformation, has only a debatable claim to fact. In the many volumes of his *Table Talk*, full of episodes that Luther embellishes in one way or another, there is not a single reference to posting, nailing or attaching anything with wax to the church door. And it is likewise nowhere to be found in his correspondence, sermons, lectures and books. What evidence does exist for this version of events comes from those who were not there. So during Luther's lifetime his secretary, George Rörer, mentions the theses being posted on church doors in Wittenberg,[15] and after his death it was Luther's closest colleague and aide, Philipp Melanchthon, who in 1546 included the story in the earliest 'official' biography, even though he himself had not arrived in Wittenberg until 1518.[16]

So let's stick to the facts. What is not disputed is that Luther wrote to Prince Albrecht. It was the letter that, in Luther's mind, was the key document, since as late as 1541 he said that he still had a copy of it close to hand.[17] And it was Albrecht's failure to answer his priest's letter that enraged and emboldened the volatile Luther sufficiently to prompt him to widen this private exchange of views between priest and archbishop. He shared his texts – the letter and the Ninety-Five Theses – with a small circle of friends and colleagues. He could not have imagined what would follow, but that decision produced the sort of instant surge of forward

ALBERTVS·MI·DI·SA·SANC
ROMANE·ECCLAE·TI·SAN
CHRYSOGONI·PBR·CARDINA
MAGVN·AC·MAGDE·ARCHI
EPS·ELECTOR·IMPE·PRIMAS
ADMINI·HALBER·MARCHI
BRANDENBVRGENSIS

Prince Albrecht, since the age of 23 Luther's local prelate as Archbishop
of Magdeburg, and the recipient of the Ninety-Five Theses.

momentum that we might now identify with a social media storm.
One of the first recipients handed the letter, and attached theses,
to a printer. Luther always vehemently denied it had been him,
and some suggest it could even have been some frustrated reformer
in Prince Albrecht's court.[18] Whoever was guilty, very quickly this
obscure friar's strongly worded challenge – not only to Tetzel's
crusade, but also to the very notion that the papacy could authorise the selling of indulgences – went viral. It was winging its way
across Germany in pamphlets, woodcuts and even songs.

It was the start of a process that would turn Wittenberg into a
major centre of the printing industry and subsequently of the
European book trade. Luther's close friend Lucas Cranach, resi-
dent in the town in one of its finest houses, played a key role in

this aspect of the publishing revolution. He had an entrepreneurial flair and had glimpsed the unrealised potential, almost a century after the advent of printing, for illustrated books directed at those with limited literacy. Cranach had a knack for popular, eye-pleasing, self-promoting presentation, and he put this to good effect with Luther's subsequent writings, with arresting title pages that featured prominently this once obscure friar's famous name, along with good-quality illustrations (produced by assistants in his studio). When combined with Luther's vigorous use of German in usually short, punchy texts, it opened up a whole new market of lay readers, those such as Luther's own parents, of humble origins, but now with a few spare coins in their pocket and sufficient reading skills to lap up such polemics about matters close to their hearts.[19]

'An insignificant clod'

Sending a private letter to Prince Albrecht as one of his priests still represented a substantial risk for Luther. Confronting the most senior cleric in the Holy Roman Empire was not something to be lightly undertaken, which explains why his text, accompanied by the Ninety-Five Theses, is so crudely and grovellingly humble.

'Most Reverend Father in Christ, Most Illustrious Sovereign, Forgive me that I, such an insignificant clod,[20] have the temerity of writing to Your Excellency. The Lord Jesus is my witness that I have long hesitated doing this on account of my insignificance and unworthiness, of which I am well aware. I do it now impudently, and I am motivated solely by the obligation of my loyalty, which I know I owe you, Most Reverend Father in Christ. May Your Excellency therefore deign to . . . listen to my request.'[21]

It is the tone of one about to tell Albrecht something that is going on behind his back. This may be a device or it may be sincere. Since Luther did not know that Albrecht's debts from purchasing the episcopal see of Mainz had caused Tetzel to be sent out selling indulgences, it is better to lean towards sincerity. There was still a naivety in Luther, untrained as he was as yet in public spats. He possessed a readiness, despite all that he had already seen, not least on his trip to Rome, to believe the best of people. Hopelessly corrupt as the circumstances of Albrecht's rise to be an archbishop twice over are to contemporary eyes, Luther would not have regarded it as unusual for a worldly prince to be appointed to head up not one but two archdioceses when in his early twenties. Despite Church rules that bishops should ideally be at least thirty, it happened regularly enough.

'Under your most distinguished name,' Luther continues, 'papal indulgences are offered all across the land for the construction of Saint Peter's. Now, I do not so much complain about the quacking of the preachers . . . but I bewail the gross misunderstanding among the people . . . Evidently the poor souls believe that when they have bought indulgence letters, they are then assured of their salvation. They are likewise convinced that souls escape from purgatory as soon as they have placed a contribution in the chest.'[22]

Luther is positioning himself as the voice of those in pews, and asks for Prince Albrecht's help in clearing up any confusion over indulgences in the mind of the faithful. When it comes to describing the cause of that confusion, however, his tone rapidly hardens and reveals not so much a letter that has been agonised over for weeks and months, but one rushed off in anger, a hallmark of Luther's output in the years ahead.

Luther offers his archbishop a charge list against sellers of indulgences that develops into a wider assault on their whole industry. 'Further, they [purchasers of indulgences] assume that the grace obtained through these indulgences is so completely effective that there is no sin of such magnitude that it cannot be forgiven – even (as they say) someone should rape the Mother of God, were this possible. Finally they also believe that man is freed from every penalty and guilt by these indulgences. O great God! The souls committed to your care, excellent Father, are thus directed to death. For all these souls you have the heaviest and a constantly increasing responsibility. Therefore I can no longer be silent on this subject.'[23]

Again there is the suggestion that his concern about indulgences is of long standing. At this point, Luther could have chosen to direct Albrecht to the attached Ninety-Five Theses and, within the context of a letter from a humble concerned friar, left him to draw his own conclusions. Instead, he launches into a brief lecture on theology, based on his conviction that the Scriptures are the best guide for all believers seeking salvation. 'Works of piety and love are infinitely better than indulgences; and yet they . . . are silent about them because they have to preach the sale of indulgences. The first and only duty of bishops, however, is to see that the people learn the gospel and the love of Christ. For on no occasion has Christ ordered that indulgences should be preached. What a horror, what a danger for a bishop to permit the loud noise of indulgences among his people, while the gospel is silenced, and to be more concerned with the sale of indulgences than the gospel. Will not Christ say, "you strain out a gnat but swallow a camel"?'[24,25]

The letter ends on a confrontational note, with a warning of trouble ahead if the archbishop does not curtail the mission of Tetzel and others of his type. 'If this is not done, someone may rise and, by means of publications, silence those preachers and refute the little book [the instruction Albrecht had issued to govern the promotion of the indulgence]. This would be the greatest disgrace for Your Most Illustrious Excellency. I certainly shudder at this possibility, yet I am afraid it will happen if things are not quickly remedied.'[26]

Is that 'someone [who] may rise' Luther himself? That is the implication of a postscript he adds, noting that he has attached his 'disputation theses so that you can see how dubious is this belief concerning indulgences, which these preachers propagate as if it were the surest thing in the whole world'. Why send the Ninety-Five Theses unless he is signalling his own willingness to lead the attack on the indulgence system? Indeed the format – as a set of propositions to be discussed and disputed in the manner beloved of Scholasticism – makes it plain that Luther is offering to present the case for the prosecution. Their inclusion signals a threat that is hardly downgraded when he signs off as 'your unworthy son'.[27]

The Ninety-Five Theses

It is not known how carefully Albrecht studied the attachment, if at all, but even if he left that task to his officials, they could have been in no doubt that Luther had the potential to cause a little local difficulty. The Ninety-Five Theses begin with an announcement that, 'out of love and zeal for truth', what follows will be debated at Wittenberg under his chairmanship. He requests that those 'who cannot be present to debate orally with us will do so by letter'. He is spreading his net wide.

'Theses' has the ring to modern ears of one thesis after another, one idea followed by something linked but separate. Instead the ninety-five are more a series of breathless bullet points, which ebb and flow between different aspects of the question, and between outright condemnation and efforts at mitigation and seeing the other side. The effect of reading them as a list can be slightly dizzying. This is no carefully structured argument; there are no sections on specific issues, nor even a framework to guide a fuller debate. Later Luther was to write much longer documents seeking to explain what exactly it was he meant by the wording he had used in some of the ninety-five. He knew, on reflection, that in places he had provided little more than a set of headlines.

One of the earliest printed versions of the Ninety-Five Theses: from
a display at the Lutherhaus in Wittenberg.

The first four theses offer an overview of Luther's own still-emerging views on sinfulness, forgiveness and salvation.

1. 'When our Lord and Master Jesus Christ said, "repent", He willed the entire life of believers to be one of repentance.'

2. 'This word cannot be understood as referring to the sacrament of penance, that is confession and satisfaction, as administered by the clergy.'

3. 'Yet it does not mean solely inner repentance; such inner repentance is worthless unless it produces various outward mortifications of the flesh.'

4. 'The penalty of sin remains as long as the hatred of self that is true inner repentance, until our entrance into the kingdom of heaven.'

For hatred of self, read contrition, precisely what Luther had already made clear in his sermons was absent in those who purchased indulgences to wash away their sins. Next, he turns abruptly to the papacy and its claim to be able to effect the forgiveness of sins by the granting of letters of indulgence. As in his handling of his archbishop, here Luther is keen to separate out actions done in the pope's name from the current incumbent on Saint Peter's throne. Later in a *Table Talk* he was even to claim that the theses were intended to help Leo X to tackle abuse. 'At that time I still regarded the Pope as my lord. I thought I had done him a favour.'[28]

5. 'The Pope neither desires nor is able to remit any penalties except those imposed by his own authority or that of the canons.'
6. 'The Pope cannot remit any guilt except by declaring and showing that it has been remitted by God; or, to be sure, by remitting guilt in cases reserved for his judgement. If his right to grant remission in these cases were disregarded, the guilt would certainly remain unforgiven.'
7. 'God remits guilt to no one unless at the same time he humbles himself in all things and makes him submissive to his vicar, the priest.'

This last thesis maintains the role of the priest (presumably, but not explicitly, in the sacrament of confession) in interceding between God and the sinner, but Luther was also touching on the extent of papal authority. Though its formal claim to infallibility in some matters of faith and morals was only officially decreed as doctrine by the Catholic Church in 1870, the papacy was long held in theory to have almost limitless teaching authority, curtailed only by its ability to impose its will. Yet here is Luther having the audacity to place on the discussion table what a pope can and can't do in regard of remission of sins.

He compounds the offence by going on to question any papal

claim to authority over what goes on in purgatory, stating in (13) that 'the dying are freed by death from all penalties, are already dead as far as canon laws are concerned, and have a right to be released from them'. Since canon law is the Church's rule book, he is asserting that Church authority cannot stretch beyond the grave and impinge on God's authority.

Next Luther dwells for a moment on what purgatory is and how it relates to heaven and hell. Given his views on the need to root beliefs in Scripture, he might have been expected to balk at purgatory as a recent invention without an agreed scriptural basis, but instead he shows his knack for finding a pithy phrase: (16) 'Hell, purgatory and heaven seem to differ the same as despair, fear and assurance of salvation.' There is, he suggests, no inevitability of getting to heaven for those waiting in purgatory, nor what he labels in (19) 'assurance', but he does then relent slightly and permits the Pope one power over purgatory.

26. 'The Pope does very well when he grants remission to souls in purgatory, not by the power of the Keys [i.e. as successor of Peter, to whom Jesus gave the keys to heaven], which he does not have, but by way of intercession for them.'

Here he appears to be voicing a doubt about the cherished Catholic notion of the apostolic succession: that every one of the successors of Saint Peter inherits his powers, including those contained in the Risen Christ's words to the apostles, as He showed them the mark of His crucifixion, 'those whose sins you forgive, they are forgiven.'[29] Yet Luther does not pause to draw out his own meaning, perhaps for fear of turning an expression of doubt into something that may be used against him. He goes back instead to propositions aimed at the shortcomings of indulgences and those who promote them.

32. 'Those who believe that they can be certain of their salvation because they have indulgence letters will be eternally damned, together with their teachers.' . . .

34. 'For the graces of indulgences are concerned only with the penalties of sacramental satisfaction established by man.'

35. 'They who teach that contrition is not necessary on the part of those who intend to buy souls out of purgatory or to buy confessional privileges preach unchristian doctrine.'

36. 'Any truly repentant Christian has a right to full remission of penalty and guilt, even without indulgence letters.'

This feels like the point where Luther pauses, as if remembering that it is an archbishop he is addressing, and clumsily switches to more diplomatic language. Despite all he has said already, he now tries to find some slight merit in indulgences, as if showing a willingness to accommodate other points of view in his planned-for disputation on the subject.

48. 'Christians are to be taught that the Pope, in granting indulgences, needs and thus desires their devout prayer more than their money.'

49. 'Christians are to be taught that papal indulgences are useful only if they do not put their trust in them, but very harmful if they lose their fear of God because of them.'

In which case, it might be asked, what is the point of them? Luther has no answer to that, and instead turns for the first time to the plans to rebuild Saint Peter's.

50. 'Christians are to be taught that, if the Pope knew the exactions of the indulgence preachers, he would rather that the Basilica of Saint Peter were burned to ashes than built up with the skin, flesh and bones of his sheep.'

This is violent language, but Luther is fleet of foot and moves on quickly to the heart of the Church's defence of the theology of indulgences – namely the notion that through the life of Jesus and of the saints, Catholicism is able to draw on a treasury of goodness to enable it to wipe away human sin.

56. 'The treasures of the Church, out of which the Pope distributes indulgences, are not sufficiently discussed or known among the people of Christ.' . . .

62. 'The true treasure of the Church is the most Holy Gospel of the glory and grace of God.'

63. 'But this treasure is naturally most odious, for it makes the first to be last.'

64. 'On the other hand the treasure of indulgences is naturally most acceptable, for it makes the last to be first.'

So rulers – the 'first', in earthly terms – prefer indulgences to the gospel because they want to maintain their power. It is a damning indictment of the whole hierarchy of the Church and indeed of the ruling elite of Europe. These theses introduce Luther as a radical reformer par excellence. His language and blunt tone throughout the Ninety-Five Theses show him speaking the language of the people, using the words they would understand (albeit rendered in Latin) and voicing their grievances. It made him a popular hero when the text of the theses, and commentaries on them, were translated into German and reached a broad audience. To Prince Albrecht and his counsellors, they must have sounded tantamount to heresy and treason rolled into one. Yet Luther does not flinch or retreat. His defence is that he is suggesting propositions for a forthcoming debate, not outlining his own views.

79. 'To say that the cross emblazoned with the papal coat of arms, and set up by the indulgence preachers, is equal in worth to the cross of Christ is blasphemy.'

80. 'The bishops, curates and theologians who permit such talk to be spread among the people will have to answer for this.'

81. 'This unbridled preaching of indulgences makes it difficult even for learned men [i.e. himself and his colleagues] to rescue the reverence which is due the Pope from slander or from the shrewd questions of the laity.'

82. 'Such as: "why does not the pope empty purgatory for the sake of holy love and the dire need of the souls that are there if he redeems an infinite number of souls for the sake of the miserable money with which to build a church?" The former reasons would be most just; the latter is most trivial.'

This is surely Luther's own question, but he puts it on the lips of others, as if something that he has been asked, and for which he has no answer. Quite how personal the theses are, though, is made plain by the two that follow, which draw directly on his own experiences in Rome.

83. 'Again, "why are funeral and anniversary masses for the dead continued and why does he [the Pope] not return or permit the withdrawal of the endowments founded for them, since it is wrong to pray for the redeemed"?' . . .

86. 'Again, "why does not the Pope, whose wealth is today greater than the wealth of the richest Crassus,[30] build this one basilica of Saint Peter with his own money rather than with the money of poor believers"?'

It is back again to Saint Peter's, but in the final flourish each closing thesis reveals the turmoil in Luther's own soul.

92. 'Away then with all those prophets who say to people of Christ, "peace, peace", and there is no peace!' . . .

94. 'Christians should be exhorted to be diligent in following Christ, their head, through penalties, death and hell.'
95. 'And thus be confident of entering into heaven through many tribulations rather than through the false security of peace.'

If Luther had felt one iota of that confidence about his own salvation, he might never have written the list.

Fuel to the fire

There is many a letter sent up a chain of command that is judged so insignificant as not even to merit a reply. Prince Albrecht might have been tempted simply to ignore Luther's approach to him and assume the whole thing would go away. After consultation with his chapter at Magdeburg and at Mainz, several factors seem to have stopped him from doing this. First, though Wittenberg could hardly be counted as among Europe's great universities, Luther was a professor of theology there, and a senior figure in his own order. To snub him by failing to respond would be to snub the Augustinians and the university's patron, Elector Friedrich.

There was also sufficient passion in Luther's letter and the Ninety-Five Theses to warn the prince-archbishop and his advisors that this was a cleric who would not be content to register his academic protest about indulgences, and then get on with his teaching responsibilities at the university. Printing now made it possible for challenging views – especially challenging views with a popular resonance – to spread more widely than ever before and cause trouble.

And then there was the unmistakable theological vigour contained in the muddle of arguments that Luther had advanced in the theses. The abuses of the indulgence system were well known and there were plenty who would agree with Luther if he were, as promised, to convene a public debate in Wittenberg. He might even attract more senior theologians to attend or write in.

What then would be the impact on Tetzel's efforts just over the border in Jüterbog, and hence on the cash flow that Prince Albrecht required to pay his debts?

The decision reached was pragmatic: to avoid the specific indulgence issue and instead take Luther at his word in requesting clarification on certain matters around the role of the papacy. The problem was handed on to Rome. This was typical, going forward, of the Catholic Church's response to Luther's challenge. Rather than concede that the sale of indulgences could be done better, a policy of delay was adopted. Luther's protest was played into the long grass by those standing on the dignity of papal authority. Leave it long enough and he would hopefully disappear. It was an ill-judged policy, though based inevitably on ignorance of the man with whom they were dealing. Though the intention might have been to drown out the protest, what it did instead was to raise the stakes and escalate the matter. Luther could not be silenced by being given the silent treatment.

The name of Martin Luther therefore arrived on Leo X's desk in the early months of 1518. Two responses are attributed to him in the Luther legend; neither is authenticated, but both have endured because they fit with the reputation of the man in charge of Catholicism. 'Luther is a drunken German. He will feel different when he is sober'. Or: 'Friar Martin is a brilliant chap. The whole row is due to envy of the monks.'[31]

The first suggests the contempt with which the German Church – and indeed Germans – were regarded in Rome. The second ascribes the whole thing to a turf war between Dominicans backing Tetzel, and Augustinians lining up behind their own man, Luther. It didn't seem to occur to Leo and his advisors that Luther was sincere in his concerns, and genuinely eager for clarification from his archbishop on the theological points he had raised. It neatly sums up the gulf between worldly Renaissance Rome and backwoods, pious Wittenberg. Who would worry about such trifles as forgiveness, the quality of contrition or salvation, when there was a basilica to be built, artists to commission and affairs of state to tackle?

Rome looks away

To the papal court, this lowly dispute wasn't worth a moment more of their time. They had their own concerns, principally forging a new relationship with France after the Concordat of Bologna, signed the previous year, which allowed the French king to appoint bishops and abbots in exchange for acknowledging the Pope's supremacy over a general council of the Church. This had been an important victory for Leo over the conciliar movement, which (like Luther but for other reasons) believed there were limits to papal authority. It sought to make the Pope answerable to gatherings of senior leaders of the Church, and had enjoyed the support of Louis XII of France when its cardinals had tried to unseat Julius at a council held in Pisa in 1512.

When the Hermits of Saint Augustine in Rome showed no enthusiasm for the task of drafting a response to Luther's complaints, it was allocated by papal officials to the Dominican Sylvester Prierias (sometimes known by his Italian name, Silvestro Mazzolini da Priero). As Master of the Sacred Palace, he was a theologian favoured by the Pope and best known for his *Summa Silvestrina*, a reference manual for confessors on the sacrament of penance. Who better, it was judged, to pen a reply to a challenge over proper contrition and the forgiveness of sins?

While a handful of archbishops, papal officials and theologians were picking over Luther's Ninety-Five Theses with undisguised disdain, among his fellow Germans his writings were provoking an entirely different response, attracting a wave of support, though probably not quite so quickly as Luther later claimed when he remarked: 'they went throughout the whole of Germany in a fortnight.'[32] By the end of 1517, copies were reported as circulating in pamphlet form, sold for a few coins, in Leipzig, Nürnberg and Basel. Luther had undoubtedly touched a nerve among his own people, long resentful at their exploitation and neglect by Rome. The demands for change, which had first been articulated sixty years previously by the Gravamina, had neither gone away, nor been properly addressed by the papacy.

Luther's *A Sermon on Indulgences and Grace*, published in 1518, written in German and going into more depth on the Ninety-Five Theses, was reprinted eighteen times before the year was out.

On the other side of the fence, among those decidedly unimpressed when they read what Luther had written, was, inevitably, Johann Tetzel. Reports suggest that indulgence sales had fallen off steeply as Luther's views became more widespread. Tetzel's order tried hard to support him, belatedly granting this pilloried non-academic a doctorate to bolster his credentials. Working with a fellow Dominican, Konrad Wimpina, more skilled than him in theology, an emboldened Tetzel even tried to take up Luther's offer of a disputation and published his own 105 theses.

When they went on sale in Wittenberg in March of 1518, students from the university set them alight. The town was solidly behind its man, though Luther worried in his correspondence with Johann Lang that such rowdy behaviour would reflect badly on him.[33] He was starting to appreciate how exposed he had suddenly become.

If he was now in the firing line, he decided he had better make absolutely plain just what battle he was fighting. So in the spring of 1518, Luther published *A Sermon on Indulgence and Grace*. Written in German, rather than the Latin of the Ninety-Five Theses, it was phrased in such a way as to make it as accessible as possible to literate German-speakers. Luther includes, for example, crowd-pleasing words such as 'prattle' to describe the abstract debates of theologians.

The arguments he deploys in the sermon are very similar to those in the Ninety-Five Theses. Once again he proceeds through a series of numbered points, but this time his argument is more structured, reinforced by references to familiar passages in Scripture. It therefore represents the first sharpening and honing of the message that had spilled out of him in no particular order in the Ninety-Five Theses.

Luther's contempt for the norms of Scholasticism is now naked. He begins the sermon with an attack on Thomas Aquinas and his elaborate theories about the sacrament of penance, being quoted to defend the sale of indulgences. Aquinas advanced, Luther says, arguments 'scarcely or not at all to be found in Holy Scripture, or in the ancient holy Christian teachers'.[34] And that, he insists, *perforce* damns what Aquinas claims. If it is not based in Scripture, or in the writings of the first Christian leaders, Luther says repeatedly, then no papal dictate can ever justify it.

That is in essence his case against indulgences: they have been invented by the Church for its own reasons. 'No one can defend the position with any passage from Scripture that God's righteousness desires or demands any punishment or satisfaction from sinners except for their heartfelt and true contrition or conversion alone – with the condition that from that moment on they bear the cross of Christ.'[35] Luther's theology of the cross was the polar opposite of indulgences. He was describing the hard, uncertain road that stretched out in imitation of Jesus' suffering in the crucifixion, while the Catholic Church was selling pain-free forgiveness and heaven for a few coppers. To back up his case, Luther quotes Jesus' absolving of Mary Magdalene from her sins in Luke's gospel,[36] as well as His forgiveness for the woman taken in adultery in John's.[37] 'Punishment', he insists, 'is in no one's power to lessen, except God's alone.'[38]

The sermon struck a mighty chord. It was reprinted fourteen times in 1518 alone, with each run being of at least 1,000 copies. In August of 1518 it was joined by *Explanations Concerning the Ninety Five Theses*, another attempt by Luther to think through the consequences of his initial outpouring of ideas, and to share them with a wider audience. Luther ignored the express order of his local bishop in Brandenburg, Jerome Scultetus, not to publish the text, and began instead with a dedication to Staupitz: 'I venture to say they are wrong who make more of the act in Latin than of the change of heart in Greek.'

The reference was to a new argument Luther advanced in the text, namely that the whole sacrament of penance was based on a

Latin mistranslation of the original Greek words in Matthew's gospel, with the injunction to 'be penitent' rendered as 'do penance'.[39] As he sought to defend the Ninety-Five Theses, Luther was expanding his arguments and his targets. In another passage in the sermon, he suggests, almost casually, that the primacy of the Church of Rome over the Greek Church was an accident of history, rather than God's plan, as Catholicism had long taught. Even when it erred, official theology taught, the Catholic Church was divinely instituted and divinely guided. It existed because God wanted it to exist. Here Luther was challenging that claim.

Though the appearance of the Ninety-Five Theses is usually credited as the moment that started the Reformation, a strong case can be made that, instead, it was the wide and rapid circulation of *A Sermon on Indulgences and Grace*, and then *Explanations of the Ninety Five Theses*, that truly made Luther's name.

PART TWO:

'The Honourable, Our Dear Respected Dr Martin Luther'

'His [Luther's] message was a stone thrown into a calm pond: the ripples spread and spread.'

Eamon Duffy, *Saints and Sinners:*
A History of the Popes (1997)

CHAPTER FIVE

Confronting Death: On a Knife's Edge

'Not at any time did I have a thought of leaving the monastery.'
Martin Luther, *Table Talk*[1]

In the modern age, talk of the separation of Church and state is commonplace. In the West, religion is regularly characterised in public discourse as an individual freedom. We are all free, if we so choose, to hold a particular set of religious beliefs just as we may choose which political party to support. But 'Church' is regarded by many as an essentially private activity, something best kept hermetically sealed off from state.

Such a prevailing mindset makes it hard to appreciate the resonance in late medieval Germany, and beyond, of the publication of the Ninety-Five Theses. The challenge they posed was not just to the lucrative trade in indulgences, but rather to the Church's integral role in every aspect of daily life at all levels of society, and indeed to that very society. To grasp the extent of Luther's rebellion at a distance of 500 years therefore requires a leap of imagination.

Indeed, it could be argued that how far he had gone only slowly dawned on Luther himself. He made a public protest on one matter, indulgences, but even as he explained his objection, he could not make it a stand-alone issue. As a result, soon the escalating list of challenges he was issuing to the Church authorities over complicated questions – notably papal authority, the paramount role of Scripture, and the place and extent of the sacraments – became greater than the sum of its parts. Luther may have started out with an overriding concern about salvation, but his protest quickly shifted from one about the means Catholicism used to peddle that salvation into a challenge to the future of the Church itself, and the system within which it operated. Luther was holding up to scrutiny the entire late medieval set-up, based as it was on the overlapping and seamless jurisdictions of Church and state.

For this was an epoch when religion permeated every human undertaking, up to and including economics, politics, statecraft and warfare. Yes, clerics still claim that is true to this day, but the now-familiar word 'secular' was only heard occasionally until the late sixteenth century, and then only in the specific context of a transfer of goods from the possession of the Church into that of others. The boundary that in twenty-first-century Western culture is all but taken for granted between religious and temporal domains was only delineated in the eighteenth century. Before that, there was no point where religion 'ended' and politics began. They were rolled together.

So, for example, the Crusades, which had played such a part in the initial growth of the indulgence trade, had been inspired at the end of the twelfth century by a profound religious passion about 'taking back' the Holy Land, where Jesus Christ had walked and talked, died and risen from the dead. So they were a religious undertaking. Yet they were also deeply political: the papacy had rallied its knights with the ambition of extending the power of the Roman Church eastwards, and asserting its claim to rule over the heads of individual princes and monarchs of Christian Europe. And so, too, in the patchwork of German states that made up the Holy Roman Empire, where the furore that followed the wide distribution of the Ninety-Five Theses was initially played out. What was in Luther's mind a religious struggle became a political issue – about the commercial activities of the Church that had given rise to Tetzel's bandwagon, and more widely about authority, taxation, serfdom, economic inequality, and the appropriate jurisdiction for the various princes and electors, as well as for their people.

The interconnections went further. Europe in the Middle Ages had a cultural and religious unity that is now hard to imagine. The papacy took no account of boundaries or earthly kingdoms in a spiritual leadership that may have been distant, erratic and subject to interference from kings and princes, but for the mass of the people was real and unchanging. It was the single focus all across Europe, and whenever dissent arose, it was crushed. And in Latin, the language of the Catholic Church, the continent had a shared way of communicating, not just in church services and documents, but between scholars universities and monasteries.

Luther's rebellion was over a particular matter of Church practice, and its theological justification, but he had raised his standard at a moment when both high and low in German society were acutely resentful of the financial demands being placed upon them by Rome, of which the trade in indulgences was just one manifestation. A substantial part of the money the Church raised was exported across the Alps, and few of its benefits were felt in Germany. Yet the designated route of protest against such abuse, via the Holy Roman Emperor to the papacy, was blocked because it was so mired in a web of political allegiances and rivalries. And in those battles, a fragmented Germany felt itself to be at the bottom of the more powerful players' lists of priorities. 'There is no nation more despised than the Germans,' Luther once ruefully reflected. 'The Italians call us beasts. France and England and all the other countries ridicule us. Who knows what God will do with the Germans; we have certainly earned a good flogging from God.'[2]

For the German masses, their disillusionment with Rome's financial demands and pastoral neglect formed part of a more general economic and social disquiet over such issues as land reform, which was to come to a head in the Peasants' War of 1524–25, the largest popular uprising experienced in Europe until the French Revolution of 1789. For the ruling class in Germany, there was also an increasing sense of restlessness at the allegiance they owed the Holy Roman Emperor, buttressed by the papacy. The claim of both ancient offices to a trans-European hegemony was starting to feel like a constraint on the ambitions of able rulers such as Elector Friedrich. It interfered with their exercise of authority, and more broadly sat uncomfortably alongside the first flowering of nationalism, encouraged by the example of early modern nation states in England, Spain and France, strong enough entities to challenge, influence, defy, and on occasion dictate to the papacy.

All these strains had been building up in the years immediately before the publication of the Ninety-Five Theses, and so what unravelled after 31 October 1517 cannot be summed up as 'all about religion', or 'all about politics'. The rulers who ended up siding with Luther against the Pope were not just 'using' religion for political ends, because they would have recognised no such division. To dissociate the two would have been like trying to separate out the hydrogen and oxygen in water. It was certainly not something of which Luther himself could ever conceive. 'World order', he pronounced, 'cannot be maintained by a body of laws alone, but through God's authority. Everything in this life is like an outline of the coming life. The princes do not force an accounting through the law, because they can't, and that's why our Lord God does it.'[3]

Accordingly, Luther had made no calculation about when and how to launch his own protest to take best advantage of a changing political, social and economic climate in Europe. With hindsight, though, he couldn't have picked his moment better. His timing quite literally saved his life.

His aim was simple. He wanted, and continued in the years ahead to want, the Catholic Church to reform itself. He had no ambition to topple it from its dominant position over the life of the continent, or set up a rival structure. He desired that it be more mindful of Scripture and therefore behaved differently.

Faced by Rome's arrogant disdain for this straightforward request, and then by its blanket condemnation of every single specific concern he voiced, what began as a personal crusade springing directly from his own *Anfechtung* grew into something so much bigger. Although he may not have fully realised it as he poured out his concerns in the Ninety-Five Theses, crucial to the case Luther was proposing was that an individual's faith and relationship with God must be separate from any obligation to the Church to which he or she belonged.

That was where he differed from Erasmus and other reformers. Happy as they were to criticise and even lampoon the Church, its theology, its rituals and especially its leaders, they did so from a position that always pulled up short of being willing to see it cast aside. In Luther's case, the Catholicism of his upbringing and monastic formation may have been a communal faith, where the sacred was experienced in the shared rituals – the Church processions to honour saints and their relics, which followed the liturgical calendar and shaped daily life in towns and villages – but his tortured beliefs were carrying him increasingly towards a vision where each individual believer stood naked before his or her God, unable to rely on the institution of the Church, the intercession of saints, the good works they had performed, or pre-paid indulgences, but only on faith that was firmly rooted in the example of Jesus Christ and the final authority of Scripture.

'Justification by faith' (or '*sola fide*') and '*sola scriptura*' were the two most familiar phrases associated ever after with Luther's name and defined his position, but both posed a challenge to the governing structures of Catholicism. So a theological dispute quickly became an institutional challenge that was overlaid by the political tensions of the age.

The gathering storm

Luther's initial reaction to the widespread attention that the Ninety-Five Theses had brought him was to carry on as normal. He got on with his daily life and work as if nothing had changed. His series of lectures on Paul's Letter to the Hebrews continued. He undertook his responsibilities in the town, in his order, and at the university. Having voiced his disquiet at the sale of indulgences, he was – perhaps foolishly – hoping that the authorities, be they Archbishop Albrecht or papal advisors, once the whole matter had been referred on to Rome, would address his concerns. He could have no idea yet that the papal court was planning to do nothing of the sort.

In the early weeks and months of 1518, however, there were plenty of fingers already being wagged at Luther. A myth was growing up around him that distorted his arguments. He was accused, for example, of rejecting as pointless all 'good works'. It is easy enough to see how this could have been deduced from what he had written in the Ninety-Five Theses, but it wasn't what he was saying. He had no desire for good works to stop, but urged them when performed to 'remain hidden and not bragged about; they should be done because of necessity, and in silence'.[4] Though fine in themselves, they would not prompt God to open the gates of heaven.

Stories were also exchanged that took Luther's objections to indulgences and embroidered into them a broader attack on every traditional ritual of the faithful. He was later to refer to a tale, freely circulating at this time, that he had deliberately and publicly smashed up a set of rosary beads, used to support a cycle of prayers to the Virgin Mary.[5] He had done no such thing, but in the telling it was a caricature of something subtler that he had been saying. Mechanically trotting out the set prayers as a way of piling up merit for the afterlife was, he believed, as much a distraction as purchasing indulgences when the real need was for true engagement and submission before God.

The rapid accumulation of legend and hearsay about Luther had one everyday consequence. For those loyal to the Pope, it painted him in the crude language of the street as a heretic, and in late medieval Europe to be suspected of heresy meant your life was in danger. It was a fate Luther faced with unusual calm. Whatever his crippling self-doubt before God, he did not at this crucial juncture lack for courage in earthly terms. The two were, of course, linked. If salvation is your only goal, then what happens in the world is necessarily seen through that filter. He may once, by his own unreliable account, have been terrified by a thunderstorm, but a better measure of the man is that, in the face of the mounting campaign against him, he neither rushed to recant, begged for mercy, nor even made himself scarce. When the call came to stand up, dispel the lies and half-truths being told about him, and defend what he had already said, Luther answered it and spoke with the passion and fearlessness of one who believes he is right. Whether such bravery came because he was in a state of denial about the extent to which his life had changed, or because he underestimated the affront he had caused to the authorities, or because he believed God was guiding him, even at this early stage of his public 'career', is hard to separate out.

The first major public challenge Luther faced came in April 1518 with the scheduled three-yearly gathering in Heidelberg of his fellow Hermits of Saint Augustine from all around the German lands. As a district vicar of eleven monasteries, he was expected to attend and play his part, and so attend he would, in spite of rumours circulating that he would be seized en route during the 350-mile journey and put on trial by the Church authorities. His courage did not, however, tip over into foolhardiness. As he set off on foot straight after the Easter celebrations in Wittenberg, he accepted the precaution of a guard, provided by Elector Friedrich, and he also took steps to travel incognito. He was in no mood to court martyrdom.

At various places en route, he was nevertheless recognised by clergy and laity alike, a tangible sign of the renown caused by the crude printed versions of the Ninety-Five Theses with his image on them that were already circulating. The reaction he met was largely positive. In Weissenfels, for example, the local priest made plain that he endorsed Luther's published position, while on an overnight stop in Würzburg, the town's bishop came out to him as a supporter of his.

The final stretch of road to Heidelberg was made by carriage, with Luther riding with his staunchest defender, his vicar-general Staupitz, as well as another old friend, Johann Lang, now prior of the Augustinians at Erfurt. A man of moderate reformist views, Staupitz may not have agreed with everything Luther had said, but he was determined as his religious superior to be seen to stand by his protégé.

Whatever else Luther might have been anticipating, on arrival in Heidelberg after what had been a nine-day journey he was treated as the man of the moment rather than an outcast. Elector Friedrich had provided a letter of introduction to the local prince, Wolfgang, Duke of Bavaria, whose territories including the Electorate of the Palatinate centred on Heidelberg. The duke fed Luther a fine meal, and then gave him a tour of his castle – quite an honour for a Catholic prince to bestow on one whose public statements were under review in Rome.

The Augustinian gathering took place at the city's university, founded in 1386 and the most prominent in southwest Germany. Most of its sessions were private, but one was open to all-comers. Luther was undoubtedly the draw, and took as his contribution to the public debate a list of forty theses he had prepared on sin, free will, God's grace and human nature. Duke Wolfgang was among those impressed by what he saw and heard. He reported back to Elector Friedrich: 'Luther had shown so much skill in disputation, as greatly to contribute to the renown of the University of Wittenberg.'

Among others in the audience was Martin Bucer, a young Dominican studying at the university. 'His answers', he reported of Luther, '[were] so brief, so wise and drawn from Scripture, [that they] easily turned all his hearers into admirers.'[6] Bucer paints Luther as calm, reasonable and resilient in defending – and even expanding – his corner. It was not always to be his approach in the months and years ahead, but thus far he appears to have been taking in his stride his overnight renown, and the criticism that he had attracted. 'He has a marvellous graciousness in response,' Bucer went on, 'and unconquerable patience in listening. In argument he shows the acumen of the apostle Paul ... That which Erasmus insinuates, he [Luther] speaks openly and freely.'[7]

Such words show that Luther's name was now routinely being paired by reform-minded Catholics with that of Erasmus, so long hailed across northern Europe and beyond as the leading advocate of change within the Church. In correspondence with their mutual friend, Johann Lang, in October of 1517, Erasmus expressed general approval of the stance taken by the friar he referred to as Eleutherius.

If Luther went down well in the public sessions, in the closed confines of his own religious order he encountered a more mixed response. Some members of the German province of the Hermits made known their fear that Luther was bringing all of them into disrepute. The order had, after all, been established by the papacy. Now Luther appeared to be attacking it. Yet in this high-minded gathering, it was not the issue of indulgences, or even that of the authority of the papacy that upset some. Instead, they questioned Luther's ever more outspoken dismissal of Aristotle, and by association Scholasticism, in favour of a new emphasis on Paul, Augustine and the Early Church Fathers. Among the most resistant to Luther's approach were members of the chapter from Erfurt. 'My theology is like rotten food to the people in Erfurt,' Luther reported in a letter home to Elector Friedrich's chaplain Georg Spalatin, fast becoming a key ally as he acted as a conduit between Luther and his prince and protector.[8]

The rift that opened with Erfurt (except in the case of Johann Lang, who sided with Luther and took over his duties as district vicar after Heidelberg) was painful, because the monastery there had been his first home in the Augustinians. It ran so deep that when, on his return journey, he stopped off in the town and tried to visit one of his old tutors, Jodcus Trutfetter ('Doctor Eisenach'), he was turned away. Stung by the rejection, the next day, when back in Wittenberg, Luther sent him a letter, claiming that the whole of his new university agreed with him, with just one exception.[9,10] His cause was now also Wittenberg's.

Rome-ward bound?

At the start of August 1518, over nine months after writing to Archbishop Albrecht, Luther received a judgement from the pen of Dominican Sylvester Prierias in Rome on the Ninety-Five Theses, made at the behest of Pope Leo X. The subtitle of the document reveals its author's disdain for this upstart from Wittenberg: 'A Dialogue against Martin Luther's Presumptuous Theses concerning the Power of the Pope'. Prierias's argument is brief – suitable, he must have judged, for such a nobody monk in the back of beyond. He simply quoted Scholastic sources to assert that the Pope was infallible in deciding both the teaching *and* the practice of the Church. If he authorised an indulgence, it was therefore beyond reproach, and anyone who contradicted that, Prierias concluded, was a heretic.

The theology that lay behind this blanket statement was rooted in the Catholic Church's claim to an Apostolic Succession – that each and every successor to Saint Peter, Jesus' chosen apostle and the first pope, had inherited his God-given authority. This was buttressed by a typically Scholastic argument that brought into play reason and logic. Jesus Christ had promised – in Matthew's gospel – to be with His Church until the end of the world.[11] Since only the Catholic Church could claim to have been around since Jesus' time to the present (the Orthodox having only, in such a scenario, come into being following the breach with Rome in the eleventh century), it must logically be the fulfilment of that promise. The outward reality of the Church's continuing existence was therefore sufficient 'proof' that the Pope had God-given authority.

Luther's repeated response to this assertion was that such a recourse to reason and outward forms impinged on the fundamental mystery of God. History cannot tell us anything about God, he insisted. Only the cross, Jesus' suffering and the Scriptures can do that.

Prierias's judgement ended with a summons. Luther was to appear in person in Rome within sixty days to answer the charges against him. The intention was clearly to make Luther quake and force him to recant. Rome had, however, misjudged its target. Instead of buckling at the knees in the face of papal might, he was instead left seething at the accusation of heresy. He was not, he protested, seeking to destroy the Catholic Church but to restore it. He held a doctorate in theology, for which he had sworn obedience to the Roman Church, and would not so lightly be dismissed and bullied.

Despite all that he had heard in the intervening nine months about the strong possibility of just such a damning verdict from Rome, Luther had still clung to a belief that the Pope would eventually thank him for taking the trouble to put him right. Prierias's response therefore came as a blow. He replied at once, with a blunt question that would be ever after always on his lips. Where was the scriptural basis for the claims made so definitively in this judgement? If the charges against him related to the Ninety-Five Theses, then they referred to what were demonstrably debating points. So why not, he asked, have a debate, and if he was shown to be wrong, he would gladly recant. To do so, though, he would require Bible references, not Scholastic rhetoric, to show him where he had embraced heresy. This was an argument where Luther evidently still believed that he could win round the Catholic Church.

Prierias's judgement had, consciously or not, endorsed an expansion of the disputed areas with Luther beyond indulgences by focusing more on what the Wittenberg friar had said about papal authority. The battleground was already shifting to what a pope could and couldn't legitimately do. 'I am sorry now that I despised Tetzel,' Luther remarked in what developed into an ill-tempered to-and-fro correspondence with Prierias. 'Ridiculous as he was, he was more accurate than you. You cite no Scripture and you give no reasons. Like an insidious devil, you pervert the Scriptures. You say that Church consists virtually in the pope . . . You make the pope into an emperor in power and violence. The [Holy Roman] Emperor Maximilian and the Germans will not tolerate this.'[12]

The aggressive tone may simply have been following Prierias's lead, but however naive he still was at this stage in his dealings with those in power, Luther could have had few illusions about his prospects of getting a fair hearing so far from home. And, if in any doubt, the news that the Roman mother house of his own order had, on 25 August, washed their hands of him should have put him in the picture. The Augustinians of Saxony were instructed by head office that Luther should be 'bound in chains, fetters and handcuffs' and rapidly dispatched to Italy.[13]

If such an abandonment surprised Luther, it shouldn't have. His studies would have taught him the bare facts of the fate of those who had the temerity to challenge the authority of the papacy. The English priest and theologian John Wycliffe (1320–84), for example, had railed against indulgences over 150 years before Luther, and, like him, had gone on to develop that argument into one against total papal power.[14] It was his work that inspired the Lollards, who had attached their 'Twelve Conclusions' to the doors of London's great cathedrals in 1395.

These propositions mirrored Wycliffe in insisting that faith must be based on the final authority of Scripture, not the unsupported pronouncements of senior clerics. Today he is best remembered as the leader of a rebellious group who translated the Bible into English. That break with tradition in a Church that resolutely stuck by Latin as its *lingua franca* and shunned the vernacular had made him a highly controversial figure with Rome. Though Wycliffe died in 1384 of natural causes before he could face a Church trial, the dispute about his teaching and works rumbled on to such an extent that thirty years later he was posthumously declared a heretic by the Council of Constance (1414–18), with the result that his corpse was disinterred on papal orders and burned.

The same council had also granted safe passage to Jan Hus (1369–1415), a Bohemian priest and admirer of Wycliffe, to allow him the chance to defend his own attacks on papal authority, on the sale of indulgences and on the paramount importance of Scripture. The connection between these three issues was well-worn territory long before Luther. Hus, however, was betrayed by the clerics who had promised him protection at Constance. He was arrested, tortured and, when he failed to recant his views, burned at the stake.

Hus's rebellion was not just recorded in historical documents in Luther's day. Those who supported his views – known as the

Hussites – still featured prominently in the Church in Bohemia (also part of the Holy Roman Empire) and were in schism from Rome. They had resisted five attempts between 1420 and 1431 to force them back into the fold.

Luther would later say that he was, at this stage, unaware in any great detail of what Hus had argued, but the continuing presence of the Hussites as a scar on the Holy Roman Empire would have made obvious to him one thing: Rome did not welcome being challenged. How best, then, to protect himself? Any promises from Catholic leaders of safe passage to Rome would be worth no more than those once given to Jan Hus. His best bet was surely his own patron, Friedrich the Wise.

Though a devout Catholic (if one who never married and instead had a succession of mistresses and illegitimate children), the Elector of Saxony had made a pledge to Luther, while Rome had been deliberating on his case, that he would make sure any subsequent proceedings be heard on German soil. This may simply have arisen out of a proprietorial sense that he must look after a professor at his own university – and now a renowned professor at that, one who was quickly making real Friedrich's dream that the name of Wittenberg University be known far and wide. Yet the elector's position was also influenced by a much wider desire throughout German lands to curtail Rome's influence in its affairs. Wilhelm Borth has, for example, argued convincingly that Saxony had a long-standing policy at this time to seek to remove itself ever more from Roman jurisdiction.[15] Here was another opportunity.

And Friedrich had also been involved in a running argument with Maximilian I, the Holy Roman Emperor, over his demand that individual rulers in the loosely connected empire be permitted more autonomy. That fight was coming to a head. Maximilian was nearing sixty years old and was haunted by the imminence of his own death (it was said that his coffin had travelled with him for his last five years). Since the role of emperor was not hereditary, but subject to an election by German princes, Maximilian was anxious to win their support for his eighteen-year-old grandson, Charles, already King of Spain. This young man, however, was not a popular choice, since his elevation would unite in one man the Spanish empire (including its vast new possessions in the Americas) that had come to him via his mother, *and* the Holy Roman Empire via his Hapsburg father, Maximilian's son. As for alternative candidates, the French had ambitions to see their own youthful monarch, Francis I, picked instead, while others – including the papacy and some German princes – were seeking a compromise candidate, so as to maintain the balance of power in Europe. Elector Friedrich had been touted in this regard.

Though Friedrich had not met Luther, and in all probability disagreed with him on some religious questions, he nonetheless pressed Rome that, rather than travel to Italy, his theology professor be questioned on German soil by the papal legate, Cardinal Cajetan, when he attended the next Imperial Diet. This regular meeting of the various rulers within the Holy Roman Empire to discuss governance matters with their emperor was soon to convene in the southern city of Augsburg.

Diet of Augsburg

When Rome agreed to the elector's request, it can only have done so confident that Thomas Cajetan was more than capable of dealing in an appropriate manner with such a minor irritant as Luther. The Church authorities, after all, had the emperor on their side. Maximilian had already expressed his disquiet to the Pope about Luther. In a letter to Leo of 5 August 1518, he had pledged 'to set a stop to the most perilous attack of Martin Luther on indulgences lest not only people but even princes be seduced'.[16] His words indicate the degree of self-interest surrounding the rush to play down and then silence Luther. Maximilian could already see that a little local row about indulgences had the potential to strain the ties that bound his ancient office to the German princes, especially at a time when the succession was in dispute.

Rome, meanwhile, continued to try to woo Elector Friedrich. In a letter dated 7 October 1518, Pope Leo addresses the Saxon ruler as a 'beloved son' of the Church, before raising with him the case of 'a son of iniquity hurling himself upon the Church of God'.[17] News had reached his ears, Leo continued, that Friedrich supported this rebel, but he had refused to give any credence to such loose talk. To avoid any further confusion, he went on, the elector must make plain his disapproval. 'We call upon you to see that Luther is placed in the hands and under the jurisdiction of this Holy See lest future generations reproach you with having fostered the rise of a most pernicious heresy against the Church of God.'[18]

In one regard, Friedrich was able to read this papal rebuke with a clear conscience. He was arranging for Luther to be questioned by a representative of the jurisdiction of the Holy See in the person of Cardinal Cajetan – though he had also taken the precaution of negotiating safe passage with the emperor for his professor.

The Italian Cajetan, a former master of the Dominican order, was the first Roman representative not to underestimate Luther. Though his own background was typical of those raised in the Scholastic tradition (he had taken the name Thomas in honour of Thomas Aquinas), at least he paid Luther the compliment of preparing for their confrontation by studying the Scriptures.

The prospect of defending himself in front of this senior representative of papal authority seems to have unsettled Luther. He may belatedly have been beginning to realise the magnitude of what he was facing, and the risks he was running. 'Now I must die,' he wrote, evidently in some distress. 'What a disgrace I shall be to my parents.'[19] Under pressure, his intestines flared up again, and on the road to Augsburg, caused him to collapse. In his own mind, his physical ailments were a sure sign that the devil was once again close at hand. His father's words, all those years before at his ordination, might also have been haunting him. Who was he, a little-known friar, to be sure that he was right and the distinguished papal legate, all the way from Rome, was wrong? Could it be the devil prompting him to cross a cardinal?

The meeting of the Diet at Augsburg had much bigger matters to settle than Luther's fate. As well as the question of selecting Maximilian's successor, Cardinal Cajetan's brief was to rally the German princes to join a fresh crusade against the Ottoman Turks, who were continuing to swallow up the remnants of the old Byzantine Empire and encroaching ever further into the Balkans. The Pope needed money to pay for an army to halt the advance, and required a tax to be levied throughout the empire. To achieve that end, he offered some minor concessions. Prince Albrecht was installed as Archbishop of Mainz and German primate with much pomp as part of proceedings. It was intended as a pat on the back from Rome to the German nobility. Meanwhile Maximilian was presented with a personal gift from the Pope – a helmet and dagger, along with the title 'Protector of Faith'.

Such flattery, though, cut little ice. The princes had long ago grown weary of papal demands. The Diet declined the call to arms and refused any new taxes. The question of the succession was left pending. Cajetan's mission had been a failure. It was against this backdrop that, between 12 and 14 October, he interviewed Luther three times.

Proceedings began with Luther entering the cardinal's lavish quarters, provided by the Fuggers, and throwing himself on the floor in front of his questioner in a gesture of abject humility. It is tempting to see this as another example of Luther playing low status to soften up his opponent, just as he had started the letter to Prince Albrecht that accompanied the Ninety-Five Theses by absolving his superior from responsibility for any excesses in the sale of indulgences carried out in his name. That, though, is to overlook both Luther's collapse before the meeting, and his whole training up to this point. He was nervous, as well he might have been, while humility before ecclesiastical authorities had been instilled in him as a first and natural instinct. Such extravagant shows of deference are how a hierarchical organisation such as the Catholic Church operated.

Morever, for all the attention that Luther was suddenly being paid, and the risk of it going to his head, he remained grounded by the image of Christ on the cross. 'In order to keep us from becoming proud or arrogant, and keep our respect for Him [God],' he wrote, 'He hung the cross and humiliation, the devil and the world, around our necks. That is why it happens that, when one seeks honours and glory in matters of theology and the Word of God, it is just like taking hot coals out of a fiery stove.'[20]

Back on his feet, his strength of purpose returned. Pope Leo had instructed Cajetan to avoid providing Luther with another platform by allowing him the debate he so desired on the Ninety-Five Theses. Instead, he must simply be told by Cajetan to recant his recent pronouncements. Luther, though, was not so easily intimidated, and Cajetan's tactic of making him stand throughout rather than sit did nothing to break his resolve. The defendant once more refused to back down until he could be convinced that he was wrong.

Cajetan needed a Plan B. A cleverer man than Prierias, he did not blithely rest on the dignity of papal authority in all matters, including indulgences. Instead, disregarding his instructions, he conceded to Luther's wish for a debate and mounted a defence of the theological principle of a 'treasury of merit', controlled by the Church, that enabled it to offer indulgences. Luther had savaged

Face-to-face with papal authority: Martin Luther argues his case before
Cardinal Cajetan, the Pope's envoy to the Diet of Augsburg, but
neither would budge an inch.

this notion in the Ninety-Five Theses. 'The treasures of the
Church, out of which the Pope distributes indulgences, are not
sufficiently discussed or known among the people of Christ,' he
had written, while 'the true treasure of the Church is the most
Holy Gospel of the glory and grace of God.' This, Cajetan
pointed out, was to contradict various papal pronouncements,
notably Clement VI's bull *Unigenitus* of 1343.

The two opponents were deadlocked. Luther would not accept
that a papal pronouncement was sufficient to prove him wrong
when there was no scriptural authority. The cardinal, with nothing more to add, felt he had adequately dealt with Luther's arguments. In any recourse to Scripture, he insisted, the Pope's interpretation was final.

Luther proposed that one way out of the impasse was to refer
the matter to other authorities. He suggested the universities of

Basel, Freiburg, Louvain and Paris. Since teaching on indulgences was not classified as doctrine, theologians should be permitted a ruling. For Cajetan, though, any referral would simply be to escalate the dispute, and to compromise his own contention that the Pope's word was final. So he tried out other more informal solutions, including an attempt to woo Staupitz over a good dinner. Luther's Augustinian superior was unmoved.

The wider ramifications of the standoff taking place before his eyes, though, registered sufficiently with Staupitz for him to tell Luther that he was releasing him from his vow of obedience as a Hermit of Saint Augustine. It was intended as a way of freeing him up to fight his battles with those higher up the ecclesiastical ladder of preferment, without always having to worry about the reputation of an order with close papal connections (a concern raised at Heidelberg), or the instructions coming from the mother house in Rome, which had taken the Pope's side against Luther. Instead, with a hint of paranoia, Luther took Staupitz's decision as a rejection in his hour of need. 'I was excommunicated three times,' he later complained, 'first by Staupitz, secondly by the pope, and thirdly by the emperor.'[21] It was the first of a series of breaks with the institutional Church that had been his home since birth.

Luther's next move was a direct appeal over Cajetan's head to Pope Leo himself, complaining about the cardinal's tactics.[22] He would come to Rome in person, Luther offered, if it didn't pose a risk to his life. In which context, he referred in his letter to an alleged plot that had just been uncovered to poison Leo himself.[23] 'I feel that I have not had justice because I teach nothing save what is in Scripture,' he concluded. 'Therefore I appeal from Leo badly informed to Leo better informed.'[24] It is an elegant phrase, but perhaps not suitable words for a minion when writing to one with so great a sense of his own importance as the Pope himself.

Such was Luther's general spirit of defiance that Augsburg was awash with rumours as to his fate. Guards on the gates were said to be waiting there to arrest him if he attempted to leave. The name and example of Hus was on many lips. With his protector Elector Friedrich already departed, Luther grew increasingly worried for his own safety. With Staupitz's help, he somehow got hold of a horse and made his escape like a thief in the night.[25]

It was the first in a series of near misses, for if officials following papal orders had got their hands on him, Luther would surely have been silenced, by one means or another. Travelling via Nürnberg, the fugitive arrived back in the sanctuary of Wittenberg on 30 October. How much had changed in the twelve months since he had sent the Ninety-Five Theses to Prince Albrecht.

On the edge of a precipice

On his return to Rome, Cardinal Cajetan busied himself with removing one plank of Luther's defence – namely that indulgences had never been declared official doctrine of the Catholic Church. On 9 November, Leo X issued the bull *Cum Postquam* ('When After'), said to have been written by Cajetan himself. There were some nods in the direction of the complaints Luther had made. Indulgences should not be seen, the bull insisted, as a substitute for attendance at the sacrament of confession, but only as a way of mitigating the penance imposed by the confessor. It also rejected the excesses seen in the sales techniques of Tetzel and others, but then got to the heart of the matter. Henceforth indulgences were to be regarded as Church doctrine. Anyone who questioned their promotion could be deemed a heretic.

Rome was finally growing anxious about dealing with the troublesome friar in Wittenberg. What was required, though, was the co-operation of Elector Friedrich, and so Cajetan sent him a damning account of his face-to-face encounter with Luther at

Augsburg. 'This beast', he reported, had 'deep-set eyes and strange ideas in his head'.[26] It was the prince's duty, he insisted, to dispatch his professor to Rome, or at least expel him into the territory of a neighbouring prince who would do the right thing.

Georg Spalatin was quick to convey this new level of threat to Luther. As was fast becoming a habit, when he found himself under pressure from the Church authorities, Luther hit back publicly with little care for diplomacy and no effort to spare the feelings of his opponents. *Acta Augustana* colourfully told his side of the story of meeting with the papal legate. Casting himself as a pious, decent German, he pictured the Italian cardinal as one who responded to legitimate enquiries about the scriptural justification for particular teachings by shouting down his questioner. But, Luther went on, playing to the gallery in Germany with its resentment of Italy's demands, he had rebuked the ignorant and insufferable Cajetan with the words, 'you need not think we Germans are ignorant of grammar'. He was turning Cajetan into a symbol of an overbearing Rome, taking Germans for granted, showing them no respect and regarding them as idiots. Cajetan was, Luther concluded, about as good an opponent as an ass playing the harp. So arresting was the image this phrase conjured up, it was taken up with gusto by the cartoonists tasked by printers with illustrating the hurriedly published accounts of the latest round in Luther's battle with authority.[27]

For his part, Luther was keen to emphasise that he did not have anything against Leo individually. His problem was with the powers claimed for the papacy. 'You are not a bad Christian if you deny the decretal [papal teaching], but if you deny the gospel, you are a heretic . . . I honour the sanctity of the pope, but I will adore the sanctity of Christ and the truth. I do not deny this new monarchy of the Roman Church, which has arisen in our generation, but I deny that you cannot be a Christian without being subject to the decrees of the Roman pontiff.'[28]

You can almost hear Luther saying, '. . . and another thing' before allowing his pen to run on to new additions to his list of complaints about the wrong-headedness of the papacy. Was this a deliberate strategy to turn his initial complaint into a Reformation? No. Luther was worked up into a lather of anger, as well he might be when his life was so obviously in danger. 'I have', he later remarked, 'no better medicine than anger. For if I want to write, pray and preach well, I must be angry. It energises my entire system, my understanding is sharpened, and all doubts melt away.'[29]

It was not in Luther's nature to be still, especially when he was under threat, and so, on 28 November, he lodged with a notary a public appeal for his case to be heard by a general council of the Church. Frustrated that the papacy would not yield an inch, he was now going over its head to invoke a disputed claim that ultimate authority in the Church resided in a general council rather than one individual. 'Therefore from Leo badly advised and from his excommunication, suspension, interdict, censures, sentences, fines and whatsoever denunciations and declarations of heresy and apostasy, which I esteem as null, nay, as iniquitous and tyrannical, I appeal to a general council in a safe place.'[30]

Luther once more linked his own fate with the unanswered frustrations of the German people. 'Before long, all the churches, palaces, walls and bridges of Rome will be built out of our money. First of all we should rear living temples, next local churches, and only last of all Saint Peter's.'[31]

He did hold back in one particular. Though he gave the text to a printer, he instructed him that it should only be published if and when he was formally banned by Rome as a heretic. The printer, though, decided to go ahead regardless. There was an irresistible public appetite to read every last word Luther wrote.

General council

How realistic was such an appeal to a general council? The cardinalate class within Catholicism – the men who, gathered as a Sacred College, voted in each new pope – was intricately linked with the various Catholic European powers who wished to influence the conduct of papacy. Even within the Italian peninsula – like Germany, a place of competitive mini-states and shifting alliances – ambitious ruling families (the Medici in Florence, the Sforza in Milan, the Petrucci of Siena) had long since developed a dynastic taste for having at least one cardinal in the family, if not a member on the papal throne. To achieve this, they worked with outside powers – the French, the Spanish or the Holy Roman Emperor, all of them simultaneously keen to stake their own territorial claims to parts of Italy and to have the Pope on their side. It was a sure recipe for conflict, continual plotting and chaos.

Each election of a new pope brought all the rival claims loudly back into play. To seize Saint Peter's throne, the successful candidate from among the cardinals would offer deals to various of the 'stake-holders', but then just as often once installed would renege or, worse, get embroiled in conflicts with those who were once his allies. Which is where general councils – and more broadly the Conciliar Movement – came in.

In the early Christian Church, there had been a pattern of calling councils when major decisions had to be made. At the Council of Nicaea in 325, for example, a gathering of bishops ruled on key questions of doctrine, including the wording of Christianity's core profession of faith, the Nicene Creed. The medieval Church had reverted to this earlier method of making rulings in the fourteenth century when the Western Schism between 1376 and 1417 resulted in there being two rival popes, one in Rome and one in Avignon, the latter effectively controlled by the French king. The cardinals gathered at the Council of Constance used their own authority finally to end the schism. Martin V, the new Pope elected in its wake, committed himself to uphold in future the conciliar ideals that had brought him to power, but he didn't keep his word. Over the course of the fifteenth century, conciliarism waned as papal power grew.

The Council of Pisa in 1511, summoned with French backing and the support of Emperor Maximilian, had been an attempt by cardinals to unseat Julius II, but it failed. Julius was forced to make a concession, summoning the Fifth Lateran Council in 1512, but by the time it ended in 1517, his successor, Leo X, had done a deal with the French king. In exchange for giving Francis I power to appoint bishops within his kingdom, the papacy won his endorsement for its supreme authority, even over a general council. The conciliar ideal had apparently been dashed, but now Luther's appeal to a general council to hold the pope to account threatened to reopen the whole dispute.

And his was not a lone voice. Again he was speaking aloud what others thought. Many would-be reformers within Catholicism shared his optimism that the best way to force corrupt Renaissance popes to change their habits would be a general council. Among them, inevitably, was Erasmus.

Hanging by a thread

His appeal for a general council was a last, desperate ploy by Luther to take control of his own fate, but the papacy refused to yield. Still his life rested in the hands of the Elector Friedrich. If he bowed to papal pressure and expelled Luther from his lands, other princes in Germany would seize him and hand him over to Rome. If he didn't, he was risking a confrontation with the head of his Church, with many of his fellow rulers in Germany, and with the Holy Roman Emperor. And all over a friar with a sharp and sometimes crude tongue who was churning out an ever-growing list of demands for reform, some of which held little appeal for Friedrich.

The elector was in a fix. His strongest instinct was that he was not sufficiently qualified to judge in the dispute between Luther and Rome, though from his correspondence with Erasmus he would have known that his professor was articulating a widespread yearning for change. And Friedrich would also have noted that the Pope himself had not so far labelled Luther a heretic, nor excommunicated him, though both judgements were believed to be imminent.

The elector returned to his initial pledge to Luther to see a verdict on his complaints reached in German lands. To that end he wrote on 19 November to Emperor Maximilian, urging him once again to make arrangements for Luther's hearing to be held close to home.

Luther was sympathetic to the very real dilemma in which Friedrich found himself. Both ruler and friar were sincere men. Neither was a schemer, working to inflame the situation. It was in that spirit that Luther wrote to the Elector and offered to leave Saxony without the necessity of being expelled. 'What am I, a poor monk, to expect if I am banished? Since I am in danger enough in your territory, what would it be outside? But lest your honour suffer on my account, I will gladly leave your dominions.'[32]

In a letter to Staupitz around the same time, Luther produced a bleak appraisal of his prospects. Friedrich, it seems, had made known his displeasure at the publication of Luther's version of the Cajetan interviews. He reported, 'The prince is very solicitous for me, but he would be happier if I were somewhere else.' He also shared with Staupitz that Spalatin, Friedrich's chaplain, had 'dissuaded me from precipitate flight to France'.[33]

Staupitz replied from Salzburg, later to become his permanent home, suggesting Luther join him there. 'You have few friends, and would that they were not hidden for fear of the adversary [the devil]. Leave Wittenberg and come to me that we may live and die together. The prince [Friedrich] is in accord. Deserted let us follow the deserted Christ.'[34]

Staupitz suggests that the elector wanted Luther to go, Spalatin that he wanted him to stay. No wonder Luther was lost as to which way to turn. A face-to-face meeting with Friedrich may have simplified matters, but that was not the way they conducted their relationship. On 25 November, Luther wrote defiantly to Spalatin: 'I am expecting the curses of Rome any day. I have everything in readiness. When they come, I am girded like Abraham to go I know not where, but sure of this, that God is everywhere.'[35]

Elector Friedrich the Wise in old age, painted by Lucas Cranach in 1525. Though his own faith was traditional Catholicism, the Elector believed that Rome had never properly addressed the questions Luther raised.

By Luther's own account, given seventeen years later in another *Table Talk*, the situation was finally resolved when a papal envoy, Karl von Miltitz (a Saxon and by some accounts a distant relative of the elector), arrived at Friedrich's court a few days before Christmas. He bore gifts from Leo, intended as bribes, including the 'Golden Rose of Virtue', a symbol of the blood spilled by Jesus Christ and a token of special papal favour. He also delivered a bundle of legal papers demanding that all princes and bishops detain Luther and send him for trial in Rome.

When Luther heard what was afoot (presumably from Spalatin), he subsequently recalled, he preached a farewell sermon and organised a last supper with his inner circle, convinced his fate was now sealed. He was within two hours of fleeing Wittenberg when a note arrived from Spalatin saying that the elector wanted him to remain and that he would protect him.[36]

It was a second near-miss for the representatives of the papacy, after Luther had slipped through the net in Augsburg a few months earlier. 'Good God,' Luther said of Friedrich's message of support, 'with what joy I read [it] and read [it] over again.'

Even allowing for Luther's habit of injecting drama into his memories, this had been a cliff-hanger. Thereafter he never ceased but to acknowledge the debt he owed Friedrich, as well as trying to discern the elector's motives in choosing the course he did. Was it a natural sense of justice? 'One could govern better with common sense and reason than with legal, written and definite rights. Our dear lord, Duke Friedrich,' he pronounced, 'was such a man, who governed according to his own sense of natural justice.'[37] Or was Friedrich guided by the hand of God? The elector was, Luther once remarked, 'truly a gift from God'.[38]

And the picture of these life-or-death days at the end of 1518 remains confused. Luther was also later to suggest that the elector had a back-up plan to hide him,[39] while in 1520 Friedrich was to claim he was ready to let Luther leave, but an unnamed papal nuncio – probably von Miltitz – told him instead to keep Luther close so he could be put under surveillance.[40] He was, he implied, doing the Pope's bidding, like any faithful son of the Church.

The truth may be simpler. After wavering, Friedrich sent a letter to Cardinal Cajetan on 18 December. In it, he endorsed neither Luther nor his theological positions, but instead justified his own refusal to act on the grounds that his professor still hadn't been given good enough reasons to recant. If they were to be provided, Luther could be handed over. The onus, therefore, lay with Rome. 'There are learned men in the universities,' Friedrich went on, 'who hold that his [Luther's] teaching has not been shown to be unjust, unchristian or heretical. The few who think so are jealous of his attainments. If we understood his doctrine to be impious or untenable, we would not defend it. Our whole purpose is to fulfil the office of a Christian prince.'

He ended his letter with an invitation to Rome to pronounce definitively on the specific questions raised by Luther, rather than on the man himself. 'His offer to debate and submit to the judgement of the universities ought to be considered. He should be shown in what respect he is a heretic and not condemned in advance. We will not lightly permit ourselves to be drawn into error nor to be made disobedient to the Holy See.'[41]

So speaks a naturally just man. It was a powerful defence for such a devout Catholic to write to his Pope. It also set the tone for the next stages in the drama. One option might have been for Friedrich to grant sanctuary on condition that Luther henceforth keep a low profile, say nothing publicly, and wait for the fuss to blow over. Yet instead here was the elector asking Rome for another set-piece debate. Even with his slight first-hand knowledge of Luther, he must have known that he was protecting someone who was not in the habit of biting his tongue. But there was also a seemingly inexorable momentum driving the whole dispute forward towards a conflagration. It had been building up thus far through Luther's often intemperate presentation of views, set against the Catholic authorities' clumsy and counter-productive attempts to corner him. Feeding it was the nerve that Luther had touched in disgruntled Germans. Now Friedrich was adding his own fuel to the fire. Anyone other than Luther might have responded by reflecting on how close he had come to being burned – literally – but that was not in his troubled nature.

CHAPTER SIX

The Leipzig Debate: Battle Lines Are Drawn

'I was thrown into battle over the gospel by God without know-ing it was happening. He simply blinded me, the way one puts blinders on a horse, when one wants it to stay on the path.'
Martin Luther, *Table Talk*[1]

Martin Luther was safe, for the time being, in the haven of Wittenberg but, outside its protective walls and embankments, events were moving swiftly. On 12 January 1519 came the long-anticipated death of Emperor Maximilian, after he caught a chill while out hunting in his native Austria. It threw the whole of Europe into a fresh crisis. Despite his efforts at Augsburg, Maximilian had not been able to settle the succession in the Holy Roman Empire, as he had wished, on his grandson, Charles, the young King of Spain. Renewed scheming began in the German lands of the empire, and beyond, with a variety of other candi-dates put forward for the vacant throne.

The seven voters were all German princes, some of them (such as Archbishop Albrecht) also high-ranking clerics. In casting their ballots they had potentially competing concerns: the extent to which Luther's ongoing clash with the papacy was accentuating discontent among their own peoples; and how far they might exploit Rome's wish to silence Luther in order to wrest from it more autonomy in their own affairs.

Other factors were also at play. To go along with Maximilian's wishes and elect Charles as Holy Roman Emperor would not just consolidate the Hapsburg family's predominant and resented role

Emperor Charles V in 1521. Instinctively opposed to Luther's reforms,
Charles was too distracted by other problems in his farflung domains
to concentrate on the upheavals in Germany.

in Germany (it had provided every emperor since 1438), but would
also create, under a single ruler, a vast swathe of territory including his Spanish inheritance, with its New World colonies, the Low
Countries (where he had grown up), and southern Italy. Charles's
inability to master the German language, moreover, indicated to
the voters that the Holy Roman Empire's needs might not be top
of his list. A popular ditty had it that he spoke to God in Latin, to
women in French, and to his horse in German. True or not, it
resonated with Germans because it once again played to their
resentment at how they were patronised by the rest of Europe.

In Paris, another young, ambitious monarch, Francis I, was
busy plotting to exploit the electors' worries. Reluctant to have
his French domains surrounded by Charles's territories, he put

himself forward as an alternative candidate to succeed Maximilian, one who would revive the early medieval Carolingian empire that had been established over France and Germany by Charlemagne, the first Holy Roman Emperor.

Either option, though, would mean a consolidation of power in the hands of one of two bitter rivals for European hegemony. There was some talk of bringing in Henry VIII of England as a compromise, but more plausible was a plan for one of the seven imperial electors to be persuaded to stand – a German answer to Germany's needs. The idea gained the backing of Pope Leo – unhappy at the prospect of the French or the Spanish monarch acquiring too dominant a position in Europe.

The candidacy of Elector Friedrich of Saxony was therefore much discussed. For his part, he tried to dampen down such a scheme, but while there was a chance that he would agree, his status was greatly enhanced. The papacy could not therefore risk alienating him over a rebellious friar at lowly Wittenberg University when there was a greater prize to be seized.

The papal legate at the Saxon court, Karl von Miltitz, was put under orders in the early months of 1519 to take a softly-softly approach – building trust with the elector at the same time as keeping Luther quiet in case he further fanned the flames of unrest. Friedrich's position on his professor of theology, meanwhile, remained unchanged. He wanted the dispute between Luther and Rome settled by a German assembly. He even nominated someone to lead it – the Archbishop of Trier, Richard von Greiffenklau zu Vollrads, another of those who would cast a vote for the next Holy Roman Emperor.

Luther, for his part, was waiting on events to learn his fate, but he was not alone. In his immediate circle were three figures of crucial importance. The first, Georg Spalatin, Friedrich's chaplain, was Luther's essential channel to the elector. The second, Andreas von Karlstadt, was his colleague in the Wittenberg theology department. The two men's outlook had been similarly shaped by visits to Rome.

Karlstadt been horrified by its Renaissance excesses during a year he spent there in 1515–16 studying canon and civil law.

Andreas von Karlstadt – a 1525 portrait: Once a colleague and friend of Luther, the two fell out. Luther called him 'arrogant, presumptuous and ambitious'.

Karlstadt had started out as the senior partner, acting as Luther's sponsor when he received his doctorate. And before Luther produced his Ninety-Five Theses, Karlstadt had been loudly lamenting the corruption of the Catholic Church and publishing theses of his own. If they agreed about the faults of their Church, though, the two clerics were possessed of very different personalities. They shared a profound religious passion, and were both easily inflamed into anger, but there was a greater recklessness in Karlstadt. Later (after they had fallen out), Luther was to describe Karlstadt as 'arrogant, presumptuous and ambitious'.[2]

The third, and most enduringly significant, was Philipp Melanchthon. Just twenty-one when he arrived in Wittenberg in late 1518 as the university's first ever professor of Greek, he was an academic prodigy who had been recommended for the job by his great uncle, the noted Humanist Johann Reuchlin. It was the same great uncle who had persuaded him to Hellenise his surname, as was the fashion in such circles, from Schwartzerdt ('black earth' in German) to its consonant-heavy Greek equivalent, Melanchthon.

Philipp Melanchthon, painted by Lucas Cranach around 1545: he was Luther's closest collaborator, and he described him as 'a scrawny shrimp' with an intellect to rival Saint Paul.

Portraits by the Wittenberg court painter Lucas Cranach the Elder reveal Melanchthon as a waif-like young man, with red hair that would thin unattractively, and an intense gaze to match Luther's. He had a speech impediment that made him – unlike Luther and Karlstadt – shy of public platforms, and a pronounced limp down one side. 'A scrawny shrimp' was how Luther described him affectionately, while comparing Melanchthon's intellect to that of Saint Paul.[3] Unlike Luther, Melanchthon was in regular contact with Erasmus and other Christian Humanists and generally his disposition was more nuanced, more open and hence, at times, more easily persuadable than Luther's.

It was over the significance of Paul's writings – and more generally of Scripture – that Melanchthon and Luther forged the closest of bonds, once the former had switched to the school of theology at the university. If Karlstadt was to be found goading Luther on to ever greater acts of rebellion, the quieter, cleverer, but more measured Melanchthon would be restraining him, urging intellectual vigour and sticking to the moral high ground at all times.

Keeping shtoom

The papal envoy Miltitz met with Luther on 5 and 6 January of 1519 in the Saxon town of Altenberg, the first of three encounters between them to take place over the next eighteen months. He had been made aware on his travels of the tide of public approval for the Wittenberg professor that was washing across German lands and beyond with the wide dissemination of Luther's writings. For every German he met who opposed Luther, Miltitz reported back to Rome, there were three who supported him. His initial efforts, therefore, were all about exploring a compromise whereby Luther could be persuaded to pipe down or, better still, express some words of loyalty to Pope Leo, if not about the authority of the papacy, that would lower the temperature. To show goodwill, Miltitz very publicly tackled Johann Tetzel, whose sales patter when hawking indulgences had prompted the Ninety-Five Theses. The Dominican was accused of immorality and corruption, and summarily disgraced. He retreated to a monastery in Leipzig and died a broken man on 11 August.

Luther was in a quandary. Did he accept Miltitz's olive branch, or did he listen to those around him who were urging him that this was the moment to push on, especially now that he had secured Elector Friedrich's protection? He gave a bullish account of this period in a *Table Talk* in the early 1530s, where he compared his younger self to a horse kept in blinders – or blinkers – so that it remains focused and beyond distraction or diversion. In this version, Luther was fixed on one course, with one goal, and God in the saddle. He could no sooner stop than turn round and run in the opposite direction.

The reality was somewhat different. The Elector's protection was neither unconditional nor for ever. He had not nailed his own colours to Luther's mast, but instead simply wanted Luther's claims examined and judged. The prospect of that judgement, while undoubtedly insignificant as far as Luther was concerned next to final judgement by God, could not be ignored. And so, in these early months of 1519, he does appear to hesitate. His conflict with Rome did not have an ever-escalating trajectory. Like Luther's own state of mind, it ebbed and flowed, and in this period there was a short-term but unmistakable dip in Luther's very public defiance of the papacy. It could have been the surfacing of an inclination to self-preservation. He was, after all, flesh and blood.

Yet, even if he pulled back a little in public, he continued to explore, to read, and to pray, and the more he did that, the more convinced he became that the Catholic Church was rotten at its core. A letter written in March reveals that, in private, his alienation was growing. 'I am studying the papal decretals . . . I whisper this in your ear. I don't know whether the pope is Antichrist . . . so does he in his decretals [pronouncements on Church law] corrupt and crucify Christ, that is, the truth.'[4]

Often confused today with the devil, with whom the Church teaches he is in league, the Antichrist is – according to Catholic doctrine – the one who denies Jesus Christ. The scriptural basis comes in the New Testament Epistles of John, looking forward to the day when Jesus will return to earth in the Second Coming. Opposing Him, it says, will be the Antichrist, a false messiah and evil through and through. 'The man who denies that Jesus is the Christ, he is the liar, he is the Antichrist; and he is denying the Father as well as the Son.'[5] And the same figure is described, though not named Antichrist, in Paul's Second Letter to the Church in Thessalonika.[6]

For Luther to use such language – albeit in a private letter – represents one more step away from the prospect of any resolution of his dispute with Rome, though once again he was not breaking new ground. The same accusation of being the Antichrist had been thrown at the papacy since the eleventh century, and not only by dissenters, but in some cases by figures later elevated by Rome to sainthood.[7]

It was against this backdrop of public reticence but ever greater private distance from the papacy that Luther set out in June for Leipzig to attend one of the great set pieces of the Reformation.

The Leipzig debate

In the midst of all the other tumultuous events of 1518, Luther had received a letter from his near contemporary Johann Eck, who had held the chair in theology at Ingolstadt University, near Munich. The two had been in contact at the start of the previous year, sharing their views on the need for reform in Catholicism. A friendship had developed, but Eck was horrified when he read the

Ninety-Five Theses. He believed that Luther had taken a wrong turn, and he sent him a forceful rebuttal. On a copy of Luther's text, he had inserted a drawing of a dagger – what he called an obelisk – next to those theses he considered wrong or frivolous. Whether the symbol indicated Eck's intention to puncture the argument offered, or represented a judgement that Luther was wielding a dagger against his own Church, is unclear. He did not intend to make public his disagreement, Eck informed Luther, but instead wanted to take up Luther's invitation, explicit in the Ninety-Five Theses, to a disputation on the issues he had raised.

While Luther's immediate fate was hanging in the balance at the end of 1518, Eck had been looking for someone to host such a debate. Most German rulers and universities were anxious to avoid deepening a dispute that was already causing them considerable anxiety, and so refused, but finally Eck persuaded Leipzig to stage the debate. Duke Georg, Elector Friedrich's Wettin cousin who ruled the other part of the family lands after their division, had long felt a keen rivalry with his relative on dynastic grounds (the Electorate had been regarded as the more desirable prize in the partition), and as one prince overshadowed by another. Where Friedrich was talked about as a candidate for Holy Roman Emperor and admired as 'the Wise', Georg was known only as 'the Bearded' on account of his facial hair. Moreover, his university at Leipzig, while older than Friedrich's upstart institution at Wittenberg, was now being eclipsed because of the attention Luther had received.

Eck's request gave him the chance to put all of that right – and cast himself as an important figure and a loyal Catholic. Duke Georg was therefore convinced by Eck that this event could achieve what all other efforts had so far failed to do – to expose the shortcomings in Luther's arguments, cause him to recant, and so restore order to the German Church. There were plenty of voices warning against. The local bishop in Leipzig, for example, was opposed, fearing it would just give Luther another opportunity to rally people. And even Leipzig University itself hesitated, so much so that Duke Georg had to transfer proceedings to the large auditorium in his Pleissenburg Castle – though moving to this new location may also have been a response to the numbers of those wanting to attend.

All Eck now required was to secure Luther's attendance, but initially the friar demurred. It may be that he had made a private oath of silence to Miltitz, or to Elector Friedrich, or even to Cardinal Cajetan, a promise to keep his counsel until the Pope pronounced a definitive verdict on his status in the Church. Luther had also grown suspicious of Eck's motives, labelling him in a letter in February to Spalatin as a 'glory-hungry little beast'.[8] Yet the opportunity finally to debate the Ninety-Five Theses, something he had wanted from the moment he scribbled them down, was ultimately just too tempting. Even so, Luther suggested a compromise. He nominated Karlstadt to face Eck, but promised he too would attend, as an advisor.

It wasn't exactly what Eck was hoping for, but, knowing Luther a little, he calculated correctly that once on the floor of the debating chamber he would be able, like a good barrister with a reluctant witness, to goad Luther by the line of questioning he took with the stand-in, and thus tempt him to speak out and condemn himself.

Luther travelled to Leipzig with Karlstadt, Melanchthon, other teachers from the university and around two hundred students, some of them armed with axe-handles. They might have been going to a local football derby, so tribal does it sound: Wittenberg versus Leipzig; Friedrich versus Georg; reformers versus traditionalists. Eck, for his part, had a detachment of bodyguards with him, said to number seventy. A riot seemed very possible. A theological dispute had become something more.

After a mass on 27 June, the debate moved to the castle, with Eck squaring up to Karlstadt, while the man everyone had come to see, Martin Luther, sat silently at his colleague's side. First there were various procedural wrangles to sort out. Eck won the argument that there should be no publications penned by participants in the disputation until after a final judgement had been delivered on what had been said by representatives of Erfurt and Paris universities. Their role as jury was stipulated by Duke Georg. Luther had argued to no avail that they were unnecessary, since Elector Friedrich was already engaged in arranging a hearing of his case before the Imperial Diet, which was assembling in the western city of Worms even as the Leipzig debate took place.

One eyewitness – thought to be Peter Mosellanus, the Leipzig professor who gave the opening address at the proceedings – has left behind a description of the combatants in the castle's auditorium. Luther, he wrote, 'is of middle height, emaciated from care and study, so that you can almost count his bones through his skin'. His tendency to pile on weight was not yet in evidence.

Karlstadt was 'smaller than Luther, with a complexion of smoked herring. His voice is thick and unpleasant. He is slower in memory and quicker in anger.' And, in case the reporter is accused of bias against one side, he is just as unkind in summoning up Eck. He was, it was reported, akin to a town crier – 'a heavy, square-set fellow with a full German voice supported by a hefty chest . . . his whole face remind one more of a butcher than a theologian'.[9]

Eck and Karlstadt set to and rehearsed already familiar arguments. The former insisted the papacy had the last say in interpreting Scripture, up to and including its recent statement on indulgences. He returned once more to Jesus calling Peter the rock on which His Church would be built.[10] This was a position that Luther (and Erasmus)[11] had already rejected, arguing as Augustine had done that the 'rock' referred not to Peter but to Christ Himself. Karlstadt repeated this line, and pointing to John's gospel to strengthen his case, picked out the passage where

Jesus tells Peter, 'Feed my sheep.'[12] 'What, then, was given to Paul?' Karlstadt wondered. 'When Christ said to Peter, "Feed my sheep", He did not mean, did He, that no one else can feed them without Peter's permission?'[13]

It is a remark that gets to the heart of Luther's objection to so much focus on Peter as the source of authority in the Church. The result was a downgrading of Paul, who, in his writings, the earliest texts in Christianity, had in Luther's opinion played a much greater role in the development of the Church. While some of Paul's thirteen letters in the New Testament may not have come from his hand, they dwarf the two short texts included under Peter's name, and were a better guide for the Christian intent on salvation.

The to-and-fro of the disputation between Eck and Karlstadt began each morning at seven. It took until 4 July for Luther to be sufficiently provoked to break his silence. What hooked him was the question of whether the papacy could be considered a human or a divine institution. It was the start of nine days of him going head-to-head with Eck.

'He is in the vigour of manhood,' wrote the same eyewitness about Luther, 'and has a clear, penetrating voice . . . A perfect forest of words and ideas stands at his command. He is affable and friendly, in no sense dour or arrogant.' This last remark cuts across every stereotype of Luther that has grown up subsequently, which casts him as a joyless man. 'He is equal to anything,' judges the reporter. 'In company he is vivacious, jocose, always cheerful and gay, no matter how hard his adversaries press him.'[14] This was the charisma that drew crowds to Luther.

Georg Benedict, a student at Wittenberg, wrote the following evaluation of Luther's debating style on the inside flap of his Bible. 'His voice could be as sharp as it could be gentle . . . gentle in tone, sharp in enunciation of syllables, words and caesuras [pauses] . . . even the worst enemies of the gospel, having heard him only once, had to admit that on the basis of the surpassing significance of what they had heard, they had not been hearing a human being but the Holy Spirit speak; and that his remarkable doctrine therefore did not originate in him but was the working of a – good or demonic – spiritual power.'[15]

That was not Eck's experience. In Pleissenburg Castle, he continued to press Luther hard on his attitude to Pope Leo, trying to exploit the gap that his opponent was always careful to leave in his criticisms between the shortcomings of the papacy and the conduct of the current incumbent. If each individual believer were to be the final judge on interpretation of Scripture, which is what Eck claimed Luther was proposing, who would lead the Catholic Church? One man, or as many as there were believers? 'Even if there were ten popes, or a thousand popes, there would be no schism,' Luther replied. 'The unity of Christendom could be preserved under numerous heads just as the separated nations under different sovereigns dwell in concord.'[16]

Is this what Luther truly believed, or was he just answering a debating point? For to strip the Pope of final teaching authority and insist on every individual believer's ability to make their own judgement on Scripture was surely, as Eck contended, a recipe for chaos.

By contrast Eck was offering a more reassuring pledge. 'I confess one faith, one Lord Jesus Christ, and I venerate the Roman Pontiff as Christ's vicar.'[17] That was the choice presented to the audience – a free-for-all, or a familiar, if flawed, structure.

Luther was not, though, investing authority solely in Scripture. He had already shown himself an admirer of the Early Church Fathers in preference to the Scholastic theologians of more recent times. So Eck next produced as evidence the Isidorian Decretals, which he claimed to be letters dating back to the first-century Church that supported the claims made for Saint Peter regarding the papacy. Though there were already scholarly doubts about the authenticity of the Isidorian Decretals, Luther went further and dismissed them (correctly it has subsequently been shown) as forgeries. Indeed, he went so far as to question whether Saint Peter had ever even set foot in Rome, despite the existence of a grave, purported to be his, where pilgrims had gathered and over which the original Saint Peter's Basilica had been erected.

Again historians and biblical scholars would today have greater sympathy for what Luther said about Peter's movements but, in an age of countless scarcely authenticated but much-prized relics of saints, his remarks would have sounded tantamount to blasphemy to some hearers. Eck was skilfully tempting Luther to reveal more about his private thoughts than perhaps Luther wanted to share.

Eck's most successful tactic, though, was to draw out and discredit Luther's position on the papacy by linking it to the fourteenth-century Bohemian heretic Jan Hus. Luther, he charged, was infected by the 'Bohemian virus'. It was an accusation that had a particular resonance for the audience in Leipzig. Many would know their own city's history and how, in the war that followed Hus being burned at the stake as a heretic, his supporters in Bohemia had invaded Leipzig and wrought havoc. Was Luther not just repeating Hus's heresy by denying papal authority, Eck suggested, in an attempt to damn his opponent by association?

It worked. Luther's knowledge of Hus at this moment was at best hazy, but he nevertheless asserted that some of what the Bohemian preacher had suggested was 'most Christian and Evangelical'. Evangelical was a significant word to choose because it was the one that Luther liked best as a description of his own theology, in preference to Lutheran, the name that Eck first pronounced during their clashes at Leipzig. Eck meant it as a term of rebuke, just as Hussite was used to damn the followers of Jan Hus. Luther was subsequently (and modestly) to fight hard against 'Lutheran'. As late as 1523, in a tract on Psalm 120,[18] he was stating once again his preference for the label 'Evangelical' – from 'evangel', or the good news of the gospels. He liked it, he said, because it indicated the paramount position of the Scriptures.

Evangelical wasn't the only word Luther used about Hus on that day. He went on to refer to the Bohemian's 'pestilential errors', but 'Evangelical' was the one that was remembered. Eck had hit on a way to win the argument.

In a break between the sessions, Luther read up on Hus and found much common ground. A more cautious man might have kept those thoughts to himself, but when Eck returned to the attack in the debating chamber, Luther retreated not one inch on what he had already said regarding Hus. Instead he compounded the bad impression he had made with the audience by suggesting that a greater willingness to listen to Hus might have done wonders for the Church.

It was an inflammatory statement, whether or not he intended it to be, and arguably reveals much about Luther's own mindset at the time. When he read about Hus and his fate, he could only see his own. By saying, if only the Catholic Church had shown a greater willingness to listen to Hus, he was really saying, if only it would show a greater willingness to listen to me. 'I believe,' he told Eck, 'that the Bohemians [those who continued to adhere to Hus's teaching, in defiance of Rome] are men and that they may be attracted by gentle words and by compromise, but that they are only hardened by being called criminal and the opprobrious name of heretics.'[19] In other words, stop attacking me and listen to the very reasonable points I am making, and together we can reform and renew the Church.

Luther went on to note that the condemnation of Hus by the Council of Constance had been general rather than a systematic refutation of his teachings, one by one. Some of these teachings,

Luther indicated, were worthy of more serious consideration. Here he was shooting himself in the foot. His appeal at the end of the previous year, when his life had been in mortal danger, had been to a general council of the Church as a higher authority than the papacy. Yet now he was arguing that just such a general council, the one that met at Constance and declared Hus a heretic to be punished by death, had been in error. So not only was he suggesting that the papacy got things wrong, now he was tarring general councils (most reformers' favourite alternative to rein in an overmighty pope) with the same brush. He quoted the recent Fifth Lateran Council, which at Pope Leo's urging had reversed the view taken at Constance on the role of councils in relation to the papacy. 'A simple layman armed with Scripture', he concluded, 'is to be believed above a council.'

Then what, Eck asked, was there left for the Church to do? 'Are you the only one who knows anything? Except for you, is all the Church in error?' It was a question Luther heard many times. His own father had asked him a version of it at his ordination, and it may have been that unhappy echo that caused Luther to come back so robustly, quoting Scripture. 'I answer that God once spoke through the mouth of an ass.[20] I will tell you straight what I think. I am a Christian theologian; and I am bound, not only to assert, but to defend the truth with my blood and death. I want to believe freely and be a slave to the authority of no one, whether council, university or pope. I will confidently confess what appears to me to be true, whether it has been asserted by a Catholic or a heretic, whether it has been approved or reproved by a council.'

As a statement of intent, it still has a force about it. The pursuit of truth – or what seemed to Luther to be truth, once its scriptural authority had been established – was all that mattered. The Catholic Church might make the same claim, but its behaviour suggested they were hollow words.

Sensing that Eck had provoked him into saying more than he intended, and that he was losing the audience, Luther tried to rescue the situation. Thus far the two protagonists had addressed each other in Latin. Luther now asked to switch to German so as to make what he was saying clear to the 'common people'. It was a phrase he liked to use. He saw himself as a spokesman for the 'common people', one of their own, siding with them against the ecclesiastical bigwigs. Central to that claim was his fluency in everyday German and his willingness to use it in formal settings where Latin was the prescribed tongue. 'I do not have a certain special, standard German language,' he once mused, 'but rather use the general common German, so both upper and lower Germans understand me.' He prayed in German a lot more than in Latin, he said, 'because the mother language is more effective'.[21]

Yet on this occasion, even in German, he had much ground to make up, and time was short. Duke Georg needed his auditorium back to entertain the princes who were returning from Worms after casting their vote for the new Holy Roman Emperor. The disputation was therefore drawn to an abrupt halt.

Eck immediately claimed victory. He had, he said, defeated Luther by revealing the depth of his Hus-like heresy, his contempt for the papacy and general councils alike, and his spiritual arrogance. He was, Eck argued, an authority only unto himself.

And Luther? He resisted Eck's victorious account, of course, but he knew that he had allowed himself to be tempted into crossing a line, not least in defending a heretic. Henceforth the same label would stick more easily to him. Even Luther's most ardent supporters would have heard the cheers of the Leipzig audience for Eck. Some would have been taken aback by their man's warm words for Jan Hus.[22] His efforts thereafter in the auditorium to clarify those remarks – whether in Latin or German – had fallen on deaf ears. Luther was now being referred to as 'the Saxon Hus'.

Potential allies

The promised judgements on the disputation at Leipzig either did not materialise (in the case of Erfurt) or took so long (Paris needed two years) that they were overtaken by events. Eck hurried from Leipzig to Rome to lap up praise as the man who had halted Luther's advance, and to demand action. Yet, for the time being, Rome was distracted. While Eck and Luther had been at it hammer and claw in Leipzig, the German prince-electors had been gathering to cast their ballots. On 28 June, the day after the Leipzig disputation began, they had opted for Charles.

The victorious young king, however, was in no position to throw himself with gusto into the challenges facing Germany – including Luther's rebellion. Instead he was to spend much of the next eighteen months in Spain, where in Castile his imposition of new taxes, his choice of advisors and his suspension of the council or Cortes had led to the Revolt of the Comuneros. It was not until 1521 that the final rebel stronghold in Toledo succumbed. In Charles's absence, Elector Friedrich remained *de facto* leader of the German princes, the key figure in Germany's affairs. All of which added to the protection he could offer Luther, but also left matters in limbo.

What is known to history as the Reformation was beginning to take shape, if not yet under that name. Luther was undeniably the leader of the opposition, loudly demanding change in the Catholic Church. His views were being heard all around Europe in pamphlets and booklets, many of them cheaply printed, and often accompanied by crude but effective cartoons and caricatures (for those who struggled with reading). One popular image likened Luther attacking the peddlers of indulgences to Jesus overturning the money-lenders' counters outside the temple in Jerusalem.[23]

In February 1519, Johann Froben, the celebrated printer from Basel who had produced every one of his friend Erasmus's books after 1513, reported that a collected volume he had made up of the Ninety-Five Theses, Explanations, and Luther's Sermon On Penitence and On the Eucharist had sold out at a speed he had never experienced before. Some six hundred copies had gone to France and Spain, others to England and Holland. One former Wittenberg student wrote to Luther that he was secretly distributing copies in Rome itself.[24]

The desire for change was certainly there, and Luther was the one best articulating it. 'At Erfurt,' he reflected in a *Table Talk*, 'when I was a young student, an old man told me there must be a change, and it will be great; things cannot go on as they are.'[25]

His rise to prominence displaced Erasmus, hitherto the most prominent voice for change. Many who had listened to him were now listening to Luther as well as, or even instead of, Erasmus. The easy assumption would have been that the two clerics were on the same side. And to an extent they were. Both wanted to see their Church reformed. Both were impatient with its obsession with rituals. Both wanted a greater focus on the Scriptures and tried to give individual believers the ability to explore them by providing more authentic versions of them. For Erasmus, that meant in 1516 producing a version of the New Testament in its original Greek, which stripped away many of the inaccuracies that had found their way into the Latin version (and which, in some cases, helped support papal claims). For Luther, in 1522, it meant translating the New Testament into German, the language his followers spoke.

Beyond that, though, there was little common ground, save the antipathy both provoked in papal circles. Where Luther railed against indulgences as a blasphemy because they had no scriptural basis, Erasmus saw them simply as an almost comical manmade excess. Where Erasmus wanted to see humankind empowered, encouraged to use its reason, intellect and creative powers,

Luther's view of life on earth remained fundamentally pessimistic. 'We are foremost poor souls, for whom it would be better if we died early and were hastily covered with dirt.'[26] If Erasmus could conceive of a kind of heaven on earth, for Luther salvation only came with death and eternal life with God.

And while Erasmus (and those who praised and protected him from the wrath of the authorities) was keen to transform the Catholic Church, he never contemplated other than that it would continue to exist, as a fixed point of authority, an anchor in an otherwise uncertain world. Luther, as he had let slip out at Leipzig, was not so sure. He owed his first loyalty to truth, not the Church. If the Church was not true, to the Scriptures above all, it was nothing.

The two realised their differences, but in 1519 they were careful to say supportive things about each other. In his *Annotations on the New Testament*, Erasmus made an oblique reference to the threat that the Catholic Church had left hanging over Luther's head. 'By how many human regulations has the sacrament of penitence and confession been impeded? The bolt of excommunication is ever in readiness. The sacred authority of the Roman pontiff is so abused by absolutions, dispensations and the like that the godly cannot see it without a sigh.'[27]

Yet defence of Luther's right to speak out, if that is what this passage was meant to be, wasn't the same as agreeing with him. Like his correspondent Elector Friedrich, Erasmus carefully kept his distance from Luther. When asked if he had read Luther's writings, he would answer that he couldn't manage German, though he managed it very well in his friendly correspondence with the elector. In a letter to the theologian Peter Barbirius, Erasmus claimed to have read fewer than twelve pages of Luther's writings.[28]

One worry for Erasmus in relation to Luther was the latter's ability to inflame German nationalism through his often crude use of language. The Dutchman was a pan-European, one who dreamt of a united Europe where rulers lived at peace under the authority of a reformed papacy. The rebellion that Luther was stoking in Germany potentially cut across that, downgrading the papacy to a less meaningful role in the affairs of the Holy Roman Empire.

Casting Luther in a nationalist light, though, is misleading. He may have articulated the widespread dismay of his countrymen and -women at their apparently unceasing papal exploitation and the inability of their rulers, divided among themselves with their own parcels of land, to resist Rome. And he was proud of his own heritage, even as it was denigrated elsewhere in Europe. 'If Germany were united, and . . . had a good and righteous lord, it would be invincible. For Germany would have national sovereignty, mineral resources, cities, production, forests, silver, soldiers.'[29]

But when those who wanted a more forceful, united Germany tried to win Luther round to their side, he rebuffed them. Around the time of Leipzig, he was being courted by two knights. The first, Ulrich von Hutten, was a romantic figure, well connected in Humanist circles, a critic of the papacy and a supporter of general councils. He deployed both sword and pen (in his satirical contribution to *Letters to Obscure Men* of 1515–17) in pursuit of a single Germany. The second, Franz von Sickingen, liked to see himself as a Robin Hood figure, distributing wealth seized from the rich to the poor, but he had also inherited a string of castles, including the Ebernburg, a vast fortress on the top of a hill above the town of Bad Münster in the Rhine Valley. A leader among the class of knights – noblemen who were one step down from the dukes and landgraves – Sickingen had his own private army and had acted as a mercenary for others. Convinced that Church taxation was making the German poor destitute, he sided with the reformist cause, and offered shelter in his castle to Luther.

'I do not despise them,' Luther said of these potential allies, 'but I will not make use of them unless Christ, my protector, be willing, who has perhaps inspired the knight.'[30] Implicit in the support proffered by Hutten and Sickingen was a willingness to take up arms in defence of the cause, however it was defined. For Luther bloodshed – unless it be his own – was unacceptable.

Another factor in his reluctance to enter into wide-ranging alliances for change – either with the knights or with Erasmus – was the loner in Luther. He had his own circle, and his broader band of supporters and sympathisers, but in his own mind he was alone in his struggles before a God he still found mysterious and often elusive. And, in his battle with Rome, he was the one being labelled a heretic, he the one whose life was at risk as a result.

At the same time, though, he was not so much of a loner as to be oblivious to the support and excitement his conflict with Rome was generating. He was grateful for it, yet his resolve remained fragile. He was forever fighting self-doubt – whether he was right, whether God would approve, or whether the devil was using him to bring down the Church. 'The more they rage, the more I am filled with the Spirit, but, and this may surprise you, I am scarcely able to resist the smallest wave of inner despair.'[31]

On his own

In August of 1519, the Hermits of Saint Augustine from across Germany met in Eisleben, Luther's birthplace, though he did not attend. Many of his fellow friars now believed his excommunication by Rome to be imminent. In the face of criticism – real or imagined – over his handling of the whole affair of his protégé, Staupitz stood down as vicar-general. He had no wish to be the one forced to hand over Luther to Rome, yet neither did he want publicly to defy the Pope. It may have been cowardice, or perhaps a sense that Luther, whom he knew so well, had embarked on a course that made a break with Rome inevitable. Staupitz wanted no part in that for himself.

In his place, the Augustinians at Eisleben appointed another Luther supporter, Wenceslaus Linck, the former prior of the chapter at Wittenberg, who had accompanied Luther to his meetings in Augsburg with Cardinal Cajetan. After the meeting, past and present vicars-general travelled to Wittenberg to see Luther. Linck made one request – and request it had to be, since Luther, though still a member of the Hermits of Saint Augustine, had been released by Staupitz from his vow of obedience. He wanted Luther to write to the pope to say that he had never intended to attack him personally. It was not the first time Luther had been asked to do this.

The meeting was his last sight of Staupitz. Afterwards the older man returned to Salzburg, his new home, and later, when Reformation fever was decimating the ranks of the Augustinians (in particular as friars married and become Lutheran pastors), he left the order and joined the Benedictines, also affected by the spirit of the times, but to a lesser degree. He died a Catholic in 1524. Writing in September the previous year, in his last letter to the man who had nurtured him at his lowest point, Luther acknowledged his debt to Staupitz, though they had ultimately chosen different courses. 'It was through you that the light of the gospel began to shine out of the darkness in our hearts.'[32]

CHAPTER SEVEN

1520: The Year of Living Dangerously

> 'No one will gain anything from me by force.'
>
> Martin Luther, *Table Talk*[1]

Excommunication remains the Catholic Church's ultimate sanction, reserved according to canon law for those guilty of 'obstinate persistence in manifest grave sin', or those 'from whose behaviour there arises scandal or serious disturbance of order'.[2] Those punished are '*ex communio*' – 'out of communion' – with their fellow believers, though since their baptism can never be revoked, they are still Christians. Instead, they are deprived of the rights that go with being '*in communio*', such as attendance at the sacraments.

Excommunication is, today, rarely invoked, but throughout the medieval period was common, capable of bringing to their knees even the mightiest of rulers. In January 1077, for example, Henry IV, the Holy Roman Emperor no less, waited for three days in the snow outside Canossa Castle in Italy for Pope Gregory VII, who was safe and warm inside, to lift his excommunication. Legend has it that the emperor wore a hair shirt, discarded his shoes and refused all food or drink in his effort to convince the Pope of his sincere repentance. Just as excommunication can be inflicted by the Church, so it can also be lifted. It is, official teaching stresses, a 'medicinal' imposition, designed to cure mistaken beliefs and bring about repentance. If Rome was hoping to use excommunication to 'cure' Martin Luther, then it was to be bitterly disappointed.

More than two and a half years after the appearance of the Ninety-Five Theses, Leo X finally issued his verdict in the bull *Exsurge Domine* ('*Arise, O Lord*') on 15 June 1520. It listed forty-one errors in Luther's writings and public pronouncements. These had been identified with the help of an expert panel, chaired by Cardinal Cajetan and including a representative of Luther's own Augustinian order. Rather than go into detail on each of the forty-one individually,³ it once again issued the sort of sweeping condemnation guaranteed to infuriate Luther. 'No one of sound mind is ignorant how destructive, pernicious, scandalous and seductive to pious and simple minds these various errors are, how opposed they are to all charity and reverence for the holy Roman Church, who is the mother of all the faithful and teacher of the faith; how destructive they are of the vigour of ecclesiastical discipline, namely obedience.'⁴

So much for any lingering hopes of a reasoned debate. The bull argued that Luther's errors were variously 'not Catholic', 'against the doctrine and tradition of the Catholic Church', and 'against the true interpretation of the sacred Scriptures received from the Church'. Where Luther claimed to be doing God's work, it restated baldly that this was the exclusive preserve of the Catholic Church 'guided by the Holy Spirit'.⁵

The papacy still did not grasp the scale of the challenge Luther was posing. A paragraph of clumsy, hollow flattery, attempting to reassure Germans of Rome's esteem, was hopelessly inadequate. 'We and our predecessors have always held this nation in the bosom of our affection ... Germans, truly germane to the Catholic faith, have always been the bitterest opponents of heresies.'⁶

The words were likely penned by Johann Eck, who had insisted on being part of the drafting committee. He might also have been responsible for the decision to match blow-for-blow Luther's tendency to crude character assassination when attacking his enemies. The friar from Wittenberg was 'inspired only by [his] own sense of ambition', likened to a serpent 'spewing out venom', and labelled 'a new Porphyry[7] [who] assails the holy pontiffs.' He was condemned as the 'wild boar from the forest', who in the Book of Psalms destroys the fertile vineyard that is the Church.[8]

As a 'true heretic', Luther was given sixty days by *Exsurge Domine* to capitulate, during which time all his existing books were to be burned. He should recant either in an open document, sealed by two bishops, to arrive in Rome within 120 days, or in person within the same timescale. If he did not, the excommunication would go ahead.

Such precise limits seem absurd when it took until October for the text to arrive in Germany, delivered by two papal representatives. Eck was one, apparently more determined than ever to triumph in his personal crusade against his former friend. The other was Jerome Aleander, director of the Palatine Library.[9] The timing of their journey north was carefully choreographed. Rome intended that Aleander, a cultivated scholar, former rector of the University of Paris, and one-time friend of Erasmus, would combine distributing the final warning to Luther among the German princes with attending the delayed coronation of Charles V as King of Germany in Aachen, Charlemagne's ancient capital. The arrival of the new Holy Roman Emperor from Spain was regarded by Rome as tactically and symbolically the right moment to stand on its dignity and loftily dismiss Luther and those who defended him.

Aleander's challenge at the coronation was to galvanise both the young emperor and his electors into taking action against the heretic, but there were faint hearts from the start. Eck didn't even go to the trouble of hand-delivering *Exsurge Domine* to Wittenberg, as he had to other seats of government around the empire. Instead he sent it by courier to the rector of the university, no doubt calculating that, following Leipzig, the town would be a no-go area for him.[10] His fear of setting foot there was no doubt increased by his having added (under the terms of a secret instruction agreed with Rome) the names of Karlstadt and two others from the university to the list of those facing condemnation by Rome.

Yet even in Leipzig, scene of what Eck had claimed as a victory over Luther in the debate just a year earlier, the papal envoy found himself forced to retreat into a cloister by public hostility. Germany was not in the mood to be told to abandon one of its own by Rome.

Elector Friedrich had received a letter from Pope Leo, dated 8 July, in advance of the arrival of the bull in Germany, once more urging him to take action against Luther who, it said, 'favours the Bohemians [Hussites] and the Turks, deplores the punishment of heretics, spurns the writings of the holy doctors [a title given to the most illustrious theologians in the Church's history], the decrees of ecumenical councils and the ordinances of the Roman pontiffs . . . We cannot suffer the scabby sheep longer to infect the flock.'[11]

This ugly image did nothing to persuade the elector. He knew, for instance, that Luther had no wish to see the Turks advance further.[12] So he continued doggedly to argue that the only way of resolving Luther's case was for a full hearing over his charges against the Catholic Church before an assembly of German representatives. To that end, he persuaded Luther to attend a further (fruitless) meeting with Miltitz, the papal envoy to the Saxon court. Behind the scenes, though, the elector is reported to have shown his contempt for the Pope's shoddy reply to the issues Luther raised. In what was taken to be a dig at the mention of a wild boar in the vineyard in *Exsurge Domine*, Friedrich is said to have sent his professor a gift of venison.

As for Luther himself, he had been hearing leaks about the bull for so long now that he could hardly be surprised at its contents.

His public line had been that, until he saw the text with his own eyes, complete with 'the original lead and wax, string, signature and seal', he refused to treat any of the rumours as genuine.[13] On 10 October, finally, he had the text in front of him of his Church's official response. He wasn't impressed. Having read it, he hit out defiantly the next day in a letter to Spalatin, attacking those he labelled as 'Roman monsters'. 'If they win,' he wrote, 'it is all over with faith and the Church . . . With my whole heart I rejoice that the noblest reason I can imagine has brought this evil to my door; I am not worthy of such holy vexation.'[14]

'It is all over with faith and the Church' may just be the angry phrase of a genuinely disappointed Luther in the heat of the moment, but it also hints at a growing despair that the Roman Catholic Church could ever be reformed. He ended his own epistle to Spalatin with the words, 'farewell and pray for me'.[15] Any outward show of fear was mitigated by an inward belief that what was happening to him was proof that God was challenging him to be truthful. Every blunt weapon used against him served only to increase his defiance and his disregard of the possibility of death.

His own formal reply to Rome's ultimatum came with *Against the Execrable Bull of the Antichrist*. You can but smile at his recklessness in choosing such a title. Rather than the Pope, however, Johann Eck was his main target: 'that man of lies, dissimulation, errors and heresy'. Eck's success at Leipzig still rankled with Luther. 'Where Eck is the apostle, there one should find the kingdom of the Antichrist.'

When it came to Leo, Luther was more circumspect, and he adopted a curious device. After all the rumours and counter-rumours about excommunication, he wrote, he had chosen to believe that the Pope could not possibly have penned the bull himself, and that it had been issued in his name without his approval.[16] It allowed him then to heap scorn on the text itself without being seen to attack Leo. 'I can distinguish', he wrote, 'between inane paper and the omnipotent Word of God . . . You impious and insensate papists, write soberly if you want to write.'

That final piece of advice was hardly one he followed himself. Of course, Leo would take the attacks in the text personally. Luther was treating him as if he were a gullible idiot, manipulated and seduced by those around him. Such an approach to the man who, by the standard practice of the time, held Luther's life in his hands was either madness or the righteous anger of one who had been pushed to his very limits. There was a streak of – at the very least – obstinacy in Luther's willingness to trade insults. He himself had been so attacked in print, yet refused to concede a single point, despite all the barbs thrown in his direction. Why should he think that such rhetoric would work with anyone else?

Perhaps he didn't. Perhaps he was just letting off steam. Now he surely knew that Leo was a lost cause. He would have to rely on the German princes to protect him.

Some among their number inevitably took *Exsurge Domine* rather more seriously than Luther, or Elector Friedrich. Emperor Charles was one. He received the papal emissary, Aleander, at his court in Antwerp, and followed the bull's instruction to the letter, ordering that copies of Luther's books circulating in the Low Countries be seized and burned in Louvain on 8 October and Liege on 17 October. These were Charles's hereditary domains and – unlike in the empire – his authority was total.

To be effective, though, such a campaign needed to extend throughout the German lands where Luther was a popular hero. That would require the support of princes, and so it was to them that Charles next turned. Aleander accompanied the imperial party from Antwerp to Cologne, en route for the coronation at Aachen, but any hopes he nurtured of a positive response quickly evaporated. Among the first they met was Prince Albrecht, Archbishop-Elector of Mainz, imperial voter and the very cleric who had first drawn Rome's attention to the Ninety-Five Theses.

He was hesitant in the extreme about joining in any book-burning frenzy.

Albrecht's natural instincts tended towards mild reform, encouraged by his correspondence with Erasmus. He was nervous, too, of how the public might react to an attack on Luther. As he dithered, Aleander muttered darkly about 'radical Lutherans' in the archbishop-elector's circle who regarded Luther 'like a friend'.[17]

Finally, though, the wavering Albrecht summoned up his courage and ordered a public bonfire of Luther's books in Mainz, only to see it halted by just the sort of popular insurrection he had feared. The official charged with lighting the flames was so worried about the reaction of the crowd that had gathered in protest that he sought their consent before starting the fire. They refused, he reported back to the archbishop, on the grounds that Luther's works had not been lawfully condemned. He did not proceed.

At Aleander's insistence, a more modest burning took place in his presence on 29 November, when the much smaller crowd present pelted him with stones. He left in fear of his life. Germany was turning on Rome.

Primary works

The papal bull threatening excommunication came in the midst of a year of extraordinary productivity for Luther. He worked ever more furiously, even manically. Over the course of twelve months in 1520, he did more to lay the practical basis for a Church to his liking than at any other time. 'When I am angry,' he was later to remark in a *Table Talk*, 'leave me in peace and let me take a break. For things are constantly coming across my path which upset me. This same thing happens to others, I believe. Therefore, you should give an angry man room.'[18] In the heightened circumstances of 1520, there was no room, no time for peaceful contemplation and compromise. Instead, in anger, he took up his quill as his weapon to lay out his programme, not so much for reforming Catholicism but for a reformed Christianity.

The tracts he authored over this period are usually referred to as his 'primary works'. If his theology of the nature of God and Jesus Christ, and the means of salvation, had already matured in his lectures on the Psalms and Paul, then it was in these texts from 1520 that he began to work through the consequences of those earlier revelations, addressing the question of whether they could ever be accommodated within the Catholic Church, something he now was starting to doubt.

The result was a recipe for radical change, but Luther would not have recognised such a description. Though cast by his critics as one keen to sweep away everything that made the Church what it was, he preferred to describe himself as attempting to go back (rather than forward) to the essence of Christianity found in the Bible and in the practice of the early Christians. 'He was driven by some spirit,' is how Melanchthon described Luther in 1520.[19]

First to be published, in May, was Luther's *Sermon on Good Works*. Written in German and structured around the Ten Commandments, it aimed to clear away any confusion around one of his key theological propositions, 'justification by faith'. If, as Luther argued, salvation could not be earned, but instead was a matter entirely down to God, beyond human endeavour, then the question arose as to whether there was any point any more in doing 'good works'.

Luther had already made plain his distaste for some of the more extreme outpourings of piety. In the *Sermon*, he clarified his position on the staples of late medieval religiosity. Practices such as praying, fasting, marking the holy days and almsgiving to the poor, all of which had a scriptural basis, should continue to be part of the daily life of Catholics. They must be undertaken, however, for themselves, not in the expectation of storing up rewards in heaven. That was a distortion of the Christian message.

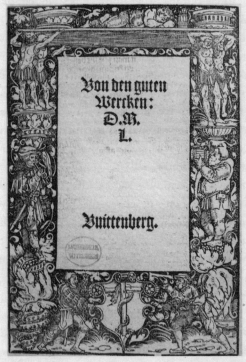

Von den guten
Wercken:
D.M.
L.

Vuittenberg.

Luther's *Sermon on Good Works*, part of an extraordinary output
of tracts in 1520. It was reprinted eight times in seven months.

'The first thing to understand', he advised, 'is that no work is
good except as God has commanded it, just as nothing is sin
unless God has forbidden it.'[20] For Luther, faith in God was always
the starting point, not the rules of the Church. Good works did
not carry an individual towards faith. Neither did they bring
anyone closer to God. It was the other way round. Out of faith
arose good works, just as out of health, the body can function.

Sermon on Good Works proved every bit as popular as his
previous writings. It was reprinted eight times before the end of
that year, six in the next.

The Papacy at Rome

The following month – just as in Rome the document threatening him with excommunication was signed by Pope Leo – Luther issued *On the Papacy at Rome against the Famous Romanist at Leipzig*. Usually known as *The Papacy at Rome*, it was written in German in just two weeks and reworked some of the arguments that Luther had already deployed, not entirely successfully, at Leipzig.

Ostensibly, 'the famous Romanist at Leipzig' was the Franciscan Augustin von Alveldt, a professor of scripture at Leipzig University who, like many other loyal theologians at Church institutions, had been busy writing papers that challenged Luther.[21] By describing him as 'the celebrated Romanist in Leipzig', massively overstating his importance, Luther wanted to belittle him. And behind Alveldt, of course, stood another 'Romanist at Leipzig', Johann Eck.

The tract was Luther's fullest attack yet on the purpose of the papacy. Christian Europe did not require a pope at all, he argued. The Church could function perfectly well as 'an assembly of hearts in one faith', present not in grand palaces in Rome, but where believers lived and worked.[22] He was describing a congregational model of Church rather than a clerical one. No hierarchy was needed, he said, because the only visible signs of the Church were the sacraments of baptism and eucharist, along with the preaching of the gospel.

True to his rule of '*sola scriptura*', this 'assembly of hearts' had its basis in a gospel passage. In Matthew, Jesus had said that 'where two or three meet in my name, I shall be there with them'.[23] Fidelity to those words, Luther claimed, placed Jesus Christ at the head of the Church, rather than the Pope, but he was not yet ready to explain how such a principle might be reflected structurally in the practice of the Church.

This led to some muddled thinking. He still, for example, supported the notion of leadership. In a regional context, that might be a bishop, but it could just as well be someone with a different title. On a bigger scale, though, the leader's task was, in Luther's words, to 'instil life. On earth there can be no head of spiritual Christendom other than Christ alone.'[24]

It left room, in practical terms, for the Pope, but not as much as recent incumbents had occupied. Indeed, the title of the tract, *The Papacy at Rome*, might be taken as implying that the Pope's role was limited to being Bishop of Rome, rather than the universal jurisdiction claimed for him. But again, there was muddle. For having apparently wished the Pope on the people of Rome, Luther went on to make public his hitherto private remarks that the papacy was the Antichrist. Backing up his point, as ever, with Scripture, he went on to contrast the Roman Pope with the high priests of Israel in the Old Testament. 'The old high priest was not allowed to own any piece of Israel's land but lived instead from contributions by the people. Why then is the pope intent on possessing the whole world? Why does he ordain and dismiss as he pleases every ruler as if the papal court were the Antichrist?'[25]

If this was his reform programme for the papacy, then it was an ambitious one. To give voice to it shows a Luther no longer willing to hold anything back for fear of the damage it might cause. Realising that the odds of Rome drawing back from excommunicating him were slim, he could evidently see no advantage in self-censorship to keep doors open that were already most likely firmly shut.

Appeal to the Christian Nobility of the German Nation

Authors often claim that one book begets the next: a thought, dilemma or character touched on briefly in one novel moves centre stage in the writing project that follows. The same process was at play with Luther in 1520. If the Pope was all but a lost cause, as *The Papacy at Rome* appeared to conclude, then as a consequence Luther needed to put some backbone into German princes and people if they were to step into the space left empty. And so, after a gap of just two months, he produced a tract on the role of temporal rulers in *Appeal to the Christian Nobility of the German Nation*.

Another unflinching epistle written in great haste, it combined religious conviction with fervent politics, a cocktail that made *Appeal* explosive. 'The time to speak out has come,' he urged in a call to action that included Emperor Charles, yet to be crowned at Aachen as Luther was writing.[26] The young king could, he proposed, be the man to cleanse the Church. It would require him to demolish the three 'walls' that 'Romanists' had erected.

The first two of the three walls he listed were already familiar from his previous writings: the Church's claim that only the successors of Saint Peter could interpret the Scriptures; and its insistence that only a pope could summon a general council. They were given new urgency, however, by being linked to a third, the radical proposition that the authority of the clergy over the laity should be abolished.

The standard medieval view (and one that persisted in Catholicism for many centuries afterwards) was that the laity were in almost all matters second-class citizens compared to the clergy. That, Luther argued, could not continue. Lay leaders, and specifically the emperor and the German princes, should not, he urged, feel they were disqualified from the task of judging Rome's inadequacies because they were not clerics. He might have added that he was empowering them to judge his own case, instead of leaving it to clerics in Rome.

Attacking the clerical culture of the Church was nothing new. The same proposition had been at the core of the Lollards' 'Twelve Conclusions'. They were specifically anti-ordination. But what

Luther was really building on were his own arguments in *The Papacy at Rome*. While blunt about how the current set-up was failing, that tract had failed to provide any real picture of how a reformed organisation might look. Here in *Appeal*, he tackled that shortcoming.

Among his proposals was one of his most enduring concepts – the priesthood of all baptised believers. 'As for the unction by a pope or a bishop, tonsure, ordination, consecration, and clothes differing from those of laymen – all this may make a hypocrite or an anointed puppet, but never a Christian or a spiritual man. Thus we are all consecrated as priests by baptism, as Saint Peter says: "Ye are a royal priesthood, a holy nation" (1 Peter 2:9); and in the Book of Revelations: "and hast made us unto our God (by Thy blood) kings and priests" (Rev. 10).'[27]

It was not, Luther believed, in the gift of the Pope or a bishop, those charged in the Catholic Church with ordaining priests, to create a superior being to anyone else. 'For, if we had not a higher consecration in us than pope or bishop can give, no priest could ever be made by the consecration of pope or bishop, nor could he say the mass, or preach, or absolve. Therefore the bishop's consecration is just as if in the name of the whole congregation he took one person out of the community, each member of which has equal power, and commanded him to exercise this power for the rest; in the same way as if ten brothers, co-heirs as king's sons, were to choose one from among them to rule over their inheritance, they would all of them still remain kings and have equal power, although one is ordered to govern. And to put the matter even more plainly, if a little company of pious Christian laymen were taken prisoners and carried away to a desert, and had not among them a priest consecrated by a bishop, and were there to agree to elect one of them, born in wedlock or not, and were to order him to baptise, to celebrate the mass, to absolve, and to preach, this man would as truly be a priest, as if all the bishops and all the popes had consecrated him. That is why [as Catholicism teaches] in cases of necessity every man can baptise and absolve, which would not be possible if we were not all priests.'[28]

Yet this fundamental equality before God had, he charged, been banished by the clerical culture of the Church. 'This great grace and virtue of baptism and of the Christian estate they have quite destroyed and made us forget by their ecclesiastical law. In this way the Christians used to choose their bishops and priests out of the community; these being afterwards confirmed by other bishops, without the pomp that now prevails.' In which context he quoted the example of the early Church, where bishops were elected by their communities.[29]

The authority that the medieval world gave to those – like himself – who had been ordained was misplaced, Luther said. He was just a man seeking salvation like any other man. His choice to live as a monk did not make him superior. He quoted Paul on the duty of the 'spiritual person', namely 'to judge all things and be judged by no one'.[30]

It was as if Luther was determined to tear down the structure of the Catholic Church brick by brick. The implications of his remarks on priesthood for the sacraments, which could only be conducted according to Catholic law, by ordained priests, was something that he would turn to later.

For now, Luther wanted to extend his destruction of the clerical–lay divide with a corresponding reform of monasticism that would reduce the number of religious orders by amalgamating them to purify their mission and direct their focus on to salvation. 'Let no more mendicant [supported by begging and gifts, rather than by lands they own] monasteries be built! God help us! There are too many as it is. Would to God they were all abolished, or at least made over to two or three orders! . . . Therefore my advice is that ten, or as many as may be required, be put together and made into one, which one, sufficiently provided for, need not beg. It is of much more importance to consider what is necessary for the salvation of the common people, than what Saint Francis, or Saint Dominic, or Saint Augustine [all the inspiration for mendicant orders] laid down, especially since things have not turned out as they expected.'[31]

And Luther was not yet done. He also proposed that priests be allowed to marry. 'We see how many a poor priest is encumbered with a woman and children and burdened in his conscience, and no one does anything to help him, though he might very well be helped. I will . . . open my mouth freely, let it vex popes and bishops or whoever it may be . . . As Saint Paul plainly says [in his Letter to Titus], and this minister should not be forced to live without a lawful wife.'[32]

Here Luther was confronting head on one of the most challenging issues in the Catholic Church at his time. The demand that men effectively should have two vocations – one to the priesthood and another to celibacy – had no clear scriptural basis,[33] and though there had long been a cult of virginity for the leaders of the Church, clerical celibacy was a man-made rule, in force since 1139 and the Second Lateran Council. Some four hundred years later, as Luther and his readers well knew, it was still being widely ignored by some – including popes.

'What nonsense is it', Luther would later exclaim, 'that marriage, which is a natural right, should be forbidden and condemned. It is the same thing as if eating, drinking, sleeping were forbidden. That would be strange! For what God has created and ordained is not within our power to exclude or forbid. We cannot be God's master.'[34] Once again the Church was making rules by claiming an authority that it did not have.

Such plain talking attracted his fellow Germans. Some four thousand copies of the *Appeal* went within days of its appearance on 18 August. Unsurprisingly, given how far-reaching were the changes it proposed, even some of Luther's inner core of supporters were alarmed by its content and its apparent wish to dismantle the Catholic world they knew. His Augustinian superior, Johann Lang, was one who wrote urging Luther to reconsider. Luther, though, was unrepentant. 'For myself, I declare that I owe the pope no more obedience than I owe the true Antichrist.'[35]

Neither Luther nor his critics could have anticipated the impact that this tract was to have in subsequent decades and centuries. If believers were essentially the same in the eyes of God, then Luther was shifting the whole emphasis of social organisation from the communal, with its hierarchies and laws, towards the individual, unrestrained by structures and institutions. It was a thought that was to have a profound influence on the development of ideas of human liberty, even human rights, once medieval Catholicism's grip on Europe had been loosened by the Reformation.

The Babylonian Captivity

The papal bull threatening Luther with excommunication had still not arrived in Germany when, in September, Luther produced *The Babylonian Captivity*. Its title alluded to the destruction of the Jewish Temple in 587 BCE, when King Nebuchadnezzar carried off the Jews into exile in Mesopotamia. The papacy had done much the same, Luther suggested, kidnapping and enslaving the Church by imposing its own rules in place of God's.

In his opening remarks, he attempted to explain his sudden burst of literary and theological energy. 'I am compelled to become more learned day by day, since so many great masters vie with each other in urging me on and giving me practice.'[36] He portrays himself as fending off enemies on all sides. And as he fought back, the blows he struck cut ever deeper. *The Babylonian Captivity* was the most challenging of this remarkable year's radical tracts, for it went further yet than *Appeal* in upending familiar worship and the practice of the faith. The most radical measure it proposed was to reduce the seven sacraments to three, or possibly two. Baptism, eucharist and penance survived (the final one only just), while confirmation, marriage, holy orders and extreme unction (the anointing of the sick and dying) were downgraded. 'The breach is irreparable,' said Erasmus when he heard what was contained in *The Babylonian Captivity*.[37] Luther had gone beyond anything Europe's other famous reformer would contemplate.

Sacraments – from the Latin word that means 'sign of the sacred' – were, and remain in Catholicism, moments when believers can encounter God's presence. As such they are the bridges that, potentially, allow the faithful to approach the divine, and are the cornerstones of the liturgical life of the Church. Their importance is perhaps best illustrated by the familiar phrase that attendance at the eucharist is receiving spiritual nourishment in the form of 'the bread of life'. These are the moments, therefore, that focus thoughts on salvation.

So Luther's desire to address their place in the life of the Church was understandable. His reservations about the degree to which those attending the sacraments can experience God is, likewise, predictable. For Luther, there was always a part of God that remained mysterious, unknowable. To claim too great a revelation around the sacraments cut across his own strongly held beliefs about the nature of God. Yet the sacraments were also held up in Catholicism as signs and instances of God's grace, and the role of God's grace was central to 'justification by faith'. It was only through faith – *sola fide* – following the Scriptures and God's grace that any individual could hope to be saved. And from that followed a conviction that, if the sacraments were to be presented as channels of God's grace, then they had to justify that billing. To which end, in *The Babylonian Captivity*, Luther applied a set of rigorous scriptural tests. Any sacrament worthy of the name must: (1) be instituted by Jesus in the gospels; (2) help each believer to know God better; and (3) be free from human attempts to manipulate it.

Extreme unction was dismissed because it rested on the authority of something the apostles did, rather than Jesus, and then only as mentioned in the Epistle of James, which Luther dismissed as a text 'not worthy of the apostolic spirit' next to the writings of Paul and Peter. In *Appeal*, he had already set out his objections to the elevation of men to the special caste of priests by dint of ordination (holy orders) by the Pope or bishops. Here, he wrote that this sacrament had been 'invented by the Church of the Pope. It not only has no promise of grace anywhere declared [in Scripture] but not a word is said about it in the New Testament.' It was not, he added, that he no longer wanted some form of ordination of priests – or pastors as he increasingly referred to them – but rather that he saw it as a 'human invention', to be treated as such, rather than as a 'sacred thing'.[38]

About confirmation – when a young person, usually on the cusp of adulthood, makes a firm commitment to the Church – Luther was especially savage. Though the laying on of hands by a bishop on each candidate mirrored Jesus' healing actions in the gospels, he concluded it was something that had been 'invented in order to regulate the duties of the bishops that they may not be entirely without work in the Church'.[39] In other words, its purpose was simply to give senior clerics something to do.

And marriage? Luther endorsed marriage as a human institution, although rather formally and coolly, but proposed that its regulation was a matter for the civil authorities because, again, he could find no basis in Scripture for it being regarded as a sacrament. 'We nowhere read that he who marries a wife will receive any grace from God; neither is there in matrimony any sign of divine institution; nor do we read that it was appointed of God to be a sign of anything.'[40]

What he was proposing was a cull. The consequence was that the status and role of the clergy, particularly in intervening between individual believers and God, was much reduced, and a greater equality of believers promoted. Nowhere is that claim of a duty to intervene seen more in the Catholic Church than in the sacrament of penance – usually known as confession. The priest can absolve a penitent of his or her sins in God's name, a power unambiguously given to the apostles by Jesus in the gospels. As He breathed the Holy Spirit into them after the resurrection, He had said to them: 'those whose sins you forgive, they are forgiven; those whose sins you retain, they are retained.'[41]

Confession had been especially significant for Luther in his days in the monastery at Erfurt, where he had been struggling under the guidance of his confessor, Staupitz, to banish his own sense of *Anfechtung*. And it was to remain a part of his life. He always, for example, retained a personal confessor. In his *Table Talk* of July 1539, he refers fondly to 'Doctor Pomeranus', his personal confessor; otherwise known as Johannes Bugenhagen, later the long-serving pastor of the Stadtkirche in Wittenberg, given his nickname because he came from his native Duchy of Pomerania to seek out Luther after reading *The Babylonian Captivity*.[42]

So penance passed the test, but Luther articulated his fierce objections to the priest-confessor making rulings on particular sins that were based on the tradition of the Church, rather than on God's word as recorded in the Scriptures. And he went further. Penitents could, he advised, confess their sins 'in the presence of any brother'. One more role of the clergy was being removed.[43]

Baptism and eucharist were the two sacraments that survived intact, though even here Luther had strong words to offer. There were already those reformers, he reported, advocating adult baptism – on the basis that a commitment to God is something that requires maturity of years. This issue was to involve Luther in great controversy with his own followers soon afterwards. Such a concession, he warned, would be open to abuse, spiritual and financial. Adult baptism would be 'sold no cheaper than parchments [indulgencies] are now'.[44] He reiterated in ringing tones the importance of baptism as soon as possible after birth – as his own had been – to cleanse the infant from the stain of original sin and usher them into the priesthood of all baptised believers 'uninjured and uncontaminated by the devices of men'. It must be, he insisted, 'free to men of every class and to all nations'.[45]

If he was recommending that baptism continue unaltered, Luther wanted reform in the Church's understanding of the eucharist – or 'the bread' as he called it, 'the first of all sacraments'. Catholicism had (and has) a particular view on the eucharist, a doctrine known as transubstantiation, developed under Scholasticism, and a good example of that school of thought's habit of tying itself up in the sort of subtle philosophical knots that, as Luther noted, are regarded by the laity as 'truly ridiculous'. 'Angels dancing on pinheads' is a phrase still heard in Catholic circles to describe the phenomenon.

What transubstantiation taught – 'a portentous word', Luther remarked, 'and a dream indeed'[46] – was that the bread and wine used at communion, in memory of Jesus' actions at the Last Supper, remained unaltered in their outward form – curiously called their 'accidents' – but simultaneously altered into the body and blood of Christ in a manner that surpasses human understanding and is a mystery known only to God. Luther judged such an opaque formula as guilty of placing believers 'in peril of idolatry', and instead proposed a typically simpler concept. 'There were real bread and real wine in which were the real flesh and real blood of Christ.'[47]

Much ink was subsequently spent by his opponents in debating how this description departed from transubstantiation, but with little everyday impact on believers. More tangible was to be the debate that later unfurled between Luther and others who shared his reforming zeal, over whether the 'real presence', as his theory was tagged, was itself too elaborate, and the bread and wine should be taken only as symbols.

Of more immediate importance – because it caused so much dispute – were Luther's words on the distribution of the euchar- ist. He damned as a 'monstrous perversion' the Catholic habit of reserving the wine at communion for clergy. The congregation – as a lower status group – received only the bread.[48] Luther demanded that this 'act of impiety and tyranny' be abolished.[49]

The Babylonian Captivity was Luther's strongest statement yet of dissent from Church practice and teaching. And it was the most passionate statement of belief he had made so far. 'I may be wrong on indulgences, but as to the need for faith in the sacra- ments,' he said, 'I will die before I recant.'[50]

The Freedom of the Christian Man

By the time his final work of 1520 appeared in November, Luther had received Rome's verdict. *The Freedom of the Christian Man* was therefore shaped by the imminence of excommunication. In its pages, he moved from dread to welcoming his censure as a new beginning, but also struggling with the practical consequences that would arise. First, though, there were formalities to get out of the way. Finally honouring his pledge, made variously to Miltitz, Linck and others, to reassure Leo that none of this dispute was personal, Luther addressed himself directly to the Pope in an attached letter, included as a foreword to the main text in printed versions. The wording he chose, however, couldn't have been further from what had been requested of him. In both Latin and German, Luther informed Leo that he had been misled by his advisors, notably Johann Eck. 'I look upon you less as Leo the Lion,' he wrote, 'than as Daniel in the lions' den at Babylon . . . Do not think, Father Leo, that when I scathe this seat of pesti- lence [the papal curia, or court of advisors], I am inveighing against your person.'[51] Like Saint Paul – from whom he drew so much – Luther believed that sharp, harsh words were sometimes necessary to shake those around him out of their complacency, whatever their rank or claimed authority. As Duke Georg (not a natural ally) noted of Luther and his circle, 'they do say what they really mean'.[52]

In such a spirit, Luther set about dismantling Leo's claim to be 'vicar of Christ', a title the papacy continues to employ to this day. 'A person is a vicar only when the superior is absent,' he wrote, and since Christ is not absent, then anyone claiming to be His vicar is 'an Antichrist and idol'. That was Leo put in his place.

The text of the treatise on Christian liberty itself represented a further, more detailed attempt to reach a definitive answer on good works. 'Justification by faith', after all, might plausibly be taken as a licence for an immoral, selfish existence, undertaken in the belief that nothing would have any impact on God's final judgement. And, in such a scenario, there would no longer be laws, structures or even morality.

'If the touch of Christ was healing,' Luther wrote, 'how much more does that most tender touch in the Spirit, that absorption in the Word convey to the soul all the qualities of the Word, so that it becomes trustworthy, peaceable, free, full of every good, a true child of God. From this we see very easily why faith can do so much, and no good work is like unto it, for no good work comes from God's Word like faith. No good work can be within the soul, but the Word and faith reign there. What the Word is that the soul is, as iron becomes fire-red through union with the flame. Plainly then faith is enough for the Christian man. He has no need for works to be made just. Then he is free from the law.'

Luther attacked those who questioned how faith could exist without good works by quoting a paradox – that the Christian was simultaneously utterly free *and* slave to all. The freedom of the Christian man, of the treatise's title, came from Jesus' sacrifice of 'His body and His very self' on the cross of Calvary. By this unparalleled act of love for humankind, Luther said, Jesus had performed a 'good work' so unique that it vanquished sin for ever. Nothing more could be required of humankind.

Yet, he still argued that, even if there was no requirement, the appropriate response to such an act of love as Jesus' was to mirror it in every human interaction. 'What Christ has is the property of the believing soul. What the soul has becomes the property of Christ.'[53] It was, after all, the oldest of all religious instructions, found in all faiths, to love your neighbour as yourself. 'Good works', Luther wrote, 'do not make a good man, but a good man does good works.'[54]

Taking up explicitly the notion of the good neighbour, he explained: 'When God in His sheer mercy and without any merit of mine has given me such unspeakable riches, shall I not then freely, joyously, wholeheartedly, unprompted do everything that I know will please Him? I will give myself as a sort of Christ to my neighbour as Christ gave Himself to me.'

And what exactly is that self-giving to consist of? Luther prescribed following the Ten Commandments (with which he himself had previously struggled) as a way of destroying pride, and therefore each individual humbling themselves before God. Only then could the door be opened to His transforming grace.

'I must even take to myself the sins of others as Christ took mine to Himself. Thus we see that the Christian man lives not to himself but to Christ and his neighbour through love. By faith, he rises above himself to God, and from God goes below himself in love, and remains always in God and in love.'

It was a powerful argument for grace, infused with a poetry that sits incongruously alongside Luther's use elsewhere of vulgar phrases. But even if the language was pleasing on the ear, and struck a chord in the heart, none of it was easy to take on board, as Luther subsequently admitted in a *Table Talk*. He had struggled and tortured himself in the monastery before accepting it. 'It is difficult for a person to believe that God is gracious to him. The human heart cannot grasp it.'[55]

Luther was approaching a final position, but there was still some distance to cover. The definition he provided of how to live out faith was in many aspects a description of a friar's routine, yet he had already voiced his doubts about monkish vows that elevated those who took them above others who didn't. And where did living like a monk leave the 'priesthood of all believers' that he had championed?

His solution was to describe a group of what he called 'true Christians' (later 'true believers'),[56] small in number in that moment, who lived guided by the Scriptures and according to the belief that salvation came only with faith. At present, he said, this group was hidden within a larger structure of an institutional Church that was itself in league with the devil. They were the equivalent of an underground cell, or even of the first Christians, hiding in the catacombs of Ancient Rome. What was needed, he said, was the sort of radical reform he had laid out throughout 1520, so that this hidden group of 'true Christians' could emerge into the daylight and guide the Church forward.

He was proposing a whole new leadership for the Church, with the 'true Christians' in the forefront as preachers, rather than the clerical rule-makers found in the current Church hierarchy. They would be ministers of the Word, exploring and explaining the 'mysteries of God' rather than controlling priests, friars and monks. It was a challenging vision, certainly idealistic, and apparently with no immediate prospect of being realised.

Neither was it one likely to appeal to the German princes who were protecting Luther from Rome. They were acutely aware of the level of popular resentment already in their lands. The last thing they wanted was for Luther to smash down the Church, which, for all its faults, had for centuries provided some form of social coherence and cement, and put in its place a radical experiment that sounded like a free-for-all. Yet Luther was now more convinced than ever before that such an outcome was imminent. On 15 December 1520, he wrote to Spalatin: 'the papacy, until now seemingly invincible, may even be rooted out beyond all hope.'[57]

That adrenalin was still pumping through his veins when he undertook a famous act of defiance on the morning of 10 December 1520, in Wittenberg. Luther, Melanchthon and a party of students from the university gathered outside the Elster Gate, the eastern entrance into the walled town, close to the Black Cloister. On the spot where the clothing and bed linen of those who had died of contagious diseases was usually burned,[58] they threw on to the flames copies of Exsurge Domine. Luther was said to be especially angry at the news of a burning of his own books in Leipzig, scene of his head-to-head with Eck. When the fire needed feeding, the crowd piled on a volume of canon law and writings by Eck and Hieronymus Emser, once a supporter but now secretary to Duke Georg and another vocal critic of reform. Luther reported his actions to Spalatin the same day, justifying them on the basis that they showed 'the papal arsonists that it does not take too much effort to burn books they cannot even refute'.[59]

He might have added that this gesture of defiance was made in the knowledge of the fall-out that would follow. Quite how far that knowledge stretched is debatable. For some this is another alternative date for the start of the Reformation. Richard Holloway, retired Anglican bishop, has written, 'he [Luther] burned more than a papal bull that day. He burned the bridges that bound him to the Catholic Church and started an international revolt described by historians as the Reformation.'[60]

CHAPTER EIGHT

The Diet of Worms: 'Here I Stand'

'I can do no other than what our dear God wills.'

Martin Luther, *Table Talk*[1]

Within a month of Martin Luther's very public act of defiance in burning copies of *Exsurge Domine* in Wittenberg, he was excommunicated by the Catholic Church. On 3 January 1521, Rome formally issued the decree censuring him, but once again there was a delay in sharing the news with Germany. It arose because of the delicacy of the political situation there, and the Pope's wish to exert as much influence as he could in fractious times. Leo was only too aware that his authority would be dented further if his definitive judgement on the heretic Luther was ignored on the ground.

For Luther, confirmation of his excommunication did not come as a surprise. For all his brave words, though, it was still a significant moment. He was now officially set apart from the Church of his baptism, the Church which he had served as a Hermit of Saint Augustine for fifteen years, and which he sincerely believed he was being guided by God to reform. Though he was never to express any regret at no longer being officially a Catholic, in some of his later tirades against 'papists' there was an unmissable note of nostalgia, at least for the 'externals' of the Catholic world he had inhabited for so long. 'The papists despised me, even though I wanted to go more than half way with them in external matters, such as vestments, celibacy, abstinence from meat, Lenten observances and so on.'[2]

Luther may have given every appearance of taking excommunication in his stride, but others were not quite so casual. By the terms of the decree, those who gave shelter to a heretic – including Elector Friedrich, Wittenberg university and, indeed, the whole of Saxony – were guilty by association, and potentially faced sanctions for their actions that ranged from the refusal of access to the sacraments right up to excommunication themselves.

In practice it was a hollow threat because Rome was in no position to act. Among the many obstacles to getting its own way was the next great event after Charles's coronation – the forthcoming gathering of the leaders of Germany with their new emperor. It was to take place from the end of January 1521 in Worms, a walled city that nestled in a bend of the Rhine, overshadowed by a vast four-towered, eleventh-century Romanesque cathedral.

Between his coronation and the meeting of the Diet, the emperor had, among other concerns, been grappling with what to do about Luther. Given his enthusiasm in the Low Countries for burning Luther's books, his own inclination cannot be in doubt, but first he needed to get the Diet to echo the Pope's condemnation of the professor from Wittenberg. That would be no easy task since the 'Luther problem' was now, in the mind of the German princes, part of a wider dispute over authority. Electors and dukes wanted to be the ones who determined what went on within their own territories. That would require a reduction in the interference by their youthful and foreign new emperor, as well as by Rome. Already they had shown that they were capable of using the case of Luther to further their overarching ambition.

For some, it wasn't only opportunism. They recognised their common ground with Luther. His *Appeal to the Christian Nobility of the German Nation* chimed with their own demands (as Luther had intended). It was now attracting popular support. In one reading, it provided a scriptural basis for German political and nationalist ambitions. There were those – Ulrich von Hutten and Franz von Sickingen in particular, with their knightly pretensions and private armies – who were keen to turn the defence of Luther into the pretext for reshaping Germany. The threat they posed was magnified in the emperor's calculations because, in that moment, he had few forces of his own close at hand and at his disposal.

The serious-minded but unimaginative nineteen-year-old Charles was torn. He was undeniably a man of strong faith. In 1556, so concerned did he become with salvation that he abdicated his various crowns and kingdoms to spend the last three years of his life in a monastery in Spain preparing himself to meet his maker.[3] So Aleander, the Pope's representative, could easily play on his natural predisposition to side with the papacy as part of the established late medieval European order (even if Leo had opposed Charles's election).

The nuncio was adamant that Luther be given no further opportunities to voice his heresy. The papal verdict of excommunication, said Aleander, should be the last word on the subject. The Diet of Worms, as an imperial body, he told the emperor, had no right to pronounce on a matter that was more properly in the Pope's domain.

Yet Elector Friedrich remained the most senior and respected among the German princes. Charles had consulted him as his 'uncle'[4] when both were in Cologne, when the Saxon prince reiterated his view that the problem with Luther was best solved by granting him a hearing in Germany. He was now pressing hard for that audience to take place at Worms.

This request, if granted, would mean that any decision on Luther by the diet would trump that of the Pope and the emperor. Next to this consideration, the bald fact that Leo had already excommunicated Luther appeared secondary. Friedrich even went so far as to abandon his usual affectation of neutrality on Luther by trying to explain away to the emperor the burning of the papal bull in Wittenberg. Luther had been gravely provoked, he wrote to Charles's advisors, and was responding in anger to hearing that his own books had been thrown on fires elsewhere in Germany. 'If now he has given tit for tat, I hope His Imperial Majesty will graciously overlook it.'[5]

BVLLA
Decimi Leonis, contra errores Martini
Lutheri, & sequacium.

Aſſiſtit Bulla a' dextris eius, in veſtitu

deaurato, circumamicta varietatibus.

Vide lector, opereprecium eſt. Adficie‑
ris, Cognoſces qualis paſtor
ſit Leo.

The Bull of Excommunication that formally censured Luther in January 1521 was issued by Rome in the build-up to the Diet of Worms.

Crucially, Friedrich had insisted that the imperial constitution – signed by Charles at his coronation – be amended to stipulate that no German could be taken for trial outside Germany, and none outlawed without the chance first to defend him- or herself. Charles's hands were thus tied.

There were also other influential voices urging the emperor to proceed cautiously when it came to Luther. Among those who had attended the imperial coronation in Aachen was Erasmus. He had also met Elector Friedrich. Despite already having declared the breach between Luther and Rome irreparable, in November 1520 Erasmus warned one of Charles's senior counsellors, Konrad Peutinger, that the 'tragedy' of Luther might end in a 'catastrophe [for] the Christian religion' unless the widely held popular resentments that he articulated were addressed.[6]

The threat of bloodshed, to which Erasmus alluded, was real. Behind the manoeuvrings of the rival courts, public sentiment in Germany was strongly on Luther's side, whether for his attacks on a bloated, corrupt, exploitative papacy, his proposals to reform Christianity, his articulation of German grievances, or his courage, as 'one of their own', a man of humble beginnings, who dared to speak up loudly about the disquiet that many peasants felt, even if it might cost him his life. Aleander has left a picture of how far Luther had captured the popular mood on the streets of Worms as the diet gathered. 'Martin is pictured with a halo and a dove above his head. The people kiss these pictures. Such a quantity have been sold that I was not able to obtain one . . . I cannot go out on the streets but the Germans put their hands on their swords and gnash their teeth at me.'[7]

In some of the crudely printed pictures that accompanied pamphlets of Luther's words, the friar's face was now often being replaced by that of Saint Paul. Another story said to be doing the rounds at the time in Worms held that some images of Luther, based on popular woodcuts, had a special quality that made them indestructible, even by the flames with which the Catholic Church wanted to kill off the heretic they portrayed. In a twist that reveals much about muddled thinking in popular religion, and its habit of ignoring fine theological distinctions, Luther was being turned into the equivalent of a Catholic saint.

Another woodcut from this period, this time by Hans Holbein the Younger, captures the simmering level of violence bubbling just below the surface of daily life. Holbein depicts Luther as the 'German Hercules', brutally wielding his club to smash the representatives of authority in the Catholic Church with the same determination with which the classical god Hercules had destroyed the many-headed hydra. With Aristotle, Aquinas, William of Occam and Peter Lombard already lying dead in a sea of blood at his feet, Holbein's Luther has Pope Leo suspended by a ring from his nose, as if leading him to his fate.[8]

Via Dolorosa

There had still not been a decision on whether to grant Luther a hearing when the diet officially opened on 27 January. There was plenty of other business to consider. The Ottoman forces were continuing their advance in southeastern Europe, and were soon to take Belgrade. The Pope continued to press unsuccessfully for donations to help him assemble a force to defend Christendom. There was, also, the usual round of patronages to dispense when the emperor was present – bishops to appoint, and ecclesiastical vacancies to be filled – all of which only served to focus minds on the anti-papal resentment felt throughout Germany, when so many of 'their' posts were still going to Italians more willing to contribute to Rome's coffers. The agenda also included items labelled 'complaints of the hard-pressed German nation'. While not directly about the Luther case, they were of a piece with the ugly mood of division and dissent he was riding in Germany. He could not be ignored.

Still Charles toyed with finding a way of avoiding Luther coming to Worms, but to do so he would have to mobilise sufficient of the German rulers to his cause. When he asked them on 19 February to approve an imperial edict excluding Luther as a heretic, the seventy or so princes, representing the component parts of his Empire, big and small, powerful and weak, collectively said no. Whatever their own faith convictions, and loyalty to the Pope who had excommunicated Luther, they knew that to deny the friar from Wittenberg a chance to defend himself might provide the spark to set off an uprising back home.

Only in March, having exhausted every other option, did Charles bow to the inevitable. He had first issued an invitation to Luther to come to Worms at the end of November 1520, but then withdrawn it, reinstated it and withdrawn it all over again, as his hopes rose and fell that the reformer's presence might somehow be avoided. Now the emperor finally accepted that it could not. He held out to Luther no prospect of a debate, rather only a public opportunity for recanting. As a sop, he addressed it, according to Luther's later recollection, with great courtesy to 'The Honourable, Our Dear Respected Doctor Martin Luther, Order of Augustine'. 'Even though I was excommunicated,' Luther noted, 'the Emperor called me honourable.'[9]

Safe passage was guaranteed. Since Luther was a heretic, there was effectively a bounty on his head, so anxious were the Catholic authorities to have him within their jurisdiction. He was therefore to be accompanied by an imperial herald (or guard) to ensure he came to no harm. It was a curiously contradictory journey across Germany. Outwardly, it had the look of a triumphant progress. In his former academic base at Erfurt, Luther was greeted by crowds lining the streets and climbing on to walls and rooftops to catch a glimpse of the friar who once walked their streets unnoticed. He stayed overnight in his former Augustinian cloister – which a few years earlier had accused him of destroying the good name of their order. At morning mass, the heretic was invited to preach.

But Luther also knew from the example of Jan Hus just how little weight to give to imperial promises of protection. The emperor who had pledged to take care of Luther was the same emperor who, in the Low Countries, had ordered his books to be burned. Having already been excommunicated by the Pope, it must have been hard to shake off the sense that what lay ahead in Worms was a foregone conclusion, that the same fate suffered by Hus now awaited him. What sustained him in confronting his enemies was his zealous and strengthening belief that his true protector was not the emperor, or even the elector, but God. He was being guided from above in all he did. His fixation on the suffering of Jesus on the cross even led him to regard the road to Worms as his own Via Dolorosa, the path taken by Christ to Calvary. Like Jesus, his fate could not be lifted from his shoulders.[10]

There were, Luther later recalled in one of the longest of his *Table Talk* narratives, various staging posts – like the Stations of the Cross, you might say, that measure out Jesus' walk to Calvary – where he paused en route and where he might have been deflected. 'As we approached Weimar,' Luther remembered, 'people were crying out that Doctor Martin had already been condemned at Worms, along with his books. And that was true.[11] I knew that the Emperor's messengers had distributed an Imperial order to be posted in all cities that Doctor Martin Luther had been condemned by the Emperor. So then the Herald [Caspar Sturm] asked me: "Doctor, Sir, are you sure you want to go?" To that I answered: "Yes, as unfortunate as it is that I have been placed under the Bann [proclamation], and that it is published in all the cities, I will obey the imperial summons."'[12]

If he doubted, he did not let it show. Where many around him seemed to be perpetually in two minds, with several agendas at play at once, Luther remained calm and focused as he journeyed on. He attributed this first attempt to derail him to Prince Albrecht, who had already vacillated on his case and was to continue to do so. The Archbishop-Elector of Mainz was, Luther subsequently alleged, keen above all to avoid the whole messy business of a hearing at Worms. His solution was that Luther would fail to answer the summons.

Next, at Oppenheim, on 15 April, Luther's young admirer from Heidelberg, Martin Bucer, appeared to suggest that together they should take a diversion via Franz von Sickingen's castle at Ehrenburg. Bucer had been taken on as Sickingen's chaplain. His master and Ulrich von Hutten were involved in a murky plot that centred on the emperor's chaplain, Jean Glapion, a Franciscan from Flanders. Posing as a moderate cleric who simply wanted to find a way to avoid a bloodbath in Worms, Glapion had won round Sickingen and Hutten to a scheme to get Luther to Ehrenburg, where Glapion promised to broker a peace deal that required only the withdrawal of *The Babylonian Captivity*, regarded as the most offensive of the publications of the previous year.

It has been alleged that Glapion was a slippery character who had little interest in such mediation and instead planned to assassinate Luther once he had him in the castle. It would undoubtedly extricate his master, Emperor Charles, from the deadlock at the diet. But quite how that would have played out with his host, Sickingen, and his assembled private army, is not clear, and therefore makes this a dubious theory. No matter. Luther was not about to take any detours. He had a healthy suspicion about Glapion's motives – why couldn't the emperor's chaplain meet him once he had got to Worms? he asked Bucer. And so he pressed on.

One final station lay ahead. By Luther's account, a message came to him from Spalatin, on behalf of Elector Friedrich, who was already in Worms. It instructed him to stay away because the whole place was too dangerous.[13] 'But I answered the messenger: "if there were as many devils in Worms as chimneys on the roofs, I would nevertheless come there". Because I was not alarmed, I was not afraid. God can certainly make one so insensitive to danger.' He added, with the benefit of hindsight: 'I don't know if I would be that foolish today.'[14]

In contemporary correspondence with Spalatin (dated 14 April 1521) Luther was in an uncompromising frame of mind. He asserted that he would get to Worms despite being opposed 'by all the gates of hell and the powers of the air'.[15] The devil and his demons, it should be noted, were prominent in his mind as among those stalking him at every turn.

When it comes to Luther's arrival on 16 April in Worms, the echoes of Good Friday become confused with those of Palm Sunday. A crowd of around two thousand had gathered in great curiosity, keen to see in the flesh the individual about whom so many had been talking and quite a number had been reading. 'Everyone crowded in the streets,' the man himself recalled, 'and wanted to see the monk Martin Luther.'[16] He was carried into the city in a humble open cart, which had been supplied to him for the journey by Wittenberg town council. It was every bit as modest as Jesus' donkey on Palm Sunday.

There was a fanfare of trumpets from the towers of the cathedral – to Aleander's fury. One legend has it that a priest reached out to touch the hem of Luther's cowl as he entered the city, like the sick and bleeding woman who, in Luke's gospel, reaches out in the crowd to feel the hem of Jesus' cloak.[17]

The day after his arrival, Luther was summoned at 3 p.m. to a session of the diet, held in a small meeting room at the bishop's palace to deter the crowds who had made such a spectacle on the previous day. Aleander made a point of staying away, unwilling to breathe the same air as a heretic, but it was here that Luther finally came face to face with Emperor Charles.

The interrogation was performed by Johann von der Ecken, an official of the Archbishop-Elector of Trier, and one who had recently organised the burning of Luther's books in that city.

Pointing to a pile of twenty-two volumes on a windowsill, von der Ecken asked Luther if they were all his.

Was he echoing suggestions that had earlier been made by Erasmus and Aleander that Luther couldn't possibly have authored so many books in so short a time as was claimed? If so, he had seriously underestimated the furious energy that could only be assuaged by Luther angrily pouring out words.

'I would have answered immediately "yes",' Luther remembered in his *Table Talk*, 'but Doctor Hieronymous Schurf [a lawyer who had been asked to represent Luther by Elector Friedrich] cried out loudly from the assembly: "somebody should read out the titles to the books".' Von der Ecken accepted the objection and worked his way down twelve German titles and ten in Latin, before asking Luther again if they were his. He replied, yes. The next question was predictable. Did he want to recant them? This show trial promised to be all over in minutes if Luther responded with his customary directness.

Instead he did something out of character. Rather than allow himself to be provoked, he addressed the emperor directly, with every bit as much courtesy as the latter had shown him in inviting him to Worms. 'Most Merciful Emperor and Merciful Princes and Lords, this is a serious and grave matter [all this according to Luther's own recollection], I am not prepared to make a statement about the books at this time. I beg you will give me some time to reflect.'[18]

Had the reality of what he was about to do suddenly hit home, as once he had stumbled when about to say the words of consecration at his first ever mass, with his father in the congregation watching him? To refuse to recant meant signing his own death warrant. Or was he desperately casting around for a way to evade the careful stage-managing designed to stop him having his say? That was certainly Aleander's verdict when he heard the news that the emperor had granted Luther a twenty-four-hour recess.

Perhaps – like many others who came into Luther's presence – Charles was genuinely intrigued by the friar's evident sincerity, seriousness of purpose, and the sense he carried with him of having God in his shadow. Among those nobles in the room in Worms was the future Christian III, Duke of Schleswig-Holstein and King of Denmark. The impact Luther made on him was to inspire Christian, against his Catholic father's wishes, to bring the new faith to his lands, finally proclaiming Lutheranism the official religion of Schleswig-Holstein in 1528 and of Denmark in 1534.[19]

The adjournment granted by the emperor gave Luther time to think, to pray, to consult those around him, including Spalatin, and to summon up his courage. To stretch the analogy of the Passion narrative,[20] it was his equivalent of Jesus' agony in the Garden of Gethsemane, when He sweated 'great drops of blood' as He prayed that the burden of His death that lay ahead be lifted from Him.[21]

Many historians reject such a generous interpretation and insist that the clever Luther was keen only to consult his team and find a way to spin things out yet further by putting the onus back on his accusers. As in many such matters, the truth is grey. Both judgements contain an element of truth. While Luther was undeniably resourceful and aware of the wider ramifications of the argument he was having with Rome and its representatives, he was also unconcerned with saving his own skin, convinced as he was that he was doing God's business. In such a context, his request for a delay might best be read as him pausing, when under extreme stress, to take the time to be sure it was indeed God's voice he was hearing.

'Here I stand'

When Luther returned the next afternoon, he was ushered into a larger room, 'for everyone wanted to hear my answer'.[22] With the emperor and princes gathered before him, at six o'clock he was asked to respond to the previous day's question. First in German and then in Latin, he confirmed that, yes, the books were his, but added that he could not recant of them all at once because they fell into three distinct categories. And with those words, he created space enough to make a speech.

The first group, he went on, were 'books of instruction regarding holy Scripture', adding, 'I find nothing bad in them.' The second were 'lectures on Christian teaching'. To recant of these, when the opinions expressed were so widely shared, would, he said, be wrong. And the third were 'contentious books . . . in which I have quarrelled with the Pope and other opposition. To the extent that they contain objectionable material, I could certainly change them . . . If I am shown my error,' he said, 'I will be the first to throw my books on the fire.'[23] It was a backhanded apology that ended up sounding like a criticism of those who would destroy his writings with flames.

The quoted words come from Luther's own description of what transpired. In other records, arguably more trustworthy since they are based on transcripts, he went further and played on the fears of an uprising in the minds of his privileged audience. 'We must be sure,' he counselled, 'that those things we do to banish strife – if in doing so we undertake to condemn the Word of God – do not rather lead to a flood of unbearable evil. Then it might be that the government of this young, noble prince Charles would become sick unto death.'[24]

When von der Ecken pointed out that there were many in the Church who would dispute his interpretation of Scripture, Luther was unrepentant. In reply to von der Ecken's request that 'candidly and without horns' he should recant, Luther gave an uncompromising defence of all his books in words that are among his most famous utterances. 'I must stand by them,' is how he remembered his reply. 'I can do no other than what our dear God wills.'[25]

There are other versions of what he said. 'Unless I am convinced otherwise by evidence from Scripture or incontestable arguments,' is how the definitive account has it, 'I remain bound by the Scripture I have put forward. As long as my conscience is captive to the Word of God, I neither can nor will recant, since it is neither safe nor right to act against the conscience. God help me. Amen.'[26]

Neither option provides the phrase most often put by history on his defiant lips that day at Worms – 'Here I stand, I can do no other.' This form of words has traditionally been said to have first appeared in biographies written after his death. More recently, however, a very similar phrase has been found in a pamphlet printed in Wittenberg immediately after the diet.[27] That still doesn't place them in Luther's mouth at the crucial moment, but does narrow the time gap.

'Here I stand': did Luther say those words when he refused to recant at the Diet of Worms in 1521, before Emperor Charles and the German Princes? – from a 1577 woodcut.

Whatever the truth, as a remark it has endured in the popular memory thereafter because it was a rallying cry that neatly encapsulated his mood at that moment.[28] Some accounts also speak of members of the emperor's Spanish entourage shouting out at Luther in protest, 'To the fire! To the fire!'[29] but now it fell once again to the conflicted Charles to decide how to proceed. It was the emperor's turn to request – and grant himself – more time before giving an answer.

In private, he had one ready the next day. He met with some of the German princes to read aloud to them a brief text he had prepared, in French, in his own hand. It began by detailing his descent from Catholic emperors, kings and dukes who were faithful to the Church of Rome, and then stated his intention to follow in their footsteps. 'A single friar who goes counter to all Christianity for a thousand years must', he insisted, 'be wrong.' He pledged to stake his 'lands, friends, body, blood, life and soul' on saving Germany from 'the disgrace of heresy'.[30] Nevertheless, Luther would be allowed to travel home, he said, honouring the promise of safe conduct, but once in Wittenberg should expect to be pursued with as much gusto as the emperor could muster.

Significantly – and to Aleander's disquiet – there were no words of vindication in Charles's ruling for the Pope's damning judgement on Luther's views, but at least the emperor's mind was made up. Or was it? Despite having expressed himself with such finality, he then agreed to further efforts being made to persuade Luther to yield some ground. He may have been hoping that the threat of being made an outlaw in his own land would cause the friar to think again. If so, he had misjudged the personality and motivation of the man he had just heard speak so fearlessly to the diet.

A more practical explanation for the emperor's apparent mixed messages lies in the events that took place on the very night he had read out his planned text to the princes. Many of them would have left the room already worrying about the popular reaction back home to an imperial crusade to capture Luther. The next morning they woke to something that confirmed their worst fears. First light revealed that the town hall and various other public buildings in Worms had been daubed under cover of darkness with the *Bundschuh*, an image of a peasant shoe that had become the symbol of a series of intermittent localised popular uprisings in the Black Forest, Alsace and Rhine Valley areas of southwestern Germany from the 1490s onwards. Now the *Bundschuh* had found its way to Worms. Or been imported there, for the shoe symbol had been accompanied by a message. It threatened that four hundred armed knights were ready to punish anyone who harmed Luther.

This promise of violence was another manifestation of the public discontent across Germany that Luther's battle with Rome had encouraged and exacerbated. The core demands of the *Bundschuh* – the abolition of feudal dues and serfdom, greater availability of communal land, and a reduction in taxes paid to rulers – also embraced disquiet at the financial impositions of the Church. The spectacle of Luther being hauled over the coals by the ruling classes in Worms for having the temerity to challenge Rome had made a cause célèbre of him.

It was against this backdrop that Charles grasped at the suggestion that a committee of delegates should try one more time to reason with Luther. If only the whole thing could be fudged! So Richard von Greiffenklau zu Vollrads, the Archbishop-Elector of Trier, was given the task of winning Luther round to a compromise. He was more gracious in his questioning than his spokesman, von der Ecken, but no more successful. When Luther once more refused to back down, the archbishop asked him what should happen next. Luther quoted back at him a line from the Acts of the Apostles: 'you should leave these men alone and let them go. If this enterprise, this movement of theirs is of human origin, it will break up of its own accord, but if it does come from God, you will not only be unable to destroy them, but you might find yourself fighting against God.'[31]

Next up were Margrave Joachim the Elder, Elector of Brandenburg (who had allowed Tetzel to peddle indulgences in his lands), and Duke Georg, host of the Leipzig debate. 'I could endure everything – the pope, princes, especially the power of the Church, and would do only what I could, but I could not deviate from Holy Scripture,' Luther recalled telling the margrave. 'I could not change them because they were not mine, but Our Lord God's.' 'Is that how you are going to proceed, that you cannot deviate from Scripture,' the margrave replied. 'Yes, that is where I stand,' Luther confirmed.[32]

It is another version of the origin of the famous remark. This second interrogation, though, appears to have left a particularly sour taste in Luther's mouth. More than a decade later, when he mentioned the margrave and Duke Georg, he predicted with unusual vehemence, even by his own standards, that both would 'go straight to hell'.[33]

The princes were left to ponder their reaction. Elector Friedrich had told Spalatin that he believed, in front of the diet, Luther had spoken well, but had been too bold.[34] The senior German prince was in a bind. To continue to protect Luther would leave the elector in contempt of the diet, but to hand him over would be an almighty climbdown and, moreover, would offend against Friedrich's conscience. Though he was to remain a Catholic until his dying day, the elector recognised that Luther had posed questions that Rome, for all its fury and indignation, had never answered.

It took over a month for the emperor's final decision to be published. The Edict of Worms made outlaws of Luther and his followers. 'His books are to be eradicated from the memory of man.'[35] The delay in its appearance was significant. It allowed some room for manoeuvre. Many of the princes had already left

Worms when the emperor finally signed it on 26 May, including Friedrich (to get treatment for his gout) and others considered pro-Luther. For some of them, the delay raised questions that were never quite answered about the legality of the edict, and therefore their own obligation to enforce it. Had they been there, might they have continued to raise objections? Or was their absence a diplomatic way of allowing the edict to be passed, without voting for it? It was said that Friedrich was never sent a copy of the edict and hence could argue that he wasn't bound by it. Was this part of some deal to spare both the elector and the emperor an embarrassing clash? There is more than a hint of a behind-closed-doors deal.

The prisoner of Wartburg

If that were the case, then Luther – consciously or not – played along. On 26 April, nine days after the emperor had retired to make his decision, and a full month before the edict was signed, Luther left Worms at the elector's urging. He had been assured – indirectly as always – that Friedrich would give him shelter whatever happened. He appears not to have known exactly what form that shelter would take, though he realised that his excommunication and the soon-to-come Edict of Worms would mean it would differ materially from the situation before, when he could freely go about his business in Wittenberg, safe behind its walls. On 18 April he wrote to his painter friend, Lucas Cranach the Elder, warning him that he may dip out of view for a while.[36]

At first, on his journey home from Worms, Luther had the imperial herald in attendance, but after three days he dismissed him in a gesture that appears to have been part of some prearranged plan. Luther's party then travelled on unaccompanied for five days, stopping overnight at Hersfeld, where the local Benedictine abbot wined and dined him and extended an invitation to preach the sermon. Although he had promised to decline such requests, as part of the emperor's pledge of safe conduct, Luther accepted. 'I had not consented for the Word of God to be bound,' he told Spalatin in a letter.[37] Perhaps he also knew that he would not be gracing too many pulpits in the near future.

On 2 May, he seized the chance again, when it was offered, this time in Eisenach, the town where he had been a schoolboy and where his mother's relatives still lived. Further down the road to Wittenberg, while passing through the Thuringian forest of his childhood, Luther and his travelling companion, Nikolaus von Amsdorf, were intercepted by two horsemen. They brandished their bows to force the rest of the party to scatter. Luther was blindfolded and taken by a circuitous route to a castle, arriving at dead of night.

Amsdorf had been in on the plan, but behind it all lay the carefully concealed hand of Elector Friedrich. Keeping Luther out of sight for the time being, he had calculated, achieved several goals at once. It was the best way to maintain the peace in Germany. It avoided seeing one of his professors put to death as a heretic. And – selfishly – it spared the elector a colossal falling-out with the emperor and the Pope. Since no one had any real idea about how the aftermath of Worms would play out across a discontented, volatile empire, it was better, Friedrich judged, that Luther 'disappeared' while all interested parties waited and watched. In the meantime, if challenged about his whereabouts, the elector could respond that his professor had been kidnapped on the road, and claim to be as worried as anyone else over what had become of him.

The morning after his capture, it dawned on Luther that he was at Wartburg Castle, on a hill above Eisenach. When blindfolded, he had been led around in a circle to disorientate him, but now the world span back into focus. Built in the twelfth century, the castle had long been associated with Elector Friedrich's ancestors, the Landgraves of Thuringia. For Luther, though, Wartburg evoked another memory. It had been a place where he had picked wild strawberries as a child.[38] For the next ten months it was to be his adult home, sanctuary, writing room, prison and torture chamber.

His only companions were two servants, who initially left his food outside his door of his room to prevent them catching a glimpse of its occupant and then spreading the news that the most famous and instantly recognisable man in the whole of Germany was in residence. There was also the castle's custodian, Hans von Berlepsch. He had been one of the two men who had seized Luther from the road. (The other was Burkhard Hund von Wenkheim, a trusted friend of the elector, with whom he had travelled on a relic-collecting pilgrimage to the Holy Land.)

Berlepsch and Luther were not natural soulmates but, in an effort to entertain his guest, the custodian took him hunting. They only went once. While he revelled in earthy language, Luther wasn't quite so keen on such earthy pursuits as killing animals. It put him in mind only of the devil, he said, 'who hunts innocent little creatures with his ambushes and his dogs'.[39] One tale from his day of sport has it that a distressed rabbit tried to make its escape from the hunting dog that was on its tail by running up Luther's trouser leg. The dog, though, wasn't about to let a piece of cloth come between him and his prey, and so grabbed the poor creature with his teeth, taking a chunk out of the friar's leg into the bargain. Luther presented the episode as a metaphor for Rome's bloodthirsty pursuit of him. In its over-eagerness to hunt down dissent, he charged, they saw the shedding of his blood as a price worth paying.

Overnight, Luther's life had been turned upside down. From being the man at the epicentre of events, the person everybody wanted to hear, see, debate with or consult, he found himself all alone at Wartburg, save for three others who had no interest in him. 'I was isolated from human contact,' he recalled, 'and no one could visit me.'[40] Even his identity was stripped away. To avoid his presence in the castle exciting the curiosity of the servants once he started stepping out of his room, he was persuaded to abandon what had become his second skin, his cowl, and dress instead as 'Junker Jörg', a Saxon knight. His tonsure was left to close over and he sported a beard.

Lucas Cranach was to paint this new-look Luther as 'Junker Jörg', but not until 1522, when rumours that he had been murdered had spread to such an extent that they threatened a riot among his followers in the streets and squares of Germany. The picture was circulated to calm nerves and show that his presence at Wartburg had become an open secret among his inner circle, and many of the German ruling classes. Cranach showed Luther in the black high-collared doublet of a minor nobleman. His beard is bushy but trimmed according to the style of the day. His eyes remain unmistakable, as arresting as ever, but his brow is less furrowed, as if unburdened, his jawline firmer, and he appears not quite so fat.[41]

If the portrait suggests he was enjoying a rest cure, the reality was very different. Luther was in a state of mental turmoil. The high of Worms had become the low of an exile he likened in letters to his confidants (once he was allowed to send them) to the fate of the Apostle John, banished to the island of Patmos whence he wrote the Book of Revelation, the apocalyptic last chapter of the Bible.[42]

Initially there had been distractions in the spacious high-ceilinged castle room he was allocated. The window looked out over the valley and he could rest and catch up on missed sleep. In the rush of the previous few years, Luther had struggled to find time to maintain his monastic discipline as laid down in the canonical hours. Never one to let himself off lightly in such matters, he would store up any missed sessions of prayer, spiritual reading and meditation and then, when an opportunity arose, tackle it as a job-lot in one long, unbroken stint. On occasion, such marathons had lasted as long as three days, uninterrupted by food, drink, or even a few hours in bed. Now he had all the time in the world to get up to date.

The broken sleep patterns resulting from the tumultuous recent events in his life were not, however, easily cured by a few days' rest at Wartburg. Indeed, Luther seemed incapable of resting at all. And with tiredness and anxiety came another of those descents into the depths that occur so regularly in Luther's life. He plunged into melancholy. His whole future lay in the balance. Even if the elector stuck to his pledge to protect him, how would that look? A lifetime in Wartburg, out of sight, out of mind? The prospect of a return to Wittenberg and the life of a professor that had been his before Worms, felt remote.

One alternative to looking forward to an uncertain future was to go back over the recent past. Luther's mind raced as he obsessively examined his conduct at Worms, asking whether he might have handled himself differently and avoided what seemed at times more like enforced silence than sanctuary. Had Worms been a missed opportunity rather than a narrow escape? 'My conscience troubles me,' he wrote, 'because at Worms, I yielded to the importunity of my friends and did not play the part of Elijah.[43] They would hear other things from me if I were before them again.'[44]

He appears to be regretting not putting his life on the line for God, as Elijah had done in the Old Testament. Yet he now decided that his fate lay solely in God's hands. Perhaps he had delayed the day by what he said, or didn't say, at the diet, but the net result once the edict appeared would be the same. He was regarded as a heretic and many would try to seize him and hand him over to Rome to be burned.

Such self-criticism, bordering on self-laceration, gives an insight into his tortured psyche. And when Luther was feeling inadequate, standing before God as a failure, his thoughts inevitably turned to the devil. 'The further one sinks into sorrow and despair, the more suitable he becomes as a tool of the devil,' he remarked in a *Table Talk*, 'for it is through doubt and despair that the devil finds an entrance to our soul and acts upon us.'[45]

The servants had brought him a sack of hazelnuts, he said, so he had something to eat between meals. He put the sack in a box in his room but then, inexplicably, in the middle of the night, the hazelnuts started jumping out. 'They rose up, and one after another struck hard against the rafters and danced around my bed. I did not know what to think. When I finally managed to get to sleep, there arose on the stairs such a clamour, as though someone was throwing several barrels down the stairs. I well know the stairs were closed off with iron gates, so no one could come up, but still several barrels were bouncing down there. I got up and went out to the stairs to see what was there. The stairs were closed.'[46]

Luther was in no doubt as to what was going on. It was the devil, paying him a call. 'Then I said: "If it is you, so be it". And commended myself to our Lord Christ . . . and laid down again in bed.'[47]

On another occasion, he saw a dog on his bed.[48] 'The devil can change himself into a beautiful white angel working for God,' he once said, 'so a man of human flesh would never recognise him.'[49] The dog, he deduced, was the devil, so he picked it up and threw it out of the window. Later, when he checked with the custodian, there was no corpse of the creature at the foot of the castle walls.[50] And again, he reported, when Berlepsch's wife came to stay in the castle, he had agreed to move and let her use his larger, more comfortable room. 'There was such a continuous clamour throughout the night,' he said in his *Table Talk*, 'that she thought there were 1,000 devils in the room.'[51]

The best-known story about Luther and the devil concerns an inkpot. Luther once remarked of his period at Wartburg that he had 'driven the devil away with ink', a clear enough reference to the various writing projects that he undertook to fill his time there, and distract himself from hearing things go bump in the night.[52] After Luther's death, on the lips of one of his former students, that remark became an account of how, when Luther was busy at work at his desk, the devil came to tempt him. To fend him off, Luther threw an inkpot at him. As the legend grew, visitors to the 'Lutherstube' at Warburg Castle would chip away at a mark on the wall, wanting what Luther himself might have disdained as a relic of himself. Soon a hole appeared, and that is what greets those who go there today.

The provenance of the inkstain is unreliable. Those wanting to attract pilgrims to the castle in the seventeenth century are reported to have fashioned a fake inkwell out of old munitions that they found stored there. But, like many of the best-known tales about Luther, it is also one of the best loved. In the early years of the nineteenth century, it delighted Jakob and Wilheim Grimm, collectively the Brothers Grimm and famous for their fairy tales, who also produced a book with an account of the inkwell incident. And a few years later it captured the imagination of the Romantic poet Samuel Taylor Coleridge, a great admirer of Luther's ability to think outside the constraints of his time. He wrote an account of the confrontation in the journal *The Friend*, with Luther launching an 'author-like hand-grenade' at Satan. For Coleridge this was Luther the poet – 'as great a poet as ever lived in any age or country' – not just writing of the eternal battles between Jesus Christ and the devil, as detailed in the New Testament, but living them out. 'He was possessed with them,' Coleridge concluded.[53]

What is certain is that Luther was so convinced of a diabolical presence at Wartburg that he told Spalatin, with a hint of paranoia, that the devil was now plotting an attack on Germany itself.

'I fear God will permit him because I am indolent.' It was all, he had convinced himself, his fault. Immodest as his claims sound, Luther was retreating at Wartburg back to those doubts and fears he had suffered as a young friar.

To modern ears, these sound like the delusions of someone having a breakdown, but it must be remembered that Luther was not unusual for the times in taking demonic possession seriously. And literally. Today's doctors might diagnose the severe bowel problems he experienced at Wartburg as a flare-up in his long-standing issues with digestion, exacerbated by the combination of stress, anxiety, uncertainty, a new diet and sudden inaction. He was confined inside the castle for the first weeks, then to the inner courtyard, and could get little exercise. Luther, though, was convinced that it was down to the devil putting him on the rack. And on the toilet.

'My excrement is so hard that I have to strain with such force to expel it that I sweat, and the longer I wait, the harder it gets,' he told Spalatin with typical directness about such bodily matters. On the same day he was even blunter in a letter to Amsdorf: 'my arse has gone bad.'[54] The elector's chaplain sensibly replied with a consignment of laxatives.

A one-man publishing industry

At the start of his time there, Luther was in no state of mind to see his enforced exile in Wartburg as an opportunity, the equivalent of an academic's sabbatical. 'I did not want to come here,' he ranted. 'I wanted to be in the fray . . . I had rather burn on live coals than rot here.'[55] Soon enough, though, he found that he had little other option than to fall back on writing. It was how he had always unburdened and calmed himself.

Once his location and status became known, as well as maintaining a lively correspondence with his circle, he also unleashed a few missiles against his critics. Eck's colleague, Hieronymus Emser, a former admirer of Luther, now a stern critic, was given the full Luther treatment in vituperative style. *Dr Luther's Retraction of the Error Forced Upon Him by the Most Highly Learned Priest of God, Hieronymus Emser, Vicar in Meissen* was awash with barbed remarks designed to shred not only the unfortunate cleric's arguments,[56] but also his whole being. If the title was intended as ironic, there was no disguising the anger seething through the text.

Most of Luther's fury, frustration and self-loathing, however, were poured into a second burst of frenzied literary activity to match his extraordinary output of 1520. In the ten months he spent at Wartburg, he produced twelve books, some sent off and published during his absence, others that had to wait on his release, and at least one suppressed by Spalatin, through whom Luther communicated with his printer.

Several of the texts picked up loose threads left hanging by his output of 1520. A tract on confession, for example, clarified the status of penance, after it had been left somewhat ambiguous in *The Babylonian Captivity*'s bonfire of the sacraments. The Pope had no power to regulate confession, Luther insisted. Neither did humankind need a cleric to place himself between the sinner and God. Those wanting to confess their sins could just as well do it before God. If they needed an audience, he prescribed doing it publicly as part of the mass, touching once again on the congregational model of Church organisation rather than Catholic system that placed clergy above laity.

If confessing was an appropriate thing to do during the mass, Luther described those things that were not in another Wartburg tract, *The Misuse of the Mass*. In *The Babylonian Captivity*, he had argued forcefully against 'private' masses for the dead, said without a congregation, usually in return for a fee, and directed at earning the deceased some remission from their time in purgatory. They were on a par with indulgences as examples of the Church trying to make God's decisions for Him. Yet Luther had previously left the door slightly ajar to such masses as a way of addressing the grief of the bereaved, if money and mitigation were removed from the equation. Now in *The Misuse of the Mass* he closed it. 'I will never again celebrate a private mass in eternity,' he wrote to Melanchthon in August as he worked on his text.

He broadened the core argument in *The Misuse of the Mass* into a familiar attack on the corruption of the clergy, but its fresher passages saw him attempt to reach a fuller definition of what exactly the mass was. Or rather wasn't. Since attending at church services was the most immediate way most believers would live out their faith, this was a key issue.

Catholicism had long taught and continues to teach that mass is a 'true sacrifice' rather than a memorial meal, recalling the Last Supper. The mass was regarded as a re-enactment of Jesus Christ's own sacrifice, and self-consciously adopts the sacrificial atmosphere within which Catholicism reads the Last Supper. This is reflected in the language – for example, the 'offerings' of bread and wine are transubstantiated into the body and blood of Jesus. And those on whom Luther had come to depend endorsed this view. The early Church referred to a eucharistic celebration as 'the sacrifice' ('*prosphora*' or '*oblatio*' in Latin), and Saint Augustine was crystal clear in describing the mass as 'the sacrifice [that] has succeeded all the sacrifices of the Old Testament, which were slain as a shadow of what was to come'.[57]

On this occasion, Luther took a different view. Precisely because of Jesus' sacrifice, which had redeemed humankind, he believed there was no need for further acts of sacrifice. Moreover, he claimed to be unable to find any scriptural basis for the Church's chosen approach, however firmly rooted it was in tradition (the canon). 'The words in the canon are plain; the words in Scripture are plain,' he acknowledged, but instructed: 'Let the canon yield to the gospel.' And if it did, he explained, the mass should be seen as an act of thanksgiving to God by an assembly of believers.[58]

Luther was more in line with Catholic tradition with his translation, completed at Wartburg, of the *Magnificat*, the song or prayer of Mary, which he endorsed and to which he attached a commentary. The words of the *Magnificat* are taken directly from the gospel of Luke, when a pregnant Mary visits her pregnant (and elderly) cousin Elizabeth,[59] so there was scriptural justification, if only in one of the four gospel sources, but Luther nonetheless warned of the Catholic tendency to elevate Mary beyond being one example among many of Christian life, and to turn her into a kind of goddess in her own right, with special influence over God's decisions. 'She does nothing; God does all things,' he insisted.[60]

Luther also worked a volume of postils – or biblical commentaries – intended as the basis for improved sermons by priests. He was an ardent believer in the paramount importance of the ministry of preaching. The priest was first and foremost a preacher, and next a pastor. If those in the pews were ever to hear the Word of God, he was convinced, they needed able preachers. He was later to remark that, of all his writings, this practical volume was one of his best.[61]

The Bible in German

And it was that same deep-rooted impulse to educate and equip each individual believer sufficiently to have a relationship with God through His word as recorded in Scripture that inspired Luther's most enduring literary feat, and arguably his greatest achievement of all – his translation of the Bible into German. It was started while at Wartburg. 'I much rather prefer that they [his other books] would all be forgotten,' he remarked in later life. 'For the entire Church is full of books, while the Bible is neglected.'[62]

To judge from his correspondence, he set out around Christmas of 1521 to change this state of affairs. Thereafter he proceeded at breakneck speed to render the New Testament in German. By the time he left Wartburg three months later, he had translated all twenty-seven of its books into the language that his fellow countrymen spoke. The pace at which he did it surprised even Luther. In January, he was complaining to Amsdorf that he had 'shouldered a burden beyond [my] power'.[63] More remarkable still was his ability to express it all with vocabulary and idioms that made it accessible to all who read it.

It was an evolving process. When he arrived back in Wittenberg from Wartburg in early March, he had with him a complete translation of the New Testament, although in draft. He had chosen the harder path of working from a Greek version (the original language in which it had been written) rather than the standard Latin text favoured by the Catholic Church. 'I have mastered neither Greek nor Hebrew,' Luther admitted in the early 1530s, 'but nevertheless I will forage into Hebrew and Greek.'[64]

He was playing down his abilities, but once back in Wittenberg he collaborated extensively on his draft with Philipp Melanchthon, who had come to the university originally to teach Greek. On 10 May, they shared their joint labours with Spalatin, and hence with Elector Friedrich. Only after that hurdle had been cleared were some early sections sent to Melchior Lotter, the Wittenberg printer most closely associated with making Luther's works publicly available.

Das Neue Testament finally appeared in September. The first print run, said to number between 3,000 and 5,000, quickly sold out. By December a second, corrected edition was ready, though the take-up was initially slower than Luther had hoped. 'Before the New Testament was translated,' he grumbled in 1532, 'every one yearned to have and read it. After it was finally translated, interest lasted only four weeks, then everyone wanted the Old Testament books.'[65]

A clue as to what was eating him came in another remark in the same year. He worried aloud that his translation (by then well underway) of the whole Bible into German wouldn't reach its intended audience. 'You have now the Holy Scriptures. Now see to it that you make good use of it after my death. It has taken more than enough of our work, but our followers will pay little attention to it. Our adversaries read more than our followers. I believe that Duke Georg [his opponent and Elector Friedrich's cousin] has read more than our nobles. For it has been noted that he once said: "if only that monk would complete his German translation and go to that place where he belongs." That is the testimonial that I have from Duke Georg and all the papists, who now use our translation.'[66] He was still complaining in the autumn of 1540. 'We have done away with the obstacles and hurdles, so that anyone can read it [the Bible – in German] without hindrance. But I am concerned that no one will read it.'[67]

Time was to prove Luther utterly wrong on this point. His German Bible had an influence far beyond anything he could have imagined. Once again, his idea in taking on the task was not an original one. Back in the fourth century, Ulfilas, a Christian bishop credited with creating the Gothic alphabet, had translated some parts of the Bible into German.[68] And in the fourteenth century, as we have seen, John Wycliffe had led the group that produced a Bible in English, and had posthumously been declared a heretic by the Church for his trouble. Erasmus should also be credited. He had produced a new Greek version of the New Testament in 1516. The second (1519) edition of this was on Luther's desk as he worked on his translation into German, with its detailed annotations especially valuable to him.

Luther's own side notes, prefaces to individual sections, and general introduction set the tone and context in which he intended his translation to be read. High up on that list was his conviction that each component part of the New Testament was not of equal worth. If it was to be an essential guide to living out their faith for individual Christians, as he had consistently taught, then he was unapologetic in offering personal recommendations on which sections to prioritise.

'In a word Saint John's Gospel and his first epistle, Saint Paul's epistles, especially Romans, Galatians, and Ephesians, and Saint Peter's first epistle are the books that show you Christ, and teach you all that is necessary and salvatory for you to know, even if you were never to see or hear any other book or doctrine.'[69] He had sufficient respect for the integrity of the whole text that he did not attempt crudely to cut out the bits that might cause readers to challenge his cherished beliefs. The Epistle of James, which he had previously dismissed as a viable basis for the sacrament of extreme unction, also contradicted him directly on the value – or not – of good works. '[It] is really an epistle of straw, compared to these others, for it has nothing of the nature of the gospel about it,' he wrote, but he left it in.[70] And the final book, Revelation, was not a favourite of his – on the grounds that its apocalyptic tale of the end of the world was too obscure to understand. 'A revelation should be revealing,'[71] he complained, but again he did not edit it out, at least in the early editions of his New Testament.[72]

The books of the New Testament that he prized most, though, received their own individual introduction. Luther's preface to Paul's Letter to the Romans is among the longest of these, and advocates daily reading of its passages. 'Every Christian should know it word for word, by heart, but occupy himself with it every day, as the daily bread of the soul. It can never be read or pondered too much, and the more it is dealt with the more precious it becomes, and the better it tastes.'

This was, of course, the Pauline letter that had first inspired him to embrace 'justification by faith'. In his translation, Luther took the liberty of translating the apostle's Greek words into German as 'justification by faith *alone*'. When challenged on this additional word, he argued that he was also conveying the ideas behind the words, and that in German that extra emphasis was necessary. Others disagreed, but he stuck to his guns and would not relent in all the subsequent re-editing he undertook right up to his death.

It was part of a never-ending search to find just the right word, tone and image to convey the original as faithfully and directly as possible to the widest audience. Luther's method was to start with a literal translation, then to work methodically through every sentence, word by word, weighing each individually until he found something that satisfied him – in terms of accuracy, sense, rhythm and accessibility. He did not want a text littered with obscure and abstract theological vocabulary that shut out readers. While only around 10 per cent of the population was literate,[73] Luther's genius was to produce a text that, when read aloud by that 10 per cent to the other 90 per cent, was not only understandable, but employed words in such a way that he endowed it with a power to move its audience.

And that was not the least of his efforts. For accuracy, when he moved on to the Old Testament, Luther is said to have visited abattoirs to make sure he was using the right German shop-floor term to render all those accounts of goats and bullocks being slaughtered on the orders of Yahweh. To check out his tone, he would loiter incognito in the streets and squares of Wittenberg, eavesdropping on the phrases and idioms used by what he would have called the 'common people' rather than the chatter in the refined corridors of the university. 'I endeavoured to make Moses sound so German that no one would suspect he was a Jew,'[74] he remarked. The whiff of anti-Semitism in his words is something which must be discussed later.

One of the greatest achievements of his translations of first the New Testament and then the Bible, historians of language have claimed, is that, because of their wide circulation and longevity, they effectively established a standard agreed form of the German language as no other book before had. Luther's aim, he recalled, was to use a version of his native tongue 'so that both upper and lower Germans may understand me. I pattern my speech after the Saxon chancellery [the Elector's administrative corps], which is spoken by all princes and kings in Germany.'[75] He acknowledged that there were many dialects throughout the German-speaking lands, some of which he had encountered on his various travels. By incorporating elements of these, he managed to produce something around which everyone could rally – in linguistic terms. 'The Brandenburg speech is light,' he once mused in a *Table Talk*. 'One hardly notices that a Brandenburger moves his lips when he speaks. They surpass the Saxons.'[76]

And even in those places where the language might exclude some, because of its geographical roots, specific idioms or long words, Luther's German Bible still drew people in by the simple expedient of including illustrations, as many as five hundred in some early editions, with the overall look they conveyed often more that of a reassuring re-creation of the German countryside than the foreign-looking environment of the Holy Land, which only a handful of readers would have seen. Old Testament passages in particular lent themselves to dramatic accompanying pictures, while the gospels and epistles were regarded as too important to offer the distraction of illustrations. The Book of Revelation provided opportunities to score points in the ongoing battle with the Catholic Church. The unnamed woman who sits on a beast whose 'seven heads' are 'seven hills' in Chapter Seventeen was depicted as a whore wearing the papal tiara amid the seven hills of Rome.[77]

Holy writing

Religion was originally passed by word of mouth: the stories told by prophets, wise men and women, the enlightened few who inspired many others, were memorised by their followers and then conveyed through the oral tradition. Next came 'holy writing' – in the case of Christianity, the Bible. It linked one generation with the next, down through centuries, and connected the eternal and the divine with the here and now. But, until Luther's time, that 'holy writing' had been accessible only to the literate few who had learned Latin. They in their turn interpreted it for those who came to listen to them, and it gave them power and control.

Now Luther was breaking that chain. Advances in printing enabled his vernacular Bible to become something the Scriptures hitherto had never been – a book, something that every literate person could read, and even the semi-literate could follow via the illustrations. No longer would they have to wait to be spoon-fed snippets from the pulpit by clerics who often had the barest grasp of Latin themselves and relied heavily on guidance notes provided by Church academics. Until Luther, believers had heard only a carefully chosen selection of the Scriptures, or had imbibed them via images, carvings and frescoes that adorned the façades and walls of their churches, or decorated the stained-glass windows. Now, they could take them home to read, study and reflect upon, their own interpretation being ultimately as valid as anything the Pope or his prelates and priests decreed suitable for their attention, or better overlooked. Just as studying the Scriptures had tackled Luther's *Anfechtung* in his early days in the monastery, now spiritual nourishment was there for the many, not just the few.

The ramifications were enormous, more than Luther could ever have imagined when he embarked on the task in Wartburg Castle. What it ultimately meant was that the medieval justification for the hierarchy and the entire structure of the Church was challenged. Neither were any longer needed to intervene between the believer and God as interpreters of Christ's words, and as mitigators on their behalf with God. Individuals could have the Bible for themselves, and that was a truly revolutionary step, and therefore a challenge, not just for the Church, but for thought itself, and all who aspired to control it.

Luther's work, begun during his lonely exile, was one of the starting points for much of what transformed the world in the centuries to come – right down to those who produced books arguing that the Church had no role in the state, or in their lives. Even the modern argument that all religion is a wholly private matter, with no role in the public square, can trace its roots back to Luther's vision of each individual standing before God for judgement, with only a Bible for guidance. Freedom to read the Bible also meant freedom to explore its tenets, freedom to find them wanting, freedom to examine their history and freedom to see them not as literal truth (in Luther's terms) but as something more figurative and ultimately neither binding nor necessary.

This was not, of course, anything Luther would have supported. He never set out to champion modern freedoms or individual autonomy, but by handing the German people a tool which enabled them to take ownership of what he saw as the most crucial relationship in their lives, he had set that ball rolling.

CHAPTER NINE

Wittenberg in Chaos:
Glimpses of a New Church

> 'This constant search for something new is the mother of all error for the people.'
>
> Martin Luther, *Table Talk*[1]

Wittenberg without Luther quickly spun into chaos. For all his clear-sightedness about the failings of the Church, and his uncompromising attitude to the need for reform, Luther also possessed a pragmatic streak. It had taken him many years of pain and torment in the monastery to arrive at his mature view as to the shape Christianity should take. And, indeed, that mature view was still developing and settling. So he understood from his own experience that others would also require time to appreciate the case for reform. While he may have been intent on forcing the institutional Church to accept change by refusing to bow to its threats or lazy arguments, he had shown no inclination to dragoon other believers to do as he said, or think as he thought. He had sufficient confidence that he was being guided by God to believe that, given time and through grace, they would come round.

The same, however, could not be said of his inner circle in Wittenberg, who were holding the fort in his absence. When their leader did not return home from the Diet of Worms, as anticipated, they faced two choices. The first was to wait patiently until he did, but in those early weeks of May 1521, even if Nikolaus von Amsdorf could reassure them Luther was safe, there was no telling how long his exile might last. That left them with the second option: to proceed. But how?

While over the previous two years, Luther had described what a reformed Catholic Church might look like, it had been a paper exercise – words not deeds. He was telling those in charge what they needed to do. And what was rarely featured in his writings was how to cope with the reaction of those many Christians who opposed his ideas and remained loyal to the traditional ways of Catholicism. Or even those who supported him on some points, but not on all.

The core group in Wittenberg took on the challenge of filling in those blanks as they searched for a practical way of proceeding that was both loyal to their leader, but also answered the rising tide of expectation that Luther's ordeal at Worms had caused both among the town's citizens, lay and clerical, and the many more beyond its walls. Four figures in particular tried to step up while Luther was away. The first was Philipp Melanchthon, Luther's closest collaborator and the cleverest among them, but by nature a deputy not a head, usually able to see both sides of an argument, but given on occasion to great surges of enthusiasm that required Luther to rein him in. Just twenty-four years old, Melanchthon was a layman, more academic than populariser.

Thirty-three-year-old Andreas von Karlstadt was, by contrast, a priest, and had originally been senior to Luther at Wittenberg University, though latterly had operated in his shadow. Such a status didn't suit his personality. An egotist and a hothead, he was all too ready to seize his chance to move centre stage.

Gabriel Zwilling, aged thirty-four, had trodden much the same route as Luther, as a Hermit of Saint Augustine in the cloisters at Erfurt and now at Wittenberg. He shared with Luther a way with words, especially when on his feet in front of a congregation or crowd, but in a crisis, such as the one that rapidly took hold of Wittenberg in the months after the Diet of Worms, he knew little of the restraint that came with Luther's capacity for self-questioning.

Instead Zwilling was caught up with Karlstadt's impatience, preferring to act rather than wait on the judgements of others, be they the emperor, the Pope, the bishops or the German princes.

The final name among the quartet was that of twenty-nine-year-old Justus Jonas, another Augustinian who had moved from Erfurt to Wittenberg in Luther's footsteps in 1521. He was a very recent convert to the cause, having previously been closely associated with Erasmus and the case for Humanist reform from within Catholicism. When Jonas had joined forces with Luther, Erasmus rebuked him for what he clearly saw as a betrayal. 'If there are things we do not like in the men whose judgement governs human affairs, my view is that we leave them to their Lord and Master. If their commands are just, it is reasonable to obey; if unjust, it is a good man's duty to endure them, lest worse befall. If our generation cannot endure Christ in His fullness, it is something nonetheless to preach Him as far as we may.'[2]

As a statement of the time-honoured principles of loyal dissent with Catholicism, Erasmus's words cannot be bettered, but they accept that there are limits to how far you can go in the cause of reform. Like many, Jonas had grown frustrated by this need to accept out of loyalty what he plainly saw as wrong. No longer willing to bide his time and inch forward in anticipation of a new, enlightened generation of Catholic leaders, he had instead set his heart on something more uncompromising that he recognised in Luther.

Jonas's decision to side with those anxious to get on with radical change rather than simply carry on discussing it in letters, papers and seminars was being mirrored across Germany and northern Europe. Lutheran ranks were swelling and, in the enforced absence of their leader, these converts looked to the inner circle at Wittenberg. That pressure grew greater still when, elsewhere, the new breed of 'Lutherans' started to face martyrdom for the cause.

The Augustinian friary in Antwerp had been a pioneer in lending vocal support to Luther since 1518 when his writings first reached it. Some of its community had studied at Wittenberg and their prior, Jakob Propst, enthusiastically backed his former colleague. But when he returned from the Diet of Worms to his personal domains in the Low Countries, where Antwerp lay, Emperor Charles was determined to give a lead to the reluctant German princes on how vigorously to tackle what had now been deemed a heresy. He therefore ordered that the Antwerp monastery be not just brought into line, but demolished. Its community was jailed and each was offered the choice of recanting, or burning at the stake as heretics.

Most backed down, but three refused to yield. Heinrich Voes and Johann Esch were to be among the first Reformation martyrs,[3] repeating Luther's arguments in their defence before being sentenced to death. After some delays, their executions took place at the start of July 1523 in Brussels' main marketplace. The charges against them were not read aloud, as was the custom, because the authorities feared hearing Lutheran doctrine would inspire those present to embrace it. Their deaths – and their faith – prompted Luther to write a *Letter to the Christians in the Netherlands*, but more memorably they inspired him in 1524 to pen a rousing hymn, 'A New Song Here Shall Be Begun'.[4]

> *At Brussels in the Netherlands*
> *God proved Himself most truthful*
> *And poured His gifts from open hands*
> *On two lads, martyrs youthful*
> *Through who He showed His power.*

It was almost as if he was celebrating their martyrdom. Or perhaps envying it. It had been the fate he had expected for himself for so long. Now others had suffered in his place and were standing before God.

Wittenberg divided

That, however, lay ahead. For Luther's colleagues in Wittenberg, in the early summer of 1521, even when they were able to establish contact by letter with their leader, the day-to-day challenges came one after another, some posed by others, some precipitated by their own actions. The first issue they grappled with was whether priests could marry. *The Babylonian Captivity* had made clear Luther's view that compulsory celibacy for priests was not required, that the vows individuals had taken at ordination could no longer be held to bind them because they had no scriptural basis. When three local priests took this at face value and announced their wedding plans, their bishop rebuked them and referred the matter up the hierarchical chain to Archbishop Albrecht in Mainz. He ordered the three men in question to be arrested.

Here was a real-life test of Luther's writings. Should the inner circle in Wittenberg prevaricate, for fear of making a bad situation with the emperor and the Pope even worse, or should they follow Luther to the letter? Karlstadt chose the latter course, taking the side of the three priests against their archbishop in a paper that argued, in line with Luther, that priests could marry, but added his own spin – namely that they needed to have a family life to make them effective in their work, so much so that matrimony should become obligatory for all clergy.

Karlstadt might be accused of overreaching himself. He would reply that he was following the spirit of Luther's writings, and even that such a radical suggestion was all of a piece with his absent colleague. Whatever the truth, Karlstadt's intervention quickly mobilised opinion. For years, many priests had been living, openly in some cases, with women, and fathering children. Here was an opportunity to restore good order and honesty to the Church. On the streets and in the pews, it was such a popular proposal that the Church authorities were in no position to resist. The three priests were allowed to marry, and many others saw a chance to regularise their positions regarding partners and illegitimate children. And for those who were leading blameless lives, but had been ordained, or taken vows, believing they had a God-given vocation to be a priest or monk, and then struggled because they felt no parallel calling to celibacy, Karlstadt offered a release from their dilemma that they seized in good conscience.

Quickly it was established in practice that vows were no longer binding. And this extended not just to priests and monks, but to nuns as well. They started to get married, often nuns to priests. For those in cloisters, it meant leaving and restarting their lives outside, but Luther's harsh words in *Appeal to the Christian Nobility of the German Nation* about the shortcomings of monasteries and religious life there spurred them on. Priests in parishes who married usually remained in place, defying their bishops who were powerless to act when faced by such overwhelming support as these men enjoyed from their congregations.

In early October, Gabriel Zwilling decided the time had come to put into practice in Wittenberg's churches another of Luther's propositions, also spelt out in *The Babylonian Captivity*: that communion in both kinds, bread and wine, should be available to all, and not just the clergy. Zwilling also demanded an end to endowed private masses said for the dead, again in line with Luther's stated position. Zwilling's principal target seems to have been the Castle Church, where the priests who cared for its collection of relics remained more strongly attached to traditional Catholicism than elsewhere in Wittenberg. They responded by steadfastly opposing his efforts.

Zwilling's response was to attack publicly from the pulpit those who stood in his way, and to urge his listeners to show their support by rebuking the recalcitrant priests when they encountered them in the street. In volatile, over-excited times, this became an incitement to anti-clerical violence. Zwilling, moreover,

declared himself reluctant to be bound any longer by any obligation to his religious order, especially when his prior in Wittenberg
refused to sanction communion in both kinds in the Augustinian
chapel. In November, he left the cloister, taking with him thirteen
of the forty-strong community.

Elector Friedrich was naturally alarmed by what was unfolding
on his doorstep. The Augustinian prior, writing to him, shared his
sense that they were witnessing a breakdown of traditional
authority. 'It has been preached that no monk can be saved in a
cowl, that cloisters are in the grip of the devil, that monks should
be expelled and cloisters demolished. Whether such teaching is
grounded in the gospel, I greatly doubt.'[5]

When Friedrich's annual display of relics went up on 1 November
in the Castle Church, they were booed and had to be hastily
removed. He might have been prepared to tolerate dissent when
Luther was posing what the elector believed to be important questions that Rome refused to answer. And he might even have encouraged Luther's defiance, because he could see a political advantage
to be gained in terms of power recouped from the papacy and the
emperor. But he was not about to put up with the dissidents threatening civil order in Wittenberg. Luther's lieutenants were playing
with fire when many among the lower orders felt so passionately
that the existing social and economic structures shut them out.

As ever, Friedrich's public approach was studiedly neutral. He
avoided saying whether he sided with the reformers or the conservative clergy of the town. Instead he appealed for a consensus to
dampen down the overheated arguments. To that end, he set up a
committee – including Melanchthon, Karlstadt and Jonas – to
look into Zwilling's activities. Privately Friedrich had little time
for Zwilling and hoped that the other three would force their
colleague to back down, but Zwilling had tapped into a public
mood of insurrection. There was too much momentum to stop
him. An ugly atmosphere took over the town.

On 3 December, a mob burst into Wittenberg's Stadtkirche, snatched missals, disrupted the priests at the altar, and even began to stone them. This wasn't what Luther had in mind when, in his *Appeal to the Christian Nobility of the German Nation*, he rejected the distinction between clerics and laity, and advocated a priest-hood of all baptised believers. Fine sentiments in writing could, however, turn nasty when translated from the page to the street.

The following day another crowd gathered outside the Franciscan monastery on the northern side of Wittenberg, incensed by that order's long-standing and public opposition to much of what Luther had proposed. They mocked the friars and smashed a wooden altar. Two days later, a smaller group returned and invaded the cloister, threatening those who confronted them with knives.

The tide of radicalism wasn't restricted to just a few hotheads. The town council – which included Karlstadt – took up the agenda of outlawing 'Romish' practices such as veneration of relics, private masses for the dead, processions and fasting. And the liturgical clean-up was to be accompanied, it demanded, by a more general purging. The council wanted a purer, holier, less tolerant Wittenberg. Sales of alcohol were to be curtailed, and prostitution banned. The teaching of Scripture must, it insisted, be lived out.

Overnight, priests who supported the reforms became pastors and preachers who ran their churches along new lines drawn up by their individual reading of Luther. One immediate consequence was to disrupt the whole system of endowments that had been the bedrock of ecclesiastical finance. Wealthy individuals or families controlled the 'living' of a church, paying for its upkeep and that of its priests, in return for a say in how it was run. If the congrega-tion was going to take over that authority, the donors were no longer going to cough up. Meanwhile some students at the univer-sity found that their abbots and bishops were no longer willing to pay their stipends to attend what had become such a notorious institution. Many were ordered home, but plenty chose to stay in Wittenberg and join the fight for a new Church.

At which point Elector Friedrich lost patience. Everything, he insisted, must go on as before, until a consensus could be reached. But Karlstadt was now riding the wave of popular rebellion and was not about to be bossed around, either by the elector or by conservative Catholic forces in Wittenberg. In a move designed to precipitate a showdown which would, he no doubt believed, lead to the final triumph of popular will, he announced that on New Year's Day he would be celebrating a reformed communion service in the Castle Church entirely in German, and that at the eucharist the congregation could receive the bread *and* the wine. The elector promptly banned the proposed mass.

Not to be thwarted, Karlstadt moved it forward and celebrated it as advertised on Christmas Day. He wore the plain black robes of an academic, rather than the vestments of a priest. There was no requirement, he told the congregation, to fast or go to confession before receiving the eucharist (as remains the Catholic practice to this day). Echoing Luther, he insisted that *sola fide* was all that was needed. 'See that Christ stands before you. He takes for you all your struggle and doubt, that you may know that through His word, you are blessed.'[6] Karlstadt stripped out any reference to sacrifice in the liturgy and almost whispered the words, 'this is my body' in German at the consecration of the bread, as if to emphasise his break with tradition. Over a thousand attended the Schlosskirche, many waiting outside. They included the entire town council.

Emboldened, Karlstadt next persuaded the council to give its blessing to his *New Order for the City of Wittenberg,* which was published in January with the aim of converting the town into a model 'Christian City'. The town was to be a beacon for all those wanting to experience a reformed Church. Among the changes required was the stripping out from churches of holy pictures and statues. In the spirit of *sola scriptura*, such paraphernalia, Karlstadt argued, offended against the fourth commandment. 'You shall not make yourself a carved image or any likeness of anything in heaven and earth beneath, or in the waters under the earth; you shall not bow down to them or serve them.'[7]

This was not an argument Luther had made. Karlstadt was operating on his own authority. He began devising his own liturgical services when he replaced weekday masses with a reading from the Psalms and then a sermon. He also outlawed all Church music, again a step that Luther had not advocated, as Karlstadt said there was no New Testament justification for it to be included. 'Relegate organs, trumpets and flutes to theatre,' he advised. 'Better one heart-felt prayer than a thousand cantatas of the Psalms. The lascivious notes of the organ awaken thoughts of the world, when we should be meditating on the suffering of Christ.'[8]

To cap a busy Christmas, on Boxing Day Karlstadt had become engaged to Anna von Mochau, the fifteen-year-old daughter of a local impoverished noble family. They married on 22 January. Elector Friedrich was invited, but did not attend. He was now as heartily sick of Karlstadt as he was of Zwilling. The following month Justas Jonas, his tonsure now grown over, walked down the aisle with Katharina Falcke.

A new complication arose, straight after Christmas, with the arrival in Wittenberg of a group of three weavers from the town of Zwickau. They had been expelled from this prosperous trading and mining centre 125 miles to the southwest after their leader, Nikolaus Storch, had claimed to see visions of an angel telling him to purify the Church by bloodshed, and establish a new leadership of the 'elect'. With little formal education, though literate, the layman Storch had started preaching about the message he claimed to have received from heaven in a series of 'corner sermons' – delivered literally on street corners. When given the support of Zwickau's radical priest, Thomas Müntzer, this had caused so much public agitation that the authorities had driven Storch and his two companions out.

The Zwickau 'prophets', as they became known, headed for Wittenberg and sought out Karlstadt and Melanchthon. They were anticipating a warm welcome and were not disappointed. Both Lutheran leaders were initially impressed by them, the normally well-balanced Melanchthon so much so that he argued to reject them was to reject God and take the side of the devil. Karlstadt meantime put them up in his house. The town council, though, was more sceptical of some of the prophets' claims, especially when, on the basis of what God had told Storch, the three began arguing against infant baptism – and hence directly contradicting Luther's teaching on the subject – in favour of baptising adults who would be born again in God.

In the Augustinian monastery that was Luther's home, Zwilling's defection had prompted much soul-searching. On 6 January, a decision was taken by the community there to allow all those who wanted to leave to do so. The cloister rapidly emptied, but that was not sufficient for Zwilling. He and others set about burning some of the sacred objects that had been kept there for veneration.

This triggered another wave of unrest in Wittenberg, with statues of saints desecrated by the removal of their hands or heads. Imagery in churches was now being deemed a distraction from the worship of God rather than an aid to it. Since God and Christ were spirit, physical representations only got in the way. Those who kept statues and religious images, both Karlstadt and Zwilling ruled, could not call themselves Christian. Citizen was being turned against citizen, and all on the basis of something that was to be found nowhere in Luther's writings.

As well as his own instinctive dislike and fear about what was unravelling in his capital, Elector Friedrich was now also coming under strong pressure from Rome and from Emperor Charles, who both had been alarmed by news reaching them about Wittenberg, to undo at once the changes that had been made to the mass lest the contagion spread beyond the walls of Wittenberg and infect other towns in Germany. Friedrich's non-confrontational pursuit of consensus evaporated. He scrapped the new ordinances agreed by the town council and ordered that the status quo before the various reforms be re-established until formal agreement could be reached between all parties. To aid that process, he banned Karlstadt and Zwilling from preaching.

While the former submitted, albeit muttering that the sanction was a result of the hidden hand of Martin Luther, Zwilling stomped out of Wittenberg, just as he had abandoned his monastery when he was challenged.[9] The town council decided the only option now was to appeal to Martin Luther to return from Wartburg.

'That unholy monk's habit'

After those first days and weeks in Wartburg, cut off from the outside world, Luther had been able to re-establish contact by letter with his followers in Wittenberg, and with Georg Spalatin, Elector Friedrich's chaplain and go-between. News started to reach him of the turmoil in Wittenberg, but much of it left him unperturbed. When he heard of the plans of three local priests to marry, for example, he signalled back his support for the step they proposed to take, based as it was on his own writings.

And thereafter he continued to welcome the marriage plans of clergy in and around Wittenberg – including several in his inner circle. But what about monks and nuns as opposed to priests? While Luther had insisted in *The Freedom of the Christian Man* that any promises made by a monk or a nun should be offered freely, and on the basis that it did not mean, as a result, they would be on a fast track to salvation, at this stage he had not endorsed them getting married. In his own case, despite his father 'begging' him 'many times' to take off his cowl,[10] Luther still assumed that he would end his days as a celibate monk.

By November, though, he had changed his position. It is tempting to speculate that he was now following events, justifying what was happening already on the ground in his name, but Luther was made of sterner stuff than that. If he objected to something, he said so. Yet, with his usual lightning speed, he had completed a tract, *On Monastic Vows*, accompanied by a letter addressed to his father and dated 21 November. It contained a belated response to the question Hans had posed all those years before, after his son's first mass. If the devil had led him into the monastery, Luther now told his father, then God had turned the situation to His advantage by using Luther's presence in the cloister to inspire in him His work towards a thorough-going reform of the Church, based on first-hand knowledge of all that was wrong. Going into the monastery, he said, had made him someone 'not of the pope' – i.e. answerable to rules set by the Church – 'but of Christ'.[11]

And now, Luther continued, in what was his clearest statement yet of his future intentions, God had 'absolved me of the monastic vow and granted me so much liberty that . . . I am subject to no one but Him alone. He is my immediate bishop, abbot, prior, lord, father and teacher. I accept no other.'[12]

The letter was written in Latin – not a language with which Hans was familiar – revealing Luther's aim as greater than settling a row in his own family. He wanted to lay to rest a dispute in the wider family of the Church. If he could break his monastic vow, then so could every monk and nun. The letter was what we might call today an executive summary, which announced briefly and pointedly to its readers, when published via Spalatin at the start of 1522, along with the main body of text of *On Monastic Vows*, that Luther was now opening the door to a radical change in monasticism. And that is precisely what followed: an emptying of the cloisters in the 1520s, with monks and nuns leaving to choose marriage and family as the context for their continuing Christian service in reformed churches. Some 800 of the 3,000 Benedictine houses in Europe closed as a result, and numbers of monks across the continent fell by over a half on pre-Reformation levels.[13]

In the body of the tract, Luther developed his argument. Monastic vows, he wrote, were all about binding those who took them to the rules, regulations and traditions of the Church, rather than to the demands of Scripture. Vows in themselves, he went on, were not necessarily bad. The real test was how they were framed. 'The liberty of the gospel governs only in relations between God and you, not between you and your neighbour,' he argued. So there were two sorts of vows: those made between individuals, for example when marrying another person, which were good (because, in the case of marriage, they protected against divorce);[14] and those made to God, which the Church had allowed to supplant Scripture. And those were bad vows because God could not be bound by man-made Church rules.

The result was, he said, dysfunctional monasteries. Luther was later to spell this out most bluntly in a *Table Talk*. 'They [monks] castigate their bodies with fasting, vigils and singing, wear cowls and scourge themselves with rods. God certainly did not order any such religious service, nor does He ask any such thing of us. Rather when His word is diligently spread in its pure form, souls will be made to know what and how one should believe. That is when they will be instructed in the love of God and the love of one another.'[15]

Luther's *On Monastic Vows* might be taken as a manifesto for the destruction of monasteries: in Wittenberg (where in January 1522 the remaining Augustinians moved out), and throughout Germany and beyond. Henry VIII's dissolution of the monasteries between 1536 and 1541, as part of the English Reformation, might be traced back to Luther (though, when Luther wrote *On Monastic Vows*, Henry was among his most fervent critics and a defender of the papacy).[16]

Luther had not, however, suggested anything so crude as closing down monasteries. To those properly run and regulated, and entered freely by those who chose them, he expressed no objection. 'And so, if you vow to take up the religious life, and if you live with men of like mind, with a clear conscience that in monasticism you seek nothing to your advantage in your relationship with God, but because either your situation has brought you to embrace this kind of life, or it appeared to be the best way of life for you, without your thinking thereby that you are better than he who takes a wife or takes up farming, then in that case you are neither wrong to take vows nor wrong to live in this way, insofar as the propriety of the vow is concerned.'[17]

And he even gave an example of 'good' monasticism in *On Monastic Vows*, quoting Saint Anthony, who in the fourth century gathered the first loose communities of hermit monks in the Egyptian desert. 'The very father of monks and the founder of monastic life, most wisely and in a Christian manner believed and taught that absolutely nothing should be observed which did not have the authority of Scripture. He knew absolutely nothing about monastic vows and ceremonial of this kind, but willingly chose to live as a hermit, and of his own will chose to live unmarried, after the pattern of the gospel. Pursuing human wisdom, his successors made this way of life into a vow, into a matter of obligation and compulsion. This way of life is but a specious copy and a mistaken observance of the rule of Anthony, which is the rule of Christ.'[18]

So Luther wanted to see a purified monasticism, returning to its original roots. Yet later, when no longer a monk, he was to abandon even this position. In a *Table Talk*, he asked his listeners to ensure, after his death, 'that you apply yourself diligently and earnestly to preserve the institution of marriage, so that the same is freely permitted to laity and pastors, and everyone who lives and breathes, so that we never again have a monastery system.'[19]

You can, of course, object to a 'monastery system' being imposed on all who feel a vocation to serve as religious ministers (i.e. clergy being required to take vows) without objecting to monasteries themselves, especially if they were reformed in their practices. And the sense that Luther never quite reached a final position on monastic life is reinforced by his own reluctance and confusion when it came to turning his back on the monk's life he had known for sixteen years. When he returned to Wittenberg in March of 1522, the Elector Friedrich, like everyone else who had read *On Monastic Vows*, assumed it was a declaration that Luther was ready to discard his cowl in favour of a black academic gown. '[He] sent me a piece of the best cloth, with the strong suggestion that I should have made from it either a coat or a cape,' Luther recalled. 'And they say he said, laughing: "wouldn't it be nice if Luther had a Spanish cape made for himself?"'[20,21] It was, though, only after another nine years, in 1532, before Luther finally 'laid aside' his monk's habit in an 'act of independence . . . to the glory of God, and the dishonour of the devil'. It had been a struggle, he confessed, and he had only been persuaded to do so because, to keep it, would have allowed 'all the papists' to say that, at heart, he didn't believe his own teachings. 'Otherwise, I could not find sufficient justification for getting rid of that unholy monk's habit. It was difficult for me.' He made his choice not on the basis of conscience, 'but because of all those others whom I wished to serve'.[22]

Back to the future

As the months wore on at Wartburg, Luther had become ever more absorbed in his writing, but the deeper he buried himself in it, the more distracting became the news reaching him from Wittenberg. So much so that he felt torn between dedicating himself to scholarship – as had, for large part, been his life up to this point – or re-entering what now was as much a political fray as a religious argument. In early December, in his nobleman's clothes and hiding behind his thick beard, 'Junker Jörg' made a fleeting visit to the town to see for himself what was happening.[23] He lodged with Amsdorf and met Melanchthon and Spalatin, pressing the latter to get on with publishing his texts, including *On Monastic Vows*. The elector's chaplain had been holding back for fear of upping tensions any further. While Luther did not endorse all that he witnessed on his brief visit, or heard about, neither did he seem overly alarmed. He published shortly afterwards a generalised exhortation against violence that urged respect for the authorities. 'Remember that [the] Antichrist . . . is to be broken without the hand of man. Violence will only make him stronger. Preach, pray but do not fight.'[24]

Yet Luther's low-key reaction is curious, when clergy were being attacked in the streets and priests stoned while at their altars. Maybe he didn't see such outbursts, or was distracted by other thoughts. Certainly, when in 1536 reformers in Cologne turned against their 'whoring priests', and a mob attacked the cathedral and chased out 'more than 200 monks and nuns', Luther condemned the actions of the crowd. 'Oh, that is not good!' he said. 'Such use of force will do great harm to the Reformation, anger many people and strengthen the tyrants. The papacy can be neither destroyed nor preserved by force, because it consists of lies. That is why it must be defeated with the Word of Truth alone.'[25]

Back in Wartburg, he was, though, still capable of being roused to anger by news that reached him. In December, he learned that nine thousand relics were about to be exhibited in a church in Halle as part of a sale of indulgences. This was right on Luther's patch, Halle being less than a hundred miles from Wittenberg.[26] In outrage, he wrote to the prelate behind the event, Archbishop Albrecht of Mainz, accusing him of peddling 'rubbish and lies'. On this matter Luther was in no mood to hide away. 'You need not think Luther is dead,' he warned the prince-archbishop, 'I demand an immediate answer. If you do not reply within two weeks, I will publish a tract against you.'[27] Such a fierce letter did elicit a placatory reply, but it still required Spalatin to step in and stop Luther from publishing the threatened tract.

By contrast, even the details of Karlstadt's reformed communion service on Christmas Day do not appear to have caused Luther undue upset. And why should they? Most of what Karlstadt put into practice was what Luther had promoted in writing. A few weeks later, when consulted about the Zwickau 'prophets', Luther was more damning than Melanchthon and Karlstadt, labelling the three mystics 'firebrands without the sword' and doubting their claims of revelations from God. 'Divine Majesty does not speak directly to men,' he counselled, speaking from his own painful experience of trying to discern the will of a God who is always mysterious.[28]

By the time the town council and elector had reached loggerheads in February, however, Luther knew he could absent himself no longer. Having initially been swept up in a burst of enthusiasm for the prophets, and all the other changes, Melanchthon suddenly regained his equilibrium and wrote to Luther in panic: 'the dam has broken and I cannot stem the waters.'[29] It required a more resolute hand. And so Luther agreed to answer an appeal directed to him by 'the council and the entire city of Wittenberg'.

It was a reluctant 'yes' nonetheless. His main focus at that moment was not events in Wittenberg but the utterly absorbing task that he had set himself of translating the New Testament into German. That, he had estimated, would take him until Easter. The castle had become less a place of custody than a peaceful haven of self-exile, where he could put to one side the distracting day-to-day details and concentrate on his own distinctive brand of popular and popularising scholarship. Already he had plans to carry his translation work further. He had spoken of taking his draft of the New Testament to Wittenberg to seek help with his Greek, and then to retreat again, this time to the country-side rather than Wartburg Castle, to set about the even bigger job of rendering the Old Testament in German, perhaps as a collective effort with those better versed in Hebrew than him.

Another disincentive to re-entering the fray in Wittenberg was that, despite the invitation from a besieged town council, Elector Friedrich opposed Luther coming back. Luther might have forgotten in his study at Wartburg, surrounded by books and drafts, that he was a wanted man, condemned as a heretic by Pope and emperor alike, and at liberty only because his prince had taken steps to protect him. Friedrich, though, was all too aware of the continuing threats, and there was a meeting of the Imperial Diet coming up in Nürnberg. To have Luther at liberty in Wittenberg, pushing on with changes that were already causing widespread unease through the Holy Roman Empire, would place the Elector of Saxony in an uncomfortable position. An invasion of his lands to seize Luther was not out of the question. Better, Friedrich concluded, that Luther remained out of sight in Wartburg.

The two debated the matter by letter, via Spalatin, after Luther gave his protector notice of his planned return. He would be, he said, in one of his rare attempts at humour, another 'relic' for the elector to add to his extensive collection.[30] Friedrich was not amused and continued to dissuade Luther, but being told he couldn't do something only ever had the opposite effect on the reformer.

'I was disturbed that the gospel was brought into disrepute at Wittenberg,' he told the elector. 'If I were not sure that the gospel is on our side, I would have given up. All the sorrow I have had is nothing compared to this. I would gladly have paid for this with my life, for we can answer neither to God nor to the world for what has happened. The devil is at work in this.'[31]

That cosmic battle between good and evil was, for Luther, more significant than any power play between earthly princes. Or the threat to his life, which was real and imminent. The devil sowing discord and distrust in Wittenberg was, he judged, a greater risk than the posse of princes who might breach the town's walls to seize him. Once again, Luther's courage should not be under-estimated.[32]

The tone he took with Friedrich was firm, almost patronising. 'I come to Wittenberg with a higher protection than that of Your Grace. I will protect you more than you will protect me. If I thought you would protect me, I would not come. This is not a case for the sword, but for God, and since you are weak in the faith, you cannot protect me.'[33]

How bold that sounds! To accuse the elector of being 'weak in the faith' was crass ingratitude for the efforts of a prince who, at key points over the previous four years, had almost alone stood between Luther and his accusers as they sought to silence him first by argument and then by force. So why say it? Was Luther allowing his pen to run away with him again? Was he just clumsy when it came to personal relationships? Or had he calculated that the high level of active support for his cause around Germany – from priests, congregations, monasteries, convents and, in some cases, whole towns – made him sufficiently strong that he didn't need a protector any longer? He may also have been revealing his displeasure at Friedrich's failure to speak up for Lutheran reforms, and his opposition to some of the attempts to implement them in Wittenberg.

All are viable readings, but the most likely explanation lies in that 'higher protection' that Luther claimed. God was guiding him and protecting him, rather than the elector, and so Luther could declare his independence of earthly powers and his total reliance on the divine. It was a position he was to adopt repeatedly in the years to come, often in flat contradiction of his actual circumstances. Once he had pinned his hopes on the Pope to reform, then the emperor to back his case, and finally Elector

Friedrich to protect him. Now he was placing everything in God's hands.

Such a conviction served him well on his return to Wittenberg on 6 March. After meeting with Melanchthon, Justas and others, he took to the pulpit of the town church on Sunday 9 March in the first of a series of eight daily sermons designed to restore calm, order and respect to Wittenberg. The crowds flocked to hear their returning hero.

His first address was on a day known as Invocavit Sunday, the first Sunday in the season of Lent, when Christians prepare over forty days for the death and resurrection of Jesus Christ at Easter. Luther reiterated the individualist core of his credo. 'Every one must fight his own battle with death by himself, alone. We can shout into another's ears, but every one must himself be prepared for the time of death, for I will not be with you then, nor you with me. Therefore every one must himself know and be armed with the chief things that concern a Christian. And these are what you, my beloved, have heard from me many days ago.'[34]

He was reminding his hearers of his own authority, and then invoking it to order an end to the division and violence in Wittenberg. 'Dear brethren, follow me; I have never been a destroyer. And I was also the very first whom God called to this work . . . Let us, therefore, let us act with fear and humility, cast ourselves at one another's feet, join hands with each other, and help one another . . . For here we battle not against pope or bishop, but against the devil.'[35]

Where Karlstadt had used the same platform to inflame, Luther now offered a new message – the balm of compromise – and reinforced it with his own leadership. He was, as he said, the first whom God had called to this work. People needed time to decide on the correct path and pace of reform, he urged the congregation that first Sunday. 'I took three years of constant study, reflection and discussion to arrive where I am now,' he told them. 'Can the common man, untutored in such matters, be expected to move the same distance in three months?'[36]

To attempt to force anyone – as had been happening in Wittenberg in his absence – was wrong. 'Haste and violence,' he said, 'betray a lack of confidence in God. See how much He has been able to accomplish through me, though I did no more than pray and preach. The Word did it all.' If he had wanted to achieve God's purpose through violence, Luther reflected, 'I might have started a conflagration at Worms'.[37]

The fearless leader of the opposition was suddenly sounding like the voice of moderation. Instead of spearheading the movement for more and more change, wiping the slate clean and starting again with a whole new Church, Luther in his eight sermons was rowing back from the forward positions on implementation of the reforms taken by Karlstadt and Zwilling. The prayers in the mass that referred to sacrifice should remain excluded, he ruled. And German would be used. But no one should be forced – as Karlstadt and Zwilling had insisted – to take communion in both kinds. They had a choice. Likewise, those who freely wanted to live by vows of celibacy should be respected, as should those who liked to fast, or see statues in their church, or go to confession with a priest. No one was to be required to change overnight patterns of worship that had been with them all their lives.

Two immediate problems resolved themselves. Gabriel Zwilling had already decamped to Zwickau, home of the prophets, after the elector had banned him. Karlstadt had remained in Wittenberg and been there to welcome Luther back, but a gulf had opened up between them. For Karlstadt, the Scriptures were not just the basis of a God-fearing life and a God-fearing community, they were a literal prescription. If they said no 'graven images', then there would be no graven images. Luther, by contrast, while just as convinced of the essential purity of the Scriptures, was not so hidebound by individual details. He was more concerned with the spirit of the law as laid down in them, rather than the letter.

Karlstadt had been unduly influenced, in Luther's opinion, by the Zwickau 'prophets' and their local priest, Thomas Müntzer, into attaching a too-high premium to individual revelation – the mystical notion that God, often in the form of the Holy Spirit, speaks directly to a chosen few so that they could relay His orders to the world. While Luther felt guided by the hand of God, he never claimed to hear His voice. God was not so direct. He kept His mystery. And so the believer must rely on *sola scriptura*, unmitigated by the sort of visions that Karlstadt seemed now to want to place above it.

There was some personal animosity mixed in here as well. Having been given his head, Karlstadt would not have been content once more to stand behind Luther. In his eight sermons, Luther made no reference to Zwilling, but he did – in the third – castigate Karlstadt. 'See to it that you can stand before God and the world when you are assailed,' he told the congregation, 'especially when the devil attacks you in the hour of death. It is not enough to say: this man or that man did it, I followed the crowd, according to the preaching of Dr Karlstadt . . . Not so; everyone must stand on his own feet and be prepared to give battle to the devil.'[38] When the university also censured Karlstadt's writings, he decided to leave Wittenberg with his young wife to take up the post of Evangelical pastor of Orlamünde, a small town 120 miles to the south in Thuringia.

However much he preferred to talk of an Evangelical movement, Luther's supporters were now increasingly looking to him, and him alone, to establish a 'Lutheran' version of the Catholic Church.

PART THREE:

'Pope' Martin

'If you study the sixteenth century, you are inevitably present at something like the aftermath of a particularly disastrous car-crash. All around are half-demolished structures, debris, people figuring out how to make sense of lives that have suddenly been transformed.'

Diarmaid MacCulloch, *All Things Made New: Writings on the Reformation* (2016)

Chapter Ten

Mayhem and Marriage: Making Choices

'I wouldn't trade my Katie for France or Venice.'
Martin Luther, Table Talk[1]

For over a decade the Augustinian friary in Wittenberg had been home to Martin Luther but, when he returned from Wartburg in March of 1522, it was much changed. Most of the community had departed, encouraged by Luther's own writings, to marry and take up posts as Evangelical pastors in nearby churches. By November, there was only one other friar, the prior, Eberhard Brisger, left living there with him. They were rattling around in a building that until recently had housed forty men. Together they raised with Elector Friedrich the suggestion of moving into a smaller property, attached to the cloister, but the prince was having none of it. His appetite for change and upheaval was exhausted.

In the town, the polarisation, coercion and outbreaks of violence that had alarmed Luther when he first arrived back had died down under his calming, authoritative influence. Though he did not retreat in his public statements from the reform agenda, neither did Luther insist everyone fall into line at once, or follow his prescription to the letter. If in principle he remained steadfast, his everyday message was one of compromise: of the need to accommodate others (including the elector) and give them time to come round to the changes. It was not, though, an open-ended promise of tolerance. When it came to the business of living out the reforms he had proposed in the Church, Luther took an

275

evolutionary approach, tinged as ever with his own certainty that God was guiding his hand towards ultimate victory.

The first sphere in which to live out the reality of that approach was locally, in the services he and others led in the churches of Wittenberg and its surrounding areas. Luther's biggest change was to switch the emphasis on to the sermon rather than the eucharist, something Karlstadt had piloted during his absence. By tradition regarded by Catholics as the summit of the mass, a moment available daily to those who attended when they could receive the 'bread of life' to sustain them, the eucharist was now to be offered only during services on Sundays. On weekdays, there would in Luther's eyes just be the bare essentials: preaching and reading from Scripture.

And when the eucharist was part of the service, Luther initially left the words that accompanied it in Latin, though most of the rest of the liturgy was in German. It was another compromise, to allow whole congregations to get used to the vernacular everywhere else in the mass, and then later extend it to the eucharistic celebration.

In 1523 Luther issued *Formulas for Mass and Communion in Wittenberg*. Despite the accusations that had been made, especially after *The Babylonian Captivity*, that he would usher in a free-for-all in worship, he showed himself capable and committed to uniformity, on his own terms.

There was a bigger shift going on. Where once Luther had written about theological questions, now he was providing a guidebook for his followers. His 'formulas' were the building blocks of what could grow to replace the dry prescriptive code of canon law. Initially better at defining himself by what he stood against rather than what he was for, Luther was now answering the challenge to show his adaptability.

The various liturgical details covered were discussed and resolved, some of them still up in the air after Karlstadt's brief and chaotic experiment. He had deemed, for example, that it was wrong, during the mass, for the priest to elevate the bread when saying Jesus' words from the Last Supper, 'this is my body', as had been the traditional Catholic way of things. Karlstadt regarded the symbolism – that the priest was standing in the place of Christ – as an act of 'idolatry', but Luther judged it perfectly permissible, if not essential.

And where with his scriptural literalism Karlstadt had turned people away from the eucharist because they were not in a fit state to receive the sacrament, Luther showed himself more merciful. Drunks and 'fornicators' could be excluded, he ruled, but for them to gain readmission should be made as easy as possible. A simple acknowledgement of their sins, rather than an elaborate confession as had been the way previously, was all that was required.

He also tried to find ways to make real at services his cherished idea of the priesthood of all believers. What made the pastor or minister stand out, he counselled, was his sermon. 'Priests are born,' he wrote. 'Ministers are made.'[2] It was detailed knowledge of the Word of God that made a minister, rather than ordination, as in Catholicism. In place of the sacrificial language and imagery that surrounded the altar, Luther suggested it should henceforth be treated as a simple table, like the table in the Last Supper, around which all were invited to gather and eat. Those who wanted could take communion in both kinds, bread and wine, but no one was to be forced, though by the following year Luther's flexibility on this matter had lessened, and he ruled that it was both or nothing. He delayed even longer, however, before publishing his prescribed text for a German-language service.

All Lutherans looked to him for guidance and he wanted to carry as many of them along with him as possible, without risking further fragmentation. His response to any dilemmas was no longer, as he had previously advised the Catholic Church, to summon a general council. Instead, he took the decisions alone, in a manner close to the hierarchical role of the papacy. But in contrast to some of those incumbents on Saint Peter's throne in his own lifetime, Luther approached the task of leadership with a combination of courage and caution, principle and pragmatism.

If his style was essentially authoritarian – and there were few other models of Church leadership available in the late medieval world – Luther also had a strong instinct towards empowerment. As had already been demonstrated by the priority he gave to making available his translation of the New Testament into German, he wanted above all to give his followers the tools to help them individually to come to know God. He did not aspire to a permanent role intervening between the two.

To make possible such individual independence would, he realised, require an entire programme of re-education of the laity, so as to break the dependency on priests, bishops and popes that had been fostered by Catholicism. Yet there was a tension. Neither did he want them, following the example of Karlstadt, to mistake the words of Scripture for God Himself. That was to turn them into a graven image. No collection of words could capture or contain the mystery of God. Any institution that claimed it could, or that its reading of the Bible could, was wrong.

In 1522 he published a *Personal Prayer Book*, intended as a replacement for popular Catholic texts then in wide circulation. There is something disarmingly simple about the prayers he recommended to readers seeking God's grace: 'Now through Your mercy,' went one, 'implant in our hearts a comforting trust in Your fatherly love, and let us experience the sweet and pleasant savour of a childlike certainty that we may joyfully call You Father, knowing and loving You and calling on You in every trouble.'[3] Luther often spoke of his own hankering for the certainties of a child's faith. '[Children] hold fast to the Word and simply know God. They believe in God for certain, just as He said and just as He promised. But we old fools suffer from heartache and hellish fire, debate the Word at length, and finally must follow their example and cling to the Word.'[4]

As befits a prayer book labelled personal, Luther revealed in one of his selections how hard he still found it to hear God's voice over the distracting clamour made by the devil. 'Silence that evil spirit – the cruel backbiter, accuser, and magnifier of our sin – now and in our last hour, and in every torment of conscience . . . Do not judge us according to the accusations the devil or our wretched conscience brings against us.'[5]

The next year he followed his prayer book with a hymn book, the first in German. If widespread illiteracy made it hard for congregations to grasp the finer points of theology, or even to read the German New Testament, Church music was a more inclusive and accessible route to knowing God. Learned words, repeated often in song, could instil faith. It was an idea with a long history in Catholicism. '*Lex orandi, lex credendi*', a Latin phrase that roughly translates as 'the law of prayer is the law of belief', held that the constant repetition of words, said out loud in the liturgy, was an effective means of instilling doctrine.

In 1529, the musical Luther came up with his best-known hymn, 'A Mighty Fortress', sometimes dubbed 'the battle hymn of the Reformation'. Its stirring words were based on Psalm 46.[6]

> *A mighty fortress is our God,*
> *A bulwark never failing;*
> *Our helper He amid the flood*
> *Of mortal ills prevailing.*
> *For still our ancient foe*
> *Doth seek to work us woe;*
> *His craft and power are great,*
> *And, armed with cruel hate,*
> *On earth is not his equal.*

His efforts in education focused especially on the young. He was keen that every village should have a school where every child could be taught in the knowledge of God. Though he had been fortunate that his parents had encouraged his education, other youngsters missed out completely, because their labour was required. And not all communities had a school.

The teacher was, in Luther's view, as important as the preacher. And, if that teaching followed, in broad terms, his own view of the Scriptures, then the school would also embed in the next generation the Lutheran perspective on Catholicism.

The Reformation spreads

If Wittenberg and its immediate environs were the first testing ground for Luther's efforts to put into practice his reforms, then stage two came as the movement he had inspired spread fast across the lands of the Holy Roman Empire and, beyond its boundaries, across northern Europe. Each day brought new requests from afar for Luther's endorsement and guidance as to what to do next to share in his vision of a rejuvenated Church.

Rapid change brings its own headaches. Popular as Luther's plans were with many worshippers, they also carried with them a sharp loss of revenue. Elector Friedrich's coffers, for example, were emptied because Luther had insisted that the lavishly endowed masses for the dead at the Castle Church in Wittenberg be discontinued, along with the sale of indulgences that accompanied the display of relics there on 1 November. Receipts from such activities were particularly missed because the elector, like other German princes, had been busy copying the example of the French, English and Spanish monarchies with their ever-expanding cast of professional, paid bureaucrats and advisors attached to the court. And a shortage of money also hit the university he had established, especially as it was now facing the reluctance of some abbots and bishops to pay for their novices and seminarians to travel to study in Wittenberg, where the Church's doctrines and traditional practices were being treated with such licence. Luther therefore found himself called upon to become an administrator, a strategist, a politician and the final court of appeal for disputes between his followers.

His plan, on arriving back in Wittenberg from Wartburg Castle, had been to finish his German translation of the New Testament and then move on to the Old Testament. That now had to be fitted around so many other pressing demands. It was not sufficient, as he might have wished, to give ordinary people a version of the Scriptures and leave them to test for themselves the truth of what they were being told by clerics and princes. As copies of Luther's New Testament circulated, there rose up a call for liberation from the Church and princely powers alike. So much so that in the neighbouring Saxon territories of Duke Georg, its ruler was demanding that those with copies of Luther's New Testament, which he regarded as an inflammatory text, should hand them over to the authorities so they could be destroyed.

Emboldened by what they had read, and by Luther's own example of defiance of pope and emperor, many refused the duke's command, and turned to Luther to defend them. But there was little practical assistance he could give, beyond a verbal assault on Duke Georg, in a letter of January 1523, describing him as a 'bladder' (i.e. full of urine).[7] It was knockabout stuff, little comfort to those facing imprisonment and even death for their loyalty to Luther.

On most money matters, Luther was also out of his depth. He had needed no money when in the cloister and the habit of living frugally was ingrained in him. Since the Hermit of Saint Augustine had seconded him to the university in Wittenberg, he received no salary. When he passed his texts to publishers, he asked for no payment, and no share of the considerable profits they made. He just wanted the texts to be distributed.

'Money', he once remarked, 'is Satan's scripture, through which he works in the world, just as God does everything through the true Scripture.'[8] On another occasion, Luther held that 'money cannot quiet hunger, but on the contrary is the cause of hunger'.[9] Fine sentiments, but not much use for priests who had married, started families and stayed in their church. The old endowments that went with the post may have dried up because the donors did not approve of the changes, and the congregation however supportive could not replace such generosity, since many were struggling themselves to eat.

Luther's solution was as simple as it was radical. In Wittenberg, he established what he called 'the common chest'. 'First, a chest with three keys shall be placed, well-kept, in the church. The money, received or otherwise solicited, would be deposited here. Second, the money would be used for all frail needy people in the congregation.'[10] If the pastor and his family were needy, it could cover his stipend, but the aim was to set up a rudimentary social security system. The original 'common chest' stands to this day in Wittenberg's Lutherhaus, the museum in the Black Cloister. By placing others in wealthy, popular churches, Luther's vision was that they would subsidise their harder-pushed neighbouring churches. With the blessing of the town council and of the elector, the scheme functioned well enough in Wittenberg, producing revenue to support three hospitals, and becoming the model for later Lutheran programmes of social engagement. But it struggled when initially tried elsewhere, where the Catholic Church also retained a foothold, and civic authorities and princes could be greedy and opportunistic.

By 1532 Luther was blaming the scarcity of good preachers, essential to the reform movement he was trying to build, on lack of money. 'The world will never believe us poor preachers, but if we had money like the papists, we would easily convert the world.'[11] Lutherans were not as generous, he suggested, as Catholics when it came to supporting their priests. It may have had something to do with not placing them on so elevated a pedestal.

In the same year, he railed again about the lack of generosity of those in the pews. 'The ingratitude of the world towards the Reformation is unspeakable and devilish. For the pastors are attacked there by persecution, here by ingratitude. And if we here in Wittenberg did not have a pious prince as defender, our people would be more plagued than the enemies of the faith. I would not want to live in any city where the pastor depended on its people for his maintenance. The entire city of Wittenberg donates no more than four pennies a year per person for our dear Reformation Church. And that is the way it is everywhere.'[12]

Church and state

If in Wittenberg the Lutherans could still depend on their prince for protection and for money, elsewhere it was more complicated. Another question Luther now had to address was how to shape the relationship between his breakaway Church and the state. This was an issue that for centuries had set popes and princes at each other's throats. The greatest standoff in the German lands, and beyond, had come with the Investiture Controversy of the eleventh and twelfth centuries, which led to fifty years of war. The dispute was ostensibly about who should make appointments to senior Church positions, up to and including the Pope, but behind that lay the whole question of how far the kings and princes could involve themselves in the regulation of churches, abbeys, monasteries, bishoprics and the like. In the backwards and forwards battle between Henry IV, the Holy Roman Emperor, and Pope Gregory VII, each side at different stages held the upper hand (with Henry's elaborate penance in the snow outside

Canossa Castle in 1077, already mentioned, just one of the twists and turns). The Concordat of Worms of 1122 resulted in victory for the papacy, with kings and rulers being given only informal influence in the appointment of bishops and abbots. That settlement, though, had been contested many times since, most recently in 1517, when Pope Leo had given the French king, Francis, a free hand in choosing bishops within his lands in exchange for his support in curtailing the powers of a general council.

As was his habit, Luther tackled the dilemma in writing. *On Secular Authority and How Far One Should Be Obedient to It*, published on New Year's Day, 1523, and penned in German to allow for wide circulation, set limits for princely authority, but also insisted that, within those limits, rulers did have a role and must be respected. In his opening remarks, Luther paired the text with his earlier *Appeal to the Christian Nobility of the German Nation*. That had laid down what princes should do, he explained. The new tract would explain what they shouldn't.

Among his no-go areas were princes seizing books, such as his German translation of the New Testament, or any other of his writings. 'For God Almighty has made our rulers mad . . . [they] have ordered people to put away books and to believe and keep what they [the princes] prescribe.'¹³ Such demands were usurping God's place, he argued.

Although the tract came with a dedicatory letter to Duke Johann, brother and heir to Elector Friedrich, Luther still aired his generally poor opinion of the ruling class. Too many spent their time, he alleged, 'doing what they please with God's Word' and 'fleecing the poor'.¹⁴ He could have said the same about the Catholic authorities, and he was, with such remarks, playing to that constituency of disgruntled lower orders in Germany whose resentment against their rulers was causing social unrest. Such people were now looking to Luther to bring about political and economic as well as spiritual and ecclesiastical changes. It was all one in the late medieval mindset.

Luther, though, sought to disentangle them. He fell back again on Saint Paul's Letter to the Romans. 'You must all obey the governing authorities,' the apostle had written. 'Since all government comes from God, the civil authorities were appointed by God.'[15] They therefore are legitimate and have their legitimate areas of operation, which Luther defined as 'extend[ing] to life and property, and what is external upon earth', but not to the spiritual domain. 'Over the soul, God can and will let no one rule but Him.'[16]

This was his doctrine of 'two kingdoms', which sought to distinguish in dualistic terms between the inner spiritual human being and the outer citizen who operated in the world. It was the starting point for the separation of Church and state that was to come, but in its first formulation was a much more moderate, accommodating approach than the path advocated by some of Luther's erstwhile followers. Karlstadt, for example, believed that only one set of laws could exist and bind humanity, and that was the Scriptures.

Luther had already referred (in 1520's *The Freedom of the Christian Man*) to a small group of 'true Christians believers'. In *On Secular Authority* he developed this thought. Such people had no need for princes and their legal codes, he said, but the 'unrighteous' did – 'to restrain the unchristian and wicked so that they must keep the peace outwardly, even against their will'.[17] And that restraint, he believed, could extend to the use of force. '[Jesus] acknowledged the sword, He nevertheless did not use it: for it is of no use in His kingdom.' Yet in this world, the sword may, he conceded, be necessary.[18]

Luther's argument was, in many respects, a traditional one – found, for example, in Saint Augustine, whose words had long been used by the Catholic Church to provide a religious justification for war and violence. Yet there is also an unmissable sense that Luther would really rather have nothing to do with the messy business of earthly matters and battles, but was only condescending to address them now out of obligation to his followers and love of neighbour. His endorsement of state power, however, up to and including violence, may have worked on paper, but it proved fragile when confronted with reality. Drawing a line, as the 'two kingdoms' theory tried to do, between private life and public morality has rarely been an easy or successful endeavour.

Luther the anti-Semite?

The flaws in Luther's formula become apparent with the publication in January 1523, a few days after *On Secular Authority*, of another shorter work of his, *That Jesus Christ Was Born a Jew*. It started out addressing the persecution of the Jews by German rulers – something 'external upon earth' by Luther's own definition – but then concluded firmly in the spiritual domain.

The essay was prompted – or even provoked – by a story doing the rounds, and originating in traditionalist Catholic circles, that Luther had denied the Virgin Birth – i.e. that Jesus' mother, Mary, was not a virgin when she gave birth to Him as the Church taught. This allegation was untrue, Luther responded, and indeed he had previously shown his respect for Mary in his translation and commentary of 1521 on the great Marian hymn and prayer, the Magnificat. But in the course of pointing out that Jesus was born Jewish – a fact many medieval Christians preferred to ignore, but with which Luther had no problem – he went on to repeat many of the insults that Christians routinely threw at the Jews, apparently endorsing such prejudices.

Yet the essay also contained his own outright condemnation of the ill-treatment of the Jews by the rulers of those lands in which they were permitted to live and trade. 'They have dealt with the Jews as if they were dogs rather than human beings; they have done little else than deride them and seize their property . . . If the apostles, who also were Jews, had dealt with us Gentiles as we Gentiles deal with the Jews, there would never have been a Christian among the Gentiles . . . When we are inclined to boast of our position [as Christians] we should remember that we are but Gentiles, while the Jews are of the lineage of Christ. We are aliens and in-laws; they are blood relatives, cousins, and brothers of Our Lord. Therefore, if one is to boast of flesh and blood the Jews are actually nearer to Christ than we are.'[19]

Any charge of anti-Semitism against Luther, on the basis of this publication, is therefore misplaced. Yet his real purpose becomes apparent as he goes on. He wanted to convert the Jews to Christianity. 'If we really want to help them, we must be guided in our dealings with them not by papal law but by the law of Christian love. We must receive them cordially, and permit them to trade and work with us, that they may have occasion and opportunity to associate with us, hear our Christian teaching, and witness our Christian life.'[20] To modern eyes, this urge to convert may read as a form of anti-Semitism. How can you respect another faith if you want to woo its believers?

But that is applying a contemporary judgement. For his time, Luther's remarks would have been seen as radical. The backdrop was a Holy Roman Empire where only a handful of cities permitted Jews to live (Wittenberg was not one, and Luther may never have met a Jew), and where, in these 'havens', with the connivance of the ruling class, violence was routinely handed out to Jews, whether it be at the end of Maundy Thursday church services, when the treachery of Judas 'the Jew', the renegade apostle, was recalled, or when economic times got hard and the Jews became an easy scapegoat on whom rulers could blame all financial ills.

The veil of the temple is rent

Since Luther's reappearance in Wittenberg, Elector Friedrich had once again been under pressure to act on the condemnation of his professor in the Edict of Worms and by the papal decree of excommunication. Luther's return from Wartburg had coincided with the next meeting of the Imperial Diet, this time in Nürnberg. It was a fractious, drawn out and ultimately inconclusive meeting, plagued by delays caused by the death of key players, and therefore lasting, with interruptions and resumptions, from 1522 to 1525. As well as Luther, on its agenda was the continuing advance of the Ottoman Turks, this time into Hungary. Charles V, with papal support, wanted to rally a German army to fight them, but had to be content with the promise of a new tax to be levied in the empire to support his campaign.

Perhaps if he had attended, Charles might have been able to impose his will, but he had his own problems in Spain, and in the newly conquered colony of Mexico, plus a war with the French (which saw him capture their king, Francis, at the Battle of Pavia in 1525). Instead he sent his younger brother, Ferdinand of Austria. This wasn't the only change in the cast list. A new papal legate, Francesco Chieregati, represented a new Pope at the opening of the diet. Leo X had died suddenly on 1 December 1521, still unable to face down Luther's rebellion.

Many of those closest to him wanted to see Giulio de'Medici, his nephew, succeed him, but others (notably the French) were busy plotting. The English cardinal Thomas Wolsey was among alternative candidates mooted. In the end a different compromise was found in the unlikely shape of sixty-three-year-old Hadrian VI, a humbly born Dutch Dominican who hadn't even attended the conclave of cardinals.[21] It was hoped that Hadrian's personal piety (he entered Rome barefoot), disdain for lavish Renaissance building projects (he halted the redecoration of the

Vatican apartments) and ascetic lifestyle might just convince some that the papacy was not as corrupt and worldly as Luther had alleged.

For all his determination to purge the excesses of the curia, however, Hadrian owed his ecclesiastical ascent to the patronage of Charles V, whose tutor he had once been, and as whose father confessor he still served. When it came to Germany, Hadrian fell in behind Charles's established but failed policy in demanding that the Edict of Worms be enforced throughout the empire against 'this petty monk'.[22] There were small but significant concessions – admitting that some of the blame for the standoff rested with corruption in Rome, and even acknowledging mishandling of the issue by the previous regime under Leo. But on the principal question of Luther's demands for reform, the Catholic authorities under Hadrian continued to offer nothing.

And, in response, neither would those German princes who had warmed to Luther and the prospect of change that he represented in their relationship with Rome and the emperor. So deep indeed was their resentment at Rome that the 'Gravamina', or list of grievances at the burdens the papacy placed on Germany, first compiled in the 1450s, was revived and circulated in 1522 at the Diet of Nürnberg.

Like Leo, Hadrian tried to appeal to Elector Friedrich to abandon Luther. It was certainly an impassioned letter. 'The veil of the temple is rent. Be not beguiled because Martin Luther appeals to Scripture. So does every heretic, but Scripture is a book sealed with seven seals which cannot so well be opened by one carnal man as by all the holy saints.'[23]

The line of attack remained the same. Rome represented tradition and Luther was simply wrong. Friedrich still did not get the explanation he had long requested as to why precisely Luther was wrong. He knew his professor wasn't 'carnal'. And so Hadrian's appeal fell on deaf ears.

By May 1522, the diet had disbanded without agreement. It reconvened later in the year, and ajourned again in 1523. On 14 September 1523, Hadrian died, his reign as short as the line of those in Rome who would miss him. His efforts to rein in excess had made him many enemies. Rumour had it that he was poisoned, but it was never substantiated.

By the time the diet gathered again in Nürnberg early in 1524, Giulio de'Medici had been elected, at the second time of asking, as Pope Clement VII, and the Renaissance bandwagon was back on track as he commissioned the *Last Judgement* for the Sistine Chapel (though he did not live to see Michelangelo start work). Regarding Germany, he was another who simply did not appreciate the danger of a schism and believed, as had his predecessors, that enough bullying of the princes there would eventually do for Luther and his Reformation.

Clement may have been a great patron of the arts, but he was a poor diplomat. His efforts to play the French against Emperor Charles, switching allegiances to suit his own best advantage, ended in failure and crushing defeat in 1527 when imperial troops marched into Rome. Drunken Lutherans among the ranks of Charles's army (religious difference mattered little to the emperor when it came to finding soldiers willing to fight) sacked the capital of Catholicism. There are stories of them parading around in looted cardinals' and even papal robes, staging mock processions and blessings under the windows in the fortified Castel Sant'Angelo where Clement had taken refuge. The crowd outside is even said to have chanted that they wanted to eat him alive. It was another low ebb for a papacy that claimed so much in terms of God-given authority. However bad the behaviour of the Lutheran troops, the experience might have given Clement pause to reflect on the extent of the popular support Luther had attracted.

Nürnberg had finally ended in 1525 without progress. Their realms ever more divided over the attitude taken to Luther's ongoing reform of the Church, many of the German princes regarded the Edict of Worms as unenforceable. The Pope had a few supporters – Duke Georg remained as staunchly anti-Luther as ever – but the majority now wanted a general council of the German Church as the only possible way of resolving the matter, with reformers and Catholics participating on an equal footing. That, though, was vetoed by Rome as an affront to its dignity. How could Luther be treated as an equal? All of which left him confined to Electoral Saxony, and his supporters free to continue to press their own local rulers for changes along the lines that Luther was enacting in and around Wittenberg.

On 5 May 1525, Elector Friedrich died at his hunting lodge at Lochau. Some accounts have it that, on his deathbed, he took the eucharist in both kinds, in the Lutheran way, something he had hitherto refused to do,[24] but that may just be wishful myth-making. Perhaps this pragmatic man was covering all bases before seeking salvation. Luther preached in German at the funeral in the Castle Church in Wittenberg, and Melanchthon in Latin.

Though he had protected his professor until the end, Friedrich had continued to avoid his company. In his last months it had become harder, because Spalatin, their go-between, had revealed to Luther that he wanted to leave the court, cast aside his ordination vows and marry. Knowing that the elector was ailing, Luther persuaded him to stay in post, but within three months of Friedrich's death, Spalatin was gone.

Perhaps Friedrich just hadn't liked the sound of the serious-minded, uncompromising friar, even if he admired his courage and wanted an answer to the questions he was asking. Many of Luther's reforms, though, offended the elector's orthodox soul. The loss of the annual display of his relics in the Schlosskirche pained him in particular. His collection, assembled over a lifetime, was now locked away in the church's sanctuary.

Outflanked

All religions are coalitions of individuals and groups. Catholicism had been remarkably successful – ruthlessly successful, indeed – in maintaining its unity over the centuries, but Luther was now the latest to challenge it by exposing its weaknesses. Yet within his own reform movement, he was also beginning to discover quite how hard it could be to marshal those who, in theory at least, share your vision.

Luther had made *sola scriptura* the foundation stone on which to build what to many appeared to be a parallel Church, but Scripture can be a distinctly unstable base. It is open, after all, to interpretation in many ways. Just as Luther's take on, for example, passages in Saint Paul's letters had not been the same as that of the Catholic theologians who confronted him, now he found himself being faced down by other Evangelicals – or 'Sectaries', another word in circulation – who had emerged in his wake, often initially as supporters, but who were now challenging his reading of the Old and New Testaments. Having already fractured Western Christianity, Luther was witnessing his breakaway movement suffer its own fragmentation.

Among those defiantly outflanking him was Andreas von Karlstadt. Since becoming pastor of the local church in Orlamünde, he had grown ever more radical, keen to act and guided only by his own literal reading of Scripture. While Luther was off the scene in Wartburg Castle, Karlstadt had used the Bible to justify his removal of statues and artworks from Wittenberg's churches. They were, he claimed, the 'graven images' forbidden in the Old Testament.

On his return, Luther had used his personal authority to stop Karlstadt's experiment, but in Orlamünde there was no one to stand in the way. Once he had banished the statues there, Karlstadt moved on to forbid the baptism of babies – placing him at odds with both mainstream Catholic practice and Luther's teaching. He noted that it was nowhere specified in Scripture, which spoke instead, he claimed, of baptism as an adult commitment.

Karlstadt used the Ten Commandments to introduce other innovations. The Sabbath in Orlamünde was henceforth to be 'kept holy', with Christians doing nothing else on Sundays but attend service and listen to his sermon. And he also went beyond Luther's acceptance of the 'real presence' of Jesus in the bread and wine at the eucharist to insist that there was nothing real about them. They were merely symbols. It was over this difference that the Reform movement splintered.

Karlstadt began to publish his views, in defiance of an agreement made at Nürnberg by the German princes to prevent the circulation of any more inflammatory texts. As a result, he was ordered by the Elector of Saxony to give up his role at Orlamünde, but his parishioners backed him in staying put. In theory, of course, Luther supported the right of congregations to choose their own pastor. In Orlamünde's case, however, it was a case of anyone but Karlstadt. Here was a classic problem of leadership.

And it wasn't the only one confronting Luther. Thomas Müntzer had once been the priest in the town of Zwickau, whence the three 'prophets' had come to Wittenberg with his encouragement. They were uneducated weavers, but Müntzer was very different in background. A man of education, he had been an early supporter of Luther, attending some of his lectures in Wittenberg. In July 1520, he had written to Luther as one 'whom you brought to birth by the gospel'.[25]

By July 1523, he had risen on the Lutheran tide to be installed by popular acclaim as both pastor and mayor of the Saxon mining town of Allstedt, where his gift as a preacher – comparable some said to Luther's – won him many disciples, but he ended up in a dispute with the local landowner who brought his case to the attention of Elector Friedrich.

Müntzer had meanwhile written to Luther to challenge him over finding a place in his theology for visions from God. While agreeing with Luther in decrying as false the claims of the Zwickau prophets to have been directed by a personal encounter with God, Müntzer nonetheless believed that Scripture was full of prophets, from Moses onwards, with whom God had communicated directly. Surely, he suggested, God's words in some visions, if shown to be genuine, could be accorded greater authority than the Word as written in the Bible?

A key component in Luther's theology was that God could only ever be partially known, through Jesus Christ. He had little time for current or past intensely religious individuals who claimed that God had revealed Himself directly to them. Their testimonies were something he had explored briefly as a young friar at Staupitz's behest, but had found them wanting.[26] God was not so easily conjured up, he argued, and so he dismissed Müntzer, and his supporters, as *Schwärmer* – fanatics, though the word in German also carries the association of a swarm.

Such intemperate and intolerant language from Luther only encouraged Müntzer and his supporters to threats of actual violence, rather than violent words, against those who disagreed with them. And Scripture provided them with plenty of examples of those chosen by God who had spilt blood in order that their view might prevail. In the Old Testament, Yahweh regularly encourages the Israelites to attack and kill their enemies.

Müntzer and Karlstadt shared common ground in rejecting infant baptism. Both, too, were keen on going further than Luther who, in their opinion, had now shown himself as too establishment, too ready to make compromises to carry all shades of opinion with him, and not truly on the side of the common man.

Both these pastors included in their oratory a particular appeal to those at the bottom of the social pack. They preached a vision of a Christian community made up of equals, akin to Luther's theory of a priesthood of all baptised believers, but made real in everyday terms. It became a new rallying cry for the discontented to vent their anger at the better-off and their rulers.

To describe the Reformation as fuelled by social and economic discontent is to present only a partial picture. Those who followed first Luther, then Karlstadt and Müntzer, and later other preachers, were predominantly from the put-upon lower classes, but not exclusively. And many of these preachers' motivations were as much about religious zeal as economic grievance. Congregations weren't drawn to hear Lutheran preachers because they saw it as a way of rising up against their rulers. They came, heard and embraced the new gospel as articulated by Luther and saw in it salvation both in the afterlife, but also in the here and now. They wanted to be saved from poverty and exploitation. To separate out the secular and religious aspects is, once again, to misunderstand the late medieval mindset.

When in March 1524 Müntzer mixed his incendiary rhetoric with visions of a forthcoming biblical apocalypse that would (as Revelation promises) see Jesus return to earth and usher in a millennium of rule shaped by justice,[27] his congregation was so fired up that they wanted it to start straight away. To precipitate the apocalypse, they went from his church to attack a popular local place of Catholic pilgrimage, the Mallerbach Chapel, where an image of the Virgin Mary was said to effect miracle cures. They burned it to the ground.

The nuns who tended the chapel escaped with their lives and sought a protector in Duke Johann, Elector Friedrich's brother and heir. While the secular authorities were puzzling over what to do to counter such outbreaks of popular unrest, Luther offered them guidance in *Letter to the Princes of Saxony Concerning the Rebellious Spirit*. If Müntzer was inciting violence, Luther wrote, he could not claim to be a minister of the Word. 'This bloodthirsty Satan' must be banished. Duly prompted, the princes summoned Müntzer to explain himself to them in August. When confronted by official might, his popular support ebbed away and Müntzer took his chance to escape.

Once he had reached a place of safety, however, his defiance returned and he took the opportunity to give Luther a taste of his own medicine. He published a blistering attack on him, entitled *An Obligatory Defence and Reply to the Spiritless Soft-Living Flesh at Wittenberg*.

Around the same time, in the spring of 1524 when he travelled to Jena, near Erfurt, Luther had encountered Karlstadt by chance. They agreed to meet in a local inn, but reconciliation was apparently the last thing on Karlstadt's mind. He angrily accused Luther of wrongly reporting him to the authorities for taking up arms, and attempting to get him banished.[28] When Luther turned up the next day in Orlamünde to see for himself what was going on in Karlstadt's parish, he found a congregation solidly behind their pastor and unmoved by Luther's own status.

To solve this essentially Church problem, therefore, he resorted to the state. It may have suited his purposes in that moment, but it was later to come back to haunt him. Karlstadt was ordered out of Saxony by the elector, without so much as a hearing. The contrast between the support given by the Saxon authorities to Luther, and his own summary dismissal, was not lost on an embittered Karlstadt.

Taking a violent turn

Karlstadt headed for the Swiss cantons, a group of thirteen territories, nominally under the authority of the Holy Roman Empire, but which had gained considerable independence by exploiting the rivalry between the empire and their other larger neighbour, France. Cities such as Zurich and Basel had proved a draw for dissenters because of their reputation for tolerance. Erasmus had decamped to the latter in 1521 from his base at the University of Louvain in the Low Countries. Emperor Charles's crackdown on Catholic dissent in his own territories had widened into a purge of anyone who disagreed with papal teaching, and Erasmus had been made to feel uncomfortable.

It was not Erasmus, however, who made the greatest impact on the newly arrived Karlstadt, but Ulrich Zwingli, who since 1519 had been a priest at Grossmünster (Great Minster) in Zurich. In the five years since, Zwingli had become the leader of the reform movement in the city, and his influence had spread into other Swiss cantons. Zwingli was initially full of admiration for Luther: inspired by the Ninety-Five Theses, he had led a protest in 1519 against the sale of indulgences in Zurich for the Saint Peter's building fund, and had seen off the vendor, Bernhardin Sanson; his oratory was powerful and his sermons were celebrated for their thorough exploration of the Scriptures, especially the writings of Saint Paul, as the prime source for Christian teaching; he was an enthusiastic supporter of clerical marriage; and he abhorred the corruption of the Church as vehemently as Luther. Like him, Zwingli had been engaged in a running battle with the Church authorities, including a series of disputations with his local bishop at Constance during 1522 and 1523. The following year, he had broken with the Catholic Church and carried most of Zurich with him.

Yet, there were areas where he went beyond what Luther proposed by way of change. It had been Zwingli's sermon, at Easter 1522, dismissing Church rules on fasting as having no basis in Scripture, and then handing round portions of sausage to his congregation, that is sometimes described as the starting point of the Swiss Reformation. Luther continued to hold that fasting had a point, though not quite as much of one as Catholicism taught. Zwingli, too, was changing the liturgy faster and more radically than Luther, replacing the mass with services according to his own rule book, published in 1525. It insisted that churches be stripped of 'graven' images and devoid of music. And his close working relationship with the city council of Zurich caused some of his opponents to accuse him of operating a theocracy there.

In theology, too, Zwingli differed from Luther. He had almost died in 1519, and attributed his survival to the intervention of the Holy Spirit. It was the passages in Paul on the role of the Spirit[29] that he prized more highly than those in which Luther had found the inspiration for 'justification by faith'. And while both men rejected the sacrificial aspect with which Catholicism imbued the mass, Zwingli was not content with Luther's continuing belief in the real presence, the notion that Christ's words 'this is my body' at the Last Supper meant that he was corporeally present in some way in the bread at communion. Instead Zwingli read the same words as meaning 'this signifies my body'. The eucharist was about symbolism.

It was on this final issue that he found common cause with the newly arrived Karlstadt. In 1524 Karlstadt published three pamphlets in Basel, attacking Lutheran teaching on the real presence. When he met Zwingli, he shared all his grievances about the wrongs he believed Luther had done him. Zwingli and Karlstadt became firm allies.

Zwingli's experiment in Zurich had gained support in some Swiss cantons, but in the more traditionally Catholic among the thirteen it was regarded as heretical. Where Luther was working in Wittenberg to coax those who disagreed with his changes to accept their worth by leading a slow process of compromise and evolution, Zwingli knew no such restraint. If agreement could not be reached, he was willing to resort to violence to win the argument.

This marked another crucial difference with Luther – and with some of Zwingli's own followers. Luther decried violence, as did some among in Zurich. A radical group, led by Conrad Grebel, read the Scripture in a different and more literal way than Luther or even Zwingli. They argued that Jesus' Sermon on the Mount required all true believers to embrace radical poverty, to put away the sword and to sever all compromising ties with civil government.[30] Zwingli's preparedness to fight, and his control of the city council in Zurich, alienated them from him. But their biggest objection was over Zwingli's refusal to accept another of their key beliefs – that baptism should be delayed until adulthood, when the individual was sufficiently mature to make a statement of commitment to Christ to accompany being bathed in water. That was what was required in their reading of the Scriptures.[31] It caused them to be known as the Anabaptists, from the Greek for re-baptise.

Zwingli, in his 1525 tract, *On Baptism*, took the opposite position (as did Luther), and defended infant baptism. He carried the Zurich council with him, but not his new colleague, Karlstadt, whose views were in line with the Anabaptists. The council in Zurich ordered that any parents refusing to baptise their infant child be punished and expelled from the city. When this did nothing to deter the Anabaptists, it went further. Anyone caught re-baptising an adult would face the death sentence.

In January 1527, the Anabaptists had their first martyr, when Grebel's close colleague, Felix Manz, was found guilty of re-baptism and put to death by drowning in Lake Zurich. As thorough-going pacifists, who took their lead from Jesus when rebuked Peter for reaching for his weapon with the words, 'put your sword back, for all who draw the sword will die by the sword',[32] the Anabaptists refused to fight back against Zwingli and his allies. As a result, many were arrested and executed. The Swiss reformer had blood on his hands.

This alarmed some of the other radical pastors in Zurich, Basel and Strasbourg – including Martin Bucer, Luther's disciple from Heidelberg, who wrote to Wittenberg, appealing for Luther's support in restraining Zwingli. Luther offered them strong words. He was scathing about Zwingli as one who had 'stumbled from the path',[33] and on another occasion accused him of 'doing nothing but seeking honours ... what he does is not good.'[34] Yet, generally, he seemed to underestimate the challenge posed by Zwingli, instead reserving his strongest language for Karlstadt, during the period the two men were working side by side in Zurich. In early 1525, Luther's *Against the Heavenly Prophets* pronounced Karlstadt 'our worst enemy'. He did go on to widen his attack to cover Zwingli, though not by name. 'If we boast that we have God's word and do not take care as to how we are to keep it, it is soon lost.'[35]

But quickly he became distracted from this substantive point and returned again to attacking the old friend who had dared to contradict him. 'I beg every Christian who observes how we bicker in this matter to remember that we are not dealing with important things, but with the most trivial ones ... each one should recognise how false and evil the spirit of Dr Karlstadt is, who, not content to ignore and be silent concerning the great and significant articles, so inflates the least significant ones as if the salvation of the world depended more on them than on Christ Himself.'[36]

It all did Luther no credit. Even Melanchthon had cautioned against such a virulent attack on Karlstadt – playing the man rather than the ball – but Luther's own resentment, fuelled by that paranoia that could bubble up inside him when he sensed betrayal, was so overwhelming that he failed to see that the actions of Karlstadt, and more significantly of Zwingli, had raised questions about his teaching that required thoughtful, compelling answers rather than crude invective. Belittling had been the tactic of successive popes when confronted by Luther, and it had only strengthened his hand. In his sweeping, quasi-papal attack on the Swiss reformers, Luther repeated that mistake. Reformed Christianity was the victim as it split into antagonistic camps,[37] demonstrating that there was not one Reformation, but many, depending on place and circumstance. Luther may have been the starting point, but it was now spreading beyond him and his control.

A marriage of convenience?

Luther had written much about marriage as he opened it in stages to clergy, monks and nuns. In late 1522, in the midst of everything else, he produced an entire tract on the subject, *The Estate of Marriage*. 'How I dread preaching on the estate of marriage! I am reluctant to do it because I am afraid if I once get really involved in the subject it will make a lot of work for me and for others.'[38] Prophetic words, for within three years he would be married himself.

In writing, his concern was robustly and earthily to sweep away the many restrictions that Catholicism had placed on marriage. '[It] is an outward, bodily thing like any other worldly undertaking [rather than, as Catholicism taught, a sacrament and something to be regulated by the Church]. Just as I may eat, drink, sleep, walk, ride with, buy from, speak to, and deal with a heathen, Jew, Turk or heretic, so I may also marry any of them.'

Given that Christian Europe felt itself at that moment under threat from the Ottoman advance, such a positive reference to the Turks should not go unnoticed, nor indeed the inclusion of Jews in his list of potential spouses. He was not, this passage suggests, by nature intolerant.

Neither did he have Catholicism's enduring dislike and suspicion of sex that caused it to place so many restrictions on the starting, the maintaining and the ending of a marriage – 'burdening us with laws' on the subject, as he was later to describe it.[39] He was much more realistic and pragmatic. If a man was impotent, he wrote in *The Estate of Marriage*, his wife could take another husband, though he did restrict her choice to her in-laws. And it worked both ways. 'When a wife is unable to satisfy her husband [sexually],' he said in a *Table Talk*, 'he can take a second, but must still care for the first.'[40] Yet, in *The Estate of Marriage*, he was as harsh in his condemnation of adultery as Jesus had been in the gospels.[41]

In the tract, he nevertheless repeated once again his reverence for the celibate life as something 'rare, not one in a thousand' and said that those who can accept it 'are a special miracle of God'.[42] Since his followers regarded Luther as a rare creature, they took this to be a reference to his own chosen path. While he was happy to preside at the weddings of those around him, he was not about to marry himself. In April 1523, for example, he had travelled to Altenberg to conduct the marriage of Wenceslaus Linck in the town where the former Augustinian provincial was now pastor.

Around the same time, on the eve of Easter Sunday 1523, a dozen nuns, inspired by Luther's teaching on the shortcomings of their vows, escaped the Cistercian Abbey at Marienthron, near Grimma, in a covered wagon driven by a local merchant, Leonard Koppe. He was risking his life by helping them. Assisting a nun to jump over the convent wall was at that time a capital offence. Since Grimma was located in the realm of Duke Georg, such insubordination against the letter of Catholicism was likely to provoke the harshest measures.

Luther left a detailed account of the sisters' flight in another essay, *Why Nuns May, in All Godliness, Leave the Convents*.[43] It did not, however, contain the wonderfully pungent detail later embroidered on to this episode – that the nuns hid themselves in empty fish barrels that were being reclaimed by the merchant after the pre-Easter Lenten season, when the convent had abstained from meat and eaten a mountain of fish instead.

Luther did mention that three of the dozen absconders headed back to their families, who were willing to welcome them home, even though they had caused scandal by their actions. The other nine, fearful of a dusty answer if they turned up on their family doorstep, headed instead for the one place they knew they would be greeted enthusiastically, Wittenberg. Among their number was Margarethe von Staupitz, sister of Luther's mentor, and Katharina von Bora, a feisty twenty-four-year-old, unafraid to speak her mind.

Her youth is poorly chronicled. Even the year usually given for her birth – 1499 – is unreliable. Her father, Hans, was a nobleman, albeit an impoverished one, and she was born, one of five surviving children, at his Lippendorf estate, south of Leipzig. Her mother died when she was small. When her father remarried, Katharina was packed off first to an Augustinian convent at Brehna and then to the Cistercians at Marienthron, where she took religious vows in 1514. The extent to which she felt a calling to religious life is unknown, but she stood in a long line of daughters of noble families, regarded as surplus to requirement, sent to convents.

It was a comfortable enough life. The abbess is thought to have been her maternal aunt and the convent owned a large swathe of the surrounding rich agricultural land, which produced a decent income and plenty of food. The cloister church meanwhile contained 367 relics, which generated more money through pilgrims and the sale of indulgences.

Quite how the Lutheran message had reached inside the cloister is unknown, though such was the spread of Luther's writings at the time that it would have been strange if it hadn't. Luther himself had visited the local Augustinian monastery in 1516 and stayed in touch thereafter with its prior, Wolfgang von Zeschau, who renounced his vows in 1522. He had two sisters in Marienthron, and they were among the twelve who escaped.

While yet another sign of the gathering pace of change in Catholicism, the arrival of nine runaway nuns in Wittenberg also posed a problem. Single women, no longer in a nunnery, could not decently set up home alone. They had, by the custom of the time, to be married. Lutheranism had no argument with that principle. Perhaps on account of her sharp tongue, Katharina was the last to find a husband. Or it may have been because she was not prepared to accept any old suitor.

For two years she lived as a guest in the marital home of Lucas Cranach the Elder. In a series of portraits produced by Cranach and his studio between 1526 and 1529, she is no conventional beauty. Her hair swept back and held tightly in place in some, or covered by an apricot scarf that wraps under her chin in another, she is forbidding, her eyes stern, her gaze fixed, if a little uneven, and her mouth displaying not even a hint of a smile, while her hands are clasped in a business-like way in her lap. Yet there is also something vixen-like about the whole assembly of her features that suggests she would be no pushover and might even be persuaded to laugh.

One student, Hieronymus Baumgartner, a pupil of Melanchthon, courted her, but then disappeared home to Nürnberg and did not return. His family is thought to have disapproved of him marrying a renegade nun of no means. Luther was taking sufficient interest in her plight – and that of the other eight nuns – to write to remind the young man that Katharina was awaiting his return. When he failed to do the decent thing, she put her foot down at being married off to a much older pastor, Kaspar Glatz. She would, she said, half in jest, half in defiance, marry only Luther or his colleague, Nikolaus von Amsdorf. Her point seemed to be that she was not opposed to marriage, even to someone older, but that if it came to what was presumably a very large age gap with Glatz, she would prefer to remain a spinster. Katharina was evidently neither a shrinking violet nor afraid to speak boldly, which would have provided common ground with Luther.

For his part, he had been quietly considering marriage, if only because so many of those around him were doing it, but had held back on the grounds that his life remained in danger. A proposal would, in this scenario, be an invitation to become a young widow. If that sounds rather abstract, then it is an indication of how, at this stage, Luther regarded the prospect of human intimacy. So much so that he laughed it off when, in 1525, Spalatin asked him once again if he was tempted to marry. In reply, Luther made another of his rare jokes, labelling himself a 'famous lover' who has had 'three wives at the same time'.[44] This was a reference to the three remaining Marienthron nuns not yet married. Of this trio, Luther went on, two were about to tie the knot, and 'the third I can hardly hold on to with my left arm'. It is a curious expression, much debated by scholars, which appears to have been in popular usage to refer to a mistress. Was Luther revealing that he had dispensed with the need for marriage and was 'in a relationship', as we would say today? There was even a rumour, when he and Katharina did marry, that she was pregnant. It was repeated by, among others, Erasmus – albeit only to question it.[45]

There is no evidence for such claims. Indeed, one remark of Luther's appears to suggest the opposite. 'The best medicine against fornication is to get married.'[46] The comment about his 'left arm' is better seen as Luther trying too hard in his own blunt (and in this case gauche) way to disown any intention of marrying. Yet two months later he had done it.

He was later to confess, with an appalling lack of chivalry, that it was another of the runaway nuns, Ave von Schönfeld, who had first caught his eye;[47] but while he was mulling over the theoretical possibility of marriage itself, she had got on with the reality and tied the knot with a pharmacist employed by Cranach.

What finally seems to have made up Luther's mind on taking a wife was a change of heart on his part about the risk of any proposal making a young widow. As the uprising known to history as the Peasants' War began to erupt in 1524, it looked more likely than ever that his life was under immediate threat. And when, in May 1525, as the conflict neared its bloody end, Luther's long-time protector Elector Friedrich died, he became ever more convinced that his own death was imminent. But now his concern was no longer the fate of any wife he should take if their marriage was short-lived. Instead it was what would look best theologically. So, drily and without emotion, he decided that he should live out for posterity his point that monks could and should marry by taking a bride himself. No one thereafter could accuse him of not practising what he preached.

It is hardly the script for a great romance. And there was a further practical, selfish motive. Relations with his father, Hans, since that dedicatory letter attached to *On Monastic Vows*, had been improving, but Hans was pressing his son to do the expected thing, now he had been freed by his own teaching to marry. Luther was later to tell Amsdorf that he had agreed to marry only 'to comply with my father's wish for progeny ... I feel neither passionate love nor burning for my spouse, but I will cherish her'.[48]

His decision made about marriage itself, there only remained the question of identifying a suitable wife to fill the vacancy. Since Katharina was the only one of the nine nuns left over, she would do. There is, therefore, no record of a romantic proposal.

A very small wedding with a handful of guests took place in the Black Cloister, the now almost empty Augustinian monastery in Wittenberg, on 13 June. Luther's confessor, Johann Bugenhagen, conducted the service, with Justas Jonas in attendance, along with Cranach and his wife Barbara, the only other woman present. It was followed a fortnight later by a much more public declaration – a *Wirtschaft*, or church celebration, followed by a communal meal. Bells rang as the couple processed through the streets of Wittenberg to the Stadtkirche, which had not so long ago been the scene of ugly protests, but was now in festive mood.

Next came the banquet in the Augustinian cloister, with Luther's parents in attendance as well as Leonard Koppe, the merchant who had liberated Katharina from the convent in his wagon. Presents were sent by the university, by the town council, and by the new Saxon Elector, Johann, who gave the couple a hundred florins, about two thousand pounds in today's money.[49] He also solved the problem of what to do with the Black Cloister by handing over this substantial four-storey residence to the newlyweds as their family home.[50] It befitted Luther's new status around Europe, though some Catholics might have preferred to see him housed in a prison, awaiting execution as a heretic.

The Luther's marital home, the Black Cloister in Wittenberg, was once the Augustinian cloister where he lived as part of a community of friars.

There were discordant voices about the marriage in Luther's inner circle. Writing on 16 June to a colleague, the already married Melanchthon implied that his leader had been softened up by nuns, and that the whole reform process would be discredited as a result.[51] His comments may have been prompted by the hurt he felt at not being among the close friends who attended the wedding itself. And Melanchthon's prediction proved spectacularly wrong. Versions of Mr and Mrs Luther portraits by Cranach were soon to be found decorating the homes of his followers where once they would have had images of the 'Holy Family' of Joseph, Mary and Jesus.

Meanwhile Hieronymus Schurff, who acted as Luther's legal advisor at the Diet of Worms, was reported as saying of the marriage, 'the whole world and the devil are laughing'. It was a variation on a line that Luther himself had used. Inviting Spalatin to his wedding party, he wrote of his betrothal: 'I have made the angels laugh and the devil weep.'[52]

Katharina von Bora by Lucas Cranach (1525): 'I feel neither passionate love nor burning for my spouse,' Luther said on their wedding day in 1525.

In Catholic circles, the jibe evidently went round that the marriage of a nun and a priest was likely to produce the infant Antichrist. Again Luther's words were being turned against him; one drawback of having a capacity for the memorable phrase. Meanwhile England's Henry VIII, who never met Luther, floated the idea in a pamphlet that his opponent's battle with the Catholic Church had been entirely driven by an irresistible wish to get married.[53] The words 'pot' and 'kettle' come to mind, but only with the benefit of hindsight.

Luther shrugged off the slurs. He was later to claim, resorting to typically scatological language, that he had used the written attacks on his marriage as toilet paper.[54] His refusal to take offence may have had something to do with how happy he was with his decision. So much so that he later wondered what had taken him so long to marry. 'I never advise anyone to delay even a day.'[55]

CHAPTER ELEVEN

The Peasants' War: Siding with the Powerful

'*One should bow down before a tree which provides him shade.*'
Martin Luther, *Table Talk*[1]

Religions offer believers – among many other things, of course – consolation in this life, and the prospect of salvation in death. That was particularly so in late medieval Europe, where daily existence was so precarious, and death correspondingly so present. Hence Christianity tended to focus hopes on a particular version of salvation – eternal life with God – rather than seeing salvation as capable of being reached in this life if, for example, current injustices and inequalities could be addressed and righted. Rather than embrace the radical social gospel for which it is nowadays known, with its 'option for the poor',[2] and stated ambition to be the 'voice of the voiceless',[3] the Catholic Church focused instead on supporting the faithful in attaining salvation after death, not in life. It did this by its careful calibration of how lives on earth should be led in order to achieve an eternal reward, and the emphasis on improving every individual's chances of making it to the hereafter by encouraging them to attend mass and the sacraments, say prayers, make pilgrimages, take part in processions and purchase indulgences.

Yet the Church did not exist in a vacuum from the society around it. There was, as already discussed, no dividing line between religion and what might broadly be called politics, economics or society, and so there was an inevitable consequence to Catholicism's particular prescription for salvation. By default and often by design, the Church was telling Catholics to accept their lot in the here and now. This made it a force for maintaining the daily status quo, something that particularly suited emperors, kings and princes, keen as they were to keep a lid on popular unrest. Hence they were anxious to win Church – and hence divine – approval for their regimes, while for Catholicism having a seat at the table of power suited its claim to universal authority.

Martin Luther had undermined that whole set-up. By his example, he had shown that the status quo was not inevitable: that Church abuses could be tackled even when the powerful, such as the Holy Roman Emperor, said they couldn't; that the clerical elite could be challenged, shown that their arguments were wrong, and that their take on Scripture was ill-founded; and that with courage and conviction change could come about in aspects of faith that touched the very core of the practice of religion. Luther had invoked the example of Jesus Christ, of Paul, of the other apostles in the gospels, and before them the prophets of the Old Testament, to examine the promise of salvation. His focus was largely eternal salvation, the otherworldly variety but, as a practical man, operating at the very centre of earth-bound power structures, he was also promoting reforms to how religion operated in the here and now. It could be improved, individuals given more control to deepen their relationship with God, strengthen their knowledge of Him through the Scriptures, and hence also over their day-to-day lives. If they didn't like their priest, for example, Luther said they could change him. Lutheranism, to all those in Germany who felt downtrodden, abused and unheard, must have sounded remarkably like a creed for their existing situation, rather than for their final destination.

And one group in particular responded to that. By the language of the street that he used, the ecclesiastical corruption and incompetence that he highlighted, and even his own relatively humble beginnings, Luther had a strong appeal for the lower orders in

Germany. Many may not have been sufficiently literate to read his sermons and tracts, nor theologically literate enough to follow the arguments he was making about *sola fide* and *sola scriptura*, but the word quickly spread that here, finally, was a churchman who understood their lives and shared their grievances. As he took his stand against the two great powers of the age – the Pope and the emperor – he excited an anticipation of more to come as his reform programme easily, almost seamlessly, became conflated with the prospect of better circumstances in daily lives, where economic woes would be addressed and that widespread sense of being excluded finally tackled. In the minds of his hearers, the religious and the political were as one.

And so, as his words flew off the printing presses, images of him, and more recently of his ex-nun wife, were distributed, and his pastors stood in the pulpits of local churches to share his teachings, Luther was celebrated by the peasant class throughout the German lands, and beyond. He played up to the image, not because his head was turned by the attention he received (he remained, following Jesus' example in the gospels, remarkably modest in his demeanour in the face of fame and infamy), but in part at least because it furthered his cause and offered him an additional level of protection from those in authority who wanted to silence him.

All of this had been bubbling away throughout his very public fight with the Church – in the streets of Worms, outside the Diet, for example, when public buildings had been daubed with the *Bundschuh*. And in 1524 it came to the boil in what is known to history as the *Deutscher Bauernkrieg* or Peasants' War. It was not a 'Lutheran uprising'; the religious revolt was part of the mix, but its causes were manifold and continue to be debated by historians today. Erupting sporadically and in no particularly organised pattern in most corners of Germany, peasants demanded the sort of liberation from punitive landowners and unjust rulers that

Luther was offering believers from the Catholic Church. By the time they had been decisively extinguished the following year, up to one hundred thousand rebels had been slaughtered by the armies of the German princes. And they did so with the explicit support of Luther who, rather than blessing the uprising as those who participate in it had expected, took the side of the ruling class. It was a key moment in his story and the shaping of his legacy.

Luther, painted by Cranach to mark his wedding day in 1525, which came as the Peasants' War drew to a bloody conclusion.

Troubled times

Luther's were troubled times across Germany. Resentment against landowners who controlled the lives of those who lived and worked on their properties had been growing for almost a century.

In some areas, including Saxony, serfdom had been abolished, in line with a more general movement in Western Europe,[4] but in the eastern parts of the Holy Roman Empire it persisted almost unchanged. Serfs or not, many across Germany existed in conditions that felt like agrarian slavery, even if not officially designated as such, and their discontent was only increased as hard-pressed landowners encroached ever more on what had been common land, taking away hitherto uncontested rights: to the free firewood that Luther's mother had collected from the forests of Thuringia; to the fish in rivers; and to pasture in the meadows for livestock.

In parallel with this restlessness in the countryside, those like Hans Ludher, who had risen to prosperity in towns from their impoverished roots in rural areas, were especially resentful. Too often they found themselves shut out of town councils and long-standing craft guilds. As society changed, the structures that governed it appeared inflexible, and the problem was compounded when the ruling elite sought to raise ever more revenue from both the artisan class and from landowners to fund their own ambitions to strengthen and professionalise their own administrations.

The ferment caused by the Reformation fed into this broader disaffection. Luther was very publicly and very successfully challenging authority – even if, in reality, his survival could also be put down to the support he received from authority figures, notably Elector Friedrich. And when he spoke out clearly and unambiguously about the grasping attitude of Rome, with its sale of Church appointments in Germany to the highest bidder to fund a building boom in Rome, he was echoing an anti-clerical bias among the lower orders at their obligation to pay their own Church taxes to those they regarded as corrupt abbots, abbesses and bishops, who owned large swathes of the countryside. They even had to concede brewing rights to monks. Luther had started to dismantle that system, by cutting out the bishops, and by encouraging monks and nuns to leave their cloisters.

The spirit of rebellion he promoted went deeper. His talk of each individual standing before God in judgement, with his or her only protection the Scriptures, stripped away the claims both of the institutional Church and more widely of all other figures claiming a God-given authority. When he talked of a priesthood of all believers, he was describing a fundamental equality in God's eyes, which readily translated to a social equality, too. His take on religion no longer held the downtrodden so firmly in their place. It inspired them to raise their eyes.

Some of his followers – or erstwhile followers – had explored and exploited this. Thomas Müntzer, for example, in the oratory that he used to rouse his congregations to action, was fond of deploying a play on the word *Bund*. In *Bundschuh*, the symbol of the peasant rebellion, especially in southwestern Germany, the *Bund* element referred to the band of leather with which the shoe was fastened, but Müntzer pointed out that another of its meanings was to refer to an association. He then mixed the two together to use *Bund* to describe a group of the peasant elect, chosen by God to build His kingdom on earth. Luther, too, had spoken of his chosen inner core of true believers, but here Müntzer made the concept more active and more directly political.

Other Lutheran pastors, often appointed to lead their churches by their congregations against the wishes of the local landowner, the local town council or the nearby abbot, were riding this wave of popular discontent and giving it a biblical underpinning. So, naturally enough, when peasant groups put together and printed lists of their demands for reform, they both echoed Luther's own words and sent the texts to him for his approval.

Of the many such manifestos from the Peasants' War, only one has survived. The 'Twelve Articles', produced in March 1525 by a self-styled 'constituent peasant assembly' that met in Memmingen, a town in Swabia in southwest Germany, begins with words that could have been written by Luther himself. 'Every municipality shall have the right to elect and remove a preacher if he behaves improperly. The preacher shall preach the gospel simply, straight and clearly without any human amendment, for, it is written, that we can only come to God by true belief.'[5] Article number two proceeds to apply those Lutheran principles to the economic core of the peasants' grievances. 'The preachers shall be paid from the great tithe. A potential surplus shall be used to pay for the poor and the war tax. The small tithe [on cattle] shall be dismissed, for it has been trumped-up by humans, for the Lord, Our Master, has created the cattle free for mankind.' And so it continues, mixing (in our eyes) the political and the religious, right up to demanding an end to serfdom, making the Christian liberty that Luther had articulated into a thing of the flesh. Article four reads: 'It is unfraternal and not in accordance with the Word of God that the simple man does not have the right to catch game, fowls, and fish. For, when God Our Master created man, He gave him power over all animals, the bird in the air and the fish in the water.'[6]

Insurrection

Some 25,000 copies of the 'Twelve Articles' were printed and circulated around Germany. By the time they appeared, the Peasants' War was underway, from Alsace in the west to Meissen in the east, though the majority of the conflict occurred in the south and west. There was little by way of organised leadership among the rebels, little co-ordination, and a variety of motivations for taking up arms. Some were local, some economic, some social, some religious. Some of those who rebelled were traditional Catholics, some were 'new' Lutherans, some from other reform-minded offshoots. Zwingli offered his support to the rising from the Swiss cantons he now controlled. And, despite it being known to history as the Peasants' War, this was by no means a straightforward class conflict.

The immediate spark for the conflagration is as hard to identify as anything else about this rising. Some point to a 'Knights' Revolt' in 1522 and 1523 in the Rhineland in the west, where groups of lesser nobility vented their dislike at losing out in the pecking order to the new merchant/burgher class in the towns. They complained that their ancestral lands were lost, their military role usurped, and that the money economy in towns replacing the existing feudal system was ruining them. This revolt was in many senses an essentially conservative and backward-looking uprising, but it may have fanned the flames of wider peasant unrest.

Another potential starting point was the demand by a Countess Helena Lupfen in the autumn of 1524, made on her ancestral lands in Stühlingen in the Black Forest region, that 'her' peasants collect snail shells. She was evidently fond of winding thread around such shells and wanted a new supply. For the peasants, however, exhausted by successive failures of the harvest, the countess's imperious and frivolous order was the last straw. They rose up in fury and their defiance quickly spread throughout southwest Germany, merging with other simmering local issues. At Kempten in Swabia, for example, fighting broke out over a dispute concerning its status as an imperial free town and the role of the local monastery.

By the spring of 1525, the Peasants' War was at its height. Perhaps the most notorious episode came on 17 April 1525. Count Ludwig von Helfenstein, a relative by marriage of Emperor Charles, and a group of up to seventy nobles were captured by a 'peasants' army' under Jacklein Rohrbach near Weinsberg. They were made to run the gauntlet and massacred. Their relatives swore revenge.

Initially, Luther's strongest instinct was to see himself as a peacemaker between the two sides in the escalating dispute. His response to reading the 'Twelve Articles', which drew so heavily on his own teaching, was to issue the tract *Admonition to Peace* early in 1525. Written in haste, as was his style,[7] it contained more angry words than pleas for calm. Addressed alike to 'princes and lords' as well as 'peasants', it castigates both groups for 'this disastrous rebellion'. He reserves special criticism for the 'blind bishops, mad priests and monks, whose hearts are hardened . . . [and who] cheat and rob the people so that you may lead a life of luxury and extravagance'. He urges them to mend their ways, reflect on the 'Twelve Articles' – which he judges fair, though flawed – and find a compromise.[8]

He is also, though, furious at being credited by some rulers with causing the whole uprising. 'Some of you are beginning to blame this affair on the gospel and say that it is the fruit of my teaching. Well, well, slander away, dear lords! You did not want to know what I taught or what the gospel is; now the One who will soon teach you is at the door, unless you change your ways. You, and everyone else, must bear witness that I have taught with all quietness, have striven earnestly against rebellion, and have energetically encouraged and exhorted people to obey and respect even you wild and dictatorial tyrants. This rebellion cannot be coming from me.'[9]

To the peasants, Luther remarks that the injustices they are suffering are an offence to God, who will judge the rulers who perpetrate them. However, he continues, 'you, too, must be careful that you take up your cause justly and with a good conscience. If you have a good conscience, you have the comforting advantage that God will be with you, and will help you. Even though you did not succeed for a while, or even suffered death, you would win in the end, and you would preserve your souls eternally with all the saints.'[10]

Though his verdict is, if anything, tilted to the peasant side, the tract sounds remarkably like an invitation to them to moderation and non-violence. And, as Luther examines each of the 'Twelve

Articles' individually, he rejects their logic. Perhaps he thought he was reclaiming his own teaching and was peeved at seeing it so misused.

To the authors of the 'Twelve Articles', however, it would have seemed as if he was twisting his words to distance himself from them. For example, when they demand the right to appoint their own pastors, Luther writes: 'The entire community should have the power and authority to choose and appoint a pastor.' Yet he qualifies it. 'If the possessions of the parish come from the rulers and not from the community, then the community cannot give these possessions to one whom they choose, for that would be robbery and theft. If they desire a pastor, let them first humbly ask the rulers to give them one.' Luther was, this sentence alone makes clear, not any sort of social revolutionary. He accepted the existing social order and could see in the 'Twelve Articles' a recipe for chaos that would imperil that order.

He was being forced to decide what relationship he wanted to have with the powerful. Would his new reformed Church follow the Catholic Church and act in concert with earthly powers, or would it stand alone and sometimes against the powerful?

Three factors influenced him. First, how could he side against the German princes, especially Elector Friedrich's heirs, when they had saved him from the fire the Catholic Church had prepared for him? Among others now at war with the peasant bands was Philipp I, Landgrave of Hesse, a leading champion of Luther's reforms since the two had first met at Worms when the prince had been just seventeen. It would have been an almighty betrayal for Luther to back those who wanted the existing system of princely authority in the German lands, as represented by the likes of Philipp, to be radically reshaped. Not that Luther was incapable, if he felt so guided by God, of committing such a 'betrayal'. As he had already displayed, Luther lacked neither physical nor spiritual courage.

The second obstacle was his belief in 'two kingdoms', already developed first in *Appeal to the Christian Nobility of the German Nation* of 1520, and three years later in *On Secular Authority*. Taking his lead from Saint Paul's Letter to the Romans, Luther upheld secular authority in this world in God's name, though within certain limits. What was 'external upon earth', he had written, was the business of princes and rulers, while matters of the soul were for God alone. That was the line he was now trying to walk, but it was proving harder in practice than he had imagined when writing the words.

The final factor was his stated view of the use of force. He had already made it plain that a pastor could never wield the sword, and he had spoken unequivocally against violence; but now violence was happening, and in some places it was happening in his name. In *Admonition to Peace*, he offered no prohibition regarding violence in the section addressed to peasants about their use of force, though he warned that rebellion risked destroying Germany. But in his second – and notorious – contribution to the debate, he tried to clarify his position and succeeded in muddying it for ever.

Before that, however, Luther made a sortie out on to the battlefield. The rebellion had spread up from the south and west and was now creeping towards Wittenberg. During the Easter of 1525 he toured Thuringia with Philipp Melanchthon. Their stated reason was to dedicate a new school in Eisleben, Luther's birthplace. Education remained at the very heart of his concerns. He had also, though, received many letters from local people articulating just the sort of grievances that were now fuelling the Peasants' War and appealing to him for support. Luther went from place to place hearing these complaints, still convinced that somehow he could intervene to mitigate the disaster he saw looming in the form of the conflict that was spreading across the whole of Germany.

The welcome he received, though, when he answered such appeals with sermons on restraint and non-violence, was not the applause he had come to expect. At Nordhausen, a city that had been among the first formally to adopt his Church reforms, some parishioners showed their displeasure at what he was saying by ringing the bells to interrupt him mid-flow. The hostility was so great that Luther was persuaded to retreat back to Wittenberg.

En route, he stopped off on 3 May to pay a call on Duke Johann in the city of Weimar. His recent experiences still fresh in his mind, Luther took the crucial step of agreeing that his prince (who would within days inherit his dying brother Friedrich's throne) needed to join the fight against the rebellious peasants. Luther's own contribution to the battle was a tract entitled *Against the Murderous and Thieving Hordes of Peasants*, completed in May of 1525. For a man opposed to violence, it is a violent document.

Luther is not wholly to blame for the incendiary title. Originally it was called *Against the Rioting Peasants*, but Luther gave his approval to the change when it was suggested by his printer. He had just heard news of the Weinsberg massacre. The time for peace-making was over, Luther was signalling. He was taking sides. There is panic in the extreme language he employed, panic even at the prospect of the rebels succeeding. He wants to make plain that any link with his teachings claimed by the rebels is false. 'Baptism does not make men free in body and property,' he writes, 'but in soul.'[11] In other words, the rebels are not free to take up arms in God's name.

Why, when they believe their cause just and can see how their current situation offends against Scripture? It comes back to the two kingdoms. Luther justifies the actions of rulers – even 'heathen rulers' – in bearing the sword to punish 'faithless, perjured, disobedient, rebellious murderers, robbers, and blasphemers'[12] by reference to a quotation from Saint Paul who urged, 'the servant of God to execute his wrath on the wrong-doer'.[13] The ruled, however, have the equivalent right to take up the sword, Luther claims. They sin when they break their oath of loyalty to their secular rulers, because they must, as Jesus Christ commanded, 'render unto Caesar what is Caesar's'.[14] Rebellion, Luther insists, is 'like a great fire, which attacks and devastates a whole land. Thus rebellion brings with it a land filled with murder and bloodshed; it makes widows and orphans, and turns everything upside down, like the worst disaster. Therefore let everyone who can, smite, slay, and stab, secretly or openly, remembering that nothing can be more poisonous, hurt-ful, or devilish than a rebel. It is just as when one must kill a mad dog; if you do not strike him, he will strike you, and a whole land with you.'

Those words – smite, slay, and stab – were to haunt him and his reputation. To label as 'mad dogs' those who believed they were following his teaching was to vilify them. Luther had opted for the forces of order and authority, and had left many of those engaged in rebellion feeling profoundly betrayed by him.

The word made flesh

Before Luther's tract could reach a wide audience, the 'thieving hordes' he had dehumanised and condemned so brutally had become slaughtered hordes. It was a bloody lesson in reality for Luther. Publication had come just days before the Battle of Frankenhausen on 15 May when, on his native Thuringian soil, the army jointly led by Luther's supporter Landgrave Philipp of Hesse, and Luther's long-standing opponent, Duke Georg, took on an unruly peasant army led by none other than Thomas Müntzer.

Thomas Müntzer – once the two men had been colleagues, but Müntzer's role in inciting the Peasants' War caused Luther to label him a 'murderous prophet'.

Müntzer had played his own part in inciting the Peasants' War. He was most likely one of the 'murder[ous] prophets who hate me as they hate you' that Luther had warned about in *Admonition to Peace*. In *Against the Murderous and Thieving Hordes*, he had explicitly condemned Müntzer as 'the archdevil who rules at Mühlhausen, and does nothing except stir up robbery, murder, and bloodshed'. The presence of Müntzer among the leaders of the revolt seems to have been another factor in convincing Luther that he was facing not legitimate demands from downtrodden Germans but 'spiritual wickedness'.[15]

Müntzer had washed up in Mühlhausen, a prosperous trading town in Saxony, where his street preaching and vivid warnings of a forthcoming apocalypse, which would instigate a thousand years of rule of earth by God in His heaven,[16] excited his hearers into joining him in rising up against what he pictured as an oppressive ruling class. This took place in September 1524, and the town council quickly restored order by the simple expedient of banishing Müntzer. He then spent some time in the southwest of Germany and in Switzerland, both hotbeds of rebellion, before returning to Mühlhausen to exploit a situation where tempers among the townsfolk were once again frayed.

From the pulpit of Saint Mary's Church, he proclaimed the assembling of a new militia, the 'Eternal League of God', to engage in battle with the princes so as to bring such chaos that it would trigger God's direct intervention in human affairs. The concept was the polar opposite of Luther's 'two kingdoms' theory. He wanted to separate out the spiritual and the political. The Eternal League of God aimed to roll the two together to such an extent that God became, in effect, a political ruler.

As the joint army of Catholic and Lutheran princes encircled Müntzer's stronghold, he led six thousand of those inspired by his apocalyptic vision to their deaths, crushed by their opponents' overwhelming numbers and superior fighting skills. Müntzer himself was captured, tortured and beheaded in Mühlhausen. To the peasants who had fallen in behind him and his vision, he remained a hero. To the same audience, Luther was the villain.

Luther did try to make amends some months later, as the Peasants' War was drawing to a close, in a document that he was initially reluctant to write, entitled *An Open Letter on the Harsh Book Against the Peasants*. Luther was not by nature one to whom the word 'sorry' came easily. His refusal to back down, or be bullied into biting his tongue on a theological point, was essential to his success, and one of his most striking qualities. But here the question was more of expressing some form of regret that his own overly harsh language might have been used to justify mass slaughter.

Luther did manage gently to rebuke the princes for being over-zealous in putting down the revolt, ignoring the part played by his own previous advice to them, 'let everyone who can, smite, slay, and stab, secretly or openly'. As an apology, however, it hardly seems adequate when one of the princes who had embraced Lutheranism, Margrave Casimir of Brandenburg-Ansbach, was reported to have ordered the eyes of sixty peasants be put out to punish them for rising up against him.[17]

And Luther certainly did not recant in his open letter of the language he had used in *Against the Murderous and Thieving Hordes*. He stood by his conviction that those who took up arms were doing the work of the devil, and no words could ever be too strong, in his opinion, in condemning Satan. Moreover, he staunchly defended the position he had adopted on using force against the state. It was, he wrote, the duty of the Christian to 'suffer injustice, not to seize the sword and take to violence'.[18] If he was essentially telling the peasants they had got what they deserved, Luther's message to rulers was one of encouragement. 'You have to answer people like that [i.e. rebels] with a fist, until the sweat drips off their noses.'

How far, it has to be asked, was Luther's vehemence in condemning the rebels inspired by his determination to sideline Müntzer? Was it sufficient to explain the difference in tone and judgement between his first statement on the Peasants' War and his second? Müntzer may have got under Luther's skin sufficiently that he should be damned by a crushing reference and cast as the devil's disciple, but Luther would have preferred, on calm reflection, to see him banished rather than executed. 'I cannot admit that false teachers are to be put to death,' he wrote in 1528, when tempers had calmed. 'It is enough to banish.'[19]

Luther's real and deeper dilemma in 1525 was about far more than a rivalry with Müntzer, or even what his one-time ally represented. If Luther was to construct a reformed alternative, or even a successor Church to Catholicism, as seemed to be the wish of those areas of Germany that had sided with him – albeit fewer in number in the aftermath of the Peasants' War, and more likely to be urban than rural – then he needed to find a way of working with, rather than against, the secular authorities. And that involved some element of compromise, even if he would never have described it as such. It was among the challenges that Luther found hardest.

Family guy

Luther's life, since the first appearance of the Ninety-Five Theses, had been lived out largely on the public stage, save for his time in seclusion at Wartburg Castle. Relentless in his energy, driven on by anger at the refusal of the Catholic authorities to give the case for reform he was making a proper hearing, he was forever speaking, preaching, lecturing or writing. While others around him had married and made homes for themselves, Luther's work had been his life, but his marriage to Katharina von Bora, despite its unpromising beginnings, was to bring him a happiness and contentment that had hitherto eluded him. As an advertisement for Luther's advocacy of priests marrying, or monks and nuns leaving their abbeys and convents, the Luthers were a poster couple.

At the Black Cloister, his one-time monastery, his wife built a home for them, and their growing family, and did her utmost to keep him on an even keel. She remodelled the Black Cloister to make it both a private place and a stage for him. There were both smaller, more intimate family rooms in the west part of the building, and larger public spaces that she filled with sufficient life to keep her husband energised. There was a regular quorum of around forty, made up of extended family, friends and colleagues who stayed as guests, plus teachers and students from the university who rented rooms and sat round the large dinner table where 'the doctor' held forth. Students were prepared to pay a premium for their accommodation for the honour of hearing Luther reflect out loud on his ongoing battle with the Church.

Which was just as well, because their financial contributions to the household coffers were, initially, much needed. Luther had never had to worry about the cost of anything, and was little inclined to start doing so now. In 1539, by which time he and Katie had six children to feed and clothe, he was breezily turning down an offer from a publisher for 400 guilders per year for the rights to his books because, as he explained, his soul was not for sale.[20] 'I have never sold a publication nor held a lecture for money,' he reflected. 'God willing, I will take my honour with me to the grave. As long as I have food and clothes, I will be satisfied.'[21]

Fine words when you are not the one tasked with providing the food and clothes. That was Katie's domain. When some of their paying guests started to follow the example set in 1531 of Conrad Cordatus, a fifty-four-year-old refugee from Catholic Austria, who had moved into the Black Cloister and begun to record Luther's often wry, unguarded *Tischreden* or *Table Talk*, she was furious. They would make money out of them, she warned, selling them to publishers. 'When someone asked the Doctor about a biblical passage,' one of the recorders wrote on 24 August 1540, 'the Doctor's wife broke in, and jokingly said: "Doctor, don't teach them for nothing! They are writing everything down." The Doctor responded: "I have taught and preached for 30 years for free. Why should I now, when I am old and weak, make a profit on it?"'[22]

His only worry was that the transcripts of his talks might reflect badly on him as verbose. 'I hate people who talk a lot, because most of the time, when it sounds like they have something really important to say, they are telling lies. For the truth, however, with which they are rarely acquainted, they use few words.'[23]

On another occasion, when Katie was again worrying about money, he treated it as a joke. 'The Hessians,' he told her, 'pray this way: "Our Father, You are in heaven, we are on earth, if You give us nothing, we have nothing, so we take out a loan, if You don't pay it off, we don't either." And that's the way things are, everything depends upon Jesus Christ, Our Lord. Money is simply a matter of fluidity, and we have hands with loose fingers. They are always open.'[24]

Among surviving documents are some that give an insight into how much difference that offer of 400 guilders per year from publishers might have made if Luther had accepted it. They record that the Black Cloister spent 300 guilders per year on meat, 200 on beer[25] and 50 on bread.[26] If that makes it sound as if they were living the high life, all alcohol and expensive meat, then the meagre figure for bread is deceptive. Luther was adamant that bread prices be kept low because they had the greatest impact on the poor. In April 1539, he even sent a written complaint to Wittenberg town council on their lack of action to ensure that bakers did not charge inflated prices.[27]

In terms of money coming in to cover these outgoings of the Black Cloister, there was the rent paid by lodgers, plus Luther's 200 guilders as his annual stipend from the Elector of Saxony. While a monk, he had received no university salary; even though he was being paid now, it was a pittance, especially for the man who had made the place famous all across Europe.

Table Talk refers to the Black Cloister having a coachman, a swineherd, tutors and a cook. They all required paying. It can have been no mean feat to balance the books, but Katie somehow managed it. Among her triumphs was the garden she developed on the former monastery's land, where she grew a crop of saffron, a prized and valuable commodity. There were pigs, cows, goats and poultry, so many that extra fields had to be acquired nearby, including one outside the Elster Gate into the town where Luther had burned the papal bull of excommunication a few years before. And Luther added to the menagerie with his faithful dog, Tölpel, whose name meant fool or numbskull. He was, Luther boasted, 'the most loyal of all animals'.[28]

Katie's need to manage the money earned her a reputation for being overly interested in turning a profit. Among those who expressed disapproval was Philipp Melanchthon's wife, also called Katharina. Melanchthon had, of course, been one of those warning Luther against his bride at the time of their wedding.

Yet Mrs Luther clearly did have an entrepreneurial flair, generating sufficient funds for a further rolling renovation of the Black Cloister between 1536 and 1541, when a bathhouse was added. By the early 1540s, she still had enough left in the pot to pay 600 guilders for a former family home at Zülsdorf south of Leipzig, a two-day journey away, after her brother Hans had been forced to sell after getting himself in a financial mess.

The popular image of the Luthers as living in genteel poverty and chaos with their children and hangers-on is misleading. They rose to be among Wittenberg's wealthiest citizens. That the credit for this achievement was largely Katie's can be judged by Luther's decision in 1541 to instruct the builders to erect a sandstone decoration over one of the main entrance doors to the Black Cloister, which he named the 'Katharina Portal'. In the same year, and unusually for the times, he appointed her his sole heir.[29]

This did not mean he was hopelessly besotted with her, but her faults were small, he judged, in comparison to the blessings she had brought him. 'Other women have far more shortcomings than my Katie. Although she certainly has enough, they are offset by far greater virtues . . . She is faithful to her marriage, that is fidelity and respect.'[30] The start of their marriage may have been more prosaic than romantic, but it undoubtedly blossomed. 'It is

God's greatest blessing when love continues to bloom in marriage,' Luther remarked. 'At first love is passionate, an intoxicating love, which blinds us, and like a drunk we forge ahead. But when we have slept off our intoxication, then there remains among the faithful true married love.'[31]

By the standards of the middle of the sixteenth century, the Luthers had a remarkably equal partnership. 'Just imagine if we did not have the female sex,' Luther once mused. 'The house and everything associated with the household would collapse; the state and society would fall apart. Thus, the world cannot endure without women, even if men could bring children into the world by themselves.'[32]

Katie was certainly fierce when it came to protecting their family life in the private quarters of the Black Cloister. When Luther's clerk, Viet Dietrich, who lived in, began giving lessons in the building, he and Katie clashed over his students overstepping the mark. Later, when Dietrich started courting one of Luther's four young nieces who lived with the couple, Katie threw him out, on the grounds that the object of his affection, Magdalene Kaufmann (known as 'Leni'), was too young.[33]

And then, of course, there were the couple's own children. Hans was born on 2 June 1526, a few days short of their first wedding anniversary. He was christened Johannes, after his paternal grandfather, but was always called Hans, or when young, Hänschen. Eighteen months later came Elisabeth, their first daughter, and then a second, Magdalena, on 4 May 1529, named after Katharina's aunt, the former abbess, who also lived with them. There was a longer gap until the arrival of their second son, Martin, his father's namesake, on 9 November 1531, followed by Paul on 29 January 1533, and the baby of the family, Margarethe, on 17 December 1534 (when Luther was fifty-one). She was christened in memory of her paternal grandmother, who had died soon after Hans Ludher in 1531. There may have been other pregnancies that ended in miscarriage, but the details of only one are recorded. In 1540, when she had turned forty, Katie lost a baby. It took her many months to recover.

The couple experienced their share of parental grief. Their first daughter, Elisabeth, died at ten months. 'I marvel that my soul is so sick,' Luther wrote soon afterwards, as if gaining new insights into his own feelings as a result of their loss.[34] The death, in his arms, of thirteen-year-old Magdalena in 1542 briefly stretched his faith in God. One account has him falling on his knees and weeping bitterly as he cried to God to save her. 'I love her dearly, but if it is Your will, Dear God, that You will take her, then I will be happy to know that she is with Thee.' It describes how he turned to her and asked, 'You would gladly stay here with me, your father, and you would also gladly go to the other Father?' 'Yes,' she replied, 'dear father, as God wills.'[35]

There is a warmth to some of these accounts of Luther as a father that belies his otherwise dour image. As a dad, he could on occasion show the tenderness that his own father had denied him. Once Luther was observed putting one of his children to bed: 'Go to sleep my little child, and be happy,' he said to the tired infant. 'I will not leave you money, but I will leave you a rich God; just be of good faith.'[36]

He was not, though, an indulgent father. The same rules that he applied in his Church reforms were part of his children's upbringing. Pastors and preachers could not, he had taught, take up weapons, and so he denied his sons the usual militaristic toys of childhood. 'Boys love deadly weapons. Therefore they should not be permitted to have them,' he ruled.[37] And he was clear, as was the pattern at the time, that his children's needs always came second to his own. On one occasion, he cut a patch out of one pair of child's trousers to mend his own. Given how tight her budget was, Katie was understandably outraged. Luther replied by explaining that 'the pants made for me by the tailor never fit right'. Domestic comforts were, it seems, making the already thickset monk into a chubby patriarch.[38]

Lucas Cranach and his assistants produced a series of 'older Luther' portraits in the 1540s, giving him a quasi-regal authority.

Building a Church

Beyond his home, Luther continued to lecture at the university and carry out the reform programme upon which he had embarked. The hostility some humbly born Germans now felt towards him, as a result of him siding with the ruling class in the Peasants' War, did not distract him from trying to provide – for those with limited literacy and education – the materials that they would need if the concept of a priesthood of all believers was to mean something in practical terms. Assisted by a group of colleagues, his work on a translation into German of the Old Testament continued, albeit intermittently between other projects. These included the preparation of two catechisms that appeared in 1529. The first, known as *The Small Catechism*, distilled the essentials of his teaching into a series of easily understood propositions (in imitation of the Catholic catechism), 'for simple folk and pastors'. Alongside the lyrics of the hymns he was also increasingly writing, *The Small Catechism* would be a basic teaching tool of his Church.

The second, *The Large Catechism*, was – as the name suggests – longer, more detailed, more precisely theological. Its audience was more the leaders of the reformed Church. Now the pillars of Luther's distinctive approach were in place, he was concerned to achieve a degree of uniformity of practice and belief in those who followed him.

There were, of course, still disputes with others in the wider Church – including an exchange of papers with Erasmus on the question of free will in 1524 and 1525. It was the theological issue that most obviously divided the two, whatever their personal feelings about each other, their conduct and their language. Erasmus argued in *On Free Will*, his most sustained attack yet on Luther, that each human being's free will, bestowed by God, could contribute to him or her attaining salvation. It was a typically optimistic approach from Erasmus – that free will would liberate humankind to do the positive things that would surely win God's approval and shape His decision about their salvation.

Luther, though, was no more an optimist than he was a Christian Humanist. His response, *On the Bondage of Will*, painted a more traditional picture of human beings as weighed down by sin, and constantly sinning more.[39] Contributing to their salvation was beyond them. It came by faith alone.

Yet the urgency had somehow gone out of the dispute between the two reformers. A measure of how little importance Luther placed on his dispute with Erasmus can be seen in the sixteen months it took him to shape his reply to *On Free Will*. Yes, he had many other things on his plate, but he had never previously let that slow him down when he was truly engaged and wanted to respond to a slight. Erasmus's rebuke to him over free will was, he must have judged, too late to change the course he had taken. Here I stand.

The questions towards which Luther was now directing his considerable gusto concerned what had effectively become his own Church within a Church. These were of presentation (how and in what format to get over its message) and of structure: how to enforce some sort of cohesion and uniformity among Lutherans now that the authority wielded by the papacy had been rejected. In February 1528, he produced *Instruction of the Visitors for the Parish Pastors in Electoral Saxony*. Just over a decade on from the Ninety-Five Theses, he had developed, with the participation of Melanchthon and Spalatin (now married and living eighty miles south of Wittenberg in Altenburg), an essential tool in making sure individual Lutheran churches and their pastors did not follow the example of Karlstadt and go their own way.

Spalatin's first calling had been (like Luther) as a lawyer. Only later was he ordained. Organisation rather than theology was his strength, and so he devised a system of visitations – inspections to be carried out of local Lutheran churches, sometimes by Spalatin himself, and based on the *Instruction*, a printed copy of which was handed out to clergy when appointed. It addressed questions about the fate of church buildings, their possessions and their endowments, and thereby sought to root the fledgling movement firmly and enduringly in the soil of Saxony.

Such a system was more urgently required than ever because, in the wake of the Peasants' War, Luther's reforms were now becoming more attractive to rulers, just as they lost some of their appeal for the rural poor. The two things were, of course, connected. Luther had, by taking sides in the war, shown himself someone with whom the princes and town councils could do business, someone who would allow them to cast off some of the most onerous ties to Rome that had long vexed them, but someone who also wished to uphold social order. In the decade ahead, much of the north of Germany was to become Lutheran, along with a smattering of cities and large towns in other areas.

Symbolic of this ever-closer bond with those in authority was Luther's warm relationship with Elector Johann. His older brother, Elector Friedrich, had, quite literally, saved Luther's life and stood by him when Rome and the emperor had been determined to try him as a heretic. Yet, officially at least, the two had never met. Their dialogue was always through a third party, and even unto death Friedrich had held fast to official Catholicism, which included faith in relics. Now, though, Johann publicly embraced Lutheranism and was happy to work wholeheartedly and directly with Luther, as shown when he decreed that the Castle Church was henceforth to follow Luther's liturgical prescriptions to the letter.

Within or without

While Luther was occupied with his reforms, their status in relation to official Catholicism remained in dispute. Rome still regarded him a heretic and clung to the belief that if only it could get its hands on him, the network of reform churches he was building would fall back into line. Luther still couldn't leave Saxon territories without risking his life. Indeed, Elector Johann felt there was such an imminent danger to Wittenberg itself that he ordered work on strengthening the walls of the town so it could better defend itself.

The person most likely to besiege it, however, was Emperor Charles, and he was busy elsewhere: fighting the French, embroiled in Italian wars, and confronting the Ottoman Turks. Whatever their loathing of Luther, the remaining Catholic princes of Germany were unlikely to act without the emperor. Some, including Duke Georg in the adjoining but separate part of Saxony, even had reason to thank Luther for his support in helping them put down the Peasants' War.

In August 1526, the Imperial Diet gathered once more, this time at Speyer, with the absent emperor's brother, Ferdinand of Austria, in charge. It reaffirmed the Edict of Worms in outlawing Luther and his reforms but, accepting the reality of the situation, ruled that such a banning order only applied to those territories still under the control of their local Catholic hierarchy, loyal to the Pope. Where Lutheranism was now firmly established, it could be put to one side. Each ruler was left to behave on the religious question 'as he would have to answer to God and the [absent] emperor'. What that meant was that Luther's Church within a Church had achieved a tacit degree of recognition, but only as an interim measure. The emperor and those who opposed Luther continued to hanker after a religious reunion of Germany, as did Luther himself, but on his own terms.

Among his supporters at Speyer was Landgrave Philipp of Hesse, who brought with him a large number of Lutheran preachers. When they were refused pulpits in the city, they took instead to the balconies of local inns and delivered their sermons to crowds of thousands gathered in the streets. Philipp matched their boldness. During the diet, he demonstrated his contempt for the Catholic Church's laws on fasting by barbecuing an ox on a Friday, by tradition the day of the week when Catholics abstained from meat. Whether Luther approved or not is unknown. His own views on fasting remained that it could have a value. Philipp's actions, indeed, were more directly in line with the practice of Zwingli.

In 1529, the diet met again in Speyer; the agreement to differ, pending a final decision, remained in place, but this time round Ferdinand was in a much more belligerent mood. The immediate cause was the advance of the Ottoman Turks into Hungary, where at the Battle of Mohacs in 1526 they had killed the Hungarian king, Louis (Ferdinand's brother-in-law), and imposed their own placeman in charge of the eastern portion of the country. The forces of Suleiman the Magnificent were now threatening Vienna. Ferdinand blamed this situation squarely on the princes who backed Luther. They had failed to come up with military and financial support requested by the Pope to drive back the Turks, he said, and had therefore gifted Suleiman victory. Now they were risking the future of the whole of Christendom to support Luther's rebellion.

This time, Speyer saw the conditions toughened around continuing with the religious truce throughout Germany. No new Lutheran 'innovations' would be allowed and the Catholic mass must be tolerated everywhere. The momentum was shifting again, fractionally, towards Luther's opponents. When the Evangelical rulers lodged a written protest at the deal, they were labelled as 'Protest-ants' by their opponents, as a catch-all that covered followers of Luther, of Zwingli and of all shades in between, including Martin Bucer at Strasbourg. It was a name that has stuck ever after.

Sensing a growing pressure from Ferdinand, some of the rulers of 'Protestant' lands decided to address theological divisions in their own ranks, so as to be able to present a united front if they were confronted with force. In October 1529, Philipp of Hesse persuaded Luther to take part in a 'colloquy' at his castle in Marburg.[40] Zwingli would also be attending. With the landgrave's support, there was no risk to Luther's safety in travelling to Marburg, since it lay in Hesse, which bordered Electoral Saxony to the south.

Still Luther did not feel much inclined to go. It may have been leaving behind his domestic comforts that was putting him off. More likely, it was a reluctance to contemplate compromise, notably over the real presence in the eucharist, with those reformers who were now outflanking him on this and other reforms. 'I know I cannot give an inch and, after reading their arguments, I remain certain they are wrong,' he told Philipp. It may sound unhelpful, especially in response to a supporter worried about external threats, but if you believe that God is directing you, as Luther did, then making compromises on theological questions is no easy matter.

Under pressure from Johann, Luther, Melanchthon and others in their inner circle did eventually set out on the two-week journey to Marburg. The elector had provided a body of guards to accompany his professor, but the difference between this trip and Luther's progress to Worms in 1521 couldn't have been more marked. Then Luther had been anxious to seize the opportunity to debate his views with Catholic representatives, even if he risked his life in the process. Now, it was as if a weariness had descended upon him. It cannot have been prompted by his scepticism that Zwingli would change his mind on the real presence. The chances of Emperor Charles being moved to abandon the Pope at the Diet of Worms had been, in Luther's judgement, every bit as remote, yet he had felt then that he must at least try to fight his corner.

So what was causing it? There may have been a resistance to Philipp of Hesse's Marburg initiative because Luther saw that reaching a theological understanding would be the first step to a military alliance between the 'Protestant' parts of Germany against those still Catholic. He wanted no part in any war of religion where blood would be shed. The fear of such a wider conflict remained high on his list of concerns for the rest of his life, as we will see. The experience of the Peasants' War, and the slaughter it witnessed, may well have haunted him.

Another explanation could be that Luther was concerned that any further compromises with those who held more radical views than him would inevitably widen the gap with the Catholic Church and set the current schism in stone. So far his stated approach had been to build a reformed Church in anticipation of Rome finally coming round and seeing the error of its ways. How willing was he was to close the door on that possibility? It was certainly a fear regarding Marburg that Luther attributed to his right-hand man, Melanchthon, in a letter to Justus Jonas. Any agreement made at the colloquy, Luther reported Melanchthon as arguing, would kill the chance of negotiating with Catholic theologians in Germany.[41]

Zwingli came to Marburg accompanied by Johannes Oecolampadius, another who took the Hellenised form of his German surname, Hausschein (which means 'house lamp'). Oecolampadius was a first-rate theologian, but one whose loyalties had moved from Christian Humanism (in 1515 he had assisted Erasmus on his Greek version of the New Testament) and then to mysticism, when he briefly became a monk, before throwing his weight behind Luther's reforms. Now, like Zwingli, he had decided he did not share Luther's view on the real presence, but regarded the eucharist only as an act of remembrance. This was the position he had taken when preaching in his base of Basel, where he had earned a reputation among Evangelicals second only to Zwingli in the Swiss cantons.

Given how entrenched both sides were, it is perhaps no surprise that they should fail to find a satisfactory formula that would enable those rulers who supported them to present a united front. Passions had run high at Marburg, and were not helped by the colloquy being cut short after just four days by news that Suleiman had laid siege to Vienna.

There was some progress signalled in the Marburg Articles, signed by all participants on 3 October 1529. Among the fifteen sections, all were agreed on 'justification by faith', on infant baptism, and on respecting 'secular authorities, laws, codes and ordinances', a dig at the Anabaptists, who were not represented at the colloquy and who would not share a table with princes. There was a statement of support for the place of the Holy Spirit who 'creates faith where and in whom It wishes' that would have pleased Zwingli more than Luther. But on the crucial question of the real presence, there was only for now an agreement to differ, a promise to work hard to find a common position, and a pledge to respect each other's views in imitation of 'Christ's love'.[42]

Luther did not stick to the spirit of the official text, however, and was heard to rebuke Zwingli: 'Pray God, that you may come to a right understanding on this matter.'[43] In other words, Zwingli was plain wrong. The Protestant cause remained divided, but not sufficiently to stop the princes continuing with their plans to build a military alliance.

CHAPTER TWELVE

Countdown to Conflict: Later Years

'A Christian must always be a cheerful person.'
Martin Luther, *Table Talk*[1]

Rain and unseasonal snow rescued the ill-prepared defenders of Vienna and enabled them to lift Suleiman's siege by the middle of October 1529, but the presence of his army of 75,000 at the city's gates had finally wrested Emperor Charles's attention away from other parts of his far-flung domains. In his battle with the French, he had emerged victorious and had managed to come to an uneasy truce with Pope Clement. In 1530, Charles became the last ever Holy Roman Emperor to be crowned in person by the Pope at a ceremony in Bologna.

From this triumphant coronation, he made his way to Augsburg to preside over the Imperial Diet, scheduled to convene at the beginning of April 1530 with the express task of restoring religious unity to Germany, and thereby liberating it from its internal divisions so that it could concentrate on supporting efforts to drive back the Ottoman Turks from the Empire's borders.

Again Luther did not press to be in Augsburg to defend his corner come what may. It would have been dangerous for Luther to travel to Augsburg, but no more so than when he had journeyed to Worms. And since when had danger deterred him? That sense of weariness was again in the air. It was agreed that Luther would gather at Easter with his closest allies (Melanchthon, Jonas and Bugenhagen) to decide their approach to Augsburg. They would meet first in Torgau and then in Coburg, the city at the extreme southern tip of Electoral Saxony, closest to Augsburg, though still 160 miles away. When the others travelled on with Elector Johann to the diet, Luther would stay behind with his clerk Viet Dietrich, in the Veste, a fortress in the city, protected by guards in case of a raid by Catholic forces.

They might, of course, have had their discussions in Wittenberg, so the choice of Coburg was a sign that Luther wanted to be somewhere from where he could travel to Augsburg in the shortest possible time if he was needed. Or if the emperor came round and declared him right in his reforms. And there was certainly an effort at Torgau, and then Coburg, to come up with a pre-prepared statement of Lutheran beliefs that would reach out to the emperor.

This was contained in the document known to history as the *Augsburg Confession*, though it did not emerge in its final form until Melanchthon was in Augsburg. Luther's mood as he approached sharing responsibility for the fate of his Reformation can be judged by a sermon he gave soon after he arrived in Coburg. He mused on Jesus Christ's suffering on the cross, linking it with the ordeal of the legendary Saint Christopher. Now best known as a patron of motorists, it was what was then a more familiar aspect of Christopher's story that Luther reflected upon – that this giant of a man had physically shouldered the burdens of the world, on behalf of God. Just as he was battling with all his might to carry a child across a raging ford, the infant in Christopher's arms announced that he was Jesus Christ, come to relieve the saint of the heavy lifting. That was how Luther saw himself, weighed down by what God had placed on his shoulders, but determined never to yield in the face of his enemies who wished to wash him away, unless given divine instruction to do so.

Seeing his colleagues set off at the start of April for the diet, Luther had every reason to feel bereft, however much he might have rationalised the choice to stay behind in Coburg. His fate, and that of all he had worked for, was now in the hands of others.

The final form of the *Augsburg Confession* would be determined by Melanchthon. And, as Luther knew, Melanchthon could not always be relied upon. Last time Luther had been removed from the action, when shut up in Wartburg Castle following the Diet of Worms, Melanchthon enthusiastically allowed Karlstadt to run riot in Wittenberg, only then to throw his hands up in horror at the result and appeal to Luther to return to sort out the mess.

Luther's thoughts appear to have overwhelmed him. He found himself unable to read and then collapsed physically. The elector's physician sent medicine to Coburg, but Luther's low only deepened when news arrived on 29 May that his father had died. 'The news shook him at first,' Dietrich informed Katie, 'but he was himself again after two days. When the letter came, he said, "my father is dead". He took his psalter, went to his room and wept so that he was incapacitated for two days, but he has been alright since.'[2]

As ever when unsettled and uncertain, Luther poured out his angst on to paper, this time in *Exhortation to the Clergy Assembled at the Diet at Augsburg*. He was determined to make his own voice heard at the diet, despite having previously agreed a collective position in the *Augsburg Confession*. By 12 May he had a manuscript with printers in Wittenberg. Because the emperor's arrival in Augsburg was delayed by two months, Luther's manifesto was already on sale as Charles neared the city. One bookseller, it was reported, had shifted five hundred copies in a few days. 'Everybody is reading it,' wrote Justus Jonas on 12 June.[3]

The text began, as was Luther's habit, with a show of humility. This was, he said, 'a mute and feeble written message'. His words were genuine in one sense: that a part of Luther, especially in moments of vulnerability, still regarded himself as that small-town monk so often lampooned by Rome. 'The reason [for writing]', he continued, 'is that my conscience drives me to pray, beseech and exhort each and all of you, in the kindliest way and from the heart, that you will not pass this diet by or use it to vain purposes.'

Launching an attack on the Catholic bishops at the diet, he argued that they could not agree to any changes without the consent of the Church. 'But who are the Church?' he continued. 'Why are we not also the Church, since we are baptised as well as you, teach, preach, have the sacraments, believe, pray, love and suffer more than you? . . . Do not keep chanting "Church, Church, Church" at us. Better for you to make certain you are the Church.'[4]

He was seeking, above all, to widen the decision-making process beyond the diet, and appealed once more for a national council of the whole Church in Germany to consider his reforms. Luther ran through familiar territory: the scandal of the sale of indulgences; the misuse of confession; and making money out of masses for the dead. He restated and defended with vigour his own views, and those of his followers, regarding clerical marriage, communion in both kinds, and the primacy of Scripture. Once again resorting to a list, he proceeded to name thirty-two issues on which the Catholic bishops had much to learn from Lutherans if they wanted to live up to their claim to be a 'true Christian Church'. These included better schools, better teaching on Christian liberty, and more instruction on how to read and interpret Scripture. If bishops didn't feel equipped to tackle such subjects, they should resign and leave it to Lutherans. If they wanted to give it a try, Lutherans could come and show them how.

It was the sort of direct, mocking, aggressive stuff that the bishops had come to expect from Luther, but was that all it was? Or did he genuinely wish to work constructively to find a way forward that would produce the religious reunion desired by so many at the diet? Later, in a *Table Talk*, Luther suggested the latter may have been the case, that at Augsburg he had felt there was an appetite among some of his Catholic foes to concede to him on some, if not all, the flaws he had highlighted in the Church. He recalled a detail he had been told of what went on at Augsburg. Archbishop Albrecht, prince and prelate of Mainz and the most senior of the German bishops, had evidently been overheard during the meeting of the diet saying that Luther had caused him to read the Bible. 'I don't know what to make of this book because everything that is in it is against us.'[5]

Luther's *Exhortation* ended on a conciliatory note. 'I maintain that you cannot do without the Lutherans, those godly heretics, and least of all can you do without their prayers, if you are going to accomplish any permanent results.' Luther couldn't, though, keep up being so constructive. 'But if you are going to force your way through this business stiffly and stubbornly (which may God forbid!), then, together with all who believe with me, I hereby call on God and all the world to witness that it is no fault of ours if you are dashed to pieces, when your pride fails you. Your blood be on your own head! We are and will be guiltless of your blood and your condemnation; for we pointed out to you your offences, admonished you faithfully to repent, sincerely implored you, and made you every offer that could serve the cause of peace, seeking and desiring nothing else than that sole support and comfort of our souls – the free and pure gospel. Thus we can boast with a good conscience that the fault has not been ours.'[6]

His use of the word 'Lutheran' may be new, but otherwise he is back on an older theme here: that the real cause of division remains the Catholic Church's refusal to budge when it is so clearly at fault. Even Hadrian VI had publicly acknowledged that there were errors in how the Church had handled certain aspects of his protests, Luther noted. As a consequence, he was arguing that finding a solution must also be in the hands of the Catholic Church. It had to bend.

Overall the *Exhortation* delivers a confused, double message: sometimes reaching out, sometimes aggressively defensive, but the loudest part was the warning shot he fired that the bishops at

Augsburg should expect no further concessions from his negotiating team. Here he was reminding his negotiator Melanchthon of how he must behave.

The text Melanchthon presented to the diet as the *Augsburg Confession* – once Emperor Charles had finally arrived on 15 June, accompanied by a thousand infantrymen – was at the opposite end of the scale in tone to passages in Luther's muddled, vehement *Exhortation*. The *Confession* was couched, typically for Melanchthon, in much more diplomatic, unthreatening and apparently reasonable terms than anything Luther would have written. Missing was any rhetoric about the shortcomings of the papacy and the dubious base on which its claims to authority rested. It is hard to imagine Luther not mentioning them.

The *Augsburg Confession*, as later edited and published by Melanchthon, is made up of twenty-eight articles, four fewer than in Luther's *Exhortation*. Twenty-one of them are statements of belief that aim to show how Luther's programme is consistent with the tradition of the early Christian Church. They are followed by seven detailing 'abuses' that have developed in medieval Catholicism that Lutherans have now moved to correct.

All the items on the list are familiar by this stage in Luther's story, but it is worth summarising them as the core principles, stripped down to bare essentials, that Luther's colleague had come up with. The *Confession* begins uncontroversially: affirming belief in one God; in how baptism removes the stain of original sin; and how Jesus was the Son of God incarnated on earth. It then moves into trickier territory for Rome: justification by faith; the role of preachers who are 'rightly called'; the place of good works as the fruits of faith and salvation, but never a price to be paid for them; the role of the sacraments of baptism and eucharist; and the limits on free will. There are also articles that highlight the difference between the Lutherans and other Evangelicals over issues such as infant baptism and the real presence.

Among the seven corrections to the Church's abuses are: making communion available in both kinds; allowing married priests; seeing mass as an act of public worship not a sacrifice; the offer of absolution for all sins, not just those revealed in confession; a commitment to fasting, but not as a way of earning salvation; the continuation of monastic vows, but not as a source of special purity; and how the powers of those in leadership roles in the Church can only come from Scripture.

There were many in Lutheran circles, some of them pastors, who might have wished that Melanchthon's list was longer, more radical or more challenging, but Luther was not apparently among them. When he was sent a final draft, before it was laid before the diet, he had signalled his approval. 'I know nothing to improve or change it,' he replied, adding, 'nor would this be appropriate, since I cannot tread so softly and quietly.'[7]

These words were, undeniably, a vote of confidence in Melanchthon's ability to judge the situation and act appropriately. Luther couldn't have been clearer in stating his support, then and later. Two years afterwards, he remarked in a *Table Talk*: 'It was God's will that the Augsburg convention take place in order to spread His Reformation . . . They have validated our doctrine; but they did not dare to classify us as heretics, but rather as a schism, while we call them the Antichrist and a horror to God. We have been given the advantage. But we are not concerned with the world. We did not start all this because of the world.'

At which point he switched from 'we' to 'I'. 'It is because of Christ's will that I ventured to do it, because he ventured to do something for me on Good Friday.'[8] In Augsburg, though, that 'I' had unambiguously become a 'we'. Lutheranism was shown to be more than one man, in revolt against his Church. Those German princes and city council leaders who were members of the diet, and who supported Lutheranism as set out in the document, signed the *Confession*. The list of names shows the extent of

Lutheranism's spread: Electoral Saxony and Hesse, the rulers of the territories of Lüneberg, Brandenburg-Ansbach and Anhalt, and the cities of Nürnberg and Reutlingen.[9]

And it was not just a matter of putting their names to a letter. When in Augsburg they had shown their support for the reforms by refusing to bow for the blessing of the papal chaplain as Charles had entered the city, or to attend the Corpus Christi procession once he was there (which marks fifty days since Easter). They also defied the emperor when he ordered that no Lutheran preachers should speak in public in Augsburg.

The Catholics in the diet feared (correctly as it turned out) that the *Augsburg Confession* would be drafted in such reasonable language as to turn heads. They therefore tried to stop it being read aloud before the assembly, but failed. On 25 June, its contents were made public, though in a small chapel in the episcopal palace that could only play host to a limited number of hearers, as a concession to those keen to lessen its impact.

Next, Charles referred the *Confession* to a group of assembled Catholic theologians. Writing from Coburg, Luther had already dismissed whatever fault they might find. 'For me personally, more than enough has been conceded. If the papists reject it, I see nothing more to concede.'[10] Melanchthon's position was different. In the fevered atmosphere of Augsburg, where an agreement seemed at least possible, he was open to argument.

It took some time for the Catholic theologians to respond. Given the compromises that Melanchthon had already made, with Luther's approval, this was probably the best chance Rome had of healing the schism, a moment when its policy of underestimating Luther, and its failure to see the scale of the threat he posed, might have been retrieved. Yet such hopes were thrown away by the theologians' document, known as the *Confutation*.

Its text was read to Luther's supporters in the diet, and yielded on almost nothing. Once again the attitude was loftily to dismiss the Lutherans, as if such words alone would cause them to recant. The arrogance stretched to refusing even to supply their opponents with a text of the *Confutation*. Instead, on 22 September, Emperor Charles pre-empted any more discussion by pronouncing that the final word had been spoken, as a consequence of the Catholic theologians' rejection of the *Augsburg Confession*. Those German rulers who had supported and sustained the rebel Church within a Church thus far now were given until 15 April 1531, directly after Easter Sunday, to return to the fold.

If the emperor appears to history overly hasty, an alternative narrative holds that at the crucial moment, Melanchthon tabled a new text, entitled *Apology*, that he had constructed on the basis of what he remembered of the *Confutation* when it was read aloud. It was his way of prolonging discussion. Charles's hand is said to have reached out to take it, just as at Worms he had, on instinct, allowed Luther an extra twenty-four hours to prepare his answer to a question about his books. But this time he was publicly rebuked by his brother, Ferdinand, sitting alongside him. The gap between the two sides was too big for any single individual to span it. The emperor's arm was withdrawn and the chance of any sort of reconciliation lost.

Luther had expected his colleagues to be away in Augsburg for a few weeks, or months at most, but they did not return to Coburg until 1 October. They discussed what had taken place for three days before heading back to Wittenberg on 4 October. By all accounts, Luther was in low spirits. He expected an attack from the emperor to be launched any day.

Fearful times

The conclusion of the Diet of Augsburg set the scene for a confrontation between those recently labelled Protestants and a Holy Roman Emperor with renewed determination to restore religious unity in Germany. Princes may take up arms, Luther lamented to his old friend Wenceslaus Linck in 1531, but there is no such option for 'a Christian who has died to the world'.[11]

The prospect of being at the heart of a battle over the reforms he had proposed in the Church therefore horrified him. He was once again challenged on his attitude to violence. While he had justified the use of force by the German rulers in the Peasants' War on the grounds that the rebels had disobeyed Jesus' clear command to 'render unto Caesar what is Caesar's', now the fight could not be isolated in the secular domain of his 'two kingdoms', but would creep into the spiritual one, too. It would be deemed a religious war – Catholics versus Protestants.

Luther's deepest instinct, as ever, was to rely on God. When challenged on how to respond to the threat posed to the Holy Roman Empire by the Ottoman Turks, he remarked: 'Pray! Because it is hopeless to rely upon weapons, only upon God. If the Turks want to do something to us, the people must simply recite the Lord's Prayer.'[12]

That is pure Luther. It is also otherworldly Luther, and by 1530 he had learnt that otherworldly wasn't always enough. After Augsburg, his supporter, Philipp of Hesse, was pushing forward with his plans to forge a 'Protestant Alliance' of the princes, cities and Swiss cantons that had embraced Lutheranism, Zwingli-ism or, in the case of Strasbourg, under Martin Bucer, something in between. That posed two challenges. The first and more obvious was once again to search for a religious formula that would unite all three 'Protestant' groupings on the vexed question of how to mark the Lord's Supper.

Luther had already revealed himself not to be given to compromise on this issue, but Philipp of Hesse quickly managed to come to an agreement over a pact of mutual defence with Martin Bucer and his allies, if not yet with Zwingli. To Luther, there was little difference between the two groups. He tended to lump them together. 'I learned from experience,' he reflected in 1538, 'to stand fast to the words: "This is my body". I never allowed myself to be swayed by their digressions, but relied upon that [gospel] passage.'[13]

That was said with hindsight. What he didn't mention was that the standoff over this theological issue was all but resolved by what might be regarded as a double blow of fate. Luther, of course, took it as divine intervention. In October of 1531 Zwingli, who had none of Luther's reservations about the use of violence in God's name, was killed on the battlefield of Kappel, defending Zurich against the five Swiss cantons that had remained Catholic, in a confrontation he had done much to provoke. The following month his chief lieutenant Johannes Oecolampadius was also dead, apparently overwhelmed by the shock of Zwingli's demise. 'It is well that Zwingli [lies] dead on the battlefield,' Luther remarked with scant Christian charity, 'for otherwise we could not have kept the Landgrave [Philipp of Hesse], Strasbourg and others of our neighbours. Oh, what a triumph this is, that they have perished. How well God knows His business.'[14] As indeed was proved when Bucer showed himself more flexible than the others and conceded a form of words on the real presence that dealt with the question to everyone's satisfaction.[15]

That left the second, equally difficult question for Luther: whether to endorse the violence implicit in the formation of the Protestant Alliance in early 1531. The Schmalkaldic League (named after Schmalkalden, the town where it was established) consisted of Philipp of Hesse, the Elector of Saxony and the other German princes and city councils who had signed the *Augsburg Confession*, plus Bucer's allies. It was undeniably a military body, another step in the establishment of a separate Lutheran Church in Germany, and a rival bloc to the Holy Roman Empire. Every member pledged to come to the assistance of others in the event of an attack by Charles V and his allies. How could Luther now draw a distinction between Church and state when it came to violence?

He struggled. In a *Table Talk*, he denied he was against violence *per se*. 'If a robber fell on me, I would always resist him, as my duty to our prince, whose servant I am. For he does not attack me because of the gospel and as a preacher, rather as an instrument of the prince. But if I were attacked because of the Word of God and as a preacher, then I must suffer it. That is where God rules, I leave everything to him.'[16] What, though, if his attacker had mixed motives, resenting Luther's loyalty to his ruler *and* Luther's preaching in equal measure, or unable to distinguish between them? Life is rarely as clean-cut as Luther's formula, as the Peasants' War, its bloody toll, and the disillusionment some of his erstwhile supporters felt in the aftermath should have taught him.

He was, once again, being drawn inexorably into another of the *de facto* arrangements with political leaders that the popes had long enjoyed with Catholic rulers. Luther, though, felt he had no alternative, if the reforms he had introduced were to survive. An uneasy formula was agreed. If rulers judged that it was right to take up arms against the emperor to protect the lands where Protestantism had put down roots, Luther conceded that it was a matter for their conscience. He would not stand in their way, though by his *Table Talk* definition they were Christians and should conclude that violence was inappropriate for them.

The basis of this compromise was a principle Luther had articulated before, namely that pastors and Church leaders could never take part in battle. There were, in this scenario, two categories of believer: the elect few who were above battle, and the rest, Christian or not, who were allowed by default to fight, on occasion on behalf of the untainted elite.

As the years passed, Luther slowly softened his attitude towards the Schmalkaldic League. It expanded when Denmark joined in 1538, followed by Brandenburg (1539) and the Palatinate (1545).

Luther was even persuaded to present his own 'Schmalkaldic Articles' to a meeting of members in 1537, but was prevented from doing so by kidney stones.[17] He had prepared a text to be adopted by the group as a negotiating position with the emperor's supporters regarding the long-demanded national council of the German Church. Such a gathering now was potentially back on the table following the election of Alessandro Farnese as Pope Paul III in 1534. But Luther's Schmalkaldic Articles were eventually sidelined, on the advice of Melanchthon. This was not because they departed from his own *Augsburg Confession*, but because Melanchthon argued that the mere appearance of Luther's name as the author of the document would inflame passions among their Catholic opponents, and make negotiating even harder.

What seems to be behind Luther's mellowing regarding his attitude to violence were his acute concerns over an impending attack. Like many who grow more anxious as they get older, there could have been a sliver of worry about his own fate, though if challenged he would surely have denied it. In the autumn of 1531, though, he had come up with a particularly grisly image, redolent of the sort of torture techniques used by the Inquisition, where he pictured his own position as being that of one crushed between God and the Catholic Church. 'I have set Christ and the Pope against each other, and as a result I have put myself between the door and the hinge. If I should be brought down, Christ will certainly raise me up again.'[18]

His real anxiety, though, was for others, as well as for the fate of the reforms he was working so hard to achieve. He fretted repeatedly from 1530 onwards about the quality of the defensive walls that protected Wittenberg. The town's ramparts, in Luther's opinion, were only fit for the task of keeping out thieves and the wild animals that wandered the north German plain. They would not deter the imperial armies.[19] 'Wittenberg scratches, scrapes, gathers everything to it and sings, "Peace, there is no danger!" But after my passing,' Luther warned in siren tones, 'dangerous times will come. Those with the long cut pants [a reference to the Spanish style of uniform, adopted by imperial forces under Charles] will increase, and it will serve them right.'[20]

In November 1538, he was again warning of the imminent threat of attack, which would also be a punishment from God. 'These are dangerous times. God will sweep out His storehouses and clean them. I pray to God that my wife and children will not live long after my death. Very dangerous and horrible times are coming. I had never foreseen such wicked times in the world.'[21]

There is, implicit in such remarks, a criticism not just of his enemies, but even of his fellow Wittenbergers. Their behaviour was not sufficient, he is saying, to keep God's protection. And his warning had an almost apocalyptic note that better suited the rhetoric of his old foe Thomas Müntzer. Perhaps Luther's concern was exacerbated because now he was a husband and father, so it was no longer just his own fate that concerned him. Indeed, later he was to say: 'I wish that I and all my children were dead! Because even stranger things are going to happen in the world. Whoever lives on will see that it becomes ever more exasperating . . .'[22]

Perhaps, too, Luther was giving way to the general insecurity of the times. Two days after he had made his apocalyptic warning, his next *Table Talk* was taken up with fears prompted by a local incident in the nearby village of Marzahna, a few miles from Wittenberg, that was clearly preying on his mind. A marauding band of thieves, under Hans Kohlhase, had targeted and destroyed the village, stringing up the local watchman.[23] Such attacks were not unusual for the period. Was Luther worrying too much?

In the short term, yes. All the military preparations Luther's princely allies were busy making proved needless. As before, Emperor Charles was quickly distracted by his many other responsibilities and campaigns, and so didn't follow up the Diet of

Augsburg with the attack on the Protestants that many had feared. The 15th of April 1531, the deadline he had set at Augsburg for the Protestant states to return to the papal fold, came and went unmarked, save by a letter from Luther. *Warning to His Dear German People* sounded a belligerent note by advancing the case for joining battle as a form of self-defence against an aggressor who wished to destroy reforms that had God's blessing.

Indeed Emperor Charles, with all his distractions elsewhere, soon showed himself more interested in calming things down in Germany than in increasing the tension. He could not fight on any more fronts, and anyway required the support of the Protestant princes on two matters: first, to agree in 1531 to his younger brother Ferdinand of Austria being named King of the Romans, and to being made heir apparent to the empire; and second, to come up with money to support the fight with the Ottoman Turks. The compromise adopted, suggested by Archbishop Albrecht of Mainz, one of the Catholic leaders with some sympathy for Luther, was to engage in more talks with the Protestants to try and seek an agreement that restored a show of unity. Melanchthon's diplomatic route might finally produce dividends.

With that agreed, Charles could continue his ongoing rivalry with the French, especially after they formed an alliance with the Ottoman Turks. There was a briefly successful excursion to Tunis on the North African coast to challenge Ottoman control there, followed by two conflicts in Italy with the French in 1535–38 and 1542–44.

Luther's Reformation was, in his lifetime, safe. The only military problems posed came from radical Dutch Anabaptists who, in 1534, seized the city of Münster in Westphalia and, under their leader, Bernhard Rothmann, once a Lutheran, proclaimed that the end of world was nigh. Only Münster would survive as the 'new Jerusalem' promised in the Book of Revelation as part of the return of God in glory.[24] They barricaded themselves in, abolished private property and sanctioned polygamy. It took a year-long siege, jointly conducted by Protestant and Catholic forces, to dislodge them. Seen in such light, Luther must have appeared to the German princes as far removed from being any sort of fanatic.

Mind, body, spirit

Luther had long been prone to angst – *Anfechtung* as he called it, or what today would surely be labelled depression. Although punctuated by moments of revelation, if not elation, it had plagued his early years at the monastery. And it had never really left him, though its signs had become harder to spot in the helter-skelter of the years between 1517 and 1525, when the circulation of his writings had put him so much in the spotlight that he had little time for anything other than a ceaseless round of writing, teaching, preaching and defending himself. The combination had largely kept the lows at bay. When they did interpose, as when the devil loomed large to drag him down at Wartburg Castle, Luther had thrown himself into work as a cure, with a furious energy that bordered on mania.

From the Peasants' War onwards, though, that momentum had slowly ebbed. Yes, he was building a Church, no small task when navigating between Catholicism on the one hand and more radical forms of Protestantism on the other, all the time leaving the door open for his reforms one day to become the mainstream. And there was his teaching and his writing and his translating. His monumental undertaking, the German-language edition of the Bible, finally appeared in 1534, though he continued to work on revising it right up to his death.

'I have so much work to do everyday that I don't have time for prayer,' he was complaining in the winter of 1542, 'and have to be satisfied with the Ten Commandments when I finally lay down, a

Lord's Prayer, and after that one or two short prayers, run through my mind a few times, and [then] fall asleep.'[25] Yet those who observed him noticed that the pace of his life was changing. 'He was in the habit of walking around,' a *Table Talk* recorder noted in June 1532, 'and would stop at a particular place and talk to himself, and pray with his hands and eyes raised to heaven. Often he would leave the table and go alone to a window and pray there for half an hour or more.'[26]

It may simply have been in that moment Luther had had a particularly tough issue to grapple with, or was searching for the absolutely right word for the chapter of the Bible he was working on, but the description sounds more general, covering a habitual stance rather than an image from a single day.

And so much had changed for him. In place of a monk's cell, there was domesticity with Katie and their expanding family. He could now live in safety in Wittenberg, having faced down an edict to arrest him as a heretic. Luther was being read widely, scrutinised in universities, and sought out by overseas visitors, including Robert Barnes, on behalf of Thomas Cromwell, Henry VIII's close advisor, wanting Lutheran support for the English king in his battle with Rome over his divorce from Catherine of Aragon.

Many who had made a similar impact on the European stage would, by the time of life Luther had reached, been tempted to rest on their laurels and enjoy the sound of their own voice. There was, granted, an element of this second in his *Table Talk* performances, but complacency was not in Luther's restless nature. Others were busy putting him on a pedestal. From 1540 onwards, Cranach's studio circulated an image of an ageing Luther, based on an earlier work, but now with greying hair, several chins and a huge physical presence that bespeaks a quasi-regal authority. Yet in person there remained about Luther an essential humility that came with his constant focus on the moment when he would meet his Maker. He refused, in modern terms, to be seduced by his own propaganda.

So, in 1540, for instance, while dining with the Elector of Saxony, Luther is said to have vigorously rejected the comparison being made by other admiring guests between him and the apostles. 'No, they were great true persons,' he protested. 'At the most God lets me stand behind the door and be His servant. And I am not even quite that.'[27] Another version of the story has Luther dismissing himself, when placed alongside the apostles, as 'a stinking afterthought', which certainly sounds more like his turn of phrase.

Luther could never rest easy. While he slept in relative safety in his bed in Wittenberg, other Lutherans in other parts of Germany, especially those with hard-line Catholic rulers, were being martyred for believing in him. He would have had to be crassly insensitive not to register his good fortune as against their plight, and to feel guilty because of it.

And that same knowledge underpinned his worries about the future. In challenging the Pope and the emperor, he had inspired princes, priests, theologians, monks, nuns, whole cities and thousands upon thousands of dedicated individuals to follow him in wanting to reform the Church. But there were those who saw him as the cause of division and disunity in Europe, which was leaving it vulnerable in the face of external threats, such as that posed by the Ottoman Turks. He had polarised Germany and the two sides were taking an increasingly militaristic stance. Where would it all end? Would reform come to Catholicism, or would Lutheranism become a separate Church, a rival to Rome, even its successor? And how many would suffer in the process? How could he mitigate that suffering or shape the final outcome?

These were questions enough to make anyone fret, and Luther had sufficient knowledge of Emperor Charles to understand that his short-term absence from German affairs did not signify approval of the compromise so far reached. And so he had to wait, the one thing all restless people find hardest of all, knowing that even such perseverance may not be enough to achieve a solution. Content as he was – and knew he should be – to leave it in the hands of God, a tiny part of Luther must have hankered for the days, so recently passed, when he was in front of the Diet of Worms, seizing the agenda and directing it.

As he waited and watched, Luther experienced a return of the physical symptoms that had accompanied his angst. In 1539, for instance, he is reported as being 'plagued' by kidney stones,[28] which may or may not be linked with his long-term digestive problems. And there were also physical collapses that could have had a psychological aspect. The pessimistic, depressive side of Luther is certainly there when reading accounts of his daily conversations in this period in *Table Talk*. Here he is in 1533. 'The world is like a drunken farmer. If you lift him up on one side of the saddle, he simply falls off the other side. Nothing can be done for the world, no matter how hard one wants. It wants to belong to the devil.'[29] And again in the same year, with a distinct echo of Saint Augustine: 'The world consists of a pile of humanity that gladly accepts all of the blessings of Our Father and in return responds with nothing more than blasphemy and every conceivable form of ingratitude.'[30]

Taking a negative view of humankind is not inevitably a sign of depression, and especially not in the late medieval times when, Renaissance Rome to one side, many believers would have concurred with Luther's view of their pitiful state before God. But then there are Luther's increasingly frequent fainting fits. In April 1527, directly after Easter Sunday, he was unable to finish giving a sermon because he was overcome with vertigo and dizziness. He seemed to recover that spring, but on 6 July suffered another collapse so severe that he believed himself at death's door.

He may have caught the virus that was sweeping across Germany at the time, and was so severe in the summer of 1527 when it arrived in Wittenberg that the university decamped en masse for safety to Jena, three days' journey to the south. The outbreak had been identified as linked to the Black Death that had decimated Europe in recent centuries and still had the power to terrify. Yet Luther refused to leave the town. He was willing, in this as in other matters, to trust in God.

Others, though, offer alternative diagnoses for his physical ailments in 1527. Justas Jonas suggested an inner-ear infection, akin to what is now called Ménière's Disease. He also described having supper with Luther on an unnamed evening in 1527, and of his host complaining of a loud noise in his ear.[31] Luther then made his way up to his bed, but collapsed in the doorway and sent Jonas to bring him some water. He returned to find Luther deep in prayer. 'O, Dear Lord, if it be Your will, if this be the hour that You have decided for me, then let it be Your will.'[32]

When Luther finally crawled on to his bed, Jonas reported him as saying: 'Lord, our almighty God, how gladly I would have poured out my blood in defence of Your word!' And later: 'You know that there are many You have given to spill their blood for the gospel. I had always believed that I was destined to spill my blood in Your name, but I am not worthy.'[33]

When a doctor was called, Jonas continued, he rebuked Luther and told him not to despair so. The professional diagnosis seemed to be that, whatever the problem, it wasn't that serious. And, indeed, after a dramatic leave-taking from his wife and one of his children, Luther suddenly announced he was feeling a little better. The following day, when Jonas called, Luther explained to him that it had been a spiritual, not a physical attack.[34]

Similar attacks came pretty regularly thereafter. Luther appears to have regarded them as manifestations of *Anfechtung*. 'If I live longer,' he promised, 'I would like to write a book about

Anfechtung, for without it no man can understand Scripture, faith, the fear or the love of God.'[35] He never made good that promise, but his remark indicated that he saw such moments as part and parcel of being a Christian. Given his reference in front of Jonas to the blood spilled by others, were they his own form of martyrdom, a shadow of what others bore in the name of his reforms? Or were they, in the contemporary language of psychology, breakdowns?

On his return from Coburg in 1530, Luther had suffered another prolonged patch of dizzy spells and complained that he couldn't cope with his workload and all the expectations he shouldered. 'I am swamped by letters from every direction. They all presume that only Luther can expedite their affairs. Hardly any messengers are able to wait.'[36]

In 1536 a planned meeting with Martin Bucer at a neutral venue had to be rescheduled for Wittenberg because Luther had fallen ill again, this time on Easter Sunday, and had told those around him that he was about to die. Once more, on a trip to Gotha in 1540, he collapsed and bade a poignant farewell to his confessor, 'Doctor Pomeranus', entrusting him with the care of his family and his burial. 'With peaceful mind and without a struggle,' Luther later recalled, 'I would have fallen asleep in Christ, but Christ wished me to live.'[37]

In Luther's mind, these collapses were a new form of trial sent from heaven to replace the ordeals he had faced at Leipzig and Worms. Yet the element of hysteria is hard to overlook. In the winter of 1542, he suffered a migraine for several days. At the supper table, he told his wife to summon home their eldest son (away in Torgau being tutored), 'because I would like to have him here when my end comes.'[38] Once again he made a swift recovery.

It is a wonder that Katharina von Bora is nowhere reported as rebuking her husband for crying wolf, for she was a woman of strong opinions who was more than able to express them. It is hard to imagine her putting up with repeated bouts of 'man flu' and saying nothing.

We know that she was given to speaking her mind to her husband, because the many lodgers who shared the Black Cloister with them reported clashes between the two. 'Domestic wrath is nothing more than a puppet show for Our Lord,' her husband once reflected aloud after the two of them had had a heated domestic in the presence of others. 'All it requires is a whack with a birch rod . . . If I can endure the wrath of the devil, sin and conscience, then I can stand my ground against the wrath of Katie von Bora. No one will gain anything from me by force.'[39]

Yet her apparent silence around her husband's repeated collapses and resurrections hints that she was more than aware that one of her roles in his life was to keep at bay his angst, *Anfechtung*, or even demons. He once recalled how, when he felt himself under assault and unable to sleep, 'then I turn to my Katie and say, "forbid me to have such temptations and recall me from such vain vexations".'[40]

Succession planning

Next to Katie, the key relationship in these later years of Luther's life was with Philipp Melanchthon. Many of those who had once been in his intimate circle had moved on to run Lutheran churches in different parts of Germany, but Melanchthon remained at his side. The two were close in most things, but it was never seamless. With Melanchthon sixteen years younger, Luther knew that he was the one who would carry his reforms forward. This accounts for why, when he was so prone to periodic collapses himself, Luther would spend time worrying about Melanchthon's always delicate health. In the summer of 1540, when some bad news caused the younger man to take to his bed 'consumed with grief and down with fever', Luther was brisk and slightly impatient. 'His worrying won't change a thing, if only I were with him. I know what a soft spine he has . . . but I have developed a thick skin. I am of peasant stock and a tough Saxon.'[41]

Luther may have been overstating his own stamina, but that 'soft spine' in Melanchthon was not principally a medical diagnosis. It was an indication that Luther continued to worry that his younger colleague was not always as robust as he might be in defending the cause of reform. It may have been a matter of style. At Augsburg and then again in 1537 with the Schmalkaldic Articles, Melanchthon had insisted on a softer, less confrontational tone than his leader. There was more flexibility in Melanchthon's approach to those who took a different point of view from the Lutherans. Where Luther's first instinct was to focus narrowly and stand his ground, Melanchthon was more the diplomat. 'Various in his works, singular in his mind,' reads the inscription on a portrait of him by Lucas Cranach the Younger, produced to mark Melanchthon's death in 1560. 'If Luther feeds the sheep through the mouth, Melanchthon tends the bees through blossoms.' The imagery may chime better in the original German, but his point is clear.

A *Table Talk* from the summer of 1531 provides a glimpse of the interaction between Luther and Melanchthon. 'You are a fine orator when you write,' Luther told Melanchthon, 'not when you speak.' That may have been his way of saying, 'you're a good number two'. The context was that Melanchthon was trying to persuade Luther to answer an attacking pamphlet by a priest from Cölln (now part of modern Berlin), and Luther was resisting – on the grounds that he couldn't spare the effort. Yet it turned out that Luther had already penned exactly the reply Melanchthon was urging in *Response to the Assassin of Dresden*. Why not just say so? Or, if he hadn't yet put pen to paper, agree to look into it? Luther, it seems, was keen to show who was in control.

For his part, Melanchthon may have been pressing the point in this incident because he was worrying that Luther's once unstoppable gush of printed works had slowed to more of a stream. He was still keeping the printers busy, but none of his tracts of the 1530s and 1540s made quite the same impact on his contemporaries as earlier texts. It also reflected circumstance. Lutheranism was now structurally, liturgically and doctrinally all but a Church in its own right in the eyes of many. And the day-to-day business of an institution makes for duller copy than leading the attacks on the status quo.

Yet there was undeniably a change in Luther, too. In the past, so much of his writing had been prompted by anger. Now he apparently had insufficient of that anger left to rouse him. Its place had been taken by anxiety, and that was as likely to make him collapse as it was to compel him to sit at his desk and commit his thoughts to paper.

There were other episodes where Melanchthon and Luther appeared at odds. In 1536 a *Table Talk* recorded another moment when, to Luther's annoyance, Melanchthon appeared to have been arguing that good works were necessary for salvation. A row loomed but then it turned out that the younger man had been misquoted.

Melanchthon was, of course, still able to travel relatively freely, unlike Luther, and would represent his leader at gatherings where he would be asked the Lutheran position.[42] Since there was no quick way of keeping in contact with Wittenberg, he would speak what he believed to be Luther's mind, and inevitably that could cause problems between them, especially when many on the Catholic side had by now identified Melanchthon as more open to persuasion than Luther. Indeed it is remarkable misunderstandings between the two of them did not happen more often.

Melanchthon's liberty may have irked Luther, as would seeing the opening he had created increasingly entrusted to another. He was not a resentful man, but he was only human. Such was the case in October 1540 when there were talks at Haguenau and later at Worms, convened at the emperor's request, to explore once again the possibility of healing the breach between the Protestants and the Catholics. Some progress was made, with the Catholics shifting their opposition to parts of the *Augsburg Confession*, and the Lutherans agreeing to discuss the doctrine of 'justification by faith'. But over such issues as papal authority, the gap was too large to close. Behind the emperor, the new Pope, Paul III, might have been more willing than his predecessors to acknowledge the strength of Luther's arguments for reform, but he was not about to downgrade his own office by convening a council of the Church. The Pope's own 'Reform Commission' had identified in 1537 some of the failings that had given rise to Lutheranism, most of them mirroring precisely Luther's own long-standing complaints, but Luther's steadfast refusal to endorse any gathering under papal direction on Italian soil to explore these issues further killed off the initiative.[43] Experience had taught Luther that anything organised under papal auspices was unlikely to give him a fair hearing. The sort of council he sought would be one where Lutherans and Catholics attended as equals.

Luther's briefing to Melanchthon on how to deal with all such promises of exploratory talks was typically belligerent. 'If the Pope would throw away his crown and step down from his Roman throne and renounce infallibility, and acknowledge that he has erred and damaged the Church and spilled innocent blood, then we would accept him into the Church. Otherwise he will always remain for us the Antichrist.'[44] It hardly gave the younger man much to negotiate with. At Regensburg in 1541 the latest attempt at reconciliation ground to a halt.

The failure once again shone a light on the fundamental decision that faced Luther, Melanchthon, and the princes who supported them. With the threat from Emperor Charles distant but real, their parallel organisation to official Catholicism was growing in size, reach and complexity. But what was its real goal? How much did they want to build a freestanding Church, and how much find a way back to a reformed Rome? The question of what constituted the 'true Church' increasingly preoccupied Luther in the 1540s.

He judged reunion possible, though only once he was off the scene. 'Those who will not accept the kernel during my lifetime will honour the shell after I am dead,' he once predicted.[45] Yet that reunion, he insisted, would be on his terms, more a surrender by Rome than a negotiation. 'I entertain no sorry picture of our Church, but rather that of the Church flourishing through pure and uncorrupted teaching and one increasing with excellent ministers from day to day.'[46] So the whole Catholic Church was going to become 'our' Lutheran Church.

In January 1542 Luther took another step along that road when he approved the consecration of the reform movement's first bishop to the vacant see of Naumburg. He couldn't have chosen a closer ally than Nikolaus von Amsdorf, who had accompanied him to Leipzig and Worms, had been in on the plot to spirit him away to Wartburg, and was even named by Katharina von Bora as her other potential husband. Yet the cathedral chapter of Naumburg opposed him, probably for the same reason as did the German bishops and the papacy, which would usually have made the decision. The Elector of Saxony had to force the appointment of the celibate Amsdorf on the diocese, and it left a legacy of unhappiness that outlived Luther.[47]

While Melanchthon was always careful in his various meetings to try to avoid causing direct offence to the Catholic Church, Luther too occasionally revealed a more conciliatory side. Asked by a colleague what he would do if he found himself at a Catholic mass, he replied: 'Don't take the priest from the altar, don't blow out the candles either. If I myself were present in the church at the time of the elevation of the sacrament, I would raise my hand just like the others [i.e. the other priests, as if he were still a Catholic priest in good standing with the Pope]. I would show respect and honour the sacrament. For the true sacrament is there in so far as what is essential. And in general the high mass in the papacy is correct.'[48]

Religion and morality

You can build a Church structure, publish teachings and appoint pastors and prelates, but you cannot insulate yourself against the difficult moral questions that will present themselves. That was Luther's experience in these later years. Events had a habit of blurring the clear distinction he tried to draw between the kingdom of the spirit and the kingdom of the prince and magistrate. As the effective 'pope' of the expanding Lutheran Church in Germany and beyond, Luther was constantly being sought out to make judgements on specific sets of circumstances. A sizeable part of the correspondence concerned marital issues, an area where Catholicism had developed an extensive set of rules and regulations, but where in the gospels Jesus is largely silent.

On questions of sexual conduct in general, Luther took a less punitive line than the Catholic Church. His remarks suggest that he himself liked and enjoyed sex (which was also true of Catholic clerics, including Pope Paul III, who had several children). More significantly, though, Luther did not follow the official Catholic line (that owes so much to his hero, Saint Augustine) of separating out the body and the spirit. Not for him any lingering shadow of medieval Catholicism's ascetic self-denial when it came to bodily pleasures, including food and drink.

On marriage, his standard line was that it was none of his concern. 'I am of the opinion that judgements in regard to marriage should be reserved to civil jurists. Since they make judgements concerning parents, children and servants, why should they not make judgments concerning married life?'[49] If marriage was, as he had argued in *On Monastic Vows*, a promise made by two individuals to each other, and (in *The Babylonian Captivity*) not a sacrament, then divorce was a matter for magistrates.

That did not mean, however, that he was washing his hands of it. In another *Table Talk*, from December 1532, he clarified this further, employing the same distinction he made over violence. Marriage was a private matter between the individuals concerned, their conscience and God. And those who abused marriage would anger God. So when Jesus states clearly His disapproval of divorce in Matthew's gospel,[50] that scriptural guidance must be heard by individuals, but that does not mean it should become the pretext for the Church authorities getting involved in what goes on in the bedroom. Luther was certainly not signalling any endorsement of what he listed as 'unchastity, whore-mongering, infidelity, unfaithfulness and adultery in spirit and substance',[51] but rather that the punishment for these sins was to be dished out by God, not by the Church.

If this sounds straightforward enough in the writing, then when it came to real life it could tie Luther in knots, and never more so than when politics intervened. Aside from the Electors of Saxony, Philipp of Hesse was among his staunchest supporters. As a young man, he had been married for dynastic reasons to the sickly daughter of Luther's implacable enemy, Duke Georg, from the other part of Saxony. It was a loveless union, and Philipp had strayed beyond its bounds repeatedly, as he confided in Luther in late 1539. He was 'constantly in a state of adultery and fornication', Luther recorded.[52] The prince was, however, ashamed of his infidelity, and believed the best way of renouncing it would be to take as his new wife the woman he loved.

Luther was not willing in Philipp's case to overlook Jesus' prohibition of divorce, but neither could he recommend

Catholicism's solution. That would be to direct the landgrave to seek an annulment of his marriage through the Roman tribunals. Their authority to judge rested on papal authority, which Luther rejected.

At the same time, he did not want to abandon Philipp to his fate. The course he therefore took is usually presented as Luther placing political needs above doctrinal purity, but it also speaks of a very human desire, informed by his own experience of a happy marriage, to reach out to someone in a difficult domestic situation.

Drawing Philipp's attention to those Old Testament patri-archs, including Abraham and David, who had several wives, Luther suggested that, in good conscience, the prince might in secret make a second marriage. While bigamy was a crime under imperial law, in God's eyes it might be a less severe sin than divorce, though a sin nevertheless. The advice was unorthodox and bespoke, and in Luther's mind was private, governed by the seal that exists in Catholic tradition on all conversations between penitents and confessors. Philipp is reported to have respected this confidentiality, though in 1540 he still summoned Melanchthon and Bucer to his castle, without explanation, and had them attend his marriage to his second wife, Margarethe von der Saale, the teenage daughter of a lady-in-waiting at his court.

They, too, kept it quiet, but Margarethe's mother, Anna, did not. When she made public Luther's private dispensation for Philipp, it caused a storm. Here was Luther permitting one rule for the rich and another for the poor, in the same old way that the Catholic Church had long operated. The episode damaged Luther's reputation for plain speaking and plain truth.[53] In a *Table Talk*, he tried to defend his actions. Philipp was acting sinfully, he acknowledged, but that did not make him unusual. 'If there is sin among us, there were also sins at the time of Christ; so very much like Judas is the Landgrave!'[54]

His point was that there was a distinction between religion and morality, with the latter ultimately a matter of judgement for God. It was another aspect of the two kingdoms theory. 'World order', he subsequently argued, 'cannot be maintained by a body of laws alone, but through God's authority . . . Everything in this life is like an outline of the coming life.'[55]

And it was on that coming life that Luther fixed his gaze when called upon to make judgements. 'The theologian', he said, 'is concerned only with teaching faith in Christ, and in that regard his main objective is to admonish everyone to do his calling according to faith; for example, the cobbler to make shoes.' He had no designs himself, he insisted, on being a magistrate. 'It is not my job to lay down instructions on how a shoe is to be made, or how a shoe is to be marketed. There are civil laws for that sort of thing.'[56]

Inciting violence against the Jews

If the Philipp of Hesse episode had an immediate and negative impact on Luther's reputation, the remarks he made in his later years about the Jews came back to scar that reputation many centuries later. In his 1542 tract, *The Jews and Their Lies*, he argued forcefully that the Old Testament should be seen primarily as a set of texts that prefaced the arrival of Jesus Christ, rather than as a collection of Hebrew Scriptures, sacred to Jews. That, in itself, to modern readers, shows a lack of respect both for the Jewish tradition, and for history, but his tract went much further.

Its language was, as the title suggests, direct and coarse. Jews were, he wrote, a 'base, whoring people, that is, no people of God, and their boast of lineage, circumcision, and law must be accounted as filth.' Of their role in money-lending, he added: 'they hold us Christians captive in our own country. They let us work in the sweat of our brow to earn money and property while they sit behind the stove, idle away the time, fart, and roast pears. They stuff themselves, guzzle, and live in luxury and ease from our hard-earned goods. With their accursed usury they hold us and our property captive.'[57] He branded them with the mark of the devil: 'full of the devil's faeces . . . which they wallow in like swine.'

Ignoring his own guidance on violence, Luther's advice to Christians, when faced by Jewish resistance to the idea of conversion, was to torch Jewish synagogues and schools, as well as forbid rabbis to preach, and confiscate all Jewish writings. The anti-Semitism of this tract was so pronounced that, in the 1930s, the Nazi propaganda machine made great play of it, finding historical justification from an unimpeachably German source for their own attitudes, and for the Holocaust. In September 1933, for example, the Nazi interior and finance ministers made a point of visiting the Black Cloister, the building decked out on their instructions with the swastika, to claim Luther as one of their own.

Was Luther, as is often claimed today, to the undoubted detriment of his enduring reputation, anti-Semitic? Absolutely, by our standards, and horribly so. But by the standards of his own time? Or even the standards of his own earlier writings?

The position of Jews in German lands in Luther's lifetime was at best tenuous. Where they were permitted to live, they were at best tolerated. They had been pushed into money-lending roles because Christian teaching on usury cast a shadow over such work, but then were regularly attacked in public for being obsessed by money, and greedy. Luther was echoing popular prejudices in his 1542 tract. That is not an excuse, of course, especially for one who had shown himself capable of standing up to the received wisdom of Catholicism.

Jews were banned completely from Electoral Saxony, but if Luther had met a Jew, he would have urged him or her to convert to Christianity. That much he had made clear in his 1523 tract, *That Jesus Christ Was Born a Jew*. That earlier document, though, is strikingly different in tone from what Luther produced in 1542. It urged greater tolerance and respect for Jews in German lands, an unusual line to take in the late medieval period in Christian Europe. Back then his hope had been that a reformed and renewed Church would prompt Jews to convert.

That hadn't happened. In his disappointment, an older, anxious and unrestrained Luther treated the Jews with the same scorn and contempt that he poured out on the Catholic authorities and those Evangelicals who outflanked him in their Protestantism. But he went further. For the Jews, in Luther's terms, had not just rejected Jesus Christ's teaching, they had rejected Jesus Christ Himself, and that for him was an unforgiveable sin.

Last orders

The tone of his attack on the Jews fits with a darker, shriller drift in much of Luther's discourse as the 1540s proceeded. His glooms became longer, his resentments more acute, and his world-changing insights fewer and further between as events proceeded around him.

Until his death in April of 1539, Duke Georg had remained a fierce champion of Catholicism in his part of divided Saxony, obliging his subjects to take an oath of loyalty to the Pope and driving Lutheranism underground. Following the early deaths of his two sons, however, he was succeeded by his younger brother Heinrich, who, three years earlier, had joined the Lutheran Church. As Duke, Heinrich – known as 'the Pious' – extended Luther's reformed faith into his section of Saxony.

Any rejoicing at this local reunion in Wittenberg, however, was short-lived. In the summer of 1541, Heinrich died, and the wheel turned again. His heir was his son, Moritz (Maurice), who reverted once more in his territories to the staunch Catholicism of Duke Georg. Moritz harboured a profound antipathy towards his counterpart in Electoral Saxony, Elector Johann Friedrich, who had succeeded his father, Elector Johann, in 1532. In this dynastic feud, Emperor Charles spotted a chance finally to bring Wittenberg to heel.

The close bond that Luther had enjoyed with Johann had continued with his son, but Elector Johann Friedrich lacked the caution of his uncle, Elector Friedrich. He determinedly proceeded with the building of a Lutheran Church, up to and including appointing its first bishop on his own authority. A disapproving Emperor Charles wooed Duke Moritz in the other part of Saxony, and developed an alliance which, he hoped, might one day enable him to support the duke in seizing the electoral lands in Saxony and reuniting it under the Catholic Church.

Luther correctly identified the danger. 'Do you think the devil is celebrating?' he asked in April 1542 of the rekindled antagonism over religion between the two branches of the Saxon house of Wettin. 'The papists are laughing behind their hands.' And Melanchthon concurred. 'Now that we have expended great effort and done much work in the Church to preserve our doctrine against the Pope and the entire world, so that no one could take it away from us, along comes this young toady [Duke Moritz] and starts a game among ourselves, so that we don't know anymore where our home is. No one will trust another for the remainder of his born days. Instead in its place the heart will be taken by opposition and hatred.'[58]

Both men sensed the gathering storm. In 1544, at a meeting of the diet in Speyer, Charles still needed the Protestant princes on side as he once again tussled with France, but once he emerged victorious from that confrontation, he returned his gaze to Germany. Efforts to seek a middle way between Catholics and Protestants, which he had previously supported, were abandoned, and the emperor reverted to his traditional role as champion of the papacy. A confrontation in Saxony was inevitable.

When it finally happened, in April 1547 at the Battle of Mühlberg, Luther was no longer around to see Elector Johann Friedrich taken prisoner, Duke Moritz installed as the Catholic ruler of all Saxony, and Wittenberg occupied by imperial troops. It was the crisis he had long been predicting and grew to engulf Germany in bloodshed.

Elector Johann Friedrich by Cranach: an enthusiastic supporter of Luther's reforms, he was defeated in battle in 1547 by Emperor Charles as he fought to defend the Reformation.

Towards the end of his life, Luther had started to tire even of Wittenberg. For years he had been complaining about the apathy and ingratitude of his fellow townsfolk. As early as October 1528 he had berated them from the pulpit for their failure to support his reform movement. 'You know that this week we will request an offering of money. I hear that no one will give anything to those who ask, but rather turn them ungratefully away. By the grace of God, you ungrateful lot, who although you thirst so greedily for money, do not give anything, you wound the ministers with evil words. I am frightened and do not know whether I will preach any more to you vulgar slobs, who cannot give four pennies a year out of good heart.'[59]

Part of his complaint was practical: that the schools he wanted to establish and the pastors he wanted to install to run churches were being starved of the necessary funds because 'Lutherans' would not give enough. Yet it ran deeper. 'You have been freed from tyrants and papists,' he raged. 'You ungrateful beasts are not worthy of this treasure of the gospel. If you don't do otherwise, repenting of your sins, I'm going to cease preaching to you, lest I cast pearls before swine or give holy things to dogs.'

So much for high-minded ideas of the priesthood of all believers. By 1545, a visibly ailing Luther was suggesting to Katie that they might move to her family property at Zülsdorf. He was turning his back on Wittenberg.

He was still in residence on 17 January 1546, however, when he preached his last sermon in his familiar pulpit at the Stadtkirche. Six days later he set off for Eisleben, his birthplace, where he had been asked by the local Duke of Mansfeld to mediate in a long-running dispute. He was greeted with great pomp and escorted to his quarters by an honour guard of a hundred horsemen.

The mediation went on from 29 January until 17 February. Among Luther's final words, in urging the parties to reach an agreement, were some that might now be read in the light of the failure of Rome and the Lutherans to mend bridges. 'We all want unity, but no one seeks the means to unity, which would be mutual love. We all seek riches, but the right way to become rich, namely through God's blessings, is sought by no one. We also want to be happy, but the means by which we may become happy, Christ, is rejected by the entire world.'[60]

On 16 February, he wrote in chalk on his bedroom wall: 'We cannot do what everyone wants; But we can well do what we want.' Again, it can be interpreted as a judgement on the schism that had opened up. Luther was not apportioning blame, but was bemoaning the failure sufficiently to acknowledge each other's positions and an over-enthusiasm for going on the attack. It was as if he was penning his last confession.

The following day, Luther was taken ill. At first Melanchthon, who had accompanied him, took it to be another 'spiritual collapse', or another bout of indigestion. Luther was convinced to rest but, when he woke at midnight, he was in considerable distress. Melanchthon and Justas Jonas gathered round the bed. 'I pray to God to preserve the doctrine of His gospel among us,' Luther said out loud, anxious even on his deathbed about what loomed over the horizon for his attempt to reform the Church, 'for the Pope and the Council of Trent have grievous things in hand.'[61]

And then he moved away from this world and focused instead on his own fate, that moment long anticipated when he stood alone before his God in search of salvation. 'I beseech you, Lord Jesus Christ, receive my soul . . . I certainly know that I shall live with You eternally and that I cannot be taken out of Your hands.' Soon after that, what is believed to have been a stroke silenced him. He died, aged sixty-three, just before 3 a.m. For one who had been threatened by his enemies with death for over a quarter of a century, he had survived much longer than many had anticipated. Including himself. Back in 1511, he had told Staupitz under a pear tree that he was not long for this world, as he tried to turn down a transfer to Wittenberg.

His coffin was displayed for two days in Eisleben, where Jonas preached a sermon, after which his body was transported back to Wittenberg. On 22 February 1546, Luther was laid to rest under the pulpit of the Castle Church in Wittenberg, where he lies to this day, with Melanchthon's grave close by. 'Though the teaching of this blessed man is still powerfully alive,' said Johannes Bugenhagen (Doctor Pomeranus), pastor of the Stadtkirche, 'there is no doubt about it – he was the angel the [Book of Revelation] talks about flying in mid heaven with an eternal gospel.'[62]

A memorial plaque to Luther on the wall of his home,
the Black Cloister in Wittenberg.

Epilogue

'All works, Great Men, Societies are bad.
The Just shall live by Faith . . .' he cried in dread.
And men and women of the world were glad,
Who'd never cared or trembled in their lives.

'Luther' by W. H. Auden, *Collected Poems*[1]

'After my passing,' Martin Luther prophesied, 'dangerous times will come.'[2] And come they certainly did. In May 1547, fifteen months after he had been buried in the Castle Church, the Imperial Army marched through the gates of Wittenberg. Emperor Charles rode up the main street to the Schlosskirche. Some staunch Catholics in his retinue were urging him to have Luther's remains disinterred so as to burn them publicly, just as the Council of Constance had in 1415 demanded that the corpse of the English Bible translator and heretic, John Wycliffe, be exhumed and put to flame.

Charles, however, resisted. Even in death, political considerations saved Luther. The emperor was in the midst of his long-delayed battle with the Protestant princes of the Schmalkaldic League, who had defied his authority as Holy Roman Emperor. The fighting had been going his way; the previous month, at Mühlberg, forty-five miles from Wittenberg, Elector Johann Friedrich of Saxony and Landgrave Philipp of Hesse, two of Lutheranism's strongest supporters, had been defeated and taken prisoner. Their allies, the rulers of the Palatinate and Württemberg, had already submitted to the emperor. Yet the war, as Emperor Charles knew, was far from over. Magdeburg and Bremen, fierce centres of Lutheranism, were still holding out against him, the latter surviving a five-month siege. If Charles was to win round waverers – and it is clear from the deal he agreed at the Diet of Augsburg the following year that he accepted the need for some show of compromise – then he had to act with some restraint.

At that diet in May 1548, Charles issued the Augsburg Interim. His success in the war, if not total, had been sufficient to make him feel he could dictate terms. Until a final ruling could be made by the Church, he decreed, Luther's followers were to be reintegrated back into mainstream Catholicism, with only some minor concessions to the reformers on matters such as married clergy and communion in both kinds.

If Charles believed that including such details demonstrated that he realised he could not entirely turn back the clock, his efforts failed to convince even the German princes who had fought alongside him. They quickly saw that the Augsburg Interim was too punitive to stand a chance of being implemented on the ground. Luther's rebellion had gone on for too long and extended too far for it ever to be wiped away by force. With the frenzied support of the printing presses, he had created one of the first modern mass movements, and it proved robust in the face of top-down attempts to close it down. The late medieval world had shifted decisively and for ever. The attachment many Germans, high- and low-born, felt to Luther's reforms had simply grown too strong to be broken.

In 1552, the German princes combined to force Charles to back down at the Peace of Passau. Elector Johann Friedrich and Landgrave Philipp were released and, in September 1555, at an Imperial Diet that Charles did not even attend, the Peace of Augsburg established ever after Lutheranism's right to exist, wherever the local ruler allowed it. The following year Emperor Charles abdicated.

The principle agreed in Augsburg in 1555 is often referred to by its Latin formulation – *Cuius regio, eius religio* ('Whose realm, his religion'). This allowed rulers the choice of which faith would be tolerated in their domains, albeit from a list of two. It was Lutheranism or Catholicism. The dividing line now hardened into a formal border, patrolled by armies.

Cuius regio, eius religio represented a breakthrough from the medieval idea that every ruler must obey the Pope, and can be seen as a first step on the road to freedom of conscience and religious liberty. Those who disagreed with their prince's choice of faith could, the Peace of Augsburg stated, move freely to somewhere more conducive to their religious beliefs.

Yet the formula ignored two realities: that, in some parts of the empire, there were both Catholics and Lutherans living side by side, who would prefer an accommodation that allowed for mutual respect rather than the injunction to fall into line or uproot their lives; and that Luther's rebellion had prompted others to found their own religious movements. What of Anabaptists, Calvinists or followers of Zwingli? Could any settlement really just label them heretics and deny them the right to exist too? Such questions came back to haunt Germany.

Home front

Katharina Luther was forty-six at the time of her husband's death, and was left alone to support their four surviving children, aged between eleven and nineteen. Though their marriage had started out as one of expediency and convenience, the Luthers' partnership had grown to become one of great love. Katharina was devastated by her loss. In a letter of 25 April 1546 to her sister-in-law, Christina, she wrote: 'I can neither eat nor drink. And in addition to that, I cannot sleep. And if I had a principality or an empire, I wouldn't feel so bad about losing it as I feel now that our dear Lord God has taken this beloved and dear man from me, and not only from me, but from the whole world. When I think about it, I can't refrain from grief and crying either to read or write.'[3]

There was a degree of overstatement about this text, one of the very few in Katharina's hand to survive. She was explaining to Christina why she was not in a position to pay for her nephew's education. But the extent of her loss, as chronicled, cannot easily be downplayed.

Luther had ordered that 'Katie' should manage his estate after his death, having seen her in action, and therefore possessing abundant confidence in her ability. Elector Johann Friedrich, though generally supportive of Luther's widow and allowing her to remain in the marital home, would not, however, allow such a break with accepted practice. He appointed male trustees to assist her, including Philipp Melanchthon.

For a short period, life at the Black Cloister continued as before, but with the emperor embarking on military action against the Protestant princes in the autumn of 1546, Katharina and her children were clearly in danger. What a prize they would be if Charles could capture them. So the Luthers followed Melanchthon and his family to Anhalt for sanctuary as Wittenberg came under threat.

Katharina returned home briefly after the town had been captured to find her crops trampled and her property plundered, but continuing conflict meant that by 1547 she was once more in exile, this time heading for Denmark, where the Lutheran king, Christian III, had granted her a pension of 50 guilders.[4] The fighting, though, made it impossible to complete the journey, and she eventually returned to war-scarred Wittenberg.

With her domestic economy in ruins, Katharina's last years were blighted by concerns over money. In August 1552 Wittenberg was once again threatened, this time by another outbreak of plague. The university was evacuated and she followed it to Torgau, where in October she suffered a heavy fall from her carriage. She died of her injuries on 20 December.

Appropriately, given their father's dislike of the sort of corruption in Catholicism that had too often facilitated the election of a dead Pope's relatives to the throne of Saint Peter, Luther's children made no attempt to take over the mantle of leadership in his Church. Instead, his oldest, Hans, became a lawyer, the profession his father had so often decried, and later was to be a royal servant. There is a certain poetic justice in this. The oldest of the next generation of Luthers had been named after his grandfather, and here he was following the career path that Hans Ludher had so much wanted for his son.

There is an account in the *Table Talk* of Martin Luther talking to his second son and namesake, Martin, while dangling him on his knee: 'If you became a lawyer, I would have you hanged on the gallows. You must become a preacher, must baptise, preach, administer the sacraments, visit the sick, comfort the grieving.'⁵ Young Martin seems to have subconsciously part-digested that directive, for while he did go on to study theology, there is no evidence that he ever became a clergyman. For his part, Paul elected to train as a physician, tending to the Elector of Brandenburg, and Margarethe, the Luthers' surviving daughter, was to marry a nobleman, Georg von Kunheim. Among their descendants was Paul von Hindenburg, the president of Germany from 1925 to 1934, who proved so ineffective in preventing the rise of Hitler.

Wars of religion?

The Peace of Augsburg quickly unravelled. The momentum was back with the Protestants: as Catholic bishops continued to convert, some violated the terms of the agreement and tried to bring over Church lands and buildings with them to Lutherism. It caused local confrontations and battles, as did efforts in some cities to restrict the liberties of minority faiths. At Donauwörth in Swabia in 1606, for example, the Lutheran majority banned a Catholic procession, causing the Catholic Duke of Bavaria to intervene.

These conflicts drew much of their energy from the continuing determination of the Pope and his allies to stamp out what they regarded as the Protestant heresy, now a many-headed hydra, and so restore unity to Christendom. There were periods of strife followed by brief lulls before it all exploded in the Thirty Years War (1618–48), once more ostensibly a confessional war, which saw the mercenary armies of the European powers pile into Germany to fight it out in God's name. The results were ruinous, bringing devastation, famine, disease and bankruptcy, and leaving between a third and a half of the population either dead or displaced. It is said to have cost the lives of 35 per cent of the population in its main central European arena of battle.

Yet to describe it as a war of religion, and thus identify it as part of Luther's legacy, is misleading. Had it been just about denomination, then it would not have witnessed the forces of the Catholic King of France lining up against the Catholic Holy Roman Emperor, or that same Catholic emperor being supported in battle by some of Germany's Lutheran princes.

The Thirty Years War finally drew to a close in 1648, when all sides were exhausted; among the many casualties was the notion that any single Holy Roman Emperor could again rule across boundaries. The Netherlands and Switzerland had freed themselves from the control of Charles V's Hapsburg descendants, who were ever more pinned back into their Austrian homeland, though in name retaining an imperial dignity. Europe was now firmly on track to evolve into a network of states, each sovereign, each defended by increasingly professional armies, and each governed by princes whose instincts were absolutist.

In Germany, the antagonism between the Lutheran states that dominated the north and the Rhineland, and the Catholic states grouped in the south and west, meant that religion was one more obstacle impeding any larger nationalist aspiration. It was only to be much later in the early nineteenth century, when the German lands had been occupied by Napoleon, that Martin Luther began to be held up as a national symbol around whom all his country-men, Catholic and Protestant, might rally to establish their distinctive and shared identity.

Another loser as a result of the Thirty Years War was the papacy, along with its claim to possess an authority that tran-scended national borders. Lutheranism had not imitated the Catholic model of a single leader, or a monolithic structure, preferring instead a coalition of local, regional and national Churches that worked together in co-operation.[6] The clear direc-tion of travel across Europe, then, was away from popes, cardi-nals and bishops dictating to kings, queens and princes. In its place, Church and state now co-operated and co-existed, but usually in a fashion that owed much to Luther's 'two kingdoms' principle. 'Luther's view of religion, as an essentially subjective and private quest over which the state had no jurisdiction,' the religious historian Karen Armstrong has written, taking the long view, 'would be the foundation of the modern secular ideal.'[7]

Lutheranism

Competing claims on Luther's legacy caused much argument in Germany immediately after his death. Indeed, the rush of pamphlets circulating, by various authors painting themselves as his true heirs, was almost as great as the tide of printed material seen during those years directly after the Ninety-Five Theses went viral.

The heart of the dispute lay in how best to react to changing circumstances. Some who had once been close to Luther, notably his former lodger Johann Agricola,[8] accepted an invitation to work with the victorious Emperor Charles on the Augsburg Interim of 1548. His participation was regarded as a capitulation to Catholicism by many Protestants, for whom Agricola became a Judas figure.

Philipp Melanchthon, as Luther's closest collaborator, distanced himself from Agricola, but his rejection of the Augsburg Interim was not a blanket one. While he could never accept it because of its downgrading of the core idea of 'justification by faith', Melanchthon did indicate a willingness to compromise with Catholicism on some other matters, less central in his eyes, so as to bring the sides closer. He suggested, for example, that the seven sacraments might be restored in a reunited Church, as long as they were regarded as rites and not ascribed any role in achieving salvation.

Until his death in 1560, Melanchthon operated as the self-appointed keeper of Luther's flame. He devoted much time to discussions with Catholic theologians, still searching for the precise form of words that would satisfy both sides, without diluting what he believed to be the essentials of Luther's message. Among subjects covered in these talks, for instance, were the place of 'good works' in salvation, and even free will.

Such meetings, though ultimately inconclusive, inevitably gave rise to suspicion among some Lutherans that Melanchthon was preparing to sacrifice doctrinal purity in pursuit of reunification with Rome. Most notable among such dissidents was Matthias Flacius, who had come to teach Hebrew at Wittenberg in 1544 when Luther was still presiding in the Black Cloister. Flacius and Melanchthon clashed repeatedly, with the former claiming that Luther's theology was being watered down by Melanchthon, and the latter replying that he knew Luther's real intentions better than anyone else.

But the greatest threat was that Lutheranism might lose its distinctive identity as other Protestant groupings gained in strength around Europe, including in Germany. By giving believers the Bible, and telling them to read it in order to have a personal relationship with God, Luther had unintentionally sown the seeds of Protestantism's own fragmentation. It only required a dozen believers to read a passage of Scripture in a certain new way and they had the basis for their own Church.

In his lifetime Luther had witnessed, and resisted, the advent of other forms of Protestantism, and the consequent dilution of the reform effort. But after his death that process of division continued within, but more significantly outside, Germany. John Calvin had only been eight years old when the Ninety-Five Theses appeared, and he went on to draw heavily on Luther's writings in his own reformed ministry in Strasbourg, alongside Bucer, and later in Geneva. But Calvin's agreement with Zwingli over rejecting the 'real presence' caused Luther to dismiss him. Such disapproval did nothing to prevent Calvinism's spread, first into France, and then beyond.

And, looking further ahead, though it was a reading of Luther's preface to Saint Paul's Epistle to the Romans on 24 May 1738 that caused the disgruntled Anglican priest John Wesley to feel his heart 'strangely warmed', the experience inspired him not to convert to Lutheranism, but rather to found his own Methodist movement. 'I felt I did trust in Christ, Christ alone, for salvation,' he recalled, 'and an assurance was given me that He had taken away my sins, even mine, and saved me from the law of sin and death.'[9]

Each new manifestation of Protestantism that came after Luther's death quoted his words on the guiding role of Scripture over tradition. To that extent, they all owed him a debt, if not allegiance. And other aspects of Luther's legacy were to prove hugely influential. His translation of the Bible into German, for instance, inspired William Tyndale's into English.

After Tyndale was executed as a heretic in 1536, his Bible was central to the English Reformation.[10] The extent of Luther's role, if any, in Henry VIII's break with Rome has been much debated, and sometimes much exaggerated. This was the same Henry who, in 1521, had been rewarded by the Pope with the title Defender of the Faith (*Fidei Defensor*), for his attacks on Luther. It is still claimed by his descendants to this day and appears as 'FD' on British one-pound coins.

And yet Henry then broke with the papacy. Had he come to regard Luther in a different light? For all that some of Henry's advisors were admirers of Luther's Reformation, and a few even travelled to Germany to experience it and him first hand, that would be to stretch the truth. Luther's challenge to papal authority may have suited the purposes of the English monarch in seeking to divorce his first wife, but it is also abundantly plain that Henry never was by any measure a Lutheran.

In the face of the new challenge of other forms of Protestantism, Lutheran representatives in 1580 agreed on and published the *Book of Concord*, intended as a set of core beliefs around which their Church gathered and which could not be compromised. It included the *Augsburg Confession* and the *Augsburg Apology* from 1530, Luther's *Small* and *Large Catechism*, and the Schmalkaldic Articles of 1537, which he had drafted.

While the Anabaptists, Calvinists and their Puritan descendants came ever more to recoil from anything that carried even a whiff of 'Romishness', Lutheranism as defined in the *Book of Concord*, with its Church music, decorations, bishops and sacraments, retained some visible connection with its Catholic past. Eisleben, the little town in Saxony where Luther had been born and had died, was even turned over the course of the seventeenth century into a centre of Lutheran pilgrimage, and styled a 'New Jerusalem' by its devotees. Pilgrimage generally involves a saint, though Luther was never accorded such a title, but Eisleben certainly had its 'holy places'. In 1997, its 'Birth House' and 'Death House' were designated a World Heritage Site.

The Catholic fightback

Once it had accepted that the Reformation Luther had set in motion could not be reversed by indifference, by threats, by force or by lining up the right strategic allies, the Catholic Church came to the realisation that it needed to find a new way of fighting back, not on Luther's terms, but on its own distinctive agenda. For some that thought dawned sooner than for others.

Since his election in 1534, Pope Paul III had been arguing for a general council of the Church, but his hands were tied by the ongoing battle for hegemony between the French monarchy and Emperor Charles, and by some senior figures in his own Church who argued that any such gathering, especially if the Lutherans took part on an equal basis, would fatally compromise papal authority. Instead Paul satisfied himself initially by appointing a commission to look at reform of the Church. He appreciated the need for change that Luther had demonstrated. In 1540, among other initiatives, he approved the Society of Jesus, led in quasi-military fashion by the Spaniard Ignatius Loyola. The Jesuits were to be at the very heart of the Catholic Counter-Reformation.

Finally, Paul managed to win agreement from all sides to a meeting at Trent in the Italian Alps, on imperial territory. The Council of Trent began in December 1545. On the agenda was both clarification of certain doctrines that had been questioned by Luther, and reform. In attendance were some cardinals who, while critical of Luther on papal authority and the sacraments, saw merit in his espousal of 'justification by faith'. In such ranks was Cardinal Reginald Pole, who in 1550 failed by a single vote to become Paul's successor. Ironically, given his subsequent role assisting Mary Tudor as Queen of England as she sought to restore Catholicism by martyring Protestants, Pole was regarded by some of his colleagues as so keen on justification by faith that they called him a Lutheran.

The discussions at Trent dragged on over eighteen years and five different papacies. There were two prolonged suspensions of proceedings, and one change of venue. When finally agreement was reached in 1563, the council voted to reject Luther's justification by faith in favour of an 'inward' justification that came about when each individual 'co-operated' with divine grace; as, for example, by carrying out good works. The Council of Trent also reiterated the seven sacraments, the status of the mass as a sacrifice, and that Christ was entirely present in the bread and wine at communion (thereby championing transubstantiation).

Yet despite this show of rejecting almost all the arguments Luther had ever made, the council also demonstrated that it had learned practical lessons from his success. It ordered, for example, improved training for clergy, especially those from Germany in the newly established Germanicum, a Jesuit-run college for priests in Rome. It urged that those ordained should spend their time preaching and teaching much more than previously. It commissioned a Trent catechism, to rival Luther's, which set out in clear terms the core beliefs and practices of Catholicism. Organisation was to be both better, and cleaner. Corruption and excess would be punished. Bishops, for instance, must henceforth live in their bishopric. More generally the air of complacency and superiority that had hung over Rome since it first encountered Luther was finally banished. The Catholic case was to be argued with new vigour. Its eventual success was no longer to be taken as read.

As a prescription, it proved an effective cure. The Council of Trent enabled Catholicism to convert large swathes of European Christianity back to itself. Rome did not capitulate to Luther, nor allow itself to be taken over by him and his followers. But fundamentally changed by him it most certainly was, though for centuries it was loath to admit any such thing.

Luther's imprint

If Catholicism proved itself reluctant even to speak Luther's name, others beyond the Churches displayed less inhibition, for better or worse. In his dramatised version of the Faust legend, about a scholar who struck a deal with the devil, Christopher Marlowe (1564–93), the Elizabethan tragedian, places his central character in *The Tragical History of Doctor Faustus* on the staff of Wittenberg University. There is much mocking in the play, published in two different editions in 1616 after Marlowe's premature and mysterious death. His targets include the Puritans, who had gone much further in their Protestantism than Luther ever did. They are portrayed as hypocrites, righteous in their beliefs, vocal in imposing them on others, but prone in private to leading the sort of lives they condemn.

But there are jibes, too, about Luther, notably around Faustus's belief that books will provide answers, when all they do in his case is deliver him into the hands of the devil. Marlowe has in his sights Luther, and his insistence that the Bible must be studied above all other books for the insight it provides into God, and for the protection it provided against the devil. 'O, would I had never seen Wittenberg,' Faustus laments, 'never read [a] book!'[11] Too much Bible, he suggests, leads not to heaven but to damnation.[12]

Marlowe's contemporary William Shakespeare shared his interest in alumni of Wittenberg. He sends Hamlet there, against the wishes of his aunt and uncle. 'For your intent in going back to school in Wittenberg, it is most retrograde to our desire,' Claudius warns him,[13] apparently worried that the bold, fearless independence of mind that the name Wittenberg would have signalled to audiences could derail Hamlet, or direct him to Protestantism and away from the Catholicism of the court in which he had been raised.

These are, for the most part, fleeting references, though much explored. The American playwright David Davalos, for instance, in his 2008 work *Wittenberg*,[14] attempted to solve the conundrum by having Luther, Hamlet and Faustus share the stage. The man rebelling against God (Faustus) confronts the man of God rebelling against the Pope (Luther), in the company of the prince searching for moral guidance (Hamlet).

Another unlikely combination places Luther with Karl Marx, the nineteenth-century philosopher and revolutionary socialist. In his

1844 *Critique of Hegel's Philosophy of Right*, best remembered now for its remark that religion is the 'opium of the people', Marx looks back on 'Germany's revolutionary past' and deems it 'theoretical'. He continues: 'it is the Reformation. As the revolution then began in the brain of the monk [or Luther as he later identifies him], so now it begins in the brain of the philosopher . . . But if Protestantism was not the true solution, it was at least a setting of the problem.'[15]

So Luther laid the foundations for social, political and economic revolution, according to Marx, by overcoming 'the bondage of piety [and] replacing it with the bondage of conviction. He [Luther] shattered faith in authority because he restored the authority of faith. He turned priests into laymen because he turned laymen into priests. He freed man from outer religiosity because he made religiosity the inner man. He freed the body from chains because he enchained the heart.'[16]

Marx acknowledged that Luther's ending the control of the Church over believers was a vital breakthrough. It internalised religious conviction, made it a matter for the individual. Yet it was just step one on the revolutionary path. Now was the moment for step two – to throw off religion altogether. Luther, for Marx, was a means to an end.

A century later it was another great upheaval, the outbreak of the Second World War, that set the poet W. H. Auden musing on why Germany had succumbed to Nazism. His first attempt at an answer, quoted at the start of the chapter, was published in October 1940 in *The Christian Century*, but later revised by Auden himself. The final version is the one quoted, and its line, on Luther's lips, about 'Great Men' being bad hints either at a moment of self-revelation on his part, or utter hypocrisy. For Luther may have accused other 'Great Men' of being bad, but Auden was pointing out that for many Germans, and certainly for the Nazis, Luther himself was a 'great man', and therefore 'bad'. In which case he could be blamed for what Germany was now inflicting on the world.

Auden's second poem took that further. 'September 1, 1939' appeared in *Another Time* in the same month as 'Luther', but was later disowned by Auden. The best-remembered line is his characterisation of the 1930s – when Auden along with C Day-Lewis and Stephen Spender had been prominent in England as left-leaning poets – as 'a low dishonest decade'.

It was a decade that had brought the Nazis to government, but Auden is concerned too with the historical roots of what was now unfolding, and here more directly points a finger at Luther as one who had 'driven mad' German culture and thus produced Hitler. It is an eye-catching accusation, but hard to know what particular crime Luther is supposed to have committed to deserve such a verdict: perhaps the appalling anti-Semitism of his later years, much used in propaganda by the Nazis; perhaps his tendency to defer to the authority of earthly rulers such as the princes who protected him, which had made Germans submissive before authoritarians such as Hitler; or perhaps the division he drew between private faith and worldly affairs, which allowed Germans to turn a blind eye to the unfolding evil of their government?

Luther's personal psychology has long held an appeal, especially for those keen to project back on to earlier ages the discipline's twentieth-century advances and insights. With so much first-hand material about Luther available, he is an inevitable target. In 1958, Pulitzer-winner Erik Erikson's *Young Man Luther: A Study in Psychoanalysis and History* drew on Erikson's distinguished clinical work and academic roles at Yale and Harvard to produce a hugely popular version of Luther's life. It told how, in the most basic terms, the Reformation was a result of the youthful trauma caused by his unhappy upbringing and the pressure his father placed on him to succeed. This provoked in Luther an identity crisis that saw him first take refuge in a friary, and then rebel against the hierarchical, patriarchal Catholic Church that had nurtured him.

Erikson had as many enthusiastic fans as he did detractors, the latter mainly drawn from academic ranks, who questioned the inferences he drew from details in Luther's life, and even some of the details he quoted to make his case. Among those by contrast impressed by Erikson's version of Luther was John Osborne, the English playwright still riding a wave of success in 1961 after his earlier epoch-changing play, *Look Back in Anger*. Osborne's *Luther*, heavily influenced by Erikson's account, was, he explained, about the power and origins of religious experience rather than the particular facts of history. His Luther (played in the original production in London by Albert Finney) was an individual thrown into a battle with authority. 'I hope it won't make a difference,' Osborne told an interviewer, 'if you don't know anything about Luther, and I suspect most people don't.' Reviews were mixed, though it won a Tony when it transferred to Broadway in 1963, and was later filmed by a cast that included a young Judi Dench as Katharina von Bora.

If neither Erikson nor Osborne found much to laugh at – or with – in Luther's story, the celebrated but irascible British novelist Kingsley Amis certainly did. He produced in 1976 a funny, award-winning but now largely forgotten novel, *The Alteration*. It wondered what present-day England would have looked like if the Reformation had never happened. Luther featured, but in Amis's account – fuelled, it should be said, by a dislike of Catholicism and hence intended as a warning of how much worse life could be – the Protestant reformer managed to come to an understanding with the Catholic Church, was elected as the reforming Pope Germanian I, and thereby ensured that Rome's religious stranglehold was maintained over Europe.

Luther's enduring legacy

Kingsley Amis's 'what if?' brings me back round to my own question, first posed amid a thunderstorm in Wittenberg: where might

Luther stand if he were a Catholic living today, or if the breach
with Rome had somehow been healed? It started off as a daydream,
and remains one, since I cannot make time work in such an
untimely fashion as to bring Luther back from the grave.

Yet it does provide a context for examining his life. Luther
started out a Catholic, was formed in Catholicism, and then
developed as an adult through the ways in which he pushed against
the Church of his birth. Even unto death, a part of him remained
Catholic, he confessed, with the status of the reform movement
he founded vis-à-vis Rome still not settled as he breathed his last.

It is often said that the great faiths that have shaped our world
only move forward through dissent. What one generation calls
heresy, subsequent ones regard as orthodoxy. That is certainly
true in the case of Luther. So – hypothetically – if he were to
return today to join in the 500th anniversary celebrations of the
Ninety-Five Theses, there is plenty in Catholic Christianity that
he would find as appealing and familiar as what is going on in his
own smaller but still vibrant Lutheran Church. He might even
take some of the credit, though self-congratulation was, attrac-
tively, not in his nature.

The Council of Trent may have largely rejected his reform
plans, but Catholicism has since embraced many of them. It likes
to develop, it frequently boasts, along a timescale measured in
centuries, not weeks, months, years or even decades. For the ener-
getic, driven Luther, such a snail's pace drove him to despair and
division, but today's Catholicism has finally caught up with its
most significant critic, borrowing his words to produce some of
its own most inspiring recent statements – notably about the
Church being the people of God and the priesthood of believers.

That's the way with words. Once said, you struggle to keep a grip
on them, and those with a particular gift for language are fated to see
their *bons mots* imitated and purloined, all without so much as a
thank you. I can imagine Luther flying into a rage about that, and

throwing off a provocatively titled riposte, but having now seen him in his last years I can just as easily picture him greeting the same realisation with a smile of recognition. His life – and lives in general – are complex. We can all be radically different people at different times.

In that chaotic period between the appearance of the Ninety-Five Theses in 1517, and the start of the Peasants' War in 1524, Luther was more given to display his angry side, in outbursts, and intemperate, often violent language. But after his marriage to Katharina von Bora, he developed if not quite a full-blown sense of humour, then at least a greater ease with himself: the ability, on occasion, to let things go, to bite his lip. It makes him a more attractive, rounded human being, but perhaps not quite such a charismatic leader as once he had been.

Every life has its stages, and its moods, Luther's arguably more than most because of that deep-seated, dark, depressive side to him that caused both his collapses and his furies. He possessed an obsessive mindset, like his great hero, Saint Paul; admirable in many ways, but alienating in others. It makes reaching a simple verdict on him impossible, and goes a long way to explaining why he is today relatively neglected in a culture that increasingly prefers black or white to grey.

What can certainly be said, without fear of contradiction, and without calling on the services of a time machine, is that Luther shaped his own age just as he shapes mine as a Catholic now, because he forced my Church to reform and save itself, at the same time as opening the door through which Protestant Christianity emerged, and continues to flourish in all its many contemporary manifestations. And he also shapes the European society in which I live. Through the ideas he espoused, on the basis of reading the Scriptures, he made the case for individual conscience, personal responsibility and accountability, and – with his formula of the 'two kingdoms' of Church and state – gave rise to modern notions of liberty, human rights and secularism. Those who discount his 'religious' legacy because they have no time for God or gods, are only free to do so because of Luther's achievements.

What is particularly striking about the story of Luther the man is how much he ultimately achieved by embarking on what was, essentially, a private journey into God, one that was moreover routine in late medieval times. He did not set out with a vision to change the Church and had no interest in refashioning society. He was not a prophet in the Old Testament sense, someone who heard the voice of God and was then impelled to act. Indeed he was suspicious of those in his lifetime who presented themselves as such.

But Luther was a prophet in that what pushed him forward was the sense, growing ever stronger inside him, that God was with him. From that belief everything else followed. It explains why, for example, he was able to show such extraordinary courage in his steadfast refusal to recant, up to and including his willingness to surrender his own life.

In the monastery, Luther's only urge had been to know and then please God in a way that he hadn't pleased his father. When he found that impossibly hard going, he turned to the Bible and, in lectures at an obscure German university, applied what he read to the current practice of his Church. It was an internal, academic debate, known to only a handful of colleagues and students. But out of it came the Ninety-Five Theses and they utterly changed the scale of the discussion beyond anything Luther could ever have imagined.

So, whether or not he brandished a hammer to pin them to the door of the Castle Church on 31 October 1517, this anniversary is an appropriate moment to choose, 500 years on, to look again at Luther's crowded, controversial but compelling life, to return him to centre stage, to explode some of the more fanciful myths that have clouded his reputation of late, and to explore those episodes that have alienated him from a twenty-first-century audience. What emerges is a man for his own age, but also for every age since, right up to the current day.

Acknowledgements

Over a lifetime it is odd which particular conversations stick in your mind when so many others evaporate. Some very happy days in my professional life were spent in the late 1990s working with the TV producer and presenter Roger Bolton, on various programmes we made together, including a long-forgotten Sunday morning show on Britain's Channel 5, when its public service remit required it to have a God-slot.

'You need to write about Martin Luther,' he told me one day, utterly out of the blue, when we should have been talking about something more pressing. Roger had grown up in the Protestant tradition and was keen to widen my Catholic horizons, so we had regularly had similar discussions. While all his other suggested subjects for further scrutiny have by now drifted out of my grasp, Luther always remained in my mind, if not quite within reach. Until, that is, the approach of the 500th anniversary of his nailing (or not) his Ninety-Five Theses to the door of the Castle Church in Wittenberg finally nailed it for me, and spurred me on to produce the biography that Roger was missing.

So my first thanks must go to him. I am also indebted to: Diarmaid MacCulloch, Professor of the History of the Church at Oxford University, for sharing his insights, and even giving me a lead on Luther that, with his encyclopaedic knowledge, he believed his fellow academics had missed for nigh on 500 years; Karen Armstrong, whose ability to bring the history of religion to life and to a wide contemporary audience remains an inspiration, and whose wisdom on this and other subjects has proved invaluable in my work; to Professor A. C. Grayling, not a known fan of religion, but one who cast a light for me in our discussion on Luther's legacy in the seventeenth century; and to the actor Joseph Fiennes, who graciously in the middle of a newspaper interview with me about his latest film stepped back into a previous screen role as Luther to share how he read the great man.

Many others have helped with specific areas of research, but special thanks go to: Simon Banner for the research he did on my behalf; Sarah Newton for her flawless German; and the Reverend Cliff Winter, retired Lutheran pastor from Wichita in Kansas, encountered on a stay in Wittenberg, and happy to share a lifetime of reflection on Luther. And there was a wonderfully enthusiastic usher at the Greenbelt Festival, who guided me to the tent where I was speaking last summer on a different subject altogether, and managed in the midst of another downpour to make me forget the rain by waxing lyrical about the connection between Luther and Marx. I was so busy jotting down a note to myself to follow it up that I forgot to record his name. Apologies and thanks.

None of this would have appeared between covers without the support, encouragement and sort of belief that drives me on by making me nervous of letting them down as shown by my agent, Piers Blofeld, my publisher, Katherine Venn, and her colleagues Rachael Duncan, Ruth Roff and Penelope Isaac at Hodder.

Finally, and always, to my family, Kit, Orla and Siobhan, for once again allowing our holidays to be taken up with Luther excursions, and Luther reading; for listening without their eyes going blank when I am explaining the specific theological points on which I have become stuck; for acting as photographer in Germany (Kit); and for everything else that matters.

Peter Stanford
London, October 2016

List of Illustrations

Photographs by Kit Stanford, unless stated

Notes

Introduction

1   The father of the Nobel Peace Prize-winning African-American civil rights leader, the story goes, travelled to Berlin in 1934 to attend a gathering of Baptist ministers and was so taken with the story of Martin Luther that he changed his own name and that of his five-year-old son, then Michael King, to reflect his admiration for the Protestant reformer.

2   *Fechten* in German means 'to fence'.

3   'Commentary on the Life of Luther', first published in 1549, and translated in full in Elizabeth Vandiver, Ralph Keen and Thomas Frazel, *Luther's Lives: Two Contemporary Accounts of Martin Luther* (Manchester: Manchester University Press, 2003).

4   Jonathan Luxmoore, 'Bishops herald Luther as a "pathfinder"', *The Tablet* (20 August 2016).

5   Christa Pongratz-Lippitt, '"Joint Festival of Christ" to be staged in Holy Land', *The Tablet* (3 September 2016).

6   As detailed in the *Libreria Editrice Vaticana*, the official Vatican record for 19 November 2008.

7   Christopher Lamb, 'Francis entertains an opening to Communion for non-Catholics', *The Tablet* (21 November 2015).

8   Peter Stanford, 'Meet the female priest defying Catholicism for her faith', *The Daily Telegraph* (4 November 2014).

9   In the run-up to the 2014 synod on the family, the Vatican sent out a questionnaire to find out what Catholics thought on a range of issues. In Germany, more than 90 per cent said they had lived together with their partner before getting married in church, and 60 per cent of Swiss Catholics backed Church blessings for gay partnerships (*National Catholic Reporter*, 4 February 2014).

10 John Worthen, *The Cambridge Introduction to Samuel Taylor Coleridge* (Cambridge: Cambridge University Press, 2010).

PART ONE
Chapter One

1   TT 6250.
2   Ian Siggins, *Luther and His Mother* (Philadelphia: Fortress Press, 1981).
3   Some researchers suggest her maiden name was Ziegler, others that this was the surname of Margarethe's mother. There is evidence that the Zieglers were prosperous burghers. See Siggins, *Luther and His Mother.*
4   Siggins, *Luther and His Mother.*
5   TT 2888a.
6   Estimates of the number of Martin's siblings varies, but most agree he had three sisters – Barbara, two years younger, Dorothea and Margarethe – and he refers in *Table Talk* to a younger brother, Jacob, who inherited Hans's business on their father's death.
7   Philipp Melanchthon, Luther's closest collaborator and, after his death, the keeper of the flame, at times favoured 1484 as the year of Luther's birth. In an age before birth certificates, there seems to have been considerable debate even in Luther's own mind as to which date was correct.
8   Lucas Cranach the Elder (1472–1553), German Renaissance painter and print-maker, who also painted Martin Luther and his wife.
9   Between the years 1520 and 1525, it is estimated that more than sixty different authors loyal to the Catholic Church took advantage of new printing methods to produce over two hundred pamphlets and polemical books attacking Luther and the new Protestantism. And Luther and his supporters answered back in kind.
10 TT 5571.
11 Thomas à Kempis (1380–1471).
12 Francis of Assisi (1181–1226), founder of the Friars Minor.
13 WA.
14 WA.
15 WA.
16 TT 137.
17 Erich Kleineidam, *Universitas Studii Erffordensis* (Leipzig: St Benno Verlag, 1992).
18 Roland H. Bainton, *Here I Stand: A Life of Martin Luther* (Massachusetts: Hendrickson, 2012, first published in 1950).
19 TT 2719.
20 TT 3358.
21 TT 5848.
22 TT 2716b.
23 TT 5173.

24 Johann Crotus, also known as Crotus Rubeanus (c. 1480–c. 1539), later rector of Erfurt; an early supporter of Luther, he subsequently reverted to Catholicism. See Otto Scheel, *Martin Luther: Von Katholizismus zur Reformation*, vol. 1 (Tübingen: Mohr, 1917).

25 *TT* 968.

26 *WA*.

27 Erik Erikson, *Young Man Luther: A Study in Psychoanalysis and History* (New York: Norton & Co, 1958).

28 *TT* 1559.

29 Letter dated 5 June 1530, *WA*.

30 Luther did not risk travelling there because his freedom of movement was much curtailed at the time, with fears that he might be seized and handed over to the Catholic authorities.

31 *WA*.

32 Though Heiko Oberman in *Die Reformation von Wittenberg nach Genf* (Göttingen: Vandenhoeck & Ruprecht, 1986) unearthed examples to show that the vulgar language employed by Luther was common in other theological treatises of the time.

33 See Erikson, *Young Man Luther*.

34 Though Paul was not one of the twelve apostles who Jesus gathered round Him in the gospel accounts, he is referred to as the Apostle Paul in Christianity in the sense that the word apostle means 'one who is sent', in this case by Jesus to proclaim His message, after his meeting with the Risen Christ on the road to Damascus.

35 Ephesians 6:4.

36 *TT* 422.

37 Ibid.

38 Quite who that 'another' might be is nowhere made clear, but Staupitz, Luther's Augustinian superior who acted as mentor, is the obvious candidate.

39 Notably his wife, Katharina von Bora, whom he regularly mentioned and often praised as, in some respects, the stronger one in their marriage.

40 *TT* 5672.

41 *TT* 3566a.

42 Erikson, *Young Man Luther*.

43 Siggins, *Luther and His Mother*.

44 Letter dated 20 May 1531, *WA*.

45 *WA*.

46 And also because Melanchthon presented her as such after Luther's death: see Siggins, *Luther and His Mother*.

47 *WA*.

48 *TT* 2982b.

49 Richard Marius, *Martin Luther: The Christian Between God and Death* (London: Harvard University Press, 1999).

50 Christopher Mackay, *The Hammer of the Witches: A Complete Translation of the* Malleus Maleficarum (Cambridge: Cambridge University Press, 2009).

51 Margin notes in Luther's hand have been discovered on Christian Humanist texts from Erfurt Library – see J. Matsuura on Luther in *Erfurter Annotationem* (Cologne: Böhlau Verlag, 2009).

52 Desiderius Erasmus, *The Enchiridion of Erasmus*, trans. Raymond Himelick (Bloomington: Indiana University Press, 1964).

53 William of Occam, *Philosophical Writings: A Selection* (Indianapolis: Hackett Publishing, 1990).

54 Marius, *Martin Luther*.

55 *TT* 131.

56 *TT* 5571.

57 *TT* 5346.

Chapter Two

1 *TT* 392.

2 *TT* 3566a.

3 *TT* 4707.

4 *WA*.

5 The fullest account of Saint Paul's conversion is in Acts 9:3–9.

6 It is the opening scene, for instance, in a muddled 2003 film *Luther*, starring Joseph Fiennes in the title role and financed in part by money from Lutheran sources.

7 *TT* 489. There was a strong Lutheran presence in Nürnberg and Luther was convinced that the devil was targeting him and his followers in particular.

8 Richard Marius, *Martin Luther: The Christian Between God and Death* (London: Harvard University Press, 1999).

9 *Summa Theologica* 11/11 q 88.

10 *WA*.

11 *TT* 149.

12 *WA*.

13 *TT* 3806.

14 This seems to have come about because Jesus was often represented pictorially as gold, the Virgin Mary as silver, and therefore Anne's womb – symbolically – was the source of precious metal.

15 *TT* 2809b.

Notes

16   Otto Scheel, *Martin Luther: Von Katholizismus zur Reformation* (Tübingen: Mohr, 1917).

17   *TT* 4707.

18   Scheel, a peerlessly thorough editor in the early twentieth century of the sources on Luther's early life, attributed the tale to anti-Catholic propaganda.

19   *TT* 3558.

20   Erik Erikson, *Young Man Luther: A Study in Psychoanalysis and History* (New York: Norton & Co, 1958).

21   Sometimes called the Austin Friars in English-speaking countries.

22   Otto Scheel (ed.), *Dokumente zu Luthers Entwicklung* (Tübingen: Mohr, 1929).

23   This phrase is a popular distillation of a longer remark made by Augustine in his commentary on Psalm 73 – 'for he that singeth praise, not only praiseth, but only praiseth with gladness: he that singeth praise, not only singeth, but also loveth him of whom he singeth. In praise, there is the speaking forth of one confessing; in singing, the affection of one loving.'

24   *TT* 4707.

25   *TT* 5346.

26   *TT* 1877.

27   Ibid.

28   *WA*.

29   In correspondence with Johann von Staupitz, *WA*.

30   Desiderius Erasmus, *The Praise of Folly*, trans. Betty Radice (London, Penguin, 2004).

31   *TT* 4414.

32   *WA*.

33   *WA*.

34   *TT* 4174.

35   *Oxford Handbook of Martin Luther's Theology*, eds. Robert Kolb, Irene Dingel and Lubomir Batka (Oxford: Oxford University Press, 2014).

36   *The Symbolical Books of the Evangelical Lutheran Church*, trans. F. Bente and W. H. T. Dan (Saint Louis: Concordia, 1921).

37   Alister McGrath, *Luther's Theology of the Cross* (Oxford: Wiley-Blackwell, 1991).

38   *TT* 137.

39   *TT* 623.

40   Sometimes also referred to as the Nominalists.

41   *WA*.

42   *TT* 518.

43   Roland H. Bainton, *Here I Stand: A Life of Martin Luther* (Massachusetts: Hendrickson, 2012, first published in 1950).

44 *WA*.

45 *TT* 518.

46 *WA*.

47 Some suggest the two had known each other as children.

48 The confession box only came into use later, so confession would usually be heard with the penitent kneeling before his confessor. See John Cornwell, *The Dark Box: A Secret History of Confession* (London: Profile Books, 2014).

49 David Steinmetz, *Luther and Staupitz: An Essay in the Intellectual Origins of the Protestant Reformation* (Durham: Duke University Press, 1980).

50 *TT* 137.

51 *WA*.

52 *TT* 94.

53 Erik Erikson describes Staupitz's efforts in *Young Man Luther* as those of a 'therapeutically clever superior'.

54 Mechthild of Magdeburg, *The Flowing Light of the Godhead*, trans. Frank Tobin (New Jersey: Paulist Press, 1997).

55 *TT* 6561.

56 *WA*.

57 Hans Schneider, 'Martin Luthers Reise nach Rom', in *Studien zur Wissenschafts- und Religionsgeschichte* (Berlin: Akademie der Wissenschaften zu Göttingen, 2011).

58 Matthew 4:1–11.

59 *TT* 6059.

60 Dr Johann Georg Walch, *The Complete Works of Doctor Martin Luther* (Saint Louis: Concordia Publishing, 1885–1910).

61 From 'Julius Exclusus' (1517) in J. A. Froude, *Life and Letters of Erasmus* (London, 1895).

62 *TT* 3528A.

63 *TT* 3528A.

64 *TT* 3428.

65 *TT* 3428.

66 *TT* 3428.

67 Heinrich Böhmer, *Luthers Romfahrt* (Leipzig: A. Deichert, 1914).

68 Ibid.

69 *TT* 527. Some accounts of his life say this was the moment when Saint Paul's phrase, 'the just shall live by faith alone', first hit him, in another lightning strike, but Luther's own account contradicts this.

70 Böhmer, *Luthers Romfahrt*.

71 *WA*.

Chapter Three

1 *TT* 1206.
2 This was the same dispute that had caused Luther to travel to Rome. He had sided with Staupitz, against Erfurt, something his fellow friars there bitterly resented, and which caused Luther to disparage them in public.
3 It may also have been that Staupitz was attempting to bolster the Augustinian presence at Wittenberg, at the expense of Erfurt.
4 *TT* 5371.
5 *TT* 1509.
6 Letter dated 26 October 1516, *WA*.
7 *TT* 3642.
8 Letter to Johann Lang dated 16 July 1517, *WA*.
9 Including Wittenberg, Dresden, Magdeburg and Erfurt.
10 Letter dated 26 October 1516, *WA*.
11 See Scott Hendrix, *Martin Luther – Visionary Reformer* (London: Yale University Press, 2015).
12 By 1591, it was said to be bigger still, with an inventory listing 17,443 items.
13 John 20:23.
14 *WA*.
15 Quoted in Roland H. Bainton, *Here I Stand: A Life of Martin Luther* (Massachusetts: Hendrickson, 2012, first published in 1950).
16 *TT* 360.
17 In his 1526 commentary on the Book of Jonah, *WA*.
18 Luther's driving obsession with death and judgement is the central thesis in Richard Marius, *Martin Luther: The Christian Between God and Death* (London: Harvard University Press, 1999).
19 In 1516 he produced a Greek version of the New Testament with accompanying notes that touched on issues of dating.
20 *WA*.
21 *TT* 3416.
22 *TT* 2462.
23 Matthew 27:46.
24 Letter dated 8 April 1516, *WA*.
25 Quoted in Bainton, *Here I Stand*.
26 *TT* 5247.
27 *TT* 352.
28 Romans 1:16–17. 'For I am not ashamed of the Good News: it is the power of God saving all who have faith – Jews first, but Greeks as well – since this is what reveals the justice of God to us: it shows how faith leads to faith.'
29 In a preface to the first volume of his collected Latin works, *WA*.
30 *TT* 13.

31 WA.

32 TT 3232.

33 In 2004, German archaeologists made headlines with their reports that, during renovations at the Black Cloister, they had uncovered the very toilet where Luther had 'started the Reformation'.

34 In their interpretations of the autobiographical passage in Galatians 1:11–2:21.

35 WA.

36 TT 146.

37 Galatians 2:16–17.

38 Galatians 2:21.

39 Galatians 3:24–25.

40 Saint Augustine, *Confessions*, trans. Henry Chadwick (Oxford: Oxford University Press, 1991).

41 *Luther: Lectures on Romans*, trans. and ed. Wilhelm Pauck (Philadelphia: Westminster Press, 1961).

42 WA.

43 WA.

Chapter Four

1 TT 5346.

2 WA.

3 WA.

4 TT 5355.

5 Eamon Duffy, *Saints & Sinners: A History of the Popes* (London: Yale University Press, 1997).

6 The claim about souls springing from purgatory was quoted by Luther in numbers 27 and 28 of the Ninety-Five Theses, and the line about the Virgin Mary was highlighted in his accompanying letter of concern to his archbishop.

7 TT 5346.

8 TT 4707.

9 The unscrupulous methods of indulgence sellers was condemned by the Council of Beziers in 1246 at the height of the Albigensian crisis.

10 In an Advent sermon preached in 1516 to fellow Augustinians in Nürnberg.

11 Desiderius Erasmus, *The Praise of Folly*, trans. Betty Radice (London: Penguin, 2004).

12 WA.

13 Julius Kostlin and Georg Kawerau, *Martin Luther* (2 vols) (Berlin, 1903).

14 See Andrew Pettegree, *Brand Luther* (London: Penguin Press, 2015).

15 Martin Treu, *Der Thesenanschlag fand wirklich statt* in 'Luther 78' (2007).

16 Erwin Iserloh, *The Theses Were Not Posted* (Boston: Beacon Press, 1968).

17 *WA.*

18 Richard Marius, *Martin Luther: The Christian Between God and Death* (London: Harvard University Press, 1999).

19 Pettegree, *Brand Luther*).

20 Others have translated the Latin *fex hominum* as 'a little shit'.

21 *WA.*

22 *WA.*

23 *WA.*

24 *WA.*

25 The quotation is taken from Jesus as reported in Matthew 23:24.

26 *WA.*

27 *WA.*

28 *TT* 5346.

29 John 20:23.

30 A reference to Marcus Licinius Crassus (115–53 BCE), said to be the wealthiest man in Roman history.

31 Roland H. Bainton, *Here I Stand: A Life of Martin Luther* (Massachusetts: Hendrickson, 2012, first published in 1950).

32 In 1541, *WA.*

33 *WA.*

34 Timothy Wengent, *Martin Luther's 95 Theses* (Minneapolis: Fortress Press, 2015).

35 Ibid.

36 Luke 7:36–50.

37 John 8:1–11.

38 Wengent, *Martin Luther's 95 Theses*.

39 Matthew 4:17, *WA.*

PART TWO
Chapter Five

1 *TT* 4707.

2 *TT* 1428.

3 *TT* 2.

4 *TT* 4162.

5 Mentioned in a sermon in Leipzig on 29 June 1519, *WA.*

6 As reported by Erasmus's friend, the Strasbourg-based reformer Beatus Rhenanus, and quoted in Roland H. Bainton, *Here I Stand: A Life of Martin Luther* (Massachusetts: Hendrickson, 2012, first published in 1950).

7   Ibid.

8   *WA*.

9   *WA*.

10 Some scholars argue that Trutfetter subsequently relented and saw Luther, though there was no reconciliation.

11 Matthew 28:20.

12 *WA*.

13 See Wilhelm Borth, *Die Luthersache (Causa Lutheri)* (Lübeck: Matthiesen Verlag, 1970).

14 Luther was certainly familiar with Wycliffe in 1520, quoting his example in *The Babylonian Captivity*.

15 See Borth, *Die Luthersache*.

16 *Opera varii argumenti* in *Erlangen Ausgabe*.

17 The phrase comes from Psalm 89.

18 See Bainton, *Here I Stand*.

19 *TT* 2668a.

20 *TT* 136.

21 *TT* 225.

22 *WA*.

23 A group of disaffected cardinals was alleged by Leo to be behind the failed attempt, though it was more imagined than real, but gave him the chance to murder their leader Alfonso Petrucci, and pack the College of Cardinals with thirty-one new appointees loyal to him.

24 Reported by Luther in a letter to Spalatin, dated 31 October 1518, *WA*.

25 *TT* 5439.

26 *WA*.

27 *WA*.

28 *WA*.

29 *TT* 2410b.

30 *WA*.

31 *WA*.

32 *WA*.

33 He had contemplated seeking refuge at the Sorbonne in Paris, where conciliar ideas were strong.

34 *WA*.

35 *WA*.

36 *TT* 1203.

37 *TT* 6955.

38 *TT* 3287a.

39 *TT* 5349.

40 *WA*.

41 *WA*.

Notes

Chapter Six

1   *TT* 1206.
2   *TT* 4187.
3   *TT* 1245.
4   *WA.*
5   1 John 2:22.
6   2 Thessalonians 1–4, 7–10.
7   As reported in a history of the Luther–Roman Catholic dialogue that followed the Second Vatican Council (1962–65), Joseph Burgess and Jeffrey Gross (eds.), *Building Unity: Ecumenical Dialogues with Roman Catholic Participation* (New Jersey: Paulist Press, 1989).
8   *WA.*
9   *WA.*
10 Matthew 16:18: 'You are Peter [Jesus said] and on this rock I will build My Church.'
11 In the commentary that went with his Greek New Testament of 1516.
12 John 21:17.
13 *WA.*
14 *WA.*
15 Quoted in Professor Martin Marty, *Martin Luther: A Life* (New York: Viking, 2004).
16 *WA.*
17 *WA.*
18 *WA.*
19 *WA.*
20 Balaam's ass (Numbers 22:28).
21 *TT* 4579.
22 In December 1999, speaking in Prague, Pope John Paul II reached a similar verdict, when he apologised for the 'cruel death inflicted' on Hus and suggested an enquiry to clear him of heresy.
23 John 2:15.
24 *WA.*
25 *TT* 1368.
26 *TT* 18.
27 Percy Allen et al. (eds.), *Opus epistolarum Des. Erasmi Roterodami* (Oxford: Oxford University Press, 1906–58).
28 13 August 1521, in *Opus epistolarum.*
29 *TT* 3583.
30 *WA.*
31 *WA.*
32 *WA.*

Chapter Seven

1   *TT* 255.
2   Canons 915 and 1339 in the Code of Canon Law, promulgated by Pope John Paul II in 1983.
3   Because, it has been suggested, the panel was divided, with different members seeing some merit in some of Luther's positions.
4   Text of *Exsurge Domine* – papalencyclicals.net/Leo10/l10exdom.htm.
5   Ibid.
6   Ibid.
7   The Roman pagan philosopher of the third century CE, who attacked Christianity remorselessly.
8   Psalm 80.
9   Forerunner of the Vatican Library.
10 Though there had been a death threat against Luther made in April 1520, with talk of a doctor who would turn up in Wittenberg to assassinate him – reported by Luther in a letter to Spalatin of 16 April 1520, *WA*.
11 See Roland H. Bainton, *Here I Stand: A Life of Martin Luther* (Massachusetts: Hendrickson, 2012, first published in 1950).
12 Though in 1543 Luther wrote a foreword to one of the first Latin translations of the Qu'ran.
13 *WA*.
14 *WA*.
15 *WA*.
16 *WA*.
17 Paul Kalkoff and Girolamo Aleandro, *Die Depeschen des Nuntius Aleander von Wormser Reichstage 1521* (Charleston: Nabu Press, 2010).
18 *TT* 2836b.
19 In a letter of 4 November, *WA*.
20 *WA*.
21 On 3 August 1520, Luther wrote to a fellow Augustinian friar: 'an ass in Leipzig is writing many books against me, and in Cremona in Italy an anonymous ignoramus whom I believe to be a member of the Preaching Friars does the same.' *WA*.
22 *WA*.
23 Matthew 18:20.
24 *WA*.
25 *WA*.
26 *WA*.
27 *WA*.
28 *WA*.
29 *WA*.
30 1 Corinthians 2:15.

31 WA.

32 WA.

33 Saint Peter, the first pope, had a mother-in-law, the gospels all report. The key scriptural justification for celibacy claimed by the Catholic Church comes in Matthew's gospel (19:10–12) where, in the context of broken marriages, Jesus talks of 'eunuchs for the sake of the kingdom of heaven', but ends his remarks with an open-ended 'let anyone accept this who can'.

34 TT 6909.

35 WA.

36 WA.

37 Bainton, *Here I Stand*.

38 WA.

39 WA.

40 WA.

41 John 20:22–23.

42 TT 4696.

43 WA.

44 WA.

45 WA.

46 WA.

47 WA.

48 There were some organisational reasons for this – for instance an over-exaggerated fear that the laity might not treat the wine with sufficient reverence and might even spill the blood of Christ. It was to take the Catholic Church 450 years to accept Luther's argument. Communion 'in both kinds' for all only became its routine practice after the liturgical changes made by the Second Vatican Council (1962–65).

49 WA.

50 WA.

51 WA.

52 Quoted in Gordon Rupp, *The Righteousness of God* (London: Hodder & Stoughton, 1963).

53 WA.

54 WA.

55 TT 137.

56 In Luther's 1523 tract, *On Secular Authority and How Far One Should Be Obedient to It*, WA.

57 WA.

58 Today an oak tree, 'Luther's Oak', marks the spot.

59 WA.

60 Richard Holloway, *A Little History of Religion* (New Haven and London: Yale University Press, 2016).

Chapter Eight

1 *TT* 15342b.

2 *TT* 4414.

3 It has been argued that Charles and Luther were in some ways similar characters, sharing a dogged single-mindedness, an inexhaustible energy and a stubborn refusal to compromise.

4 They were cousins.

5 *WA*.

6 9 November 1520, in Percy Allen et al. (eds.), *Opus epistolarum Des. Erasmi Roterodami* (Oxford: Oxford University Press, 1906–58).

7 Paul Kalkoff and Girolamo Aleandro, *Die Depeschen des Nuntius Aleander von Wormser Reichstage 1521* (Charleston: Nabu Press, 2010).

8 Looking with twenty-first century eyes, the woodcut appears to be supportive to Luther. Holbein the Younger did have his studio at the time in the city of Basel, where Reformation sentiment ran high. But in Wittenberg the depiction of their professor was taken badly, the animal-like way he went about killing his opponents seen as a reference to Pope Leo's characterisation of him as a wild beast in the vineyard.

9 *TT* 2783a.

10 *WA*.

11 During the early weeks of the diet's meeting, Luther's books were being burned in the streets of Worms, though Aleander complained they were replaced as quickly as they were seized. 'Everyday it rains Luther books in both German and Latin.'

12 *TT* 5342b.

13 The elector is recorded as having been in two minds about whether Luther should attend, such were the dangers to his life.

14 *TT* 5342b.

15 *WA*.

16 *TT* 5342b.

17 Luke 8:43–46.

18 *TT* 5342b.

19 Robert Scribner, Roy Porter and Miklaus Teich, *The Reformation in National Context* (Cambridge: Cambridge University Press, 1994).

20 An anonymous pamphlet was published within months of the Diet of Worms, entitled *The Passion of Doctor Martin Luther*.

21 Luke 22:44.

22 *TT* 5342b.

23 Ibid.

24 Adolf Wrede, *Deutsche Reichstagsakten unter Kaiser Karl V* (Göttingen: Vandenhoeck & Ruprecht, 1962).

25 *TT* 5342b.

26 *WA*.

27 See Peter Marshall, Professor of History at Warwick University, writing in the *Literary Review*, July 2016.

28 Roland Bainton used it as the title of his book.

29 Wrede, *Deutsche Reichstagsakten*.

30 Ibid.

31 Acts 5:38.

32 *TT* 5342b.

33 *TT* 1340.

34 E. S. Cyrian (ed.), *Georg Spalatin Annals Reformationis* (Leipzig, 1718).

35 Wrede, *Deutsche Reichstagsakten*.

36 *WA*.

37 *WA*.

38 *TT* 5353.

39 *WA*.

40 *TT* 6816.

41 Luther is said to have sat for the portrait when he made an undercover visit to Wittenberg in December 1521.

42 Biblical scholars believe it unlikely that the John of the gospels could also be the John who penned Revelation, since authoritative dating of the latter book would make him over a hundred years old when he wrote it.

43 The Old Testament prophet who, in the First Book of Kings, risks his life by challenging those who worship the Canaanite god, Baal, to turn instead to Yahweh.

44 *WA*.

45 *TT* 2840a.

46 *TT* 6816.

47 Ibid.

48 Medieval Christianity believed the devil could transform himself into almost any animal, and a malign link was made between dogs and Cerberus, the three-headed hound in Greek mythology who guarded the gates of hell on behalf of Hades, god of the underworld, often conflated with Satan.

49 *TT* 912.

50 *TT* 5358b.

51 Ibid.

52 *WA*.

53 John Worthen, *The Cambridge Introduction to Samuel Taylor Coleridge* (Cambridge: Cambridge University Press, 2010).

54 *WA*.

55 *WA*.

56 Luther was a master of the crushing put-down. Hearing in the early 1530s that someone he did not rate was getting a doctorate, he remarked (*TT* 1043), 'we will once again make a new theologian out of an otter'.

57 Saint Augustine, *The City of God*, trans. Henry Bettenson (London: Penguin, 2003).

58 *WA*.

59 Luke 1:46–55.

60 *WA*.

61 *WA*.

62 *TT* 3945.

63 *WA*.

64 *TT* 1040.

65 *TT* 2761b.

66 *TT* 2790b.

67 *TT* 5324.

68 His translations of the gospels and Saint Paul's letters survive to this day, and some claim that he completed a Germanic version of the whole Bible, though others dispute this.

69 *WA*.

70 *WA*.

71 *WA*.

72 He later was to make efforts to remove Revelation, James's Epistle and others, but they continue to be included in Lutheran Bibles, albeit grouped at the very end.

73 See R. W. Scribner, 'Oral Culture and the Diffusion of Reformation Ideas', in Helga Robinson-Hammerstein (ed.), *The Transmission of Ideas in the Lutheran Reformation* (Worcester: Irish Academic Press, 1989).

74 *TT* 2771a.

75 *TT* 1040.

76 Ibid.

77 When Elector Friedrich saw these illustrations, he demanded that the papal reference be removed in subsequent editions, which it was, but after his death Luther allowed it back in.

Chapter Nine

1 *TT* 2761b.

2 Percy Allen et al. (eds.), *Opus epistolarum Des. Erasmi Roterodami* (Oxford: Oxford University Press, 1906–58).

3 The third, Lampertus Thorn, languished in prison, where he died in 1528.

4 Carter Lindberg, *The European Reformations* (Oxford: John Wiley, 2010).

Notes

5   Nikolaus Müller, *Die Wittenberger Bewegung 1521* (Leipzig, 1911).

6   Hermann Barge, *Andreas Bodenstein von Karlstadt* (Leipzig: Friedrich Branstetter, 1905).

7   Exodus 20:4–5.

8   Barge, *Andreas Bodenstein von Karlstadt*.

9   Zwilling ended up as pastor at Torgau, seat of Elector Friedrich's younger brother and heir, Duke Johann.

10   *TT* 4414.

11   *WA*.

12   *WA*.

13   *Encyclopedia of Monasticism*, ed. William Johnston (London: Routledge, 2000).

14   Matthew 19:9.

15   *TT* 903.

16   In 1521, Henry VIII published an attack on *The Babylonian Captivity*, entitled *Defence of the Seven Sacraments*. He was rewarded for his efforts by Pope Leo with the title 'Defender of the Faith'.

17   *WA*.

18   *WA*.

19   *TT* 6913.

20   *TT* 4414.

21   Emperor Charles had introduced Spanish fashions to Germany and they were in vogue at the time.

22   *TT* 4414.

23   It has been suggested that one reason for the journey was to sit for Cranach for the portrait of Junker Jörg.

24   From *A Sincere Admonition to All Christians to Guard Against Insurrection and Rebellion*, *WA*.

25   *TT* 3473a.

26   Today the revived University of Wittenberg operates in partnership with the University at Halle.

27   *WA*.

28   *WA*.

29   *WA*.

30   *WA*.

31   *WA*.

32   All the more so since those who, in the recent past, had promised to come to his rescue, Sickingen and Hutten, were now off the scene, the former killed in a fight with his own prince-bishop, and Hutten in exile in Zurich.

33   *WA*.

34   From the first of the 'Invocavit Sermons', *WA*.

35 WA.
36 WA.
37 WA.
38 WA.

PART THREE
Chapter Ten

1   TT 49.
2   WA.
3   WA.
4   TT 18.
5   WA.
6   By 1537, so popular had Luther's hymns become, that they began to find their way, at first unacknowledged, into Catholic hymnals, where they remain to this day. One story has it that this hymn was first sung by Luther and his companions as they entered Worms in 1521 to attend the diet.
7   WA.
8   TT 391.
9   TT 3145c.
10 WA.
11 TT 1445.
12 TT 2724b.
13 WA.
14 WA.
15 Romans 13:1.
16 WA.
17 WA.
18 WA.
19 WA.
20 WA.
21 He was the last non-Italian pope voted in by the cardinals before the Polish John Paul II in 1978.
22 Eamon Duffy, *Saints & Sinners: A History of the Popes* (London: Yale University Press, 1997).
23 Quoted in Roland H. Bainton, *Here I Stand: A Life of Martin Luther* (Massachusetts: Hendrickson, 2012, first published in 1950).
24 Martin Brecht, *Martin Luther: His Road to Reformation*, trans. James Schaff (Philadelphia: Westminster Press, 1895).
25 Peter Matheson (ed.), *The Collected Works of Thomas Müntzer* (Edinburgh: T&T Clark, 1980).

26 And, as a result, the Lutheran branch of Protestantism continues to have little time for such quiet, introspective contemplation to this day.

27 Revelation 20.

28 Luther had done so according to a letter of 4 July 1524. *WA*.

29 '[God] is the one who has given us the qualifications to be administrators of this new covenant,' Paul had written in his Second Letter to the Corinthians (3:6–7), 'which is not a covenant of written letters but of the Spirit: the written letters bring death, but the Spirit gives life.'

30 Matthew 5–7.

31 They were not the first to take this stance. It had previously been adopted, for example, by some of the Hussites in Bohemia.

32 Matthew 26:53.

33 *TT* 1340.

34 *TT* 5122.

35 *WA*.

36 *WA*.

37 Though it should be added in mitigation, that later, when Karlstadt and his family were caught up in the Peasants' War and in fear of their lives, Luther put his written animosity to one side and gave them shelter in his own home for eight weeks.

38 *WA*.

39 *TT* 414.

40 Ibid.

41 Matthew 5:28: 'If a man looks at a woman lustfully, he has already committed adultery with her in his heart.'

42 *WA*.

43 *WA*.

44 *WA*.

45 Martin Treu, 'Katharina von Bora, the Woman at Luther's Side', *Lutheran Quarterly* (Summer 1999).

46 *TT* 12.

47 *TT* 4786.

48 *WA*.

49 Prince-Archbishop Albrecht, often Luther's opponent, sent twenty florins.

50 Eberhard Brisger, the only other remaining friar, left in 1525 to marry.

51 Treu, 'Katharina von Bora'.

52 *WA*.

53 Treu, 'Katharina von Bora'.

54 *WA*.

55 *TT* 4886.

Chapter Eleven

1 *TT* 92.

2 A phrase used, most notably, by the Catholic liberation theologians of Latin America from the late 1960s to the 1990s, and an approach that has characterised the papacy of Francis, who has said he wants Catholicism to be a 'poor Church, for the poor'.

3 Again a phrase used by Francis, but best known on the lips of Archbishop Oscar Romero of San Salvador, who was murdered at his altar in 1980 for supporting the rights of the poor against the ruling elite in his native El Salvador.

4 Wat Tyler's Rebellion of 1381 in England, so nearly successful, began a process there that was largely completed by 1500.

5 From a translation of the original text held in the State Archives at Memmingen.

6 Ibid.

7 The editors of the Weimar edition note the unusually confused punctuation.

8 *WA.*

9 *WA.*

10 *WA.*

11 *WA.*

12 *WA.*

13 Romans 13:4.

14 Luke 20:25.

15 *WA.*

16 As promised by the Book of Revelation.

17 Rudolf Endres, 'The Peasant War in Franconia', in Bob Scribner and Gerhard Benecke (eds.), *The German Peasant War of 1525* (London: Allen and Unwin, 1979).

18 *WA.*

19 *WA.*

20 *TT* 4690.

21 Ibid.

22 *TT* 5187.

23 *TT* 2401.

24 *TT* 2731b.

25 Inspiring Katie at one stage to run a small domestic brewery.

26 *TT* 5650.

27 *TT* 4349.

28 *TT* 2849b.

29 Though Saxon law would not allow women to take on such a role, and on his death in 1546, his wishes were overridden and a male guardian appointed.

30 *TT* 49.

31 *TT* 3530.

32 *TT* 1006.

33 After the death of Luther's sister in 1529, her four daughters lived in the Black Cloister. Leni married from there in 1538.

34 *WA*.

35 *TT* 5494.

36 *TT* 2848a.

37 *TT* 3415.

38 *TT* 4531.

39 *WA*.

40 Colloquy was originally a word for a religious gathering to discuss theological viewpoints, though is nowadays more usually used in a secular context.

41 In a letter dated 14 June 1529 from Luther to Justus Jonas, *WA*.

42 *WA*.

43 *WA*.

Chapter Twelve

1 *TT* 522.

2 *WA*.

3 *WA*.

4 *WA*.

5 *TT* 6509.

6 *WA*.

7 *WA*.

8 *TT* 2425.

9 Because of references to the real presence, some in the Swiss contingent stuck with Zwingli and refused to sign, but submitted their own separate statement, while Strasbourg, Constance, Memmingen and Lindau put their names to another version, this time of twenty-three theses, drafted by Martin Bucer.

10 *WA*.

11 *WA*.

12 *TT* 5398.

13 *TT* 2793.

14 *WA*.

15 A final concord was agreed in May 1536 between Luther and Bucer.

16 *TT* 2666b.

17 His text was later incorporated into the Lutheran *Book of Concord*, the authoritative collection of Lutheran doctrinal statements, first published in 1580 to mark the fiftieth anniversary of the *Augsburg Confession*.

18 *TT* 67.

19 Though he also worried about the Elbe flooding and causing destruction in the town (*TT* 2880a).

20 *TT* 3453.

21 *TT* 4084.

22 *TT* 5506.

23 *TT* 4088. Kohlhase was finally caught in 1540 and put to death, though he went on to become a folk hero in some German legends.

24 Revelation 21:2.

25 *TT* 5517.

26 *TT* 3222b.

27 *TT* 429.

28 *TT* 4479.

29 *TT* 631.

30 *TT* 1072.

31 *TT* 2922b.

32 Ibid.

33 Ibid.

34 *WA.*

35 *TT* 1289.

36 *WA.*

37 *TT* 4991.

38 *TT* 5537. Hans, then sixteen, was being tutored by a Lutheran pastor in Torgau.

39 *TT* 255.

40 *TT* 1557.

41 *TT* 5096.

42 Melanchthon, for example, met the Protestant reformer John Calvin at such a gathering, but Luther was not able to attend.

43 It took Paul until December 1545 finally to launch the Council of Trent, which went on to become the starting point for the Counter-Reformation.

44 *TT* 5310.

45 *TT* 2076.

46 *WA.*

47 In 1547, the 'official' Catholic candidate, Julius von Pflug, replaced Amsdorf, who retired but remained a champion of Luther's doctrine, later clashing with Philipp Melanchthon over what he saw as the latter's attempt to dilute Luther's legacy.

48 *TT* 803.

49 *TT* 414.

50 Matthew 5:32 and 19:9.

51 WA.

52 WA.

53 The criticism even drove Philipp of Hesse back into the arms of the emperor.

54 *TT* 5096.

55 *TT* 2.

56 *TT* 109.

57 WA.

58 *TT* 5428.

59 WA.

60 *TT* 6962.

61 Already gathering in the town in the Italian Alps at the Pope's invitation.

62 Revelation 14:6.

Epilogue

1 Written in 1940, but taken from the subsequently amended version that appears in *Collected Poems* (London: Faber and Faber, 1976).

2 *TT* 3453.

3 Martin Treu, 'Katharina von Bora, the Woman at Luther's Side', *Lutheran Quarterly* (Summer 1999).

4 Other Lutheran rulers, including Duke Albrecht of Prussia and Duke Christoph of Württemberg, had offered her financial support in educating her sons.

5 *TT* 1422.

6 In 1947, when the World Lutheran Federation was established, there were 138 member churches.

7 Karen Armstrong, 'The Myth of Religious Violence', *Guardian* (25 September 2014).

8 Agricola had taught at Wittenberg and accompanied Luther to Leipzig, but the two fell out in 1536.

9 Recorded on a monument outside the Museum of London.

10 Tyndale shared Luther's belief in justification by faith and may even have visited Wittenberg in 1524. His execution followed him opposing Henry VIII's divorce.

11 Christopher Marlowe, *The Tragical History of Doctor Faustus* (London: Routledge, 1965).

12 Others have noted parallels in *The Tragical History of Doctor Faustus* between the voice of its central character and Philipp Melanchthon, notably the scholar Clifford Davidson in his paper, 'Dr Faustus of Wittenberg', *Studies in Philology*, 59 (1962).

13 William Shakespeare, *Hamlet*, Act 1 Scene 2.
14 Premiered by Philadelphia's Arden Theatre Company.
15 Joseph O'Malley (ed.), *Marx's Critique of Hegel's Philosophy of Right* (Cambridge: Cambridge University Press, 2009).
16 Ibid.

Index

Page numbers in *italics* refer to figures.